**W9-DIS-826**

# The Central & East European Handbook

Regional Handbooks of Economic Development
Prospects onto the 21st Century

*The China Handbook*
*The India Handbook*
*The Japan Handbook*
*The Central and Eastern Europe Handbook*
*The CIS Handbook*

Forthcoming

*The Southeast Asia Handbook*

# The Central & East European Handbook

## PROSPECTS ONTO THE 21ST CENTURY

**Patrick Heenan, Monique Lamontagne,** Editors

Glenlake Publishing Company, Ltd.
Chicago • London• New Delhi

AMACOM
New York • Atlanta • Boston • Kansas City • San Francisco • Washington, D.C.
Brussels • Mexico City • Tokyo • Toronto

This book is available at a special
discount when ordered in bulk quantities.
For information, contact Special Sales Department,
AMACOM, a division of American Management Association,
1601 Broadway, New York, NY 10019.

*This publication is designed to provide accurate and authoritative information
in regard to the subject matter covered. It is sold with the understanding
that the publisher is not engaged in rendering legal, accounting, or other
professional service. If legal advice or other expert assistance is required, the
services of a competent professional person should be sought.*

ISBN: 0-8144-0571-1

*Printing number*

*10  9  8  7  6  5  4  3  2  1*

# Contents

## International Relations

## Appendices

# Editors' Note

The region examined in this book now comprises 15 independent states, but it comprised just seven, along with territories occupied by an eighth, as recently as 1991. Until just two years before that, all these countries were governed by Communist regimes. It can be argued that the transition from Communism and the almost simultaneous collapse of the Soviet, Yugoslav, and Czechoslovak federations are sufficient to justify treating these countries as a single group. In fact, however, there is no consensus on the name, the nature, or the boundaries of the region in question. Where does central Europe end, and eastern Europe begin, and do they overlap with northern Europe anyway? Is there an east-central Europe that can be distinguished from southeastern Europe? Where should we place Russia, or at least its European regions, or Belarus, Ukraine, or Moldova? In any case, now that the Soviet bloc has passed into history, is there any reason to speak of a single region that remains significantly different from other parts of Europe?

One response to such questions has been to revive a much older division of Europe into two unequal parts: the West and center, traditionally seen as the realm of Catholicism (and Protestantism); and the East and Southeast, the homelands of Orthodoxy (and other Eastern Christian churches). Yet this division is not grounded in historical realities and it has had disastrous consequences. An excessive emphasis on differences in ascribed religious affiliations, in an ever more secular continent, can obscure the imperial, national, and economic factors that have always prevented unity within each version of Christianity. Even more dangerously, those who uphold these differences tend to downplay, or even deny, the enduring coexistence of varieties of Christianity in most areas of Europe, as well as the contributions of Jews, Moslems, and other non-Christians to all European societies and cultures. Nor is this merely a historical curiosity, or a topic for detached academic debate. Nazism and Serbian nationalism are by no means the only European ideologies to have been nourished by such prejudices.

Religious beliefs, and the ideologies that exploit them, have tended to tear the peoples of this region apart. It is their common history that brings them together, for better and for worse, and gives substance to the idea of a single region distinct from western Europe. From the 15th century onwards, the major countries of western Europe set about creating sea empires that helped to shape the destinies of every continent on the planet. Meanwhile, the countries of central and eastern Europe – here including several that are not covered in this book – were divided and conquered by the Turkish, Austro-Hungarian, Russian and German empires, and remained dependent until a few of them achieved autonomy in the 19th century. It was after World War I, and the collapse of the four empires, that the region examined in this book took on a recognizable form, as nation-states were revived (Poland), reorganized (Albania, Bulgaria, and Romania), separated from former subject peoples (Hungary), or newly created (Czechoslovakia, the three Baltic states, and the former Yugoslavia). Between the two world wars, all but Czechoslovakia succumbed to various forms of dictatorship; all were then conquered by, or entered alliances with, the new empires of Fascist Italy, Nazi Germany, and the Soviet Union.

Following the defeat of Italy and Germany, and the expansion of Soviet control, it then became customary in the West to talk of a unitary "Eastern Europe," a term that was often understood as including the Soviet Union itself, even though most of its territory was in Asia. This usage reflected the very real similarities among the regimes imposed on the region, but it took no account of the distinctiveness of Yugoslavia and Albania, the Soviet occupation of the Baltic states, or the divergences in economic performance and political development among the countries forcibly allied to the Soviet Union. Thus, for many in western Europe and North America, it was only after 1989 that the differences among these countries, and indeed within them, became interesting and important.

Nevertheless, the 15 countries discussed in this book can reasonably be viewed as forming a single group, separate both from the EU and from the former Soviet republics of the CIS (examined in *The European Union Handbook* and *The CIS Handbook*, respectively). Given that no one country can assume the kind of role that Russia and Germany fitfully play in their respective regions, all 15 have opportunities to develop as independent states, even at the same time as the facts of economic life require increasing cooperation. Attempts to make the transition from state control to markets, and from various types of Stalinism to liberal democracy, have not gone smoothly or easily anywhere in the region. In many cases, they have been diverted and corrupted, and in Serbia they have been blocked altogether. Yet the political and economic development of almost all these countries is generally strikingly advanced in comparison to that of Russia and other countries now in the CIS, where the Stalinist system lasted much longer and its effects went much deeper. Accordingly, we have chosen to treat the Baltic states as parts of this region, since their period of captivity under the Soviet regime was too short to destroy their national identities or their historic connections with their neighbors. We have also chosen to exclude eastern Germany (the former "German Democratic Republic"), because, however heavy the burden of its recent past may still be, its unification with western Germany in 1990 has set it on a separate path of development from the other former Communist countries. We readily acknowledge that there are valid arguments for other definitions of central and eastern Europe.

We also acknowledge that no single book can hope to provide a complete account even of one of these countries, let alone of the whole region. Our goal here has been to discuss a defined range of facts and issues, as concisely, accessibly, and evenhandedly as possible. The book is aimed at students, scholars and the general public alike.

We would like to thank all those who have helped in the making of this book. Our contributors have been patient and cooperative throughout; their contributions include not just the chapters in their names, but large parts of the appendices. Our academic advisers all did useful work, recommending contributors and helping to shape the structure of the book. Dr Marian Wisniewski of the University of Warsaw and Dr Vladimir Handl of the University of Birmingham also provided some invaluable assistance, and we are grateful to Dr Graham Field and to many others who took an interest in the project. Finally, Roda Morrison has once again supplied valuable editorial support at every stage.

## Linguistic Conventions

The country widely known as FYROM – an abbreviation for the Former Yugoslav Republic of Macedonia – is referred to simply as Macedonia in this book. The 14 other countries in the region are also referred to by their generally accepted names in English. In seven cases, these closely resemble their names in their own main languages, but in seven others they do not: Albania (Shqipëria), Croatia (Hrvatska), Estonia (Eesti), Hungary (Magyar), Lithuania (Leituva), Poland (Polska), and Slovakia (Slovensko). Similarly, most national and regional units within states are referred to by their generally accepted names in English: for example, Montenegro (Crna Gora) and Kosovo (Kosova to its historic Albanian majority, Kosovo i Matohija to Serbs). The following cities are also referred to by names that have become customary in English: Belgrade (Beograd), Bucharest (Bucureşti), Munich (München), Prague (Praha), Tirana (Tiranë), Vienna (Wien), and Warsaw (Warszawa). Other place names are rendered in the most appropriate language.

Readers should note that the word "region" is unavoidably used with three different meanings: the countries of central and eastern Europe viewed as a single group; the major subnational unit in many of these countries (often equivalent to "province"); and an unofficially defined socioeconomic area.

Individuals with Hungarian names are cited with personal name first, family name second, although the reverse is normal in Hungarian.

The ethnic group often still referred to as "Gypsies," reflecting a nonexistent connection with Egypt, are referred to here by their preferred name, "Roma."

Finally, throughout this book, the organizations that controlled the countries of central and eastern Europe up to 1989 are called "Communist Parties" for ease of reference. However, their claim to have any connections with the Communism of Karl Marx and his followers – or even, in most cases, with the Communist Parties that existed in the region before World War II – is highly debatable. Further, they were never parties in any sense familiar in liberal democracies, as they were instruments of the Soviet government and/or domestic dictatorships. In any case, they used a variety of different names at different times, from the "Polish United Workers' Party" to the "League of Communists of Yugoslavia."

## Currency Symbols

| | | | |
|---|---|---|---|
| AL | lek (Albania) | Lit | litas (Lithuania) |
| BL | lev (Bulgaria) | MD | denar (Macedonia) |
| BM | marka (Bosnia-Herzegovina) | RL | Romanian leu (plural, lei) |
| CrK | kuna (Croatia) | ST | tolar (Slovenia) |
| CzK | Czech koruna | SK | Slovak koruna |
| DM | Deutschmark | US$ | US dollar |
| EK | kroon (Estonia) | YD | dinar (Yugoslavia) |
| F | forint (Hungary) | Z | Złoty (Poland) |
| Lat | lat (Latvia) | | |

## Abbreviations

The following abbreviations are used throughout this book:

| | |
|---|---|
| CIS | Commonwealth of Independent States |
| Comecon | Council for Mutual Economic Assistance (1949–91) |
| CSCE/OSCE | Conference on Security and Cooperation in Europe (1975–94)/ Organization for Security and Cooperation in Europe (since 1995) |
| EBRD | European Bank for Reconstruction and Development |
| EU | European Union |
| GATT | General Agreement on Tariffs and Trade |
| GDP/GNP | Gross Domestic Product/Gross National Product |
| IMF | International Monetary Fund |
| NATO | North Atlantic Treaty Organization |
| OECD | Organization for Economic Cooperation and Development |
| UK | United Kingdom (when used as an adjective) |
| UN | United Nations |
| US | United States (when used as an adjective) |

In other cases, the meaning of each abbreviation or acronym is stated at its first appearance within each chapter.

**National Frontiers and Capital Cities in Central and Eastern Europe**

# Context
# and
# Prospects

## Chapter One

# Poland

## *Andrew H. Dawson*

Since 1989, the Poles have made remarkable progress in sloughing off the malign effects of 40 years of Soviet domination. Nevertheless, the goals that they have set for themselves have not yet been accomplished in full.

### History to 1989

For centuries, Poles have seen themselves as members of a nation in its own right that is part of both eastern and western Europe. They have taken badly to domination, from whatever source, and commemorate with gratitude those foreigners who have supported Polish independence, from Napoleon I, who established the Grand Duchy of Warsaw, onward. The last 200 years have been particularly painful. The dismemberment of their country between 1772 and 1795, and its subjugation by Prussia, Russia, and Austria throughout the 19th century, were followed by another partition and occupation by Nazi and Soviet forces between 1939 and 1945, and by Soviet domination from the late 1940s to 1989. Periodically, the Poles have demonstrated their opposition to external control, from Kosciuszko's uprising of 1794 to those in Warsaw in 1943 and 1944. More recently, they opposed Soviet control and the Communist form of economic management in the Poznań uprising of 1956, at Gdańsk in 1970, in further troubles in 1976, and in the Solidarity (Solidarność) uprising of 1980. Notwithstanding several changes of leader over that period, the Communist authorities lost much of the credibility that they might once have enjoyed. The imposition of martial law in 1981, and the murder of a troublesome priest,

Father Popiełuszko, by military police in 1984, destroyed what was left. The economy stagnated. Eventually, the regime was obliged to concede free elections for a revived Senate and a minority of the seats in the Sejm, the lower house of the National Assembly, in June 1989. It was trounced. The principal opposition party, Solidarity, won 99 of the 100 seats contested in the Senate and almost all those open to free election in the Sejm, and the first post-Communist government in central and eastern Europe was formed. It was only later in the year that the Berlin Wall fell and other Communist regimes started to collapse.

Polish aspirations in 1989 were clear. The vast majority of the population wished to replace the system of Communist control and central planning with a plural parliamentary democracy, an independent judiciary, a more market-based economy, and the right of private citizens to engage in business. Poles also wanted to join NATO and the European Community (now the EU). However, at that time no country had made the transition from Soviet central planning to the free market, and doubts were expressed as to whether such a change would be possible. In particular, doubts were cast on the ability of the peoples of central and eastern Europe to cope with the social dislocation that economic transition was likely to cause. Doubts were also expressed as to whether they could develop the legal and financial infrastructure necessary for the establishment of an economy based on private ownership of property.

Much, however, has been achieved. Indeed, Poland has become something of a model for other former Communist countries. In particular, the constitution has been reformed, macroeconomic stability has been established, the private sector of the economy has quickly surpassed the public sector in importance, and social stability has been maintained in the face of considerable change, involving a great deal of individual hardship.

## The Constitutional Settlement

Fundamental to the changes that have occurred has been the successful establishment of a plural democracy, in the face of considerable difficulties. As one of their final acts, the Communists enacted an electoral law that instituted proportional representation in its purest form. The first fully free post-Communist elections produced a Sejm composed of a large number of political parties, few of which had many seats, creating severe problems for the formation and survival of governments. There have been several administrations since 1989, all of which have been coalitions or minorities. However, the threshold of votes for representation in the Sejm has since been raised to 5%, and the number of parties represented has shrunk drastically. After the 1997 elections, there were only five. The electoral process has generally worked smoothly. The elections of 1993 brought to power a left-of-center government, led by the Democratic Left Alliance (SLD), a party composed largely of former Communists, but that of 1997 produced a more right-wing administration, dominated by Solidarity Electoral Action (AWS). Similarly, the first presidential election by universal suffrage, in 1990, installed Lech Wałęsa, the Solidarity leader; the second, in 1995, saw his defeat and replacement by Aleksander Kwaśniewski, a former Communist. Further, although administrations have varied in their enthusiasm for the post-Communist transformation of Poland, there has been no wish to return to Communist practices and there is much common ground between the major parties. This fundamental constitutional stability has rested in no small part upon the maturity of the electorate, which has drawn a line under events in the Communist era, and accepted that most of those who were members of the Communist Party, but who now espouse social democracy, are not thereby debarred from public office.

## The Reform of Local Government

Another example of the rapid maturing of plural democracy has been the recent reform of local government. As part of its transition from Communism, Poland has been reorganizing the constitutional relationship between the country's tiers of government, and redrawing the map of local authorities. During the Communist period, local authorities were legally branches of central government, possessing few, if any, independent powers. That arrangement was overturned in 1990, when elected commune (*gmina*) councils were empowered to raise revenue and undertake action not reserved to other authorities. However, it was acknowledged that one, and perhaps two, further tiers of directly elected local authorities would be needed if the principle of subsidiarity was to be effected, for communes, with an average population of 15,000, are far too small to provide the more specialized local public services. Little progress was made between 1993 and 1997, when the SLD and its coalition partner, the Peasants' Party (PSL), could not find a structure that would favor both of them. Following the 1997 elections, in contrast, the new, more united administration made proposals for the completion of the reform.

Since it was reconstituted after World War I, Poland has made use of several types of local government unit. After World War II, the country was divided into 22 regions (*województwa*), accompanied by a lower tier of around 390 counties (*powiaty*). However, both the counties and the "large" regions were replaced in 1975 by a single tier of 49 much smaller regions. By 1998, all the major political parties had agreed to return, at least in principle, to the earlier model. It was also agreed that the financial relationship between the center and the regions should become more transparent. Under the Communists, there was scope for individual politicians to influence the flow of funds from central government to regions, and a widespread belief that the system was corrupt. It was therefore agreed that all regions should receive the same fixed proportion of the national taxes (on income and value added) raised within them, on the grounds that more elaborate systems of central government grants, related to the particular needs of individual regions, would be more difficult to understand and more open to manipulation by interested parties. However, it followed that each region should be sufficiently large to be able to generate the income required to provide such services as policing and economic development. It was doubtful that the smaller of the 49 regions – 15 had populations of less than 500,000 – would have been able to do this.

Initially, the AWS government proposed that there should be 12 regions and around 320 counties, a structure that would have gone far to meeting these requirements. In such a structure, all regions could have been large, both in area and population; all could have had broadly based economies, which would be better able to cope with downturns in individual industries than smaller, more specialized areas; and all might have included a city that could act as a focus for the area around it. Moreover, such a structure could have accommodated many of the problems that have arisen as Poland has transformed its economy, by bringing together areas of high and persistent unemployment with those that have fared better.

However, the initial proposal ran into stiff opposition, founded on the country's political geography. The principal opposition party, the SLD, which has strong support in many of the middle-sized cities that might serve as centers for regions, wished to see a much larger number of them. Some of those living in regions that would have disappeared under the government's proposals objected to the possibility that they would be incorporated into larger units suffering, or likely to suffer, from severe social and economic problems, as they feared that they would be called upon to subsidize such areas. Others pointed out that their regions were well-established and widely recognized entities, underpinned by a significant historical or cultural status within Poland. The Catholic Church supported the city of Częstochowa, which is the country's most important site of pilgrimage, in this regard. Others were concerned that the loss of status of their cities as seats of regional authorities would inhibit attempts to attract custom and investment. During the spring and summer of 1998, there was much public protest, but eventually a compromise was reached, in which the major parties agreed to 16 regions. The first elections for the new authorities passed off smoothly in October 1998.

## Economic Restructuring

Post-Communist Poland inherited a large monetary overhang of personal savings, accumulated by households that had earned money but could find little within the highly regulated Communist economy to spend it on. The country had also incurred substantial hard currency debts to governments and banks in western Europe, north America and elsewhere during the 1970s and 1980s. The currency, the złoty, was not convertible. Drastic action – called "shock therapy" by some – was taken by the first post-Communist government to solve these problems. In 1990, trade, including foreign trade, was freed from most central controls, and the majority of price controls were scrapped. Prices rose rapidly, thus destroying the overhang. Negotiations were launched with the country's foreign creditors, as a result of which its debts were either rescheduled or canceled. The IMF provided a large standby fund to underwrite the value of the złoty on world currency markets, and the currency became convertible at a rate that proved to be sustainable. Speculators did not attack, and the government did not need to draw on the IMF guarantee. What is more, these early achievements have been sustained. Despite considerable economic disruption within the country in the early 1990s, and a substantial unrecorded element within the economy, the government has been able to collect most of the taxes it has levied and maintain its budget discipline. Inflation has fallen rapidly from the extraordinary levels of that period to around 10% a year in 1998, while the currency, which has declined slowly in value, has proved to be more stable than many in supposedly more soundly based market economies. Poland has also been one of the most successful of the former Communist countries in attracting foreign direct investment.

The effect of shock therapy on the domestic economy was also dramatic. The replacement of central planning by the free market exposed enterprises to the discipline of paying the real costs of their activities, while obliging them to produce goods of a quality which would persuade customers to buy, at prices that they could afford. There were sharp falls in demand for all except essential products. Industry was also affected by the reform of the arrangements governing international trade. The restoration of the right of individuals and firms to own and run their own businesses was accompanied by that of their right to import and export, and many people took the opportunity to import western brand-name products, thus undermining the demand for goods produced in Poland. At the same time, the government, which had, in effect, been a major customer, especially of the industries supplying armaments and infrastructure goods, reduced its demand substantially. Comecon, which had managed trade among the countries of the Soviet bloc, collapsed, taking with it much of the previous trade between Poland and other countries in central and eastern Europe. Levels of output fell sharply in many industries, and workers were laid off. Some enterprises collapsed. Employment fell from 17 million in 1989 to just over 14 million. Unemployment, unheard of under central planning, reached almost 3 million people, or around 17% of the workforce.

The structural impact of these changes was marked. In 1989, around 30% of Polish employment was in manufacturing and mining. In contrast, by 1993, at the nadir of economic decline, that proportion had fallen to around one quarter. The proportion in trade – the most buoyant of the service industries – had, however, grown from 9% to 14%. There was also a substantial change in the relative sizes of the public and private sectors, brought about by a sharp decline in the number of jobs in all parts of the public sector, other than education and health, and an increase in those in private

enterprises, especially retailing, construction, transportation and manufacturing (see Table 1.1). By 1993, only 43% of employment was in the public sector.

These changes affected the country very unevenly, from the regions of Warsaw and Poznań, where the rate was around half the national average, to some parts of the north, where between one quarter and one third of the labor force were out of work. There were also variations within regions. For instance, the jobless rate in the city of Warsaw was only around one quarter of that for the nation, and it was also low in many other cities, such as Katowice, Kraków, and Wrocław. It was, however, very much higher in Łódź and Radom, in many of the smaller and middle-sized cities, and in rural areas.

This pattern reflected the structural changes. The growth in services appears to have bolstered the largest cities. On the other hand, the slump in manufacturing and mining seems to have affected some cities, and especially those in Upper Silesia in the northwest, much less severely than others: it may be that these areas, in which the state sector of the economy remains large, will prove to be particularly vulnerable to any new wave of reform. It should also be noted that there has been a significant shake out in agriculture, affecting not only the relatively small public sector, but also farms in private ownership. It is, perhaps, for this reason that unemployment appears to have struck some of the regions in which the proportion of jobs in the private sector in the late 1980s was relatively high just as severely as some of those that were heavily dependent upon the public sector.

Changes of such magnitude and rapidity, involving considerable individual hardship, tend to destabilize societies, yet there has been no public unrest in Poland. The economy, which began to grow again in 1993, has continued to do so at a pace that has led to a steady decline of unemployment, to around 9% in 1998, when the standard of living exceeded that of the late 1980s. However, the process of transition is not yet complete. The pace of reform was checked in 1993, following the installation of a left-of-center government; and, although some of the public sector has been privatized, many large industrial enterprises remain, in effect if not in name, in public ownership.

## Coalmining

This is especially true of coalmining. Under the Communist model of development, the highest priority was accorded to increasing the output of fuel, and Poland built up large export markets in bituminous coal, not only among other Comecon members but also in western Europe. Polish miners were among the country's highest-paid workers. However, labor productivity was abysmal. Further, several of the mines, including those which were being sunk in the 1970s and 1980s in the newly discovered Lublin field, faced such difficult geological conditions that they could never have covered their costs in a market economy. The removal of government subsidies to the industry, the fall in demand from the country's heavy industries, the more efficient use of fuel brought about by economic reform, and the disruption of the industry's markets in the Soviet bloc led to the closure of all the pits in the small Lublin and Wałbrzych fields, a sharp fall in employment in the industry in general, and the prospect of closures in Upper Silesia.

By the mid-1990s, however, few closures had occurred, even though three quarters of the Upper Silesian mines had been losing money, the industry's debts had soared, and its taxes remained largely unpaid. In 1990, the government was advised by the US consultants Arthur Andersen to close up to 15 pits, and in 1993 the World Bank offered to meet some of the social costs if at least nine were shut. There has been talk of halving the workforce over a period of 10 years. In 1996, the government announced a further cut of 18% in the output of coal and the closure of 20 mines by the end of the century. However, it proved to be incapable of action on such a scale, let alone privatization. Instead, it fell back on attempts to introduce some sort of internal market within the industry – attempts that failed to balance the books – and indicated that it did not intend to privatize industries such as coal that it considered to be "strategic" (see Riley and Tkocz). In short, Polish governments appear to have had no realistic answers to the problems that the reform of the economy has created for the industry, and have proved politically unable to choose between radical restructuring, which would be necessary before substantial amounts of private capital can be attracted, and a return to overt public subsidy.

## The Ursus Tractor Works

Similar problems have also occurred in many of the other industrial "dinosaurs" of the Communist period, including the Ursus tractor works. Ursus is a city of around 40,000 people on the southwestern edge of Warsaw. Its tractor factory was founded in the late 19th century, destroyed during World War II, and reconstructed during the 1950s. As a large state-owned monopoly supplier of around 55,000 tractors a year, not only to Poland but also to other Comecon countries, it came to typify the industrial development of the postwar period, and, with 25,000 employees, it was the dominant economic and political force in the city. During a period of limited economic opening to the West in the 1970s – in an attempt to attract capital investment – it acquired a license from Massey-Ferguson of Canada to build one of that firm's large tractors, and there was talk of raising output to 100,000 a year. This did not happen, and the machine that it did produce was more suited to huge collectives than to the small, privately owned farms that accounted for three-quarters of the country's cultivated land. Nor did the factory have a happy workforce, acquiring a reputation during the 1980s as one of the country's most important centers of anti-Communist agitation.

In the immediate aftermath of the fall of the Communist government, some Ursus directors showed that, contrary to western views of Communist management, they were capable of considerable initiative, rapidly hiving off the factory's more profitable activities by forming "private" companies that employed the factory's workers and "used" (that is, stole) its materials. That process, however, was quickly outlawed, and the plant remained in public ownership. By 1991, sales of tractors had fallen below 10,000, and the government, desperate to cut the wages bill, established a restructuring consortium to rid the enterprise of the most unproductive activities and halve the workforce. That consortium turned to the European Community and the British government for advice, and was told to make even greater reductions in the number of jobs. The fall of the right-wing government in 1993 led to the removal of the consortium's leader and the adoption of a less draconian plan, based on sales targets of 35,000 tractors by 1995 and 50,000 in 1996. In the event, these proved to be unattainable, not least because of the unsuitability of the factory's principal product for the domestic market. Production remained at very low levels, the enterprise's debts continued to grow, and opportunities for even such simple forms of diversification as the provision of spare parts for the existing model were neglected. Workers took to the streets to demand more subsidies, reducing still further the likelihood of attracting the foreign investment that will be required if new types of tractor are to be produced or the enterprise's debts restructured. Meanwhile, the management was urging the government to hobble the private manufacturing of tractors by imposing tariffs on parts imported from Belarus by smaller private producers for assembly into machines more suited to Polish conditions, at much higher levels of labor productivity. The government obliged, but only to the extent of noting that the manufacture of machinery, like that of food, textiles, furniture and pharmaceuticals, is deserving of special protection from foreign predators, and reversing its earlier policy of cutting tariffs. It was not, however, prepared to go so far as to exclude imports. In other words, the Ursus factory has proved to be too important to be allowed to founder but too expensive to save. It has become one of the biggest public sector loss-makers, and is being strangled by its debts.

Ursus is not the only loss-making state enterprise. Notwithstanding "shock therapy," around 3,000 enterprises were still in public ownership in 1993. In 1995, the government transferred 500 of the largest to 15 national investment funds, each managed by groups of Polish and foreign banks, in the hope that such "arm's length" organizations would be able to achieve the restructuring that has proved to be so difficult for politicians. Some enterprises may survive, but others have already been broken up. It is anticipated that some or all of the equity will eventually be sold to the public.

## Farming

The problem of farming is quite different. Among the countries of central and eastern Europe, only Yugoslavia and Poland failed to collectivize their farms under Communism. Poland abandoned the attempt in the aftermath of the Poznań uprising in 1956. However, the Communist authorities showed little sympathy for farmers, subjecting them to discriminatory charges, and obliging them to obtain equipment and fertilizer from, and to sell much of their output through, state-owned enterprises. After a series of land reforms between the wars, and then in the immediate aftermath of World War II, the industry was dominated by small peasant holdings. Although many people left the land during the Communist period, to take up jobs in cities, this structure changed little. Difficulties were placed in the way of farmers who wished to enlarge their holdings, and the opportunities for investment were limited. There were numerous large holdings only in the areas that had belonged to Germany before World War II, in the north and west of the country, where large estates had been seized by the Polish government in 1945.

As a result of the economic reforms of 1990, many of the state farms, which had been heavily subsidized, collapsed. The high levels of unemployment in the north of Poland are the result. At the same time, the market for farm products was disrupted by the collapse of trade with other countries in central and eastern Europe, and the opening of the country to food imports of much higher quality from the rest of the world. Faced with high levels of unemployment in the cities, farmers found that they were unable to leave the land. While western investors were willing, and in some cases eager, to invest in other parts of the economy, there was no significant inflow of foreign capital to agriculture. There was considerable distress in some rural areas.

Since then, the government has provided some protection for farmers, but little else has changed. Agriculture continues to employ one of the largest proportions of the workforce in any European country – around 26% – but produces only around 7% of the country's GDP. If the Polish economy continues to grow rapidly, there will be some opportunity for people to leave agriculture, allowing the enlargement and intensification of holdings, and improvements in the standard of hygiene and the quality of products. However, very great changes will be required, probably requiring many years, before the gap between employment and productivity can be bridged.

## The International Dimension of the Economy

One of the principal Polish aspirations in 1989 was to become more firmly connected with western Europe, and Poles were relieved when two of the more important organizations binding them to other Communist countries in the region – Comecon and the Warsaw Pact – collapsed in the early 1990s. They were also relieved to see some further waning of Russian power, exemplified by the breakup of the Soviet Union in 1991, although they have been alarmed by the increasing instability of Russia, Ukraine, and Belarus. All Poland's post-Communist governments have sought to strengthen ties with western Europe, and in this they have had some success. By the mid-1990s, Poland had achieved a spectacular turnaround in its pattern of international trade. In 1997, it was invited to join NATO – a process completed in March 1999 – and in 1998 it began negotiations on EU membership.

Under Communism, the quantity of trade, especially with countries outside Comecon, was rather low. Trade was also characterized by an emphasis on primary and simply processed goods. In 1985, Polish trade amounted to 31% of GDP (see Główny Urząd Statysyczny 1998a). Trade in primary and simply processed goods accounted for around 36% of the total, and manufactures for the rest. Mineral fuels were by far the principal item of both exports and imports. The most important trading

partner was the Soviet Union, with which 27% of trade was conducted, followed by West Germany, East Germany, and Czechoslovakia. Trade with other Communist countries in Europe accounted for 48% of the total.

Between 1985 and 1990, Polish trade fell sharply, but then recovered, to amount to 44% of GDP by 1995. By that date, trade in primary and simply processed goods had sunk to 23% of the total, while manufactures had risen to 77%. Mineral fuels had been displaced as the most important item in both imports and exports. There has also been a marked reorientation of trade. Unified Germany's share of the total rose from 13% in 1985 to 32% in 1990, while trade with other ex-Communist countries of central and eastern Europe declined sharply, to 17%.

Much of this change has been associated with the growth of the private sector in the Polish economy. Private trade, which had been illegal before 1990, accounted for 64% of all trade in 1995, and a higher proportion of it has been with established market economies than with ex-Communist countries. However, the private sector has been responsible for much of the increase in imports, and has accounted for the whole of Poland's large trade deficit. In contrast, the public sector has continued to trade extensively with other transition economies, and particularly with Russia, where it accounted for 62% of Poland's total trade with that country. Moreover, trade by the public sector has been largely in balance. However, worsening economic problems in Russia and Ukraine since the mid-1990s have undermined that position.

Problems over trade have made Poland's effort to enter the EU more urgent. Immediately after the fall of Communism, Poland indicated that it wished to join what was then the European Community, and an association agreement was signed in December 1991. However, it was not generous (see Messerlin). Polish access to markets for a range of "sensitive" goods – food, chemicals, steel, and textiles – was severely restricted, and Polish workers were not allowed to participate in the single labor market. Some technical and other aid was offered, but the substantial resources associated with the Community's common agricultural and regional policies were not made available. In spite of Polish pressure, it was not until November 1998 that the EU began serious negotiations with a view to admitting Poland and four other transition economies, and some of its leading members indicated that they were unlikely to gain entry before 2005 at the earliest. It is not clear what level of support for agriculture and the poorer regions will be available within the EU by that time.

## Effects on the People

In some parts of central and eastern Europe, the collapse of Communism has led to killing, the destruction of shelter, shortages of food, and reductions in medical services. Even in places in which such extreme events have not occurred, it has sometimes been accompanied by inadequate institutional reform and economic stagnation. Fortunately, Poland has avoided these extremes, but stresses have been very great.

For example, there is evidence of increasing levels of ill health related to insecurity, and it has been reported that around 40% of children and young people have medical problems (see Firlit-Fesnak). Life expectancy at birth fell sharply for males, and to a lesser extent for females, during the first two years of the transition (see Główny Urząd Statysyczny 1998b). However, the longer-term picture is quite different. While the early Communist years produced a marked improvement in life expectancy for both males and females – the figure for males rose from around 59 years in 1952 to 67 in the mid-1970s – no further improvement was achieved during the last 15 years of Communist rule. By 1996, in contrast, it had risen to 68 years. Similarly, female life expectancy, which also declined slightly in the 1980s, has been improving again since the early 1990s, reaching 77 years in 1996.

More particularly, since 1991 there have been some marked falls in the standardized death rates associated with some of the more common diseases. Deaths from circulatory diseases for men, which had risen from 722 per 100,000 in 1989 to 759 in 1991, and from 731

to 752 for women, had fallen by 1996 to historic lows of 636 and 670 respectively. Similarly, deaths from accidents and other external causes, which had risen from 122 per 100,000 for men in 1989 to 139 in 1991, had also fallen, to 114 by 1996. The steep decline in infant mortality that was occurring before 1989 has continued; the rate has more than halved since 1980, dropping from 255 per 10,000 live births to 191 in 1989 and 122 in 1996. Similarly, after a period between 1990 and 1993 in which no improvement was achieved, the steep reduction in tuberculosis has been resumed. In contrast, death rates from cancer have continued to climb since the 1980s.

However, there are exceptions. Although care must be taken in the use of nonstandardized death rates at the regional level, the former region centered on Łódź – an old industrial city that has faced severe problems of economic and social adjustment – appears to be one of the least healthy places in the country. The 1996 death rate, at 13.5 per 1,000 of the population, was far in excess of the national average (10), and considerably greater than the next highest (11.6). It should be noted that the two regions recording that level were both adjacent to Łódź. The Łódź region has had the highest death rate continuously since the mid-1980s, and the gap between it and the national average has been widening. More particularly, both men and women recorded a much higher incidence of deaths from circulatory diseases and cancer there than in the Polish population as a whole.

## Conclusion

In several important regards, Poland has set the pace for post-Communist institutional and economic reform. There has been a substantial restructuring of the economy, but the process is far from complete in either the primary or the secondary sectors. Nevertheless, economic growth has been robust, standards of living have been rising, and the health of Poles has begun to improve again. Unlike the 1980s, when Polish society was in disarray and its economy was stagnant, the post-Communist future seems to be bright.

# Further Reading

Bossak, Jan W., *Poland: International Economic Report*, Warsaw: Warsaw School of Economics, 1995

An annual survey of the state of the Polish economy

Firlit-Fesnak, Grazyna, "What About Social Policy? Social Effects of System Transformation in Poland," in K. A. Wojtaszczyk, *Poland: Government and Politics*, Warsaw: Elipsa, 1997

A discussion of some of the social consequences of Poland's economic transformation since 1989, by a Polish academic

Fitz, Ryszard, *The First Polish Economic Guide*, Warsaw: Common Europe Publications, 1997

A substantial guide to recent economic development and investment opportunities in Poland

Główny Urząd Statystyczny, (1998a) *Rocznik Statystyczny Handlu Zagranicznego 1998*; (1998b) *Rocznik Statystyczny Ochrony Zdrowia 1997*, Warsaw: Główny Urząd Statystyczny, 1998

Annual reports on international trade and social development, compiled and published by Poland's Chief Statistical Office

Messerlin, Patrick A., "The EC and Central Europe: The Missed Rendezvous of 1992?" in *Economics of Transition*, Volume 1, 1993

A critical assessment of the association agreements signed by the EU and some of the countries of central and eastern Europe shortly after the fall of the Communist regimes (and since replaced by more far-reaching "Europe agreements")

Radetzki, Marian, *Polish Coal and European Energy Market Integration*, Aldershot and Brookfield, VT: Avebury, 1995

Riley, R., and M. Tkocz, "Coalmining in Upper Silesia Under Communism and Capitalism," in *European Urban and Regional Studies*, Volume 5, 1998

A detailed study of the development of the Upper Silesian coal industry up to and after 1989

World Bank, *An Agricultural Strategy for Poland*, Washington, DC: World Bank, 1990

An assessment of the problems and potential of Polish agriculture in the late 1980s

*Dr Andrew H. Dawson* is Senior Lecturer in Geography at the University of St Andrews in Scotland.

## Table 1.1 Changes in Employment in Poland, 1989–93 (% except as shown)

|  | Private Sector | Public Sector | Total |
|---|---|---|---|
| Agriculture | −8 | −66 | −17 |
| Mining, energy and manufacturing | +10 | −40 | −26 |
| Construction | +51 | −75 | −35 |
| Transport | +23 | −39 | −30 |
| Trade | +77 | −69 | +34 |
| Education | −42 | −2 | −3 |
| Health care and social welfare | +32 | −3 | −1 |
|  |  |  |  |
| Total workforce | +9 | −35 | −16 |
| Total workforce (thousands) | +687 | −3,463 | −2,776 |

Source: Główny Urząd Statystyczny, *Poland: Quarterly Statistics*, and *Rocznik Statystyczny 1994*, Warsaw: Główny Urząd Statystyczny, 1994

Chapter Two

# Hungary

*Mark Pittaway*

## The Change of System

The change of system in Hungary in 1989 was not the product of a spectacular political upheaval or mass demonstrations, as in the rest of the region, but it was driven by processes similar to those operating elsewhere. Throughout the 1980s, economic stagnation was gradually transformed into a withdrawal of trust in the institutions of the socialist state. As early as July 1985, this was evident in elections to the National Assembly, when some non-Communist candidates were elected, for the first time anywhere in the Soviet bloc, while several political leaders failed to win seats. Even where functionaries were successful, many of them were aware of the quiet but growing distrust in the government across much of society. This awareness of the weakness of their position, combined with their fear that the uprising of 1956 might be repeated, gave an impetus to reformist opinion within the Communist Party itself. This explains the willingness of the Party to lead the process of reform, thus ensuring both the success of negotiated revolution in 1989, and the strength of ex-Communist political forces in the new Hungarian Republic.

As in the rest of the region, from the beginning of the 1980s Hungarian society had been marked by increasing political activity. New, unofficial organizations sprang up, consisting of pacifists, Christians, environmentalists, and human rights activists, which formed the background to growing intellectual opposition to the regime. Their cooperation bore fruit in 1985 with a meeting of the intellectual opposition at Monor, close to Budapest.

The following two years witnessed the unofficial publication of political programs calling for democratization and the application of market principles to the economy.

By 1987, the old guard within the government had been replaced with a new technocratic administration, led by the former Budapest party secretary, Károly Grósz. This government aimed to solve the problems of the economy through the adoption of a radical program of reform that added up to an unspoken public admission of the seriousness of the crisis. It aimed to restrict the money supply, reduce the public debt, and close the balance of payments deficit. The reforms included a major transformation of the tax system, through the introduction of income tax; an attempt to commercialize the state-run banking industry, in order to allow more efficient allocation of capital; a reduction in subsidies to loss-making state industries; and the tacit abandonment of the policy objective of full employment. However, the program stopped short of a radical marketization of the economy, and criticism of its provisions was fed by considerable popular discontent as living standards fell.

Increasingly, the opposition began to form itself into political groupings. Conservative and populist intellectuals formed the Hungarian Democratic Forum (HDF) in September 1987; a group of anti-Communist students at the Budapest University of Economics founded the Alliance of Young Democrats, known by its initials in Hungarian as Fidesz, in March 1988; and around the same time the liberal opposition formed the Network of Free Initiatives, which eventually became the Alliance of Free

Democrats (AFD). The monopoly of the Communist labor unions was broken with the foundation of a free union in the universities and the research institutes of the Academy of Sciences.

The Communist Party responded to the growing pressure from society by dismissing its leadership. János Kádár, who had been its Secretary since the suppression of the 1956 uprising, was replaced by Grósz in May 1988, and a new generation of technocratic functionaries came to dominate its decision-making bodies, the Central Committee and the Politburo. In the fall, a new government was formed under the western-educated technocrat Miklós Németh. At this point, the opposition groups transformed themselves into political parties, and demanded free elections in which they would be able to try to replace the Communists. The HDF, the AFD, and Fidesz were joined in November 1988 by the first of the "historical" parties that claimed the legacy of those that had existed before the imposition of Communist rule up to July 1948. Thus, the Independent Smallholders Party (ISP) proclaimed itself the successor of the Smallholders Party that won the first free postwar elections in 1945, and in the first few months of 1989 it was followed by a revived Christian Democratic Peoples' Party (CDPP) and a refounded Social Democratic Party of Hungary.

This process was given enormous impetus by the first significant measures of real political reform. On January 11, 1989, the National Assembly passed laws guaranteeing freedom of association and freedom of assembly. These gave the new parties, unions, and other organizations a secure legal basis, and made the creation of a multiparty system inevitable. It was the mass demonstrations on Hungary's national day, March 15, that represented a clear turning point, in that they persuaded the regime to begin negotiations with the emergent non-Communist political forces. On March 22, these new political movements formed the Opposition Round Table, designed to prevent the Communist Party from trying to maintain its power by dividing the opposition. Next came the National Round Table, established in June and comprising representatives of the

Communists, the Opposition Round Table, and various social organizations that were beginning to distance themselves from the ruling Party.

In January, the Central Committee of the Communist Party had also finally recognized the events of 1956 as a "popular uprising," rather than labeling them a "counterrevolution" as it had for the previous 33 years. This opened the way for the reburial of Imre Nagy, the reformist who had been Prime Minister during the uprising and who had been executed in 1958, chiefly for attempting to take Hungary out of the Warsaw Pact. This ceremony occurred on the 31st anniversary of his execution, June 16, 1989, and was followed by the death of János Kádár just over two weeks later. An era had ended: even before the revolutions elsewhere in central and eastern Europe, Hungary was already constructing its post-Communist political order.

The negotiations in the National Round Table proceeded over the summer of 1989, and final agreement was reached in September on an overhaul of the Constitution and the Constitutional Court, the functioning of political parties, multiparty elections, and the penal code. A new republic was declared on October 23, 1989, the 33rd anniversary of the outbreak of the 1956 uprising. Some of the parties, notably the AFD and Fidesz, objected to certain provisions in the agreement, especially those relating to proposals that would give the President strong executive powers. They collected sufficient signatures to force a referendum on these issues, which was held in November 1989 and which overturned the clauses on the presidency. Thus, Hungary acquired a new polity centered on a relatively powerful National Assembly.

Opinion polls taken during the summer of 1989 indicated that the Communist Party would be the likely winners of the first free elections, but three by-elections to fill empty Assembly seats indicated that public opinion was considerably more anti-Communist than the polls suggested. The Party itself was in a state of organizational collapse. Intellectuals within its apparatus had organized themselves into "reform circles" that promoted the democratization of the Party itself, and the opposition they generated among Party conservatives led to the formation of several warring platforms. These conflicts came to a head at the Party congress held in October 1989, where a majority of delegates voted the Party out of existence, reconstituting it as the Hungarian Socialist Party (HSP) with an explicitly social democratic program. Despite its open commitment to reform, the HSP rapidly lost support, in part because of a series of scandals relating to illegal police surveillance of opposition figures.

The collapse in support for the HSP was also driven by the dramatic events across the region. On September 11, 1989, the Foreign Minister, Gyula Horn, allowed 60,000 citizens of East Germany who were staying in Hungary to travel to the West, precipitating the wave of change that swept the region. By the end of the year, Communist regimes had fallen in all of Hungary's neighbors, with the exceptions of the Soviet Union and Yugoslavia. These events gave the opposition a greater degree of confidence, and undermined the authority of the HSP. Its last act in power was to draw up treaties with the Soviet Union guaranteeing the withdrawal of Soviet troops from Hungary.

## The Post-Communist Political System

The Constitution of the Republic of Hungary is a substantially amended version of the 1949 Constitution, which laid down the fundamental legal bases of the "dictatorship of the proletariat" at the beginning of the Stalinist years. The changes made in 1989 allowed the introduction of a multiparty system and the rule of law. Initially, the introductory clause stating that Hungary was a "people's democracy" was replaced with the statement that "Hungary is a republic, based equally on the principles of bourgeois democracy and democratic socialism." In 1990–91, however, the reference to "democratic socialism" was replaced with an assertion that the republic is based "on the rule of law." The Constitution guarantees many basic human rights. There is pressure from certain quarters, especially the liberal AFD, to conduct a root and branch revision of the Constitution.

The Constitutional Court, comprising judges appointed by the National Assembly for nine-year terms, has been very active in striking down legal provisions that it believes to be unconstitutional. Most spectacularly, it struck out several elements of a package cutting social welfare benefits targeted at families in June 1995.

The President of the Republic, who is elected by the National Assembly for a five-year term, has the power to sign or reject laws, formally appoints the government and its members, and decides on the dates of Assembly elections. Árpád Göncz, elected to the post on August 3, 1990, was reelected to a second term on June 19, 1995. There is considerable speculation about Göncz's successor: many commentators expect that the governing coalition will support the candidacy of the ISP leader József Torgyan (see below) when the election is held in 2000.

The government, headed by the Prime Minister, is formally appointed by the President of the Republic, but is directly accountable to the National Assembly, meaning, in practice, the party or parties with a majority in it. Ministerial appointments must be confirmed by the Assembly, and the government can be removed only by a constructive vote of no confidence by the Assembly.

The National Assembly comprises just one chamber, with 386 members, who sit for a term of four years. All citizens over the age of 18 are entitled to vote. Members of the Assembly can be elected in one of three ways: directly from one of the single-member constituencies; through being included on a county list of party candidates; or through inclusion on a national list. This complex system is designed to secure proportional representation of the population.

## The Course of Politics, 1990–99

The first free elections since 1947 were held in two rounds in March and April 1990. The HSP was utterly defeated, winning fourth place with just over 10% of the votes cast. In the first round, the HDF won first place by a narrow margin over the AFD, with the ISP taking a strong third place. Two more parties, Fidesz and the CDPP, also entered the National

Assembly. In the second round, assisted by anti-Communist rhetoric and a gradualist program of economic reform, the HDF and its allies, the ISP and the CDPP, together won a landslide victory. They were thus able to form a conservative coalition government, with József Antall as Prime Minister.

This coalition's tenure of office was not to be a happy one. It took office in the midst of an economic crisis, and was dogged by disputes between those who saw themselves as Christian democrats and their radical nationalist colleagues. This dispute led to a split, with the leader of the radical nationalists, the anti-Semitic writer István Csurka, leaving the HDF in 1993. The government was also undermined by another dispute, over the restitution of agricultural property confiscated under the Communist regime, that split the ISP. Its radical wing followed the party leader, József Torgyan, out of the government, while supporters of compromise remained inside. The government found itself accused of authoritarianism over its attempts to pack the state-controlled media with its own political appointees, while its strident nationalist rhetoric in relation to Hungarian minorities living in neighboring countries attracted widespread criticism. On top of all this, Prime Minister Antall was seriously ill with cancer, and died in December 1993. He was replaced by his Interior Minister, the authoritarian conservative Péter Boross. The coalition government became deeply unpopular for the rest of its term of office.

In the elections of 1994, the HSP staged a remarkable comeback, winning an absolute majority of seats but not of votes, and its leader Gyula Horn, who had been Foreign Minister in 1989, formed a coalition government with the AFD. In spite of a faltering start, this government pursued a technocratic liberal policy of reforming the economy. Lajos Bokros, a respected banker who was appointed Finance Minister in 1995, presided over a dramatic package of tax rises combined with savage cuts in welfare spending. Although Bokros resigned in February 1996, his policies were continued, and were augmented with a policy of widespread and rapid privatization, including the sale of energy utilities to foreign investors.

These policies were highly unpopular, and led to a fall of 9% in real incomes during 1995. However, living standards stabilized in 1996, and increased throughout 1997 and 1998.

The reforms were not enough to save the government when it sought reelection in May 1998, following a series of damaging corruption scandals. The HSP retained its position as the largest political force in the country in the first round, but this concealed major changes to the party system and a significant swing to the right among middle-class voters. The CDPP, damaged by splits, failed to win any seats, while the HDF was only able to retain any seats at all because of an electoral alliance with Fidesz. The extreme right-wing Hungarian Justice and Life Party (HJLP), led by István Csurka, the anti-Semitic writer who had left the HDF five years before, won over 5% of the votes cast, and its first seats in the Assembly, on the basis of an explicitly anti-Semitic program. Fidesz, repackaged as a center-right party in the mold of the British Conservatives, took 28% of the vote, while Torgyan's ISP increased its support. Support for the HSP's coalition partner, the AFD, collapsed, and for the first time since 1989 right-wing parties won over half the votes cast in the first round. This translated into a comfortable but not overwhelming second-round victory for the center-right parties.

The new coalition government formed by Fidesz, the ISP, and what remains of the HDF, is headed by the Fidesz leader Viktor Orbán (born in 1963). Largely composed of little-known technocrats, the government has broadly continued the economic policies of the Horn government, although it has taken a harder line with the banking industry. It has also sought to remodel the welfare system, in order to support the traditional two-parent family, and has sharply increased the number of police on duty as part of a drive against crime. Its attempts to tighten state control of the media, highly reminiscent of the period between 1990 and 1994, are a major cause for concern at present, but its chances of reelection depend much more on the performance of the economy.

Local elections in October 1998 broadly confirmed the results of the May elections, but revealed a sharp difference in voting behavior between Budapest, which voted for the left, and the rest of the country. More worryingly, they also demonstrated a growing willingness among lower middle-class voters in urban areas to vote for the extreme right. Nevertheless, with just six parties in the National Assembly – examined below in order of the number of seats they now hold – Hungary is still a relatively stable liberal democracy.

## The Hungarian Socialist Party (HSP)

The HSP has broad popular support across all age groups and social classes, although its support is particularly concentrated among urban working-class voters; it generally performs very poorly among the very young and the very old. It lost power in May 1998 not because of its own performance – it retained its share of vote, and polled more votes than any other single party – but because of the poor performance of its liberal coalition partner, the AFD. In the summer of 1998, Gyula Horn resigned as party leader, and was succeeded by the former Foreign Minister, László Kovács.

Over the course of the 1990s, the HSP's program has shifted from social democracy to what might be characterized as a technocratic-liberal position. It has abandoned its support for generous family welfare benefits and state-guaranteed pensions, having introduced means testing for the former and moved in the direction of promoting private sector provision of the latter. In government, it supported massive privatization, and high taxation of those on relatively low incomes, as well as consumers in general. It advocates a policy of pacification with Romania and Slovakia over the issue of Hungarians living in those countries, and is strongly committed to Hungarian membership of the EU and NATO. Kovács has been closely associated with these policy shifts.

The HSP will find it very difficult to benefit from any decline in the present government's unpopularity, as it is discredited as far as much of the electorate is concerned. Its appeal to left-wing voters was seriously undermined by the social and economic policies it implemented in government between 1994 and 1998. This was compounded by the HSP's involvement in several corruption scandals, which have raised questions about the way in which its Communist past translates into collusion in corruption through the various links that are widely believed to exist among state agencies, big business, and organized crime.

## The Alliance of Young Democrats (Fidesz) and the Hungarian Democratic Forum (HDF)

The HDF, the first non-Communist party to be founded in Hungary in the 1980s, has never recovered from the collapse in its support after its years as the largest party in the first democratic government. In contrast, Fidesz has expanded, collapsed, and then recovered, entering government just over 10 years after it was founded by a group of university students.

Fidesz came to prominence as a political movement in the fall of 1989, when it joined with the AFD in refusing to sign the Round Table agreement and campaigning against a strong presidency. In 1993, it reformed its structures, adopting an identifiably conservative program and driving out prominent politicians from its liberal wing. Its leader, Viktor Orbán, was widely distrusted and came to be seen as power-hungry as a result of these struggles. These factors resulted in a spectacular defeat for the party in the 1994 elections, when it won exactly 7% of the vote and only 20 seats. Since then it has staged a remarkable comeback, repackaging itself as a modern conservative party. For the 1998 elections, Fidesz positioned itself very skillfully, outflanking the HSP on the left with policies to abolish student tuition fees and restore cuts in child benefits, while using anti-Communist rhetoric and promising demonopolization of utilities privatized by the HSP-AFD government. It won the largest number of seats, but not of votes, as a result, carrying the remnants of the once powerful HDF along with it.

## The Independent Smallholders Party (ISP)

Since 1991, the fate of the ISP has been bound up with the personality of József Torgyan, a powerful right-wing demagogue who used questionable tactics to get himself elected as its president in that year, thus provoking a major split. The matter was brought to a head when Torgyan attempted to withdraw from the government of the day over the restitution issue (see above), and expelled a majority of the ISP's members in the National Assembly in early 1992. In 1993, in contravention of a legal ban on parties being named after living individuals, he attempted to set up a Torgyan Party, with his wife as president and his face as the party symbol, and when registration was denied he loudly complained of his personal rights being breached. Despite this rebuff, and the lack of any election manifesto to speak of, Torgyan and the ISP won 8.85% of the votes, and 26 seats, in 1994. Exit polls showed that he took votes largely from older and poorer male voters strongly disillusioned with the economic situation.

Torgyan's right-wing populism put him in a strong position to profit from the unpopularity of the HSP-AFD coalition government and its free market economic policies. A powerful public speaker, he has advocated at various times a default on Hungary's foreign debt, cuts in taxation, and a large-scale "calling to account" of former Communists who have benefited from privatization. The ISP also has a strongly nationalistic platform, and has vociferously opposed the treaties of understanding that the Horn government signed with Romania and Slovakia, which renounced Hungarian territorial designs on Transylvania and southern Slovakia. Several senior ISP politicians have made thinly veiled racist statements about minorities living inside their country and the inhabitants of neighboring states. Agnes Maczó, an ISP member who was Deputy Speaker of the National Assembly, found herself at the center of a storm in the spring of 1997, when she made comments that were interpreted as blaming Jews for Stalinism. Torgyan himself has been accused by the Interior Ministry of being a secret police informer during the Communist period, although it has not made public any documents that might support this allegation.

After the 1998 elections, the ISP joined the new center-right coalition, and Torgyan became Minister of Agriculture. Because of the

ISP's populist nature, questions must be raised about how long its support for the government will last, and about the effects that its participation will have on economic and social policy in the long term.

## The Alliance of Free Democrats (AFD)

The AFD broke out of its original base among Budapest intellectuals to become a mass party during the referendum campaign in November 1989 (see above). In 1991–92, it was plunged into internal divisions between its founders and the representatives of the mass membership, which were resolved when one of the Budapest intellectuals, Iván Petö, became party president, while others, paradoxically, retreated from their front-line roles in the party's internal affairs. Gábor Kuncze, who was relatively little-known, led the AFD's election campaign in 1994, when it retained its position as the country's second largest party, winning 19.76% of the votes cast. In the HSP-AFD coalition government, Kuncze served as Deputy Prime Minister and Minister of the Interior, while the AFD as a whole played the role of guarantor that the government would remain committed to a radical, market-based restructuring of the economy and the welfare system. This commitment, coupled with the perception among right-wing voters that the AFD's leadership was dominated by people of Jewish origin, made the party increasingly unpopular. The 1998 elections saw its support slump to 7.72% of the votes cast. This has created a crisis within the party, and there is a ferocious debate under way about its future.

## The Hungarian Justice and Life Party (HJLP)

The HJLP is by far the most significant of the extreme right-wing parties in Hungary. It was founded by the notorious anti-Semite and former HDF vice-president István Csurka, after he was expelled from that party in 1993. Csurka has written that Hungary is the victim of a Jewish conspiracy orchestrated in New York, Moscow, and Tel Aviv, and the HJLP's program calls for vigorous action to combat foreign influences, including strong restrictions on the rights of non-Hungarians to own property. It performed poorly in the 1994 elections to the National Assembly, winning only 1.58% of the votes cast, but it then formed an alliance with József Torgyan's ISP. In late 1994, the two parties together won 9% of the votes cast for the Budapest city assembly and took second place to the HSP in Pest county. The HJLP's newspaper, *Magyar Forum*, is widely available, and since 1994 the party has consistently shown that it can organize large demonstrations in the capital.

In the 1998 elections, the HJLP entered the National Assembly, taking 5.3% of the votes cast. It performed especially well among urban, elderly, middle-class voters angry at the decline in the purchasing power of their pensions. In the local elections in October 1998, it demonstrated that it has the potential to expand further, winning around 20% of the vote in some of the outer districts of Budapest. Because of the lack of credibility of the HSP, it is the HJLP that is likely to benefit from any discontent with the center-right coalition government.

## The Post-Communist Economy

The beginnings of Hungary's transformation into a market economy can be found, not in 1989, but at the end of the 1970s. Hungary's external debt had approached crisis proportions, and from 1978 onward policy shifted toward austerity and the gradual legalization of the private sector. Small-scale private entrepreneurship was legalized and encouraged in the early 1980s, leading some social scientists to speak of an emerging "socialist mixed economy" by the middle of the decade. Subsidies were gradually cut from 1979, and serious attempts to rationalize loss-making state enterprises began in the mid-1980s. From 1988, it became increasingly clear to policymakers that further progress could not be made without more far-reaching austerity policies and more radical marketization.

Large-scale privatization began in 1989, although not without controversy. Anger was directed at "spontaneous privatization," in which managers effectively transferred the ownership of their companies to foreign investors, often with tacit state approval, under terms preferential to themselves. During 1990 and 1991, the institutions of a market economy were put in place with the creation of new procedures for financial services, a stock exchange, and an independent central bank. A bankruptcy law was introduced at the same time, but was not implemented until 1992. Finally, a State Property Agency was created to supervise large-scale privatization.

These attempts to introduce the institutions of a market economy did not occur under the most auspicious circumstances. As a result of the collapse of Communist regimes elsewhere in central and eastern Europe, and at the insistence of the IMF, the system of trade based on the Russian ruble collapsed. As a result, the markets for much of Hungary's industrial and agricultural output disappeared overnight. This coincided with the end of the 1980s boom in western Europe, and with the introduction of severe austerity policies elsewhere in the region. A severe recession followed: GDP fell by 20% between 1990 and 1992, and unemployment reached 11% in 1993, while real wages fell catastrophically. Government attempts to reduce subsidies met with unrest, most dramatically when a plan to increase the price of gas was abandoned in 1990 after taxi drivers blockaded key transportation routes in protest. The recession combined with accelerating inflation, which exceeded 20% by 1993.

However, during the years of recession the budgetary situation improved. The external debt burden fell, the budget deficit was reduced, and the balance of payments fell. In 1993, the government, faced with the prospect of elections the following year, began to stimulate the economy by relaxing its control of public expenditure and easing credit restrictions. Despite success in attracting foreign direct investment – until 1994 Hungary attracted around two thirds of all such inflows into the region – the economy was not transformed. Inflationary pressures grew throughout the economy as the balance of payments deteriorated.

It was this situation that the HSP-AFD coalition government inherited in 1994. Public opinion surveys revealed that the HSP owed its election success to growing skepticism among voters about the desirability and feasibility of market-based transformation, while the directors of large state corporations could exert considerable influence within the HSP in the direction of delaying reform. However, technocrats within the HSP, led by the new Finance Minister, László Bekési, joined with the AFD to call for an acceleration of market-based reform, combined with decisive measures to ease the balance of payments problem. Bekési managed to put through a package of mild tax increases, spending cuts, and moderate devaluation in the second half of 1994, but these failed to ease the situation.

Bekési resigned in frustration at the beginning of 1995, and a crisis ensued. There was a significant problem of capital flight during the first two months of the year, and the possibility of a currency crisis loomed large. The new Finance Minister, Lajos Bokros, a technocrat and banker, insisted that he be given the authority to deal with the situation, and the Prime Minister, Gyula Horn, who is believed to have argued for a social democratic approach, gave way. In March 1995, an austerity package was unveiled, designed principally to restore the confidence of investors and the IMF. It sharply increased taxes and cut welfare spending, means-testing family allowances and abolishing supplementary child support. Bokros also began to draw up detailed medium-term plans to reduce welfare expenditure, which included a greater role for the private sector in pensions and health services. Tuition fees were introduced in higher education, and a round of large-scale public sector staff cuts was announced. The Hungarian currency, the forint, was sharply devalued and was then subjected to a rolling series of smaller monthly devaluations. Finally, in order to reduce imports an 8% levy was introduced. Microeconomic transformation also accelerated in 1995. Responsibility for privatization was removed from the Ministry of Industry and Commerce, and given to a new Privatization Ministry. As a result, privatization speeded up with the sale of Hungary's energy utilities to foreign investors during 1995 and 1996.

The Bokros package, as it had become known, became the major political issue in Hungary during 1995. It led to a general fall in real wages, depressed demand, and led to zero growth in 1995 and for much of 1996. The welfare cuts hit poorer families especially hard. Strikes and demonstrations by public sector workers increased, and opinion polls pointed to a recovery by the right-wing opposition parties. Worried about public unrest and their own prospects of reelection, the HSP-AFD government began to slacken the pace of reform in 1996. Bokros resigned and was replaced by Péter Medgyessy. The economy began to grow in the second half of 1996. By 1998, economic growth was estimated to be around 4%; inflation fell below 20% in 1997 and continued to fall in 1998. Yet this picture of general improvement concealed several underlying problems.

Hungary has successfully adopted a strategy based on attracting a substantial proportion of foreign direct investment. It has become a significant automobile producer as a result of investment by Suzuki at Esztergom, General Motors at Szént Gotthard, Audi at Györ, and Ford at Székesfehérvár. Meanwhile, Székesfehérvár as a whole has been held up as an economic success as a result of large-scale investment not only by Ford but also by IBM and Philips. However, this has led to regional imbalances: Budapest and the Northwest of the country attract the bulk of foreign investment, leaving the Southwest and Northeast severely depressed. Most new investment has been "greenfield" (on completely new sites), leaving many labor-intensive producers crisis-ridden. For example, Ikarusz, which produced most of the Soviet bloc's buses under Communism, suffered severe problems during the mid-1990s, while steel production has fallen, with surviving plants complaining of having no money to invest in modernization. The banking industry remains debt-ridden and prone to crisis. Revelations about Posta Bánk, then the country's second largest bank, led to the mass closure of accounts by its customers in 1997, and it was allowed to fail in 1998.

By early 1998, it was becoming clear that the improved economic position was coupled with a recurring deterioration in the balance of payments. Medgyessy's explanation that this was simply a symptom of Hungary's success in attracting foreign investment was less than convincing. Instead, it seemed that wealthier consumers were spending their rising incomes on imported goods, while Hungary's overall trading position had been improved, but not transformed, by foreign investment.

The prospects for the Hungarian economy are difficult to assess. Hungary has largely reoriented its exports toward the West, but the effects of the financial crisis in Russia in 1998 suggest that the degree to which it has done this is exaggerated by official statistics. The last months of 1998 were characterized by the collapse of a large number of companies, particularly in the food-processing industry, while the center-right government, in office for only a few months at that point, provided subsidy packages to some heavy industrial companies tied into Russian markets. A greater cause for concern lay in the dependence of some of Hungary's immediate neighbors on those same markets, which may well have indirect negative effects on Hungary too.

## Conclusion

Since 1989, Hungary has made steady progress toward the creation of a functioning democratic polity and a market economy. Of course, this process has not been free of problems. Despite notable successes, such as the country's ability to attract foreign direct investment, there are a series of major structural problems relating to the distribution of that investment and the imperfect transformation of what used to be the state sector. In the political sphere, a broadly democratic political system has been established, and there have been three peaceful transfers of power as a result of free elections. Despite the ejection of some minor parties from the National Assembly in 1998, the party system is broadly stable. Hungary has also made considerable progress toward establishing a state fully based on the rule of law.

Nevertheless, there are several questions that must be raised about Hungary's transition. It is clear that a majority of Hungarians remain committed to a mixed economy and a strong welfare system, entailing a degree of state intervention significantly greater than has been envisaged in any government's reform program. There is also considerable public disquiet about increasing inequality, corruption, and organized crime, and a lack of trust between the population and their politicians. There has been a perceptible rise in the influence of political extremists, especially on the far right of the spectrum. Accordingly, while an overwhelming majority of Hungarians support the democratic political order, it is possible that politics in the first decade of the 21st century will be more turbulent than in the last decade of the 20th.

## Further Reading

Balogh, István, *Törésvonalak és Értekválasztások: Politikaitudományi Vizsgálatok a Mai Magyarországról* [Broken Lines and Choices of Values: Examinations of Contemporary Hungary from the Point of View of Political Science], Budapest: MTA Politikai Tudományok Intézete, 1994

An excellent collection of articles on the emergence of the new democratic system just before the HSP's election victory in 1994

Bihári, Mihály, editor, *A Többpártrendszer Kialakulása Magyarországon, 1985–1991: Tanulmánykötet* [The Development of the Multiparty System in Hungary, 1985–91], Budapest: Kossuth Könyvkiadó, 1992

An essential collection of articles on the early stages of party formation

Bozóki, András, editor, *Tiszta Lappal: A FIDESZ a Magyar Politikában 1988–1991* [With a Clean Sheet: Fidesz in Hungarian Politics, 1988–91], Budapest: Fidesz, 1992

A comprehensive collection of documents about Fidesz, showing its transformation from a youth movement into a quasi-party between 1988 and 1991

Bruszt, László, *A Centralizáció Csapdája* [The Trap of Centralization], Szombathely: Savaria University Press, 1995

A thoughtful collection of articles on the sociopolitical dynamics of the transition process, by an academic on the center-left of the Hungarian political spectrum

Csizmadia, Ervin, *A Magyar Demokratikus Ellenzék, 1968–1988*, Elsö Kötet, *Monográfia* [The Hungarian Democratic Opposition, 1968–88, Volume One, Monograph], Budapest: T-Twins Kiadó, 1995

A comprehensive history of urban dissidents in Hungary from the end of the 1960s to the eve of the change of system, based on interviews and extensive archival research

Földes, György, *Hatalom és Mozgalom (1956–1989): Társadalmi-politikai Erőviszonyok Magyarországon* [The State and the Movement, 1956–89: State-Society Relations in Hungary], Budapest: Reform Könyvkiadó-Kossuth Könyvkiadó, 1989

An original analysis of the malfunctioning of the reform Communist model in Hungary, from the perspective of a young reformer within the Party

Földes, György, *Az Eladósodás Politikatörténete, 1957–1986* [The Political History of Indebtedness, 1957–86], Budapest: Maecenás Könyvkiadó, 1995

A history of Hungarian public finance in the Communist years, based on extensive archival research, this is the best introduction to the economic legacy left ·by the Communists to the new republic in 1989.

Gombár, Csaba et al., editors, *Kormány a Mérlegen 1990–1994* [Government in Balance, 1990–94], Budapest: Korridor, 1994

An informative collection of articles analyzing the performance of the conservative coalition government between 1990 and 1994

Gombár, Csaba et al., editors, *Question Marks: The Hungarian Government 1994–1995*, Budapest: Korridor, 1995

A strange collection of journalistic articles dealing with the first few months of rule by the HSP-AFD coalition

Halpern, Lászlá, and Charles Wyplosz, editors, *Hungary: Towards a Market Economy*, Cambridge and New York: Cambridge University Press, 1998

An excellent collection of articles and easily the best introduction to the economics of the transition

Hankiss, Elemér, "Demobilization, Self-Mobilization and Quasi-Mobilization in Hungary, 1948–87," in *East European Politics and Societies*, Volume 3, number 1, 1988

Hankiss, Elemér, *East European Alternatives*, Oxford: Clarendon Press, and New York: Oxford University Press, 1990

Hankiss, Elemér, "The 'Second Society': Is There an Alternative Social Model Emerging in Contemporary Hungary?" in Ferenc Fehér and Andrew Arató, editors, *Crisis and Reform in Eastern Europe*, New Brunswick, NJ: Transaction Publishers, 1991

This and the previous two works by Hankiss form a highly influential analysis of the system change in 1989.

Pittaway, Mark, and Nigel Swain, "Hungary" in Bogdan Szajkowski, editor, *Political Parties in Eastern Europe, Russia and the Successor States*, Harlow: Longman, and New York: Stockton Press, 1994

An introduction to Hungarian politics between 1988 and 1994

Ripp, Zoltán, *Szabad Demokraták: Történeti Vázlat a Szabad Demokraták Szövetségének Politikájáról (1988–1994)* [Free Democrats: A Historical Analysis of the Politics of the Alliance of Free Democrats, 1988–94], Budapest: Napvilág Kiadó, 1995

A useful history of the AFD, written largely from the journalistic record

Stark, David, "The Micropolitics of the Firm and the Macropolitics of Reform: New Forms of Workplace Bargaining in Hungarian Enterprises," in Peter Evans, Dietrich Rueschemeyer, and Evelyne Huber Stephens, editors, *States versus Markets in the World System*, Beverley Hills, CA: Sage, 1985

Stark, David, "Rethinking Internal Labor Markets: New Insights from a Comparative Perspective," in *American Sociological Review*, Volume 51, 1986

Stark, David, "Coexisting Organizational Forms in Hungary's Emerging Mixed Economy," in Victor Nee and David Stark, with Mark Selden, editors, *Remaking the Economic Institutions of Socialism: China and Eastern Europe*, Stanford, CA: Stanford University Press, 1989

These three articles by David Stark are interesting and informative on aspects of the spread of the private sector during the 1980s.

Swain, Nigel, *Hungary: the Rise and Fall of Feasible Socialism*, London and New York: Verso, 1992

The best general introduction in English to the Hungarian economy up to 1989

Szalai, Erzsébet, *Útelágazás: Hatalom és Értelmiség az Államszocializmus Után* [Intellectuals and the State in Hungary After State Socialism], Szombathely: Savaria University Press, 1994

A collection of this writer's pioneering articles on the sociopolitical dimension of privatization

Szelényi, Iván, et al. *Socialist Entrepreneurs: Embourgeoisement in Rural Hungary*, Cambridge: Polity Press, and Madison: University of Wisconsin Press, 1988

A good guide to the emergence of the private sector in the 1980s

Tökes, Rudolf L., *Hungary's Negotiated Revolution: Economic Reform, Social Change and Political Succession, 1957–1990*, Cambridge and New York: Cambridge University Press, 1996

An unwieldy but interesting account of the roots of the system change

## Periodicals

The author has used material derived from the Hungarian national press in the preparation of this chapter, especially *Figyelö, Héti Világgazdaság, Magyar Hírlap, Népszabadság,* and *Népszava.*

*Dr Mark Pittaway* is a Lecturer in European Studies at the Open University in the United Kingdom. He has worked extensively in Hungary, gaining access to recently opened archives on the Communist past, and is working on a book on industrialization and social change during the first decade of Communist rule.

Chapter Three

# The Baltic States

*Wayne C. Thompson*

The disintegration of the Soviet Union in 1991 enabled the Baltic states to be the first countries directly controlled by the Soviet regime to regain their independence. All three faced myriad challenges, such as being severed from their traditional markets, introducing new currencies, establishing their own military forces from scratch, negotiating the departure of former Soviet troops and cleaning up the environmental damage they had caused, adopting new constitutions and sets of laws, and organizing their first democratic elections since the 1930s.

This dramatic turn in history did not automatically eradicate the legacies of an overbearing Soviet empire. In order to maintain control over a sprawling multinational region and promote industrialization, the Kremlin had intentionally mixed peoples and capriciously changed borders. All three Baltic states were left to deal with the residual problems: Who belongs to the restored sovereign states with a claim to automatic citizenship? Can a democracy deny full rights to sizable minorities who were living and working in the country at the time of independence? Where should borders be drawn? How extensively and quickly can a Soviet-style economy be converted to a free market? Do the newly independent states belong to a Russian "sphere of influence," and do they owe special deference to their powerful neighbor? How can the new small states find military security?

In the 1990s, the Baltic Sea became one of the most important and complicated areas in the new Europe. It links nine European countries, including two of its largest, Russia and Germany, and some of its smallest. Democracy

is practiced in each, but in some, particularly Russia, it is new and fragile and is accompanied by a weak rule of law and much corruption. Economic and informal ties are thriving all around. Along the western littoral are some of the world's most prosperous nations; along the eastern littoral is poverty, especially in Russia, but also in the Baltic states and Poland. Eyes are on the Baltic states because the ways they are grappling with fundamental problems of economic transformation and modernization provide insights and inspiration for other post-Communist countries.

Through the Baltic states one can also observe how the West will deal with an uncertain and truncated Russian colossus, which still instills fear and wariness in all other Baltic Sea states. This region is the gateway to Russia and contains one of Europe's most complicated geopolitical challenges: how to provide protection for Estonia, Latvia, and Lithuania. Their security is a kind of political and moral litmus test for the extent to which Russia has genuinely changed and has shed its age-old imperial aspirations.

It should be noted that these three states have as many differences as similarities. They are all small in geography and population, they have a history of repeated foreign domination and of only a few decades of independence (entirely within the 20th century), and they have experienced humiliation and exploitation by the Soviet Union. Nevertheless, they are three very different nations, with separate languages. Estonian is a Finno-Ugric language related to that of Finland, a country with which Estonia has very close relations. Latvian and Lithuanian are ancient

Indo-European languages. The three are mutually incomprehensible. There are differing ethnic mixes, as well as cultural heritages. For example, the Catholic Church has played a special role in Lithuania, while religion is less important in Protestant Estonia. Finally, these three countries had little experience or inclination to cooperate closely with each other before the late 1980s. Even today their cooperation, although extensive, is pragmatic and has its limits.

## History

The Baltic states have experienced a succession of foreign masters: Danes, Germans, Swedes, Poles, and Russians. During the Great Northern War, which began in 1700, the Russian Emperor Peter the Great conquered the area around Riga (now the capital of Latvia), and what is now Estonia, in 1710. Under the Treaty of Nystad (1721), which ended the war, Russia formally acquired two extra provinces: Estonia (then comprising only the northern part of the modern state) and Livonia (consisting of what are now southern Estonia and northern Latvia). Russia went on to annex Courland (now northern Lithuania) in 1795. For most of the 19th century the Russian emperors supported reforms that enabled the Baltic peoples to develop their national culture. This ended in 1881, when Alexander III came to power and ordered a policy of Russification. Russian was declared the official language and the medium of instruction, and the Russian Orthodox religion was imposed. This strict program of Russification was terminated after the Russian Revolution of 1905.

World War I created the conditions for their independence. When the Russian empire fell in 1917, the Baltic states supported the Provisional Government in Petrograd (as St Petersburg was then called), and pressed for self-government. Estonia was allowed to unify the ethnic Estonian lands, and in the Treaty of Brest-Litovsk, signed with Germany in March 1918, the Bolshevik government renounced claims to the Baltic states. Germany, with some support from the local ethnic German elites, occupied the entire Baltic coastal area and

threatened to annex it, but as German soldiers had to withdraw, Bolshevik troops rushed back in, forcing the Baltic peoples to fight them to gain their independence. In Estonia, for example, Bolshevik forces supported the creation of a Communist provisional government, based in the Northeast of the country, in March 1919. The Estonians defeated the Bolsheviks in January 1920, in one of the few military victories in their history, and signed the Treaty of Tartu with Soviet Russia on February 2, 1920. This drew the border along the military front lines and recognized Estonia's independence, sovereignty, and neutrality "forever." Unlike the Treaty of Brest-Litovsk, which had been dictated by Germany (and was accordingly annulled by the Treaty of Versailles in 1919), this was a bundle of diplomatic instruments that constituted a lasting mutual recognition of each signatory country as an object of international law. Similar treaties were signed with Lithuania on July 12, 1920, and with Latvia on August 11.

Between the world wars, the Soviet Union, like other European countries, peered anxiously at a restless and expansive Germany, and it sought to protect itself. On August 23, 1939, the Soviet Union and Germany signed a nonaggression pact that contained a secret protocol dividing central and eastern Europe into spheres of influence: Finland, Estonia, Latvia and (one month later) Lithuania were assigned to the Soviet Union. This freed Moscow's hand to attack Finland in November 1939 and ultimately force it to make territorial concessions, while remaining independent. It also enabled Stalin to issue ultimatums to the Baltic states in 1939, and again in 1940, to accept Soviet troops on their soil. He then demanded governments loyal to the Soviet Union. With small numbers of their own troops surrounded on their own territories by superior numbers of Soviet troops, and noting that 25,000 Finns had died in the unsuccessful effort to thwart a Soviet invasion, they did not dare resist.

Believing he could temporarily stave off disaster for the Estonian nation until the frightening political situation improved, President Konstantin Päts signed a document accepting Stalin's demands. He and most other Estonian leaders were then deported to the Soviet

Union. The new Moscow-controlled government, aided by local Estonian Communists – numbering only 133 in the entire country – staged legislative elections, during which no mention of any impending annexation by the Soviet Union was made. Only Communistdominated organizations were allowed to nominate candidates, and deputies obedient to the Communists won 92.8% of the votes. The new "People's Assembly" formally asked to join the Soviet Union on July 22, 1940, and was accepted on August 6, 1940. The other Baltic states were led through the same procedure and met the same fate in August 1940. Russia continues to insist that all three had voluntarily joined the Soviet Union.

Interrupted only by German occupation from 1941 to 1944, the Baltic states spent the next half-century as disgruntled but relatively prosperous republics of the Soviet Union. Encouraged by Mikhail Gorbachev's reform proposals, which permitted more free discussion and toleration than ever before in Soviet history, they seized the opportunity, first to enlarge their self-determination within the Soviet Union, and then to gain complete independence. In 1988 "popular fronts," composed of both Gorbachev Communists and nonCommunist democrats and nationalists were formed, first in Estonia and then in Latvia and Lithuania (for the consequences of tensions among these dissident groups, see Blaney pp. 240–9). On August 23, 1989, 2 million Estonians, Latvians and Lithuanians formed a human chain from Tallinn to Vilnius to dramatize their demand for freedom. With large and articulate exile groups, especially in the United States, the three peoples were able to mobilize considerable international sympathy and diplomatic support for their aspirations. This was especially facilitated by the fact that all western democracies, except Sweden and, briefly, Australia, had refused to recognize the Soviet Union's annexation of the Baltic states in 1940.

Lithuania became the first Soviet republic to declare its independence on March 11, 1990, followed by Estonia on March 30 and Latvia on May 4. On May 12, the heads of all three countries signed the Declaration of Concord and Cooperation reestablishing the Council of the Baltic States (founded in 1934).

Gorbachev indignantly rejected these demands for independence and even ordered that Interior Ministry troops use force against dissidents in the streets of Vilnius on January 13, 1991, killing 15 of them. A week later, six persons were killed in Riga, and the threat of violence also hung over Estonia. Boris Yeltsin, President of Russia, supported the Baltic states' calls for freedom, and Gorbachev ultimately joined him in agreeing to sign a new union treaty on August 17, 1991. This treaty, along with the prospects of Baltic independence, precipitated the Moscow coup attempt against Gorbachev on that day. The failure of the insurrection, after only five days, prompted most countries in the world to recognize the independence of the Baltic states. The Nordic countries and the European Community (now the EU) were first, followed by the United States on September 2, and the Soviet Union on September 6, 1991. On September 17, 1991, the Baltic states, which had belonged to the League of Nations, were admitted to the UN.

## Political Systems

All three newly independent states proceeded rapidly to hold free elections, and to establish the kind of institutional and legal conditions that place them within the western political model. They have all developed multiparty systems in which democratic procedures are respected. Despite frequent changes of coalitions and cabinets, they have maintained underlying political stability while demonstrating that power can be transferred peacefully from one coalition government to another. In Latvia and Lithuania, but not in Estonia, parties of former Communists have been able to win power, but they relinquished it when they no longer had the voters' support.

### Estonia

An Estonian constitutional assembly with a wide popular and political base, and led by the democratic nationalist segment of the independence movement, prepared a new constitution. Remembering the autocratic government that emerged in the tumultuous 1930s, the majority rejected the Constitution of 1938, with its strong executive, and adopted instead a parliamentary system, rather than a presidential one. The new Constitution, and a law denying automatic citizenship to non-Estonians who had moved to the country after 1940, were submitted to a referendum on June 28, 1992, three months before the first legislative elections, and were accepted overwhelmingly.

The political heart of Estonia is the unicameral 101-seat legislature, the Riigikogu, elected by proportional representation every four years. The politician who can assemble a majority coalition in the Riigikogu becomes Prime Minister, the most important political figure. The Riigikogu elects the President for a four-year term, although an exception was made for the first post-Soviet presidential election, when first-round votes were cast by the citizens. The prestige of Lennart Meri, President since 1992, is so great that the presidency has gained a level of importance and authority that the drafters had not intended. A multilingual philologist and specialist in Finno-Ugric languages, he is the son of a prewar President. He and his family had been deported to Siberia from 1941 to 1946, an experience that helped him decide never to join the Soviet Communist party. He was Foreign Minister and Ambassador to Finland before winning the presidency.

Only Estonian citizens can vote in national elections, but non-citizens who are legal residents are permitted to vote in local elections. Although only citizens can stand as candidates, non-citizens can have an input into that level of government closest to them. This is important especially in areas with large Russian-speaking populations, such as the Northeast around Narva, and in the capital city of Tallinn, where 40% of the residents are not native Estonians.

Of importance is the number of exiles who have returned to play important political, military, and economic roles, although some individuals who lived in comfortable western exile during the Soviet period sometimes experience resentment among certain segments of the population. They must learn to be tactful in offering more efficient foreign ways of doing things. In Estonia the individual who won most votes in early elections for the Riigikogu was a US citizen, Jüri Toomepuu, while one of the losers in the first presidential election was a US political scientist, Rein Taagepera, who was founding Dean of Tartu University's School of Social Sciences. Estonia's first Defense Minister was Hein Rebas, a Swedish Army reserve officer, and a retired US Army colonel, Alexander Einseln, commanded its defense forces. Its first Ambassador in Washington, DC, was Toomas Ilves, who was born in Sweden and moved to the United States, where he became a commentator for the Estonian service of Radio Free Europe. From 1996 to 1998 he was Estonia's Foreign Minister, but he then resigned the post to engage in electoral politics.

## Latvia

With some alterations, Latvia readopted on July 6, 1993, its Constitution of 1922, which calls for a stronger presidency than in Estonia. The President is elected for a three-year term by the unicameral legislature, the Saeima; its 100 members serve three years and are elected by proportional representation in five constituencies. Parties must win at least 5% of the votes to obtain seats. Non-citizens are not permitted to vote in national or local elections.

Returned exiles have been prominent in Latvia, as in Estonia. Latvia's first ambassador to the United States, Stasys Lozoraitis, was a US citizen, as was Gunars Meierovics, a leader in one of the country's most successful parties, "Latvia's Way."

## Lithuania

Lithuania's Constitution readopts the strong presidential system of the prewar republic. The President is popularly elected every five years, and establishes the country's foreign and domestic policy. He or she may issue decrees, declare a state of emergency, and return laws passed by the unicameral legislature, the Seimas, for reconsideration. Next in order of importance is the Chairman of the 141-member Seimas. Its deputies are elected for terms of four years; 71 are elected by direct vote and 70 by proportional representation.

The President appoints the Prime Minister, who must retain the support of a majority in the Seimas and is responsible for day-to-day operations, as well as for maintaining diplomatic relations with foreign countries and international organizations.

In January 1998 a former senior official of the US Environmental Protection Agency, Valdas Adamkus, was elected President of Lithuania. A narrow majority of voters hoped that his know-how and international connections would firmly root their future in the West. In his words: "I want to see Lithuania as a democratic country so that the younger generation will grow up under western cultural influence" (quoted in *The European*, February 2, 1998).

## Populations

All three countries have small populations. According to official estimates for 1998, Estonia's was 1.454 million (with 506,000 in Tallinn, the capital); Latvia's was 2.7 million (915,000 in Riga); and Lithuania's was 3.69 million (582,000 in Vilnius). Today, only Lithuania is largely ethnically homogeneous.

In their respective countries in 1934, ethnic Estonians constituted over 88%, Latvians 75.5%, and Lithuanians 84%. Russians were the largest minority in both Estonia (8.5%) and Latvia (12%). They enjoyed citizenship, language guarantees, their own schools, and cultural autonomy. After they had been bullied into the Soviet Union in 1940, the demography of the three republics changed. When Soviet rule ended in 1991, 2.3 million Russians were left behind.

Around 80% of Lithuania's population are ethnic Lithuanians. Only 9.4% of the residents are Russian, living mainly in cities. In 1940, the country acquired a sizable minority of Poles, now numbering about 260,000, or 7% of the total, and residing mainly in Vilnius and in the rural Southeast, through its acquisition of Vilnius and the surrounding area. Its Communist leaders skillfully prevented a large influx of Russian-speakers, enabling it to grant almost universal citizenship to all residents in 1991 without risking a loss of control over the nation's destiny.

This is the kind of automatic citizenship – the "zero option" adopted by most former Soviet republics – that Russia demands of Estonia and Latvia, where the situation was very different. Estonians constituted 97% of the country's population in 1945, after Russia had incorporated predominantly Russian-speaking areas in the East, 72% in 1953, 64.7% in 1979, and 61.5% in 1989. By 1999 this had risen to 65%, due to Russian outmigration after independence, leaving an ethnic mix of 28.7% Russians, 2.7% Ukrainians, 1.5% Belarusians, 1% Finns, and 1.9% other nationalities. The situation was even worse in Latvia, where the non-Latvian population reached almost half by 1991, an astonishing 63% in the capital city, Riga, and a majority in the six next largest cities. By 1996 only 56.7% of the country's residents were Latvian, while 30.3% were Russian, 4.3% Belarusian, 2.7% Ukrainian, and 2.6% Polish. Massive inward migration of Russians, and outward deportation of native Estonians and Latvians, had dramatically changed their demographic mix and threatened their national survival.

Many Russian-speakers find themselves in a dilemma. For many, return to Russia or any other former Soviet republic is unthinkable. Their jobs, residences, friends and relatives have long been in the Baltic states, and there is economic chaos and political instability to the East. Most want to stay. In Estonia, for example, a poll conducted in the Northeast of the country in 1995 indicated that only 1% were willing to leave, although one third were keeping open the option of repatriating (Tartu University pp. 3, 10).

Although Russian-speakers lead largely separate lives in Estonia and Latvia, they bear little hatred or deep aversion toward Baltic nationals. Another poll in 1995 showed two thirds of non-Estonians expressing a liking toward Estonia and Estonians (Howell p. 3), and a poll conducted in 1994 indicated that over half the Russians had never "experienced or witnessed any unpleasantness by Estonians to Russians," and 38% only "infrequently" (Ministry of Foreign Affairs number 9). In September 1993, 74% of Russian-speakers in Estonia described relations with Estonians as good, a feeling reciprocated by 50% of

Estonians, while 58% disagreed with the contention that "minorities are being badly treated here." The corresponding figures for Latvian and Lithuanian Russians finding relations with the majority nationality good were 63% and 88% respectively; for minorities being "badly treated," 43% and 70% respectively disagreed (Ministry of Foreign Affairs number 4). Clearly, ethnic tensions are not only far below the threshold of violence, but they are diminishing, as non-Estonians and non-Latvians are adjusting to the requirements established in the citizenship laws.

Other polling data from 1995 indicated that most Russians in Estonia do not agree with assertions from Russia that they need to be protected by Moscow, either in the form of "peacekeeping forces," military bases or pressure, or the maintenance of Russian political, military and economic influence in the former Soviet republics. Half the Russians in Estonia found the government in Estonia better than that in Russia, while only a fourth found the Russian government better, and 82% agreed that Estonia offers better opportunities to improve living standards than Russia does. Two thirds said that conditions for "people like me" are worse in Russia; the comparable figures for Latvia and Lithuania were 59% and 61% respectively. Six out of 10 Russians in Estonia wanted Estonia to be "an independent country with relations with all countries," while 18% favored "union with Russia and other republics of the former Soviet Union" and 3.5% a "restoration of the Soviet Union." Only 2.9% believed that northeastern Estonia should belong to Russia. (All figures in this paragraph are from Ministry of Foreign Affairs number 8.) In fact, Russian claims to protect the Russian-speakers in the Baltic states hurt them because they strengthen doubts about their loyalty and suspicions that they form a "fifth column."

## Citizenship in Estonia and Latvia

Devising citizenship policies that are both acceptable to Estonians and Latvians, and tolerable for Russians, is the most persistent political problem in relations with Russia, and the one that elicits the most visceral resistance from Moscow.

For Estonia and Latvia the question of citizenship was of vital importance. With large Russian-speaking minorities, both faced the prospect of continued heavy Russian influence on most aspects of policy if all residents were granted either automatic or dual citizenship. In 1995, two thirds of non-Estonians in Estonia wanted one or the other of these options, but only 3.5% of Estonian respondents agreed (Tartu University pp. 3, 11–12). Both options were rejected in Estonia, as in Latvia. This was not only a question of control over the two nations' affairs, but a matter of principle. In the Estonian and Latvian view, the majority of Russians had been permitted to settle in Estonia or Latvia in order to implement Moscow's policy of occupation after it had forcibly annexed the two countries in 1940. On what basis could occupiers and their descendants expect to be recognized as citizens?

Russia adamantly denies that the Soviet Union had ever "occupied" the Baltic states and that their joining was involuntary, despite some admitted pressure at the time. Although a very different regime rules in Russia after the collapse of the Soviet Union, the UN has acknowledged Russia as the successor to the Soviet Union, and Russia is therefore cautious about renouncing what was done under Communist rule. It fears that concessions could open Pandora's box of claims against it, and provide a precedent for other newly independent republics, or even nations within the present borders of Russia, such as Chechnya. It has never apologized for the Soviet Union's actions in 1940 or subsequent crimes, nor has it ever hinted that the occupation might have been illegal. A majority of Russians in Estonia agree with the Russian position that the country had voluntarily joined the Soviet Union and had never been annexed (Howell pp. 32, 42). The fact that the Baltic peoples accepted their fate without armed resistance in 1940 lends some credibility to the Russians' interpretation.

Determined to remain masters in their own houses, Estonians and Latvians based their citizenship laws on the notion of legal continuity of their prewar republics. They imposed severe restrictions, granting citizenship automatically only to pre-1940 residents and their descendants. In Estonia one sixth of the Russians qualified; subsequent naturalization of more than 103,000 non-Estonians raised this to over one third by 1998, while the proportion rose to about 40% in Latvia. Confronting criticism that Russian-speakers were being made permanent non-citizens, both Estonia and Latvia opened citizenship to all persons who met certain criteria. In Latvia, these included residency for at least 16 years, extending back into the Soviet era, except for ex-Soviet military and security personnel, and their families, stationed in the country. In Estonia, the residency requirement was for only two years. Both countries also stipulated that an applicant for citizenship must be willing to take an oath of loyalty and to demonstrate competence, but not fluency, in Estonian or Latvian, languages that are difficult for them to learn because they are not related to Russian. They must answer basic questions in Estonian and Latvian about the Constitution; in Estonia they may look at the text and answer the questions.

Few Russians can meet the language requirements in either country without major effort. In 1989, only 13% of Russians in Estonia and 22% in Latvia had a good command of the national languages. The others had seen no need to learn them, because Estonians and Latvians had been expected to speak Russian well, and most did so. There was an outcry after independence in 1991 that the new language restrictions were unfair violations of human rights. Neither countries' citizenship laws discriminate on formal ethnic grounds, but since the immediate effect was the disenfranchisement of most ethnic Russian residents, many saw it that way.

The rights of those who do not speak the national languages are greater than in some other small nations that fear absorption and destruction of their cultures. Parents are free to send their children to Russian-language schools, although a law enacted in Latvia in 1998 calls for the phasing in of Latvian as the sole language of instruction in public schools over 10 years. A similar law required Estonian to be the language of instruction in all secondary schools by the year 2000, but it will

not go into effect until at least 2007. Russians face no restrictions on using their language at the workplace. It is an advantage to speak Estonian or Latvian, and the defense forces and many categories in the civil service are blocked to non-citizens. Article 50 of the Estonian Constitution states that where more than half of the permanent residents in a locality are members of an ethnic minority, such as in the overwhelmingly Russian-speaking Northeast of Estonia, they have a right to deal with the state and local authorities in their own language. In both countries state radio and television are broadcast in Russian. There are Russian-language theaters and a wide variety of Russian newspapers and magazines is available. Many university courses are taught in Russian. As of the academic year 1996–97, all curriculums at Estonian universities required some course work in Estonian, but almost all examinations in the universities could be written in Russian if the student preferred.

The Estonian and Latvian position on citizenship is grounded in notions of citizenship widely held in the rest of the world. Like most countries, they have chosen the *jus sanguinis* ("law of blood") as the principle for conferring citizenship: descent from an individual of a particular nationality. Every child with at least one parent who is an Estonian or Latvian citizen has the right, by birth, to citizenship. Thus, they offer citizenship to anybody who follows certain procedures, learns the national language, and demonstrates a basic knowledge of the political system. This latter requirement points to a deeper aspect of genuine citizenship: it should involve more than merely endowing an individual by law with certain rights and the expectation that he or she will perform certain duties. In the fuller sense, a citizen is a person who feels a moral commitment and loyalty to the state, and who is willing to put aside some aspects of self-interest in favor of the interests of the community at large. Both countries want citizens whose primary loyalty is to Estonia or Latvia (where 71% were Latvian citizens in 1996), not to any other state.

Russian leaders were incensed by these laws. Yeltsin felt especially betrayed by Estonia, since he had supported its independence over Gorbachev's opposition. He had publicly appealed to Soviet troops not to obey orders to attack civilian targets and, at great risk, he had traveled to Tallinn, narrowly escaping kidnapping by loyal Soviet military, to sign the Moscow-Tallinn Agreement of January 12, 1991. Article 3 of this agreement obligated Estonia to offer citizenship to any Russians wanting to be Estonian citizens and living in Estonia on that date. Since this was signed at a time when it was not yet clear that Estonia could become a separate state and when the citizenship issue was still largely irrelevant, the new leaders of a free Estonia decided not to implement it. Russia believes that Estonia's reneging on a formal signed agreement created the conditions for today's bad relations between the two countries.

Complaints from some of the 25 million Russians living in the newly independent former Soviet republics do not fall on deaf ears in Moscow, where a wide assortment of political leaders and groups can be expected to exploit them for their own purposes. The adoption of Estonia's citizenship laws was met by a continuous thunder of warnings from Russia. Yeltsin declared in 1993 that Estonia seemed to have "forgotten about some geopolitical and demographic realities, but Russia has the ability to remind it about them" (as quoted by Ott and Kirch p. 22). On December 31, 1995, he warned of countermeasures to alleged discrimination against Russians in the "near abroad," a term used in Russia to describe the newly independent former Soviet republics along Russia's periphery (as quoted in Ministry of Foreign Affairs number 12; see also Lieven p. 306).

Resentments both in Russia and in the Baltic states, stemming from the citizenship laws, adversely affect bilateral relations, and place a burden on sensitive negotiations with Estonia and Latvia, which Moscow has singled out as unfriendly nations. Russia denied Estonia "most favored nation" status in trade and doubled its customs charges, while Russian propaganda attempted to portray Estonia to the international community as a rogue state that serves as a conduit for drugs, and supplies arms and nuclear materials to the Irish Republican Army. When Russian retirees demonstrated in Riga against their treatment, Boris Yeltsin targeted Latvia's lucrative oil transit business, cutting oil exports by 15% through the Latvian port of Ventspils. Yuri Luzhkov, the Mayor of Moscow, has compared Latvia to Pol Pot's Cambodia (as quoted in the *Economist*, October 10, 1998).

Both Estonia and Latvia feel international pressure to relax their citizenship laws in order not to antagonize Russia. In October 1998, 53% of Latvians voting in a referendum approved of giving automatic citizenship to all children born in Latvia since 1991. Adopted by elected Parliaments, the citizenship laws appear reasonable by western standards, and the policies of Estonia and Latvia toward minorities have been more successful in easing ethnic tensions than in most post-Communist states. International organizations, such as the UN and the Council of Europe, have also generally accepted the laws, despite Russia's energetic efforts to have Estonia and Latvia condemned for human rights violations. These bodies have been used by both sides to internationalize their bilateral problems. They first aired their differences at the CSCE (now OSCE). Estonia brought up the matter of Russian troop withdrawal, and Russia raised the issue of human rights. At Russia's initiative, the CSCE appointed a High Commissioner to monitor human rights developments in the Baltic states, and opened offices in Tallinn and Riga (in December 1992 and February 1993 respectively).

## Foreign and Defense Policies

The Baltic states can be counted among the winners of the Cold War. Their peoples share a common fear and mistrust toward Russia. They hold Russia responsible for their loss of independence in 1940; for the loss of about one fifth of their populations to deportation, execution, or exile; for the reminders of Soviet rule in their countries, such as gray, unaesthetic buildings and environmental destruction; and for the fact that their economies fell far behind those of their neighbors, the Nordic countries, during 51 years of subjugation. Although they strive to work constructively with Russia, they are not inclined to show the kind of fealty to which Russia is accustomed.

Many Russians have difficulty adjusting to the new reality and claim the right to pliant ex-dependencies, which should adopt a deferential attitude. Some Russians are not yet ready to tolerate the prospect that the Baltic states are free from Moscow's sphere of influence. Article 61 of the Russian Constitution includes a right of intervention and a role as protector of 25 million "diaspora" Russians, whom it officially calls "compatriots." The Baltic states are troubled by such claims of special privileges in its "near abroad," as well as by a Russian offer in February 1993 to provide "peace-keeping" troops to hard-pressed neighbors; a proposal on May 17, 1996, to enlarge and tighten the CIS in a way that would bind the former Soviet republics more closely to Moscow (which the Baltic states perceived as a taunt and summarily rejected); and an overwhelming majority vote in the State Duma, the lower house of the Russian Federal Assembly, on March 15, 1996, to declare the dissolution of the Soviet Union invalid. Not only the Baltic states, but the United States and Yeltsin himself rejected that resolution.

In June 1996 the Estonian and Latvian governments became wary of Russia's military buildup in the Pskov region, which borders both countries, and were disappointed that the United States approved an amendment to the Conventional Forces in Europe (CFE) Treaty that permits Russia to beef up its forces on its flanks. This accord smacked of superpower dealings over the heads of smaller nations. In 1998, as a reminder to the Baltic states of how vulnerable they are, Russia carried out a war game called "Operation Return" near the Estonian border, in which its troops took over a small country (*Economist*, December 19, 1998).

With Estonia at the EU's doorstep and NATO determined to expand its membership Eastward, Moscow has decided that it would be wiser to reassure the Baltic states that it is no threat to them and that they do not need to join NATO for self-defense. In December 1997, Yeltsin announced plans to cut Russian naval and land forces around them by 40%. Less welcome was his suggestion that Baltic security be separated from that of the rest of Europe, and the transatlantic tie, and be based on bilateral security guarantees with Russia, an idea the three governments, joined by Finland and Sweden, quickly rejected. The Baltic states insist there can be no purely regional solutions to Baltic security. Such offers, proposals, and assertions frightened the Baltic states. They prompted them to abandon their earlier ideas of neutrality, which would put them in the same security vacuum as they had found themselves in during the 1930s. Feeling insecure, and knowing that no western power would defend them militarily without a formal guarantee, the Baltic states have made it known that they wish to enter NATO and the EU. They regard NATO as the only alliance capable of thwarting any future Russian expansionist temptations or attempts to restore "spheres of influence."

All three states have joined a network of international governmental organizations to internationalize their security concerns until they can become NATO members (see also Appendix 4). They joined the UN and the CSCE in September 1991, the Council of the Baltic Sea States (CBSS, which includes Russia) in March 1992, and the North Atlantic Cooperation Council (NACC) in December 1992, as well as its successor, the Euro-Atlantic Partnership Council (EAPC), in 1997. They also became associate members of the Council of Europe, in 1993, but later attained full membership; and they have been associate members of the Western European Union (WEU) since 1994. In January 1998, Riga hosted a Baltic summit of the leaders of all five Nordic nations, the three Baltic states, Germany, Poland and Russia.

In January 1994 Lithuania became the first of the three to apply officially for NATO membership, followed shortly after by the other two. Lithuania also forged a "strategic partnership" with Poland in June 1997, and created with it a joint battalion, LITPOLBAT, that is interoperable with NATO and prepared to contribute to its security interests. Because Lithuania provides the only logical "land bridge" between Russia and its enclave of Kaliningrad, Moscow views Lithuania's NATO application as a provocative act, but all three Baltic states noted the wording of the NATO summit declaration in January 1994:

"we expect and would welcome NATO expansion" (as quoted by Hansen p. 10). With quiet encouragement from the United States, Denmark has become the most visible champion of the Baltic applications to NATO.

All three states quickly joined NATO's Partnership for Peace program as a concrete means for integrating Baltic defenses, achieving NATO standards, and demonstrating the value of their contributions to western security efforts. They have joined in creating the Baltic Airspace Surveillance Network (BALTNET), an airspace radar monitoring system steered by Norway that could in the future be integrated with those of NATO and Finland, a country with which Estonia operates a joint coast guard and marine surveillance service. The Baltic Squadron (BALTRON), led by Germany and headquartered in Tallinn, is interoperable with NATO, and is organized to clear mines and engage in such international naval exercises as "Open Spirit 98." The Baltic Battalion (BALTBAT), with support and guidance from the United Kingdom and the Nordic countries, and with a rotating trinational command structure, is trained to participate in UN peacekeeping operations, such as in Bosnia-Herzegovina with Danish soldiers. A permanent Baltic Defense College (BALTDEFCOL), supported mainly by the Nordic countries to provide Baltic officers with interoperable training in English, is located in Tartu, Estonia.

The military forces of all three countries also participate in NATO maneuvers. In July 1998, Lithuania hosted 5,000 soldiers, including units from the United States, Denmark, Norway, Germany and all three Baltic states, with Russians, Ukrainians and Belarusians present as observers. Lithuania's Deputy Defense Minister, Povilas Malaksuskas, underscored the goal of all these cooperative efforts: "to make Baltic membership in NATO a logical inevitability" (see Coleman).

The United States has communicated that it would like to see Russia and the Baltic states develop good neighborly relations. This was made most explicit on January 16, 1998, when President Bill Clinton endorsed in principle their desire to join the Atlantic alliance by signing with the three Baltic Presidents a "Charter of Partnership." Although it is not a guarantee of future NATO membership or US protection and sets no timetable for membership, it puts on record Washington's "real, profound and enduring interest" in Baltic security, and the conviction that the three new democracies have as much right to join NATO as do the three post-Communist countries that actually joined in 1999 (Poland, Hungary, and the Czech Republic). In return, the Baltic states committed themselves to work toward good relations with all their neighbors, including Russia.

Although Russian leaders express no fundamental objection to Baltic membership in the EU, NATO is another matter. They reject assurances from Baltic governments that NATO is not directed toward Russia. Russians are divided on how they should react to NATO enlargement. Nevertheless, many moderate and extremist political elements in Russia maintain that NATO presence so close to Russia is unacceptable. A stream of invective is directed to the Baltic states. All three of the leading candidates in the first round of the Russian presidential election in June 1996 felt the need to cover their nationalist flanks by making inflammatory statements about Baltic hopes to join NATO. Yeltsin said on September 8, 1995, that if NATO expands, "the flame of war would burst out across the whole of Europe" (Ministry of Foreign Affairs number 12). He repeated in a letter to President Clinton on June 20, 1996, that "even a hypothetical possibility of extending NATO's sphere of operation into the Baltic states" is out of the question (as quoted in *Postimees*, July 11, 1996). A few days later, following the visit by the three Baltic Presidents to Washington, DC, he swore that "Russia will not withdraw from the Baltic region" (as quoted in *The Baltic Times*, July 4, 1996). Yeltsin asked Clinton at a summit meeting in Helsinki in March 1997 for a promise never to admit the Baltic states to NATO, a request Clinton rejected on the grounds that Russia has no veto over NATO membership and that no European democracy is excluded (*Washington Post*, January 15, 1998).

The Baltic states do not face an immediate threat from Russia. As Birthe Hansen and Bertel Heurlin concluded in 1998, "in terms of security, never before have the Baltic states been in a situation where they could be assessed so secure as in the present environment" (Hansen and Heurlin p. 83). The Baltic states and Russia desire outside help in many forms to solve their economic, environmental, and security problems. They therefore cannot overlook the views of major foreign countries or international organizations, such as NATO or the EU, who counsel compromise, in their own interests and for the sake of peace and political stability in the region.

## Borders

The rapid unraveling of the Soviet Union left numerous border uncertainties all around the periphery of the former empire. Any compromises in any one set of border negotiations could be invoked as precedents in countless other talks. A small country has only a few borders to fix. All Baltic countries found themselves embroiled in frontier disputes, not only with Russia, but with each other. Where should the frontiers be that divide these new states from each other, and especially from Russia itself? It made no sense to discuss this while all were ruled from Moscow, but the question now affects the neighbors' foreign relations, and is charged with symbolism and emotions, especially in Estonia. Few issues are more important for sovereign states than their borders. Talks about them are bound to be highly political and emotional, especially between a country with few power resources and a long memory of domination, and a negotiating partner that has controlled or strongly influenced the other for two and a half centuries. The embattled Russian government in Moscow, facing nationalist charges at home that the empire had not been vigorously defended, is loath to make any concessions on the borders that remain. Yeltsin emphasized on September 8, 1995, that "the border is unchangeable. We don't need foreign land, but we can't give away any single meter of our own land either" (as quoted in *The Baltic Observer*, September 14, 1995).

With strong western support, all three Baltic states negotiated the withdrawal of Soviet troops from their territories, by August 1993 for Lithuania, and by August 1994 for Estonia and Latvia. However, they have no international support for an uncompromising position on borders with Russia. For example, no western country has shown an interest in the restoration of Estonia's prewar borders, and Carl Bildt emphasized to Estonia, when he was Prime Minister of Sweden, that recognition by the Nordic countries and the UN was based on the borders existing in 1991, not those of 1939 (Lieven p. 378).

All three Baltic states have had difficulties defining their maritime borders with Russia and with each other. In 1996, Estonia even briefly sent a warship to back up its dispute over a sea border with Latvia. Nevertheless, agreeing to maritime borders is somewhat easier than land borders, because negotiators are drawing new lines, and there exists much international law that can be applied. By October 1996, Estonia had reached an agreement on its maritime border with Russia. It was complicated only by the fact that Finland had to agree to any lines drawn in the Gulf of Finland, but Russian negotiators announced that no sea agreement would be signed until the thornier land negotiations had been completed. It is on the land border between the two countries that a settlement is especially urgent for Estonia.

In 1945 both Estonia and Latvia lost territory to Russia but could do nothing to prevent it. Latvia's border differences with Russia are minor, and Lithuania has no land disputes with its neighbors (Belarus, Poland, and the Kaliningrad enclave of Russia). The major Lithuanian-Russian issue was Russian transit rights for its military forces in Kaliningrad. An informal agreement was reached in 1991 to allow Russian troops to cross Lithuania by rail only, with a maximum of 180 soldiers on any one train and their weapons in a separate car. Lithuanian soldiers can inspect these rail transports to ensure that these stipulations are being followed.

Estonia's losses east of the Narva River and in the southeastern Petseri district amounted to 5% of its total land area. Independence in 1991 raised the question of where the permanent border should be drawn. On September 12, 1991, Estonia declared the border changes forced on it in 1945 to be invalid, but it realizes that it does not have the power to restore the old border. In any case, it is hesitant to accept back more than 2,000 square kilometers of territory, inhabited almost entirely by Russians. In the absence of a treaty both sides worked with the line actually patrolled by the border guards. Estonia maintained the position that the Treaty of Tartu (1920) should be the basis for negotiations. Since the forced Soviet military presence in Estonia in 1940 had been a violation of Estonian sovereignty and of international law, the Treaty had always remained in force, and Estonia's prewar sovereignty was not invalidated by Soviet annexation and occupation. The Final Act of the 1975 Helsinki Agreement supports the principle that European borders are inviolate. This had been the basis of the troop withdrawal agreement with Russia in 1994, establishing the principle that the Soviet military presence had been a violation of Estonia's sovereignty and of international law. Russia rejects this interpretation, which would make the period of Soviet rule "illegal."

However, Estonia knows that the EU and NATO are unlikely to accept it as a member as long as it has an outstanding border dispute and other serious disagreements with Russia. Neither of these international organizations has ever officially stated this, but representatives have offered unmistakable hints. Gebhardt von Moltke, NATO's Deputy General Secretary for Political Issues said in Tallinn in 1995 that "Estonia's outstanding border issue with Russia would have to be solved peacefully . . . before membership would be possible" (as quoted in *The Baltic Independent*, October 20, 1995). The same message was communicated to the Estonian government on May 6–7, 1996, by Klaus Haensch, President of the EU's European Parliament (*The Baltic Times*, May 9, 1996).

The overriding desire to join first the EU and then NATO made it clear to the Estonian government that a change in its negotiating strategy toward Russia was essential and that there was no longer any need to tie Russian recognition of the continuity assured by the Treaty of Tartu to the signing of a border agreement. Indications from the EU that Estonia was a serious contender for admission, successful negotiations to establish visa-free travel with the Nordic countries, and the absence of any serious international objections to Estonia's citizenship laws indicated that almost no countries questioned the continuity of Estonia's statehood or its sovereignty.

Therefore, with most of the technical border questions already solved, Estonia accepted an agreement with Russia on October 7, 1996. The text made no mention of the Treaty of Tartu, and it placed the border where Moscow had fixed it by unilateral decree in 1945. However, in January 1997 Yevgeni Primakov, then Foreign Minister of Russia, announced that Russia would not sign the agreement until the two countries could hold bilateral talks aimed at changing certain pieces of Estonia's domestic legislation. Estonians were reminded again how their citizenship law profoundly affects their relations with Russia.

## Economies

The Baltic states have been significantly more successful than the members of the CIS in making the transition from the Soviet command economy to market economies. They had always been the most prosperous areas under the Soviet regime, and had become the most enthusiastic practitioners of Gorbachev's *perestroika*, so they were well-prepared to reform their economies when the opportunity came in 1991. They were the first ex-Soviet countries to introduce their own national currencies, to free prices, wages and trade, to reduce government subsidies and inflation, and to sell off state enterprises. Visitors to any of the three states now find increasing signs of prosperity everywhere.

Of course, this has not developed at equal rates, and the lowering of many citizens' living standards, especially of those on fixed incomes, cannot be ignored. High inflation in the early post-Communist years, affecting such essentials as rent, heat, food, and day care, as well as such free-time activities as culture and entertainment, have caused many to change their lives only grudgingly and, at times, to reflect on the ways in which things were materially better under the old regime. In Latvia and Lithuania, resentments caused by "shock therapy" have occasionally helped former Communists to win elections. The young and well-educated, along with some well-placed members of the former Communist elites who have benefited from privatization, are generally doing well, but older people, large families, and single women are all struggling. The social welfare net that most western European democracies have built up over the past few decades does not yet exist, mainly because the states cannot afford it but also, in the case of Estonia and Latvia, because their Constitutions explicitly mandate balanced budgets.

At the close of the 20th century, the Baltic states are enjoying, along with Poland, the fastest economic growth rates in Europe. Estonia's economy grew by an estimated 10% in 1997, while Latvia's and Lithuania's each grew by an estimated 6%. Unlike Russia, all three countries produce a variety of goods that western consumers want to buy, from cars, ships, and clothing to medicines and beer. They have dramatically shifted their trade from the former Soviet Union toward the prosperous West, especially the Baltic Sea area, where there are around 70 million consumers. For example, between 1991 and 1997 Estonia's trade with Russia declined from 95% of its total trade to 18%, and two thirds of its imports, and over half its exports, are now with the EU. All three states have free trade agreements with each other. Official unemployment rates are also low in all three, and a thriving shadow economy means that real unemployment is even lower.

The Baltic states are making relatively good progress toward establishing the rule of law, including reliable and impartial commercial law, although the process is not yet complete. A whiff of corruption hangs over the privatization programs, which are largely finished. Such corruption exists in the political and economic systems in all three states, and all are experiencing organized crime, as well as skyrocketing crime rates in general. However, these problems are far below the levels found in CIS countries. Indeed, one reason why Estonia was elevated to the "fast track" for eventual membership of the EU was that it was judged to have one of the cleanest public administrations in the post-Communist world.

## Estonia

Estonia, which resumed positive GDP growth in 1995, is now the acknowledged "tiger" among the Baltic states, and indeed one of the leading economies among all 27 countries emerging from Communism. In 1992, it became the first former Soviet-controlled territory to abandon the ruble by introducing (in fact reviving) its own currency, the kroon, which it tied to the Deutschmark. It reduced its inflation rate from a dizzying 1,000% in 1992 to under 10% in 1999. In terms of purchasing power, it is the richest post-Communist country, along with the Czech Republic, while its official unemployment rate, at 3.3% in 1999, is impressively below the EU average of 10.9%. It quickly privatized the bulk of its economy, and two thirds of its GDP is now generated by the private sector. Railways, ports, and energy utilities are on the auction block.

Estonia also enjoys the highest foreign investment per capita and the highest credit rating among post-Communist countries. It is attractive to investors, among other reasons, because of its flat rate of 26% for both personal and corporate income taxes, its lack of tariffs and general openness to trade, and its habit of treating foreigners and Estonians alike in business. A country that is three-fourths urban, it is on its way to becoming a predominantly information-based service economy, with native Estonians constituting the minority of the labor force in manufacturing. Despite severe financial limitations, its university system is producing a labor force equipped to deal with high technology: Estonians use the Internet more than any other post-Soviet people, and twice as much as the French or the Italians. This is an addiction it has in common with its most important trading partner and source of investment, Finland, a country with which it shares close and unique linguistic and cultural ties. Giant Finnish firms, such as the state oil company Neste, department store chains, such as Stockmans, and hundreds of small and medium-sized businesses find Estonia a congenial place to do business. Sweden is also an important trading and investment partner close at hand.

According to the Estonian Customs Office, in 1997 Estonia's exports were divided principally among Russia (17.8% of the total), Finland (15.6%), Sweden (13.4%), Latvia (8.7%), and Lithuania (6.2%), while 30.9% of its imports came from Finland, 11.7% from Russia, 9.6% from Sweden, 9.2% from Germany, and 4.2% from the United States. Thus, despite the host of political problems between Estonia and Russia, as discussed above, Russia still plays a significant role. However, Estonia is determined to minimize its economic dependence on Russia, and it relies far less on its eastern neighbor for energy than Latvia and Lithuania do. It buys more from the West and continues to extract oil from shale, which is an infamous polluter, but which still is its largest industry, ahead of mineral fertilizers, shipbuilding, and the processing of forest products. It has no nuclear power plants (nor does Latvia; but Lithuania does). To give both Germany and Russia a stake in its prosperity and stability, Estonia has granted Ruhrgas from the former country and Gazprom from the latter partial ownership in its gas industry, a move that has slightly warmed its chilly relations with Russia.

Agricultural production and processing employ about 28% of the population. This is one sector in which privatization has been slow, partly because nationalist pressure postponed the free sale of land. Only persons who can trace their Estonian citizenship to before 1940 can buy land, although there is a legislative effort to change this. Most farm land is still organized into collective and state farms, but all supervision by the state has been removed. Farmers have been the hardest hit by Estonia's almost totally open economy, and consumers must look hard in grocery stores to find Estonian-grown products.

Estonia has won the praise of many private businesspeople and bankers, as well as that of such international agencies as the EBRD and the EU. As mentioned above, in September 1997 the EU placed Estonia on the fast track toward membership, alongside Poland, Hungary, the Czech Republic, Slovenia, and Cyprus.

## Latvia

Latvia, the most industrialized of the Baltic states, comes next after Estonia in terms of economic success. Its trade has shifted from about 80% to the other Soviet republics to 80% toward the West. Most of its former collective and state farms have been converted to cooperatives, but there are few private farms. It lags behind Estonia in foreign investment, and although its privatization program is nearly complete, it has had greater problems. In 1995 it suffered a severe banking crisis, when a third of its banks collapsed. On the positive side, it has the best port in any of the Baltic states – Riga – as well as a stable currency, the lat; only 3.7% inflation as of early 1999; and an official unemployment rate of 7.4%, well below the EU average.

By the standards of post-Communist countries in general, Latvia is doing very well. For that reason, there is some resentment of the fact that it was excluded in 1997 from the fast track for accession to the EU, and must wait for the next round to be reconsidered.

## Lithuania

Lithuania is the poorest and least industrialized of the Baltic states, although it is no longer a predominantly agricultural country. Despite some privatization in agriculture, collective farms still are the rule, although the state's role in them has dwindled. With approximately a fourth of the land covered by trees, it is not surprising that forestry products are an important source of income for those living in rural areas.

Lithuania's currency, the litas, has become steadily more solid since it was launched in June 1993. In the early years, inflation ran as high as 1,400%, but by 1999 it had fallen to 4.4%. The country's 5.4% unemployment rate is half the EU average. Privatization was well advanced by 1996, and in 1998 Lithuania completed one of the largest privatizations in central and eastern Europe, selling off 60% of Telekomas, its fixed-line telecommunications monopoly. It is confidently turning its privatization efforts to shipping and ship repair, oil refining, gasoline station networks, and television and radio. Investment is pouring into its port of Klaipeda, a free economic zone catering to much of the former Soviet Union. From 1995 to 1999, cumulative foreign direct investment in Lithuania doubled every year, with the United States as the leading source. Free trade agreements cover 60% of Lithuania's trade, and its major trading partner is the EU, which accounts for over 40% of its trade turnover. Thus, as in Latvia, the EU's decision to leave Lithuania off the list of countries offered fast-track accession to the EU has aroused resentment.

## Conclusion

All three Baltic states will enter the 21st century with some major challenges left to be faced. For the sake of their prosperity and security, all three are seeking economic and military integration with the West, but are facing determined Russian opposition to their joining NATO. Their need for the security that such integration might provide stems from the long-standing Russian claim to predominance over the nations along its periphery. None faces an imminent threat to its newly regained independence, but all must remain on guard, to ensure that they do not lose a part of their sovereignty. That would be the case if Russia were able to restrict their ability to make their own decisions, such as on joining a military alliance.

Estonia and Latvia face both foreign and domestic political problems that are sometimes in conflict with each other. To preserve their languages and cultures, and survive as nations, they have chosen to restrict their citizenship and create strong motivation for members of ethnic minorities to recognize the Estonian or Latvian character of the restored republics. While continuing with this policy, they must always calculate Russia's response and adjust it to what Russia would be willing to tolerate. Estonia desires to finalize a border agreement with Russia in order to live in peace with it, and to accelerate its integration into the western world.

## Further Reading

Blaney, John W., editor, *The Successor States to the USSR*, Washington, DC: *Congressional Quarterly*, 1995

The Baltic states occupy one chapter in this general overview, which includes parts on security and economic issues, key international relations, and regions and nationalities.

Bremmer, Ian, and Ray Taras, *New States, New Politics: Building the Post-Soviet Nations*, Cambridge and New York: Cambridge University Press, 1997

Chinn, Jeff, and Robert Kaiser, *Russians as the New Minority*, Boulder, CO: Westview Press, 1996

A broad study of ethnicity and nationalism in all the post-Communist states that have ethnic Russian minorities, in which one chapter is devoted to the Baltic states. Its strength is comparison.

Coleman, Fred, "The Kaliningrad Scenario," in *World Policy Journal*, Fall 1997

Dreifelds, Juris, *Latvia in Transition*, Cambridge and New York: Cambridge University Press, 1996

A good general introduction to contemporary Latvia

Gerner, Kristian, and Stefan Hedlund, *The Baltic States and the End of the Soviet Empire*, London and New York: Routledge, 1993

A book that describes the emergence of independence in the Baltic states as a result of the disintegration of the Soviet Union

Haas, Ain, "Non-violence in Ethnic Relations in Estonia," in *Journal of Baltic Studies*, Volume 27, number 1, Spring 1996

A detailed explanation of why ethnic relations in Estonia are tense, but have nevertheless remained peaceful

Hansen, Birthe, and Bertel Heurlin, editors, *The Baltic States in World Politics*, New York: St Martin's Press, and Richmond: Curzon, 1998

A collection that focuses on the external policies of the Baltic states, with chapters on Russia, NATO, relations with the United States, and other topics

Hiden, John, and Patrick Salmon, *The Baltic Nations and Europe: Estonia, Latvia and Lithuania in the Twentieth Century*, Harlow and New York: Longman, 1991

A thorough presentation of the historical dimension of the Baltic states' struggle for independence and sovereignty

Howell, Margie, editor, *Estonia and Russia, Estonians and Russians: A Dialogue*, Stockholm: The Olof Palme International Center, and Tallinn: The Institute of International and Social Studies, 1996

A study that focuses on Estonia's primary domestic political problem

Laar, Mart, *War in the Woods: Estonia's Struggle for Survival 1944–1956*, Washington, DC: Compass, 1992

This is a gripping narrative by a former Estonian Prime Minister and historian at Tartu University on the mistreatment of the Estonian population, which led to a loss of a fifth to a fourth of the prewar population, as well as resistance to Soviet rule until 1956.

Laitin, David D., *Identity in Formation: The Russian-speaking Populations in the Near Abroad*, Ithaca, NY: Cornell University Press, 1998

A skillful synthesis of data and history, transformed into persuasive theoretical insight, this book takes the reader deep into the complex problems of Russians in the "near abroad."

Lieven, Anatol, *The Baltic Revolution: Estonia, Latvia, Lithuania and the Path to Independence*, New Haven, CT: Yale University Press, 1993

The best general treatment of the Baltic states' history and their liberation from Soviet rule

Ministry of Foreign Affairs of Estonia, *Reflections of Estonia*, Press Releases, numbers 4, 8, 9, and 12, Tallinn: Ministry of Foreign Affairs, various unstated dates from 1993 to 1996

Misiunas, Romuald, and Rein Taagepera, *The Baltic States: Years of Dependence 1940–1990*, Berkeley: University of California Press, and London: Hurst, 1993

One of the best sources for the Baltic states under Soviet and German rule

Oliver, Dawn, and Derek Heater, *The Foundations of Citizenship*, New York and Brighton: Harvester Wheatsheaf, 1994

A theoretical work that provides background on what constitutes citizenship in political theory, as well as in international law and practice

Ott, Attiat F., and Aksel and Marika Kirch, "Ethnic Anxiety: A Case Study of Resident Aliens in Estonia (1990–1992)," in *Journal of Baltic Studies*, Volume 27, number 1, Spring 1996

A statistical study of non-Estonians' attitudes and feelings in the early years of independence

Park, Andrus, "Ethnicity and Independence: The Case of Estonia in Comparative Perspective," in *Europe-Asia Studies*, Volume 46, number 1, 1994

One of Estonia's best-known political scientists (now deceased) puts Estonia's citizenship laws in an international perspective.

Raun, Toivo U., *Estonia and the Estonians*, Stanford CA: Hoover Institution, 1991

The best history of Estonia and its people

Shoemaker, M. Wesley, *Russia, Eurasian States, and Eastern Europe 1998*, Harpers Ferry, WV: Stryker-Post Publications, 1998

Contains very current basic facts and astute, annually updated analysis

Silver, Brian D., and Mikk Titma, "Support for New Political Institutions in Estonia: The Effects of Nationality, Citizenship, and Material Well-being," in *Problems of Post-Communism*, Volume 45, number 5, September/October 1998

This article presents the results of a survey on the effect of citizenship on Russian-speakers' attitudes in Estonia, and concludes that the mere fact of citizenship does not change attitudes dramatically.

Smith, Graham, et al., editors, *The Baltic States: the National Self-Determination of Estonia, Latvia and Lithuania*, London: Macmillan, and New York: St Martin's Press, 1994

A focused study of these three nations, edited by specialists on Soviet and post-Soviet affairs

Taagepera, Rein, *Estonia: Return to Independence*, Boulder, CO: Westview Press, 1993

The best available book on the initial years of Estonian independence, written by a political scientist who was a candidate in free Estonia's first presidential election

Tartu University Market Research Team, *The Attitude of Town Residents of Northeastern Estonia Towards Estonian Reforms and Social Policy*, Tallinn: Open Estonia Foundation, November 1995

A comparative study based on surveys conducted in 1993, 1994, and 1995

Vardys, V. Stanley, and Judith B. Sedaitis, *Lithuania: The Rebel Nation*, Boulder, CO: Westview Press, 1996

A good general introduction to contemporary Lithuania.

Vetik, Raivo, "Ethnic Conflict and Accommodation in Post-Communist Estonia," in *Journal of Peace Research*, Volume 30, number 3, 1993

A competent treatment of the ways in which violence has been avoided in independent Estonia

---

*Wayne C. Thompson* is Professor of Political Science at the Virginia Military Institute.

---

Chapter Four

# The Czech Republic and Slovakia

## *Martin Myant*

## The Background: Czechoslovakia, 1918–89

Czechoslovakia was formed out of the collapsing Austro-Hungarian empire in 1918. Czech national awareness had grown rapidly in the latter part of the 19th century, as economic development, starting in agriculture, spread into light and engineering industries. It drew inspiration from a long history and past prominence in central Europe, and was expressed in a cultural life that broadly followed Viennese or other Germanic models in education, music, theater, literature, and sport. The Slovak nation was less clearly defined. A recognized written language distinct from Czech did not appear until 1843, and Hungarian domination in the latter part of the 19th century had been geared towards assimilation, leaving minimal scope for independent cultural development. Slovakia was also economically less advanced, with an economic structure based on small-scale peasant agriculture. Slovak national development was therefore heavily dependent on links to the more mature Czech nation. When the Czechoslovak state was founded, leading Slovak politicians welcomed the centralization of political power in Prague, fearing that, if they were given the choice, much of the rural population might have opted for Hungarian rather than Slovak nationality.

The interwar republic acquired a reputation as an island of democracy amid totalitarian and autocratic regimes, but it was ultimately weakened by national tensions. Although great inequalities persisted, Slovakia underwent significant development, both economic and,

in particular, cultural; with it came hostility to the dominance of Prague, and growing support for a Catholic nationalist movement. Meanwhile, the German minority in the Czech lands (Bohemia and Moravia) had never welcomed the creation of Czechoslovakia, although its political representatives had accepted it as a fact after 1918. However, after the Nazis came to power in Germany in 1933, support grew for their allies, particularly in the parts of Bohemia bordering Germany. In 1938, Nazi Germany dismembered Czechoslovakia, with the acquiescence of Britain and France. Frontier areas were incorporated into Germany, and much of southern Slovakia was incorporated into Hungary. In 1939 Bohemia and Moravia were invaded and forced to become a "protectorate," and an autonomous "clericofascist" Slovakia emerged, allied to Germany.

The Czechoslovak state was restored following the defeat of Nazi Germany in 1945, and its liberation was predominantly carried out by the Soviet army. There were a number of important differences between the new Czechoslovakia and the state formed in 1918. The victorious powers agreed that Germans would be expelled if they could not prove antifascist activity – a process largely completed by 1948 – while Hungarians were also expected to leave Slovakia, although this policy was formally abandoned after 1948, leaving a substantial Hungarian minority. Slovakia was given new recognition, following the active participation of Slovaks in an uprising against the Nazis and their collaborators in August 1944. However, hopes of a fully equal arrangement, based on federation, were not fulfilled.

The new republic also moved firmly to the left. Large-scale industry was nationalized in 1945, and the Communist Party emerged with 38% of the votes cast in elections in 1946. Its popularity was based on a widespread feeling that the interwar republic, and its ruling groups, had failed to deliver social justice or national security, and had in many cases collaborated with the Nazi occupiers. It was understandable that the Soviet Union, as the victor over the Nazis, could appear as a model to follow. There was also substantial opposition to Communist dominance, but other political forces were defeated in February 1948, when the Communists established a monopoly of power.

Czechoslovakia was then firmly incorporated into the Soviet bloc. Economic policy was focused on completing the nationalization of industry, collectivizing agriculture and restructuring industry towards engineering, steel and raw materials. In the early 1950s Czechoslovakia became the leading producer of machinery and armaments for what was becoming known as "eastern Europe." Later years saw some restoration of the light industries that had been strong in the past, and the development of motor vehicle and consumer electronics production, partly for domestic consumption and partly for export within the protected Comecon area. However, the economy remained semiautarkic, with trade limited to specific products and specific markets, mostly in the East. Productivity and product quality fell progressively behind world levels. Advanced market economies took 44% of Czechoslovakia's exports in 1948; this proportion fell to 17% by 1953, the point of maximum Cold War isolation, but such countries still accounted for only 31% of exports in 1989, and by then there was a strong bias towards raw materials and simpler semimanufactures, such as steel.

Open opposition to Communist rule was of less significance than in neighboring countries. Communist power was consolidated fairly easily, not least because of continuing fears of a revival of German expansionist ambitions. The postwar expulsion of the German population created a strong base in Bavaria for movements demanding a return of confiscated land and property, and the alliance with the Soviet Union seemed to many to be the best guarantee of Czechoslovak independence. However, the reduction in Cold War tensions and the exposure of Stalin's crimes in the Soviet Union opened the way for gradual liberalization within the ruling Communist Party.

A change in leadership in January 1968 initiated the "Prague Spring," bringing Alexander Dubček to power around a loose alliance of economic reformers and advocates of a more open cultural life. Behind this movement lay a deep lack of interest in, or even cynicism about, the alleged benefits of socialism, but there was no strong pressure for a reversal of 1948 and a return to multiparty democracy. Reform was to involve an end to censorship and liberalization, rather than full democratization of political life. It remains unclear where this attempt to combine an effective monopoly of power for the Communist Party with wider political freedoms would have led. In the event, it was ended by a Soviet-led invasion in August 1968.

The invasion had profound effects on political and economic development, and marked a crucial watershed in postwar development. A small minority welcomed the invasion. During the period of "normalization" that followed, voluntary resignations and a purge of the Party led to the loss of about one third of its membership. Supporters of the reform movement were removed from their jobs or demoted, and subjected to continual petty restrictions, affecting, for example, their children's education.

Czechoslovakia remained permanently isolated from the mainstream of European development despite a feeling, especially in the Czech lands, that it rightfully belonged there. Slovak sensibilities were less completely offended, as 1968 did see the conversion of Czechoslovakia into a federation. This reform, at least nominally, gave Slovaks equal status with Czechs, and each nationality now had its own legislature and government, alongside the federal institutions. However, there was never again a serious effort to reform the Communist system from within. Those in power were completely opposed to any thoughts of a "third way," while the active opposition, albeit it was numerically weak, gradually shifted towards total hostility to any notion of socialism.

Economic development was centered on reincorporation into the Soviet bloc. Czechoslovakia sought minimal loans from the West and concentrated on exporting to other Comecon countries, but growth was rapid throughout the early 1970s, thanks partly to cheap Soviet oil. This helped for a time to reduce the appeal of active opposition, which never found a base in social discontent. Nevertheless, by the end of the 1970s the weaknesses of central planning, and the costs associated with isolation from the advanced countries of the world, meant that economic growth effectively ceased, while living standards stagnated. There was, however, no source for a real economic collapse, nor was there a basis for a strong social movement that could bring about political change.

There were differences between the two parts of the federation. Communist power brought movement towards equalization of economic conditions between the Czech lands and Slovakia, partly through a deliberate policy of locating new industries in less developed rural areas. In Slovakia, the national income per capita moved from 63% to 88% of the Czech level between 1948 and 1989. Thus, although by the later 1980s the Communists were broadly discredited in both parts of Czechoslovakia, in the Czech lands it could be blamed for setting back practically all aspects of national development. In economic terms, Czechoslovakia had fallen behind the advanced countries of western and central Europe, while cultural life had been cut off from the outside world. In Slovakia, however, the postwar years were the first period of rapid economic growth. There was also much less sense of a pre-Communist identity to which the country could return.

## The Velvet Revolution and After, 1989–90

Change came in the "velvet revolution" of November 1989, but only after the fall of the Berlin Wall. Police repression in the wake of a small, officially sanctioned demonstration on November 17 was followed by street demonstrations of rapidly increasing size, and two one-hour general strikes. The weight of public opinion proved enough to press the authorities to yield, and to allow the creation of a government of "national understanding" on December 10, with a majority of members from the former opposition. Václav Havel was elected President on December 29 by the Federal Assembly formed under the old voting system. The elimination of Communists from positions of power was then very rapid, and Dubček returned as Chairman of the Federal Assembly. Several Communists in the new government resigned their Party memberships, including the new federal Prime Minister, Marián Čalfa.

The leading forces in the revolution were Civic Forum, in the Czech lands, and its sister organization, Public Against Violence, in Slovakia. Both had been hastily formed during the events of November 1989. The core of both movements was created by active dissidents, but they rapidly took in prominent figures from economic research, education and cultural life, within loose and often ad hoc structures. Local organizations took initiatives in transforming government and administrative bodies, and there were some changes in enterprise managements. Both broad movements decided to remain united in contesting the first free elections, held on June 5 and 6, 1990, in which only parties gaining more than 5% of the votes cast could gain representation in the Federal Assembly and the two republican legislatures (see Table 4.1).

Civic Forum was successful in the Czech lands, with no serious rival, but the position in Slovakia was slightly different. The elimination of the Communist system alone was a less powerful source of political identity, and Public Against Violence did somewhat less well. There was also a large vote for the Christian Democratic Movement, led by Ján Čarnogurský and other former dissident activists, and a significant showing for Slovak Nationalists, who harked back to the heritage of the wartime Slovak state. Much of their propaganda indicated hostility to other nationalities, especially the Roma, who made up around 1.4% of the total population of Slovakia (as estimated in 1993). The Hungarian minority, 10.8% of its population (also as of 1993), voted overwhelmingly for specifically Hungarian parties.

The elections were followed by the creation of new federal, Czech and Slovak governments, excluding all Communist representation. Their programs included firm commitments to a "return to Europe," to the consolidation of democracy, and to speedy, market-oriented economic reform, although differences had already emerged as to how this last goal was to be implemented.

## Political Developments, 1990–92

The success of Civic Forum posed questions about its future. It had previously been assumed that it would disappear as a more "normal" party structure took shape, but this was clearly still some way off. Voters in mid-1990 were showing their support for the end of Communist rule, and for the general direction of democratic and market-oriented reform, but a clearer political differentiation of society was yet to take shape. Some leading Civic Forum figures started speculating on the possibility that the movement could claim a permanent role in political life, perhaps as an alternative to clearly defined political parties, but this was to prove a blind alley.

The clearly established parties as of mid-1990 appeared to be either peripheral or distinctly unattractive to much of the population. The best-organized parties existed as survivals from the Communist period. The largest, the Communist Party itself, followed a different course in the Czech lands and in Slovakia. In the former, it set itself the aim of becoming a "modern party of the left," but failed to convert itself into the kind of post-Communist formation that emerged in Poland or Hungary. One group within it harked back to the heritage of the "Prague Spring" as the basis for a philosophy distinct from social democracy; an opposing group paid lip service to the need to change, but effectively resisted any criticisms of the Party's past. This ultimately proved to be the majority position, and efforts to change the Party's name were repeatedly defeated. The Party nevertheless retained support among the older generation, to whom liberalization and the opening of borders seemed less relevant than fears over economic security and the possibility of German domination.

Satellite parties had also been allowed to exist between 1948 and 1989, as long as they agreed with the policy decisions of the ruling Communist Party. They came to the 1990 elections with organizational bases, finances, and printing and publishing facilities, but they were weakened by the need to explain away their collaborationist past. The most important, the Czech People's Party, which had derived from a long-established party with links to the Catholic church, linked up with Catholic dissident groups, and was represented in the first post-Communist government. It was weakened by accusations that leading figures had cooperated with the former security police, and by the emphasis placed on religious affiliation by some of its leading representatives.

Clarification of the political structure depended largely on divisions within the movements that had led the velvet revolution. Again, the key points of division differed in the two parts of Czechoslovakia. In the Czech lands, Civic Forum divided over its internal structure, the treatment of the Communist past, and strategy for economic reform. The federal Minister of Finance, Václav Klaus, pressed for a pure market system with minimal government involvement, and believed that Civic Forum should be converted into a clearly defined political party capable of pushing his program through against the expected opposition. He built support within Civic Forum by effectively allying with advocates of a strongly anti-Communist policy, and won election as the movement's Chairman on September 15, against a close ally of President Havel. He went on to win a majority for conversion into a clearly right-wing political party, on January 12, 1991. The alternative position was less clearly defined. Its adherents favored maintaining the broad character of Civic Forum, possibly as something distinct from a rigid and disciplined political party. They also took a more cautious view on economic reform, and some expressed fears that anti-Communist rhetoric could be leading towards abuses of individual human rights. The outcome was a formal split into two organizations, the Civic Democratic Party (ODS) led by Klaus, and the Civic Movement, led by the Foreign Minister, Jiří Dienstbier.

The ODS established a more coherent organizational structure and a clearly defined political profile as a right-wing free-market party. Anti-Communist rhetoric was in line with part of Czech public sentiment, although it was less relevant to the Slovak public, and former Party members occupied high positions across the new political spectrum. Nevertheless, for part of the ODS anti-Communism played a special role in defining an uncompromisingly right-wing identity, as distinct from the more liberal and tolerant Civic Movement. Opinion polls quickly showed that the ODS was taking the bulk of the former Civic Forum supporters, but the Civic Movement retained more government posts.

The ODS took the lead in winning majorities in the Federal Assembly for a number of new laws. One such law, passed in October 1991, imposed a ban on holding office in the state administration, the media or state-owned enterprises on former secret police informers, members of a number of former Communist organizations, and those who had held office in the Party above a certain level, even if they had not been proved guilty of any criminal act. Alexander Dubček refused to sign the new law, even after it was pointed out that as an elected figure he would not be personally affected, although he could not work as an administrative employee. A further law, passed in December 1991, allowed for prison sentences of up to eight years for supporting or making propaganda for Communism.

The two organizations that emerged out of Civic Forum agreed to work together within the coalition government until fresh elections in June 1992. The fragmentation of Civic Forum also led to distinct identities for other political groupings. Some prominent figures joined the Social Democratic Party, which had been recreated in December 1989 and had at first been dominated by the older generation who had been members before 1948.

## Slovakia, 1990–92

At the time of the collapse of Communist power the breakup of Czechoslovakia did not seem a likely event. There were differences between the Czech and Slovak parts of the federation, but they did not appear to be fundamental. In economic terms the two parts were very similar, with very much the same structural weaknesses. Slovakia probably gained from the federation, both through direct budget transfers and through incorporation into a larger economic unit with potentially close links to western Europe. The early disputes seemed largely to be minor, or purely symbolic, such as the question of whether the country's name should have a capital "S" or a small "s" in the middle.

From the Czech side this all appeared rather trivial, but in Slovakia there was a strong desire to gain initial recognition on the international stage as something distinct from the Czech identity that had dominated in the old Czechoslovakia. With this came skepticism about the economic reforms (discussed below) being developed in Prague and pushed through the Federal Assembly by Klaus. Ideas began to emerge of a distinct economic strategy appropriate to Slovakia, although they were never very specific. In fact, the differences between the two economic structures were relatively small. Slovakia did have a larger share of heavy armaments industries, which suffered a particularly sharp decline, and it also had a bias towards larger enterprises that processed raw materials, but these could often enjoy some prosperity as their simple products quickly found export markets in western Europe. The biggest economic difference was not in inherited structure but in prospects for completely new growth. There was less potential for tourism in Slovakia, and greater geographical distance limited the scope for contract work for German companies. Weaker traditions of private entrepreneurship also contributed to a much slower development of small-scale services.

A distinctive Slovak political development took clear shape after the 1990 elections. Broadly, four positions emerged. The first was for immediate independence. The second, advocated by Čarnogurský and the Christian Democratic Movement, was for independence at a future date after joining what is now the EU. The third, represented by the new Slovak Prime Minister, Vladimír Mečiar of Public Against Violence, was for substantially greater powers for the Slovak government, particularly over economic affairs. The fourth was for the existing arrangements, and was associated with support for the economic reform proposals coming from Prague.

Even the Communist Party developed differently in Slovakia, partly because it had more activists from the younger generation than its Czech counterpart. A transformation into the Party of the Democratic Left was successfully achieved in 1991, albeit with a sharp drop in membership, and past internal conflicts were largely forgotten. Instead, the new Party sought a foundation in rather cautious claims of Slovak specificity, rather than emphasizing its own Communist past.

The crucial personality in Slovak politics was Mečiar, whose political agenda increasingly centered on enhancing the Slovak national identity. He gained immense popularity with his irreverently anti-Czech rhetoric, but was accused, even from within his own Party, of fomenting unnecessary conflicts. Threatened with removal, he formed his own Movement for a Democratic Slovakia (HZDS) on March 6, 1991. On April 23 he was removed from office by the Slovak legislature and Čarnogurský was appointed Prime Minister. The rump of Public Against Violence, firmly identified with the fourth of the above positions, was left with dwindling support, while Mečiar speculated about a future arrangement of relations between the two republics that would give clearer recognition of Slovakia's status. This headed towards a conception in which a new constitution would have to start from recognizing Slovakia's independent status. The powers of a central authority, within a confederation rather than a federation, would then be derived from the two constituent republics, rather than a central authority devolving power to the two republics. Nominally at least, the bulk of leading Slovak politicians wanted a common Czechoslovak state, but they were setting terms that caused exasperation on the Czech side.

Leading Czech politicians had no understanding of such ideas, let alone sympathy with them. A growing body began to hope for a separation that would, they assumed, leave the Czechs free to pursue rapid economic reform, and to gain quick acceptance into the EU. Public opinion was expressed in petitions calling for the continuation of a common state, but behind this lay the assumption that Slovaks should be blamed for being unreasonable, rather than a criticism of Czech politicians for being less understanding. President Havel joined this trend, expressing the strong view that there should either be a continuation of the federation or a complete separation. By the spring of 1992 it appeared that no politician able to influence events could understand the point of view of the other part of the federation.

## Elections and Separation

Elections for the Federal Assembly on June 5 and 6, 1992, were fought in the shadow of separation (see Table 4.2). Klaus and the ODS were clearly victorious in the Czech lands: the Civic Movement failed to win representation, while second place went to the Communist-dominated Left Bloc. In Slovakia, Mečiar's movement triumphed, while second place went to the Party of the Democratic Left.

The Czech Social Democrats and Communists were opposed to the breakup of Czechoslovakia, as were the Slovak Social Democrats and the Party of the Democratic Left, but none of these parties was able to play any role in government. The victors in both republics presented themselves as firmly in favor of maintaining a common state, but on very different terms. They also disagreed sharply on economic policy. Thus, the only feasible federal coalition had to bring together Klaus and Mečiar in one government, and the only basis for agreement between them was an acceptance that they could not agree.

Both leaders therefore decided to support a federal government that would have the sole task of negotiating a speedy and harmonious end to the federation. Although opinion polls continued to show that this was supported by only a small minority of the population, there were no significant demonstrations of public opposition, and the Federal Assembly finally gave its approval on November 25. The separation took place on January 1, 1993.

The two new republics could then pursue their fates independently. Separate institutions, currencies and international representation were established quickly, and, although some property disputes dragged on through the 1990s, the process of separation was remarkably free from serious acrimony. It was hoped at first that economic relations would continue to be very close, perhaps through linked currencies and a customs union. Some Czech politicians even dampened down fears with reassurances that everything would continue exactly as in the past.

## Economic Reform

The main task facing the federal and national governments elected in June 1990 was the implementation of economic reform. The first proposals were worked out by expert commissions from February 1990 onwards, and a full set of proposals was presented to the Federal Assembly in July 1990. It was effectively a compromise between two different conceptions. Klaus's position dominated the opening sections, which emphasized macroeconomic liberalization and stabilization. There was to be the speediest possible freeing of previously controlled prices and international trade, combined with restrictive monetary and macroeconomic policies in order to choke off the expected inflation: this was effectively the standard IMF package for countries faced with macroeconomic imbalances. There was also to be a start to privatization, with the possibility of using the voucher method to enable effectively free distribution of shares to the population. Other sections, reflecting an alternative conception that envisaged a more active role for the state in restructuring enterprises before privatization, referred to policies for key industrial sectors.

The proposals were criticized by a number of economic experts, who expressed particularly strong doubts over voucher privatization, but Klaus was able to win the approval of the Federal Assembly on September 17, 1990, and enjoyed effective control over their implementation. On January 1, 1991, the prices of goods accounting for more than 80% of consumer spending were deregulated, while rents, energy prices and public transport charges remained under state control. Trade was largely freed

from administrative controls, and partial convertibility of the currency was introduced.

Devaluation of the currency led to an immediate increase in the prices of imported goods, contributing to a rapid burst of inflation. Wage increases were held in check by government controls, with the result that domestic demand and living standards fell sharply. This coincided with the collapse of trade among Comecon countries, leading to a sharp fall in industrial output and in overall GDP (see Table 4.3).

There has been some debate over the significance of these falls in GDP. There may have been scope for significant growth in unrecorded activity in the "gray" economy, suggesting that recorded GDP figures understate the real situation. A boom in tourism enabled a significant proportion of the population, especially in Prague, to rent out rooms in private homes, giving a significant boost to their incomes. This was also a period of rapid structural change, both in the economy and in personal consumption. New small businesses, allowed under a law passed in April 1990, appeared in services and trade. The number of people classified as self-employed stabilized at around 10% of the active labor force of the Czech Republic by 1994, while almost as many again were registered as entrepreneurs, although they also had other, more important sources of income. The freeing of imports also led to rapidly rising consumption of modern consumer goods. There was a significant shift away from spending on previously subsidized goods, such as meat, towards color televisions and motor vehicles.

On balance, it is clear that there were losers from the economic changes that followed the velvet revolution. Employment declined in traditional industries, and new firms were not attracted to areas scarred by environmentally destructive activities, such as coalmining. Opportunities for those beyond retirement age, many of whom had previously worked, also largely disappeared. However, there were also many who gained from the new arrangements. New job opportunities appeared, particularly in the cities, both in new businesses and in expanding sectors, notably financial and other services. It is likely that the aggregate GDP figures both overstate the extent of the fall, as it was felt by the population, and obscure the extent to which a large part of the population, despite government rhetoric about the need to "tighten their belts," actually experienced clear gains from the start of the transformation onwards.

The available figures also give some indication of the differences across the federation. The fall in recorded GDP was smaller in the Czech Republic than in Slovakia, where unemployment rose much more rapidly, partly because many Slovaks had worked in the Czech Republic and were among the first to lose their jobs. There was also less growth of new firms in Slovakia, particularly in its more remote rural areas, and the proportion of self-employed people stabilized at slightly above half the Czech level. The breakup of the federation also hit Slovakia harder, as it had been more dependent on the economic links within Czechoslovakia.

## Privatization

Privatization began before the breakup of the federation, although even then it was administered by the separate national governments, not by the federal government. The first steps were taken in late 1990, when some of the property confiscated after February 1948 was returned to its original owners or their heirs. Next came the "small" privatization, in which small businesses were auctioned off to individuals. The more important step was the "big" privatization, based on a law passed on February 26, 1991. This allowed for the transfer of state property into private hands by a variety of different methods, depending on proposals worked out by the management of the enterprise concerned. Other proposals were also allowed, so that groups of employees or outsiders could also make bids, but the final decisions rested with the government. In practice, the management of the enterprise was usually successful. In some cases they opted to buy a controlling interest, requiring credit from a bank, but more frequently privatization involved the voucher method.

This was implemented in two waves in the Czech Republic, but in just one wave in Slovakia. Individuals could buy books of vouchers for a nominal sum. Despite some initial hesitation, three quarters of the adult population took part in the first wave and a slightly lower proportion in the second wave. Investment funds could also bid for shares, after acquiring voucher points from individuals. They claimed to offer more secure investments, based on their ability to spread risk and their expertise in selecting the most promising enterprises. In practice, 70% of all voucher points were invested in such funds in the first wave and a slightly lower proportion in the second wave. Each enterprise was given a nominal value, and voucherholders (funds and individuals) then used their voucher points to make bids for shares. Wherever supply and demand matched, an enterprise was considered sold; where they did not match, the enterprise was entered into a further round of bidding, at a new price.

By 1998, Czech privatization had been completed, apart from utilities, public services, energy, transport, a small number of specific manufacturing firms, and a number of large banks. Almost 80% of the assets allocated for privatization were in units converted into joint stock companies: 48% of their shares were exchanged for vouchers, but a further 27% remained unsold.

Voucher privatization had far-reaching consequences, both political and economic. Its economic impact included its effects on enterprise restructuring, consumer spending and the balance of payments. Most immediately, however, it had political consequences, in consolidating the position of the ODS in the Czech Republic, by giving it an image as a determined and decisive party of government, firmly committed to a break from the past. More immediately, it offered the population a cash bonus. Voucher books were bought for the nominal price of CzK1,000, equivalent to less than one quarter of average monthly earnings at the time, but the shares were quickly sought by somewhat mysterious buyers at prices well above that level. It was estimated that about one third of shares had been sold within two years of receipt. This enabled individuals to boost their private consumption, supporting the boom in spending on imported consumer goods that followed the liberalization of imports (as mentioned above), and it also encouraged a feeling of rising living standards that helped keep Klaus popular through to the middle of the 1990s.

The economic consequences for enterprises have been evaluated with an increasing degree of negativity. The naïve hope had been that "active" owners would rapidly impose rationalization and improvements in efficiency, but the distribution of shares to the population, and their subsequent sale, led to an unstable and rapidly changing ownership structure. The ultimate purchasers included Czech banks, foreign investment funds, largely from the United Kingdom, and some rapidly emerging Czech financial empires, often with unclear sources of initial capital. They typically brought no new sources of finance for enterprises that desperately needed modernization if they were to compete in the new market environment. If anything, owners were more likely to seek short-term gains by insisting on the largest possible dividend payments.

In some cases, the activities of new owners clashed even more clearly with the long-term interests of enterprises. Voucher privatization was implemented with such haste that an adequate legal and regulatory framework was still lacking as shares were traded. It should be added that this was partly a matter of deliberate policy, as the free market purists controlling economic policy distrusted all forms of regulation. The consequence, however, was the phenomenon of "tunneling," whereby owners, or managers freed from direct control by active owners, could remove the wealth of enterprises or funds for their own private purposes. A report issued by the Czech Ministry of Finance in November 1997 identified 15 different ways in which this was being done. The costs to the economy are impossible to quantify exactly, but tunneling must have led to a loss of resources available for investment, and it damaged the reputation of the Czech Republic among potential investors.

Other forms of privatization brought slightly different consequences. Enterprises sold directly to private owners were frequently even less favorably placed, as the purchase was typically based on a credit that had to be repaid. Many of these firms were soon facing bankruptcy.

However, sale to a foreign company often brought enormous gains. The first major example was the Škoda car company, sold to Volkswagen of Germany in stages from April 1991. With foreign ownership came investment, modernization, and access to markets abroad. The same story was repeated in other firms in engineering and light industry. There were a few disappointments, and in some sectors inward investors had little or nothing to offer, as domestic firms could already compete internationally. The main problem, however, was that direct inward investment remained at a relatively low level. By 1997, foreign-owned firms accounted for only 8.7% of employment in manufacturing, mining and energy, and for only 13.3% of output.

## Economic Recovery in the Czech Republic, 1993–98

Economic growth in the Czech Republic peaked in 1995 and gradually slowed down over the following years (see Table 4.3). The breakup of the federation caused a drop in output in some industries, and forced a redirection into new markets, delaying economic growth. In the political sphere, however, the right-wing parties gained a much freer hand. They could press ahead with the second wave of voucher privatization, and the accelerating growth in the middle of the decade enhanced their international standing. Klaus could live his dream of putting the Republic ahead of other countries in the race for economic reform, and sought international recognition before the others did.

Czechoslovakia had already rejoined the IMF in September 1990. It signed an association agreement with the European Community (now the EU) in December 1991, which gave some immediate freeing of access to the markets inside the Community, and encouraged an assumption that full membership could follow eventually. Both IMF membership and associate status were transferred to the two successor states, and "Europe agreements," extending the association with the EU, came into force in both states in February 1995. The Czechs, however, felt themselves to be moving ahead when their Republic became the first former Communist country to be accepted into the OECD, in December 1995, shortly after the government had introduced full current account convertibility of the currency. This all fitted with Klaus's proud boast that the transformation into a market economy was complete. The outside world seemed convinced, and the Czech Republic enjoyed the best credit rating among the former Communist countries.

This optimism lasted for only a few more years. Growth rates slowed down as the current account deteriorated alarmingly, mainly because of the failure of much of Czech industry to compete successfully in international markets. Foreign-owned firms generally did well, but Czech-owned companies were constrained by lack of finance for investment, and by poor or unimaginative managements. Very often, when they did have financial strength, they squandered it on diversification into the purchase of other unsuccessful enterprises, rather than development of their own products.

The only means to penetrate western European markets involved switching towards less sophisticated products. Engineering firms moved from finished railway locomotives, vehicles, or production plant into simpler components that were made under contract for western firms. Textile and footwear firms switched from making finished products, for export to the east, to engaging in outward processing trade for western European, mostly German, companies. These were in general less profitable activities than selling under one's own brand name. They also had limited potential for expansion, and export growth was too slow to cover the increase in imports.

The balance of payments was helped for a time by the growth in tourism, the inflow of portfolio investment associated with voucher privatization, and lending by foreign banks to Czech enterprises. These, however, tended to exhaust their potential, and alarm bells were sounded by the growing current account deficit, which reached 7.6% of GDP in 1996. This led, in early 1997, to rumors of imminent devaluation, and thus to serious pressure on the Czech currency, which the government had sought to hold at a fixed exchange rate since January 1991.

Under pressure from the IMF, and despite the reluctance of Klaus, who continued to insist that the economy was essentially in good shape, the government adopted an emergency package in April 1997. The current account was to be restored to balance by cuts in domestic consumption, led by reductions in state spending equivalent to about 4.6% of the planned level. This package was quickly judged inadequate and, this time in the face of even more resistance from Klaus, a further package was adopted in May that roughly doubled the proposed budget cuts. It coincided with a final failure by the central bank to maintain the value of the Czech currency, which was left to float on May 27.

These measures could never offer a long-term solution to the Czech economy's problems. The cuts in consumption led to a further reduction in the rate of GDP growth, which was negative in 1998. The balance of payments quickly improved, but no new basis had been created for improving the economy's competitiveness.

## Economic Recovery in Slovakia, 1993–98

Slovakia suffered more than the Czech Republic did from the immediate effects of separation, but economic growth was quickly restored and, on a number of standard indicators, the country appeared to be fairly successful. Behind this apparent success, however, lay the roots of long-term instability. The fundamental problem, as in the Czech Republic, was the failure to develop a competitive economic structure that could provide enough revenue from exports to pay for the population's growing demand for imported consumer goods. The weakness became apparent very early, as economic difficulties led to the imposition of surcharges on some imported goods, and then to devaluation of the Slovak currency in July 1993. This followed discussions with the IMF, but stood in contrast to the earlier agreement with the Czech government to maintain existing parities. Devaluation helped exports of basic industrial goods, such as steel, paper and heavy chemicals, but the base of the Slovak economy was very narrow. In 1996,

38% of exports were from just five enterprises that had grown up under central planning and had benefited from substantial past investment.

There was less inward investment than in the Czech Republic. The most significant single case was Volkswagen's purchase of the Bratislava car factory, which was then integrated into the German firm's overall operations as an assembly plant. Unlike Škoda in the Czech Republic, the factory had no independent brand name and provided little stimulus to other firms based in Slovakia. There was some rhetoric about distinctive Slovak policies, aimed at the development and diversification of the economy, and there was much formal recognition of the need to develop new industries, but proposals for change remained largely on paper.

The second wave of voucher privatization had been delayed in Slovakia, and was effectively abandoned in 1994 in favor of the transfer of assets to friends and political allies of Prime Minister Mečiar, at still undisclosed prices. This approach avoided some of the problems associated with Czech privatization, as ownership was quickly stabilized while prices were probably low enough not to burden the new owners with unmanageable debts. By 1996, the private sector accounted for 64% of employment in Slovakia, compared with 57% in the Czech Republic. However, the Slovak approach to privatization was less successful at ensuring that ownership passed to competent individuals.

Slovakia continued to suffer from large current account deficits, which exceeded 10% of GDP in 1996. By the autumn of 1998, the economy was facing a renewed crisis, as the country's largest enterprise, the Košice steel company, was approaching financial catastrophe. The owners were accused of tunneling funds abroad, while their previous business strategy had amounted to flamboyant diversification into hotels, soccer clubs, and other areas in which they had no expertise.

## The New Czech Politics, 1993–98

The breakup of the Czechoslovak federation freed the hands of the Czech right-wing parties.

The coalition government formed at the federal level in June 1992 continued in office, with some adjustments, after January 1, 1993. It was still headed by Klaus and dominated by the ODS, but it also included representatives from the neoliberal Civic Democratic Alliance and the Christian Democrats. The opposition in the lower house of the new Czech Parliament, the Chamber of Deputies, was divided among far-right Republicans, Social Democrats and Communists.

Klaus's eventual fall reflected both immediate problems and the consequences of longer-term trends. Three factors gradually dented his popularity. The first was the worsening performance of the economy, culminating in the stagnation of 1997. The second was the declining interest in the anti-Communist rhetoric that had been so prominent in the early years after 1989. The ODS had played on fears of a possible return to the past, but that appeared less relevant as time went on. The third was the growing awareness of widespread corruption. There had been a few cases even at the start of privatization, but they had seemed less important than the general direction of government policy. Gradually, however, cases of tunneling (as discussed above) became almost daily news items, and it was less certain that identification with the reform strategy could be considered a guarantee of popularity.

These factors contributed to a gradual realignment of political allegiances, associated with a clarification of social differentiation. Inequalities in earnings were still small by western European standards, but workers in mining, manufacturing and energy, and employees in the public services, whose pay had fallen relative to the national average, increasingly identified with opposition parties. The Social Democrats, with their strongly "European" image and their clearly stated ambition to lead a government, were the main beneficiaries (see Table 4.4). Shifts in political allegiances led to major gains for the Social Democrats in the elections in 1996, ensuring that the ODS-dominated coalition government could not hope to continue without their tacit acceptance.

However, Klaus's final fall was precipitated by a scandal over his own party's funding: it appeared that the ODS had been secretly supported by individuals who had benefited from privatization decisions. Klaus tried to bluff his way out of this latest difficulty, but was deserted by his former close allies. He resigned as Prime Minister on November 30, 1997, as the coalition fell apart. The ODS suffered internal divisions and defections, and Klaus was accused of failing to face up to the need for honesty on party funding. The dissension led to the appearance of a new party, the Union of Freedom.

A caretaker government was formed on January 2, 1998, under Josef Tošovský, the governor of the central bank, and early elections were scheduled for June. Despite further revelations of financial irregularities, the ODS retained a respectable level of support. However, the bitterness of the conflicts within the former coalition made it impossible to recreate it. Instead, a Social Democrat government led by Miloš Zeman took office, based on a minority of seats in the Chamber of Deputies, but with tacit support from the ODS. There was no certainty that it would be able to implement significant changes in policy, or survive for anything approaching a full term.

## The New Slovak Politics, 1993–98

Political life in Slovakia after January 1993 was dominated by Mečiar's attempts to consolidate his own position of personal power. The government formed in June 1992 contained only one representative of another party, a Slovak Nationalist, and he resigned in 1993. Mečiar also came into conflict with members of his own HZDS, which led to the removal of the Foreign Minister in March 1993 and a series of battles with the president, Michal Kováč.

In March 1994, Kováč instigated a vote of no confidence in the unicameral legislature, the National Council. Following its success, a new government was formed, bringing together the Christian Democrats, the Party of the Democratic Left, and three groupings of former HZDS members. It also had the tacit backing of the Hungarian representatives. However, in the early elections held in September 1994, Mečiar and the HZDS won

35% of the vote. He returned to power with the backing of the Slovak Nationalists and a left-wing group that had broken away from the Party of the Democratic Left.

The period that followed saw Mečiar using constitutionally dubious measures to weaken and destroy opposition. The state security police appear to have been involved in the bizarre kidnapping of President Kováč's son in August 1995, which remains officially unexplained. A strongly nationalist flavor to policy included support for the revival of the cultural legacy of the wartime Slovak state, and a language law, passed in November 1995, which reduced the status of Hungarian. There was no official effort to counter the racist attitudes to the Roma that have been openly propagated by leading figures in the Slovak National Party. The main cost to Slovakia was international isolation. The EU turned down its application to begin negotiations on full membership in July 1997 and restated the same decision in November 1998, citing the poor consolidation of democracy as the principal reason.

By 1998, however, a broad coalition of opposition forces had been established. In September, it defeated the HZDS in elections for the National Council (see Table 4.5), despite the obstacles placed in its way by the media, which were strongly biased towards the HZDS, as well as attempts by Mečiar to prevent the registration of the main opposition movement, the Slovak Democratic Coalition. In the event, the Coalition, led by the new Prime Minister, Mikulas Dzurinda, became the largest group in the government that took office in October 1998. It includes Christian Democrats, Social Democrats, and a number of other groups, some of which emerged out of the HZDS; its partners in government are the Party of the Democratic Left, the Party of Civic Reconciliation, and the Hungarian Coalition. Together, these groups command more than the three fifths of votes in the National Council required to amend the Constitution. They began in January 1999 by amending it to introduce a system of direct election for the presidency (in two rounds of voting), replacing the previous system of election by the National Council itself. The first such election, in May 1999, was won by the government's candidate,

Rudolf Schuster (with 57% of the votes cast in the second round). His main rival for the post was Vladimír Mečiar (with 43% in the second round).

## A Future in the EU?

By the end of 1998, both of the chief architects of the breakup of Czechoslovakia had fallen from power. In both cases, their promises of great national advance had been fulfilled very partially at best.

Klaus's boasts of a successful economic transformation of the Czech Republic looked hollow, as economic growth turned first to stagnation and then, in 1998, to decline. However, claims that political life is now stable and consolidated appear more credible. The political parties that dominate the Czech Parliament have fairly clearly defined and stable social bases, and seem likely to dominate political life for some time to come. The way is also open for membership of the EU, following the launch of detailed negotiations in November 1998. It is not clear when they will be completed. The Czech government no longer tries to claim precedence over others in central and eastern Europe, but it is likely to remain in the first group from the region to win full acceptance.

Mečiar's legacy to Slovakia appears more clearly negative. Slovak national pride could for a time be helped by independent statehood, but the economic future is very uncertain. There have also been other heavy costs, in the form of delay in consolidating the political structure and international isolation. The new coalition government spans a political spectrum from Čarnogurský's strong allegiance to the Catholic Church to the Party of the Democratic Left's pragmatic "post-Communism." They were brought together by their common desire to remove Mečiar, but have already displayed major divisions, for example over the position of the Catholic church in the education system. Particularly in view of the serious economic situation, it may prove extremely difficult to keep a stable government united around the difficult tasks of winning confidence abroad, broadening the base of the economy, and promoting harmony among nationalities. Statements by Prime Minister Dzurinda and other leading government figures have suggested that, with Mečiar out of power and then defeated in the presidential election, they foresee early acceptance into the EU. Unfortunately, Mečiar's legacy, and the general immaturity of Slovak political development, may take some time to overcome.

## Further Reading

Czech Statistical Office, *Statistical Yearbook of the Czech Republic*, Prague: Scientia, annual publication

This useful publication, in Czech and English, is also available on disk. It provides detailed statistics on economic and social life, with historical series back to 1960.

Economist Intelligence Unit, *Country Reports*, London: The Economist, quarterly publications

The reports, each around 10,000 words long, provide up-to-date information on economic, political and business developments in the Czech Republic, the Slovak Republic (as they call it), and many other countries.

Kaplan, Karel, *The Short March: The Communist Takeover in Czechoslovakia 1945–1948*, London: Hurst, and New York: St Martin's Press, 1987

An account of the Communists' establishment of their monopoly of power by a Czech historian, based on detailed use of archival sources

Mamatey, Victor, and Radomír Luža, *A History of the Czechoslovak Republic, 1918–1948*, Princeton, NJ: Princeton University Press, 1973

A solid account of the interwar period

Musil, Jiří, editor, *The End of Czechoslovakia*, Budapest: Central European University Press, 1995

A wide-ranging study, showing the differences between Czech and Slovak development from 1918 onwards as a background to the breakup of the federation

Myant, Martin, *The Czechoslovak Economy 1948–1988: The Battle for Economic Reform*, Cambridge and New York: Cambridge University Press, 1989

An account of declining economic performance against the background of political development

Myant, Martin, *Transforming Socialist Economies: The Case of Poland and Czechoslovakia*, Aldershot and Brookfield, VT: Edward Elgar, 1993

A critical assessment of the economic strategies pursued by Czechoslovak and Polish governments after 1989

OECD, *Economic Surveys*, Paris: OECD, biannual publications

Assessments of economic developments and prospects in the member states of this organization, including the Czech Republic, as well as in its "Partners in Transition," including Slovakia

Skilling, H. Gordon, *Czechoslovakia's Interrupted Revolution*, Princeton, NJ: Princeton University Press, 1976

Still the most complete account of the events of 1968, although more information is now available

Smith, Adrian, *Reconstructing the Regional Economy: Industrial Transformation and Regional Development in Slovakia*, Cheltenham and Northampton, MA: Edward Elgar, 1998

A critical assessment of the economic transformation in Slovakia, with detailed studies of the armaments industry

Statistical Office of the Slovak Republic, *Statistical Yearbook of the Slovak Republic*, Bratislava: Veda, annual publication

This is issued in Slovak and English, with accompanying disk, and gives detailed statistics on economic and social life, with historical series back to 1960.

---

*Dr Martin Myant* is a Reader in the Department of Accounting, Economics and Languages at the University of Paisley in Scotland.

---

### Table 4.1   Results of Legislative Elections, June 1990 (% of total votes cast)

|  | Federal Assembly (Czech) (Slovak) | | Czech Legislature | Slovak Legislature |
|---|---|---|---|---|
| Civic Forum | 51.6 | – | 49.5 | – |
| Public Against Violence | – | 34.9 | – | 29.3 |
| Communist Party | 13.6 | 13.6 | 13.2 | 13.3 |
| Christian Democratic Movement | – | 17.8 | – | 19.2 |
| People's Party – Christian and Democratic Union | 8.7 | – | 8.4 | – |
| Society for Self-governing Democracy in Moravia and Silesia | 8.5 | – | 10.0 | – |
| Slovak Nationalist Party | – | 11.2 | – | 13.9 |
| Hungarian Christian Democrat Party | – | 8.5 | – | 8.7 |
| Social Democrats | 4.0 | 1.7 | 4.1 | 1.8 |
| Farmers' Party | 3.9 | 2.3 | 4.1 | 2.5 |
| Greens | 3.3 | 2.9 | 4.1 | 3.5 |
| Democratic Party | – | 4.0 | – | 4.4 |

**Table 4.2   Results of Legislative Elections, June 1992 (% of total votes cast)[1]**

|                                                          | Federal Assembly (Czech) | (Slovak) | Czech National Council | Slovak National Council |
|----------------------------------------------------------|:---:|:---:|:---:|:---:|
| ODS                                                      | 33.7 | – | 29.7 | – |
| Movement for a Democratic Slovakia                       | – | 33.7 | – | 37.3 |
| Left Bloc – Party of the Democratic Left                 | 14.4 | 14.2 | 14.1 | 14.7 |
| Christian Democratic Movement                            | – | 8.9 | – | 8.9 |
| People's Party – Christian and Democratic Union          | 6.0 | – | 6.3 | – |
| Society for Self-governing Democracy in Moravia and Silesia | – | – | 5.9 | – |
| Slovak Nationalist Party                                 | – | 9.4 | – | 7.9 |
| Hungarian Christian Democrat Party                       | – | 7.4 | – | 7.4 |
| Social Democrats                                         | 5.6 | – | 6.5 | – |
| Republicans                                              | 6.4 | – | 6.0 | – |
| Liberal Social Union                                     | 5.9 | – | 6.5 | – |
| Civic Democratic Alliance                                | – | – | 5.9 | – |

1 Only parties that won more than 5% of the total votes cast are included. Other parties won no parliamentary representation.

**Table 4.3   Economic Performance of the Czech and Slovak Republics, 1990–97 (%)**

|                                                  | 1990 | 1991 | 1992 | 1993 | 1994 | 1995 | 1996 | 1997 |
|--------------------------------------------------|:---:|:---:|:---:|:---:|:---:|:---:|:---:|:---:|
| *Czech Republic*                                 |  |  |  |  |  |  |  |  |
| Change in GDP (at constant prices)               | –1.2 | –14.2 | –6.4 | 0.5 | 3.4 | 6.4 | 3.9 | 1.0 |
| Registered unemployment (as proportion of the workforce) | 0.73 | 4.13 | 2.57 | 3.52 | 3.19 | 2.93 | 3.5 | 5.2 |
| Change in consumer price inflation               | 9.7 | 56.6 | 11.1 | 20.8 | 10.0 | 9.1 | 8.8 | 8.5 |
| *Slovakia*                                       |  |  |  |  |  |  |  |  |
| Change in GDP (at constant prices)               | –2.5 | –14.6 | –5.4 | –1.9 | 4.9 | 6.8 | 6.9 | 3.4 |
| Registered unemployment (as proportion of the workforce) | 1.6 | 11.8 | 10.4 | 14.4 | 14.8 | 13.1 | 12.8 | 11.6 |
| Change in consumer price inflation               | 10.6 | 56.0 | 10.7 | 23.1 | 13.6 | 9.6 | 5.8 | 6.1 |

**Table 4.4  Results of Elections for the Chamber of Deputies in the Czech Republic, June 1996 and June 1998 (% of total votes cast)[1]**

|  | 1996 | 1998 |
| --- | --- | --- |
| ODS | 26.9 | 27.7 |
| Social Democrats | 26.4 | 32.3 |
| Communists | 10.3 | 11.0 |
| Christian Democrats | 8.1 | 9.0 |
| Union of Freedom | – | 8.6 |
| Republicans | 8.0 | – |
| Civic Democratic Alliance | 6.4 | – |

1 Only parties that won more than 5% of the total votes cast are included. Other parties won no parliamentary representation.

**Table 4.5  Results of Elections for the National Council of Slovakia, September 1998 (% of total votes cast)**

| | |
| --- | --- |
| Slovak Democratic Coalition | 26.3 |
| Party of the Democratic Left | 14.7 |
| Party of Civic Reconciliation | 8.0 |
| Hungarian Coalition | 9.1 |
| Slovak Nationalist Party | 9.1 |
| Movement for a Democratic Slovakia (HZDS) | 27.0 |

## Chapter Five

# Bulgaria

*John Bristow*

## The Communist Period

As it pushed the Axis forces westwards, the Soviet Army crossed the Danube into Bulgaria on September 8, 1944, and the following day the first Communist-dominated government was installed. It was eventually headed by Georgi Dimitrov, who had received international attention in 1934 as a defendant in the Reichstag Fire trial in Germany, and had subsequently taken refuge in Moscow, where he became Chairman of the Communist International (the Comintern). Dimitrov died in 1949, but by then all the political elements of Communist hegemony were in place. Dimitrov's brother in law, Vulko Chervenkov, took over in 1950, but in 1953 the death of Stalin and the subsequent reorientation of Soviet policy fatally weakened his position. In March 1954, his most important post – General Secretary of the Party – went to the man who came to personify Communist Bulgaria, Todor Zhivkov. Zhivkov inherited and maintained a regime especially noteworthy for two characteristics: extreme loyalty to the Soviet Union – he offered Bulgaria to the Soviet Union, as its 16th republic, but the offer was declined – and harsh internal repression. Right up to the 1960s, Bulgaria could boast the same kind of lethal labor camps as the Soviet Union.

Economic strategy was also based closely on the Soviet model. Economic progress was to be based upon rapid industrialization, although at the time the Communists came to power industry accounted for less than 20% of total output. This was to be achieved by concentrating a high proportion of investment in that sector through the planning mechanism, with a high investment ratio financed through forced saving. The supply of labor to industry would be increased by the collectivization of agriculture and the large increase in agricultural productivity that this was expected to achieve. The institutions through which this strategy was to be implemented were, as regards nonagricultural activities, put in place very rapidly. By the end of 1947, all industrial enterprises were in state hands, the banks were merged into a single state bank, and international trade had become a state monopoly. Agricultural reorganization was more difficult. In 1944, there were more than 1 million farms with an average area of barely 4 hectares. The main instrument of consolidation was to be the collective farm (referred to in Bulgarian by its initials, TKZS). By the end of the 1940s, only 11% of arable land was in the hands of the state, but the pace accelerated in the next decade until, by 1958, 92% of such land was in the hands of the collectives. By that date, the collective farms had been grouped into fewer than 1,000 units, with an average area of more than 4,000 hectares.

The result of all this was a dramatic change in the structure of economic activity. In the 12 years to 1960, the share of industry in total output rose from 23% to 48%, and its share in total employment rose from 8% to 22%. The obverse of this trend was a fall in agriculture's share of output from 59% to 27%, and in its share of employment from 82% to 55%. These trends persisted throughout the Communist period until, by 1989, industry accounted for 57% of output and 38% of employment, while agriculture's shares were 12% and 18% respectively.

Initially, the development strategy was successful. Growth was achieved by devoting a large proportion of resources to investment, by transferring labor from agriculture to industry, and by taking advantage of the economies of scale available following the consolidation of both manufacturing and farming into large units. However, the limits of this "extensive" development were reached by the 1960s, when it became necessary to improve total factor productivity if growth was to be maintained. This proved impossible, and growth rates slackened significantly. Annual real growth averaged 11% in the 1950s, 7.5% in the 1960s, 7% in the 1970s and little more than 3% in the 1980s.

The impact of the development strategy on the living standards of the mass of the population is a complex issue, and this complexity is reflected in the ambiguity of popular attitudes towards the eventual transition to a market economy. Before World War II, Bulgaria had been among the poorest nations in Europe, with income per capita barely 20% of Germany's, only 45% of Czechoslovakia's, and 60% of Hungary's. Nor was the country a democracy. Although it could plausibly be argued that average material wealth would have been greater in 1989 if the previous 45 years had been lived under a capitalist rather than a Communist economic system, the latter produced not only a standard of living markedly higher than those living before the war had experienced but, more significantly, it produced social benefits that would not have been generated under capitalism. The mass of people had a degree of security, through full employment and high levels of provision of state-funded health care, education, and pensions, and many now mourn its passing.

The lack of access to consumer goods was recognized as politically dangerous by the regime and periodically the plans provided for some expansion in this area. By the 1980s, however, economic dissatisfaction began to mingle with political dissatisfaction, the former fueled by images generated by mass media and foreign tourists, and the latter by what was happening in Poland and in the Soviet Union. The key event was the internal Party coup that overthrew Todor Zhivkov on November 10, 1989. The proximate cause was the appallingly adverse international publicity created by his persecution of the Turkish minority, and his repressive reaction to massive demonstrations sparked by protests against environmental conditions. He had simply become an embarrassment to his colleagues and, importantly, to the Gorbachev regime in Moscow. Transition can be said to have begun with his disappearance from power, after he had been the effective boss of the country for 35 years.

## Politics in a Free Bulgaria

A number of important changes occurred within three months of the fall of Zhivkov. The Union of Democratic Forces (UDF) was established as the main opposition coalition, bringing together a large number of political and other interest groups. The Constitution was amended to remove the special position of the Communist Party. The latter changed its name to the Bulgarian Socialist Party (BSP). Finally, a multiparty forum was set up to design new electoral laws and related institutions.

In the first free elections for the unicameral National Assembly, held in June 1990, the BSP and its associates won 211 and the UDF 144 of the 400 seats. The BSP's overall majority should not be interpreted as the result of nostalgia for Communism. First, the BSP was simply more effective at fighting elections. It used its well-established party structure to good advantage, and also had the benefit of the UDF's complete inability to understand electoral politics. Notably, the UDF antagonized the Movement for Rights and Freedoms (MRF), a party representing the Turkish minority that would have been an invaluable ally against the BSP, especially in those constituencies where the election went to a second round (that is, where no candidate received an absolute majority of votes in the first round). Second, the BSP received huge blocs of votes from rural dwellers, who were anxious about future land policy, and from pensioners, whose interest lay in short-term social protection rather than long-term economic reform.

A government was not formed until September, by which time the Chairman of the UDF, a sociology professor named Zhelyu Zhelev, had been elected as the country's President by the National Assembly. The government lasted barely two months in the face of popular unrest and party fragmentation, and in December a new government was formed, with a nonparty figure, Dimitur Popov, as Prime Minister. What was expected to be merely a caretaker administration survived for almost one year, and initiated the process of economic transition.

On the political front, one urgent task was the construction of a new Constitution, since the existing one had not been designed from scratch for a parliamentary democracy. The major features of the Constitution, which came into force in July 1991, include a National Assembly reduced in size; a simpler electoral system, based on proportional representation through party lists; and direct presidential elections. October 1991 saw the first elections under this new Constitution. The outcome was that the UDF won 110 of the 240 seats, the BSP and associates 106, the remainder going to the MRF. In January 1992, Zhelev was returned as President in a direct election. The UDF/MRF coalition government, led by Filip Dimitrov, was very active, putting in place laws on land restitution, banking and privatization, but it fell foul of factors that have become all too familiar in Bulgaria. The UDF itself was an unstable coalition, as its only unifying force was distaste for the old regime, and its main identifying feature was an unwillingness to compromise even within itself, let alone with its supposed partner, the MRF.

The coalition lost a confidence vote in October 1992, and, after two months of searching, President Zhelev found another nonparty figure who could receive the support of a majority of the National Assembly as Prime Minister. This was Lyuben Berov, an economist, and his appointment created the nice coincidence that three contiguous countries (Bulgaria, Greece, and Turkey) simultaneously had economics professors as Prime Ministers. The economist who has written this chapter would like to claim that policy-making in these countries was improved by this experience – but cannot honestly do so.

Once again, Bulgaria found itself with a government not generated by elections, and not even from within the Assembly. It was supposed to be a "government of experts" – for example, the Minister of Finance was another erstwhile academic economist – but its level of expertise proved disappointing, and it was a victim of its lack of connections with the Assembly. It relied on a bloc representing most of the BSP and the MRF, with some mavericks from the UDF. Managing repeatedly to construct a kind of revolving majority in the Assembly, it survived for one year and nine months, at the end of which, in September 1994, an exhausted Berov resigned. Elections were scheduled for December, and an interim government was put in place under the director of the Privatization Agency, Renata Indzhova, the first woman to become Prime Minister of Bulgaria (and only the second in any post-Communist country).

The elections were catastrophic for the UDF, which lost 41 seats to a combination of the BSP and new groups. The BSP finished with 125 of the 240 seats, and went on to form democratic Bulgaria's first single-party government. The BSP's leader, Zhan Videnov, became Prime Minister at the age of 35. The BSP's victory was a result of popular disillusionment with both economic and political features of transition, and mirrored what had recently happened in Hungary, Lithuania, and Poland. The BSP was also assisted by the organizational incompetence of the UDF who, it should be remembered, had not been in government for two years.

Although the BSP government also lasted for about two years, it was brought down by two factors: economic mismanagement, and its well-known association with the corruption and crime that have disfigured Bulgarian life. The former will be reviewed later, but the latter deserves a word now.

All societies need control mechanisms – which take the form of effective legal and judicial systems, and a substantial degree of social commitment on the part of the populace, politicians, and officials – to restrict the consequences of individual greed. All post-Communist countries have suffered from the fact that the old mechanisms collapsed before any new mechanisms became effective. None is without its scandals over privatization of state assets or ineffective banking control. Russia is famous for its "mafia," and Bulgaria's experience has been very similar. "Informal" privatization, the abuse of official power in the formal privatization process, corrupt banking practices, the diversion of foreign grants and loans, and the overt crime that accompanies such a lawless environment – including businessmen shooting competitors – were all facilitated by a network of contacts based on the old Communist apparatus that linked those with political, official and economic power. Nobody was immune, but the BSP, all of whose influential members were former Communist officials, was, both in fact and in public perception, linked to this network. The flaunting of their wealth by these elements, in the face of the appalling effects of the economic crisis of 1996 on the mass of the population, was too much for even an exceptionally stoical electorate to bear.

Although Videnov's government could still have maintained the support of a majority in the Assembly, and there was no constitutional obligation to hold elections until the end of 1998, even the government recognized that it had lost legitimacy. The popular swing against the BSP had been reflected in the presidential election of November 1996, when Petur Stoyanov of the UDF defeated the BSP's candidate; there were serious street demonstrations and presidential pressure for new elections; and the major international financial agencies were refusing to do business.

In the elections of April 1997, the UDF won a clear overall majority, with 137 seats, while the BSP's representation collapsed to 57 seats. The remaining seats went to various groups, at least one of which (Euroleft, a centrist party formed by BSP defectors) could be relied on to support a UDF government. What, at the time of writing, has turned out to be the most effective government so far was formed under the leadership of Ivan Kostov, who had been Minister of Finance in the Popov government of 1990–91, and in its successor UDF government, and who is arguably the most impressive Bulgarian politician of his generation.

## Transition to a Market Economy

Although some elements were put in place in 1990, Bulgaria's economic transition is usually taken to have begun on February 1, 1991, with a "big bang" package of liberalization measures:

- the freeing of most domestic prices;
- the elimination of most quantitative restrictions on foreign trade;
- the liberalization of foreign exchange dealings, with internal convertibility of the national currency, the lev, and the establishment of a single, market-determined exchange rate; and
- a severe reduction in producer and consumer subsidies in the state budget.

The country began the process with exceptionally adverse initial conditions. First, there was a substantial monetary overhang, which caused the level of prices to explode on liberalization. Second, there were huge foreign debts, and a moratorium on foreign debt service had been in place since early 1990. Until a rescheduling agreement was arrived at in July 1994, these debts provided a severe fiscal constraint, and effectively isolated the country from foreign bank credit. Third, Bulgaria had been abnormally dependent on Comecon. According to official figures, 80% of its exports went to other Comecon members, and 65% to the Soviet Union alone. When that institution collapsed, Bulgaria faced two problems that have yet to be overcome. As a result of the move to international prices, there was a very marked deterioration in the terms of trade, since the Soviet Union had been providing materials, especially energy, at artificially low prices, and had imported from Bulgaria at artificially high prices. Then, the real economic decline in all former Comecon countries in the early 1990s had an especially pronounced effect on demand for Bulgarian output. The need for, and the difficulties of, trade reorientation have been a central feature of the country's transition process. Bulgaria faced no problems that were not experienced elsewhere in central and eastern Europe: it was simply that the country had all of them at once, and to a degree not shared in other countries.

## Inflation and the Exchange Rate

Bulgaria's initial experience was similar to that in all the other countries that adopted a "big bang" approach to liberalizing prices and foreign exchange, that is, all of post-Communist Europe except Hungary and Romania: an explosion of the level of prices, and a massive nominal devaluation. Thus, in February 1991 alone, the domestic price level more than doubled, and the lev lost almost 90% of its value against the US dollar. The situation then settled down, but where Bulgaria has been different from most of the rest of central and eastern Europe, although not from Russia, is that there has not been a smooth stabilization over the subsequent years (see Table 5.1).

Early 1991 was of course dominated by the immediate effects of the liberalization measures of February. The echo effects of the liberalization, through inflation-linked wages and the effects of devaluation on domestic prices, persisted throughout the year. Apart from the effects of a dramatic increase in prices for energy, which were still under state control, in May 1992, a long period of comparative stability then began. However, the fundamentals of the economy, such as the balance of payments, did not significantly improve, and the lev began to weaken considerably in late 1993. The Bulgarian National Bank (BNB) used its reserves to support the currency but eventually had to give up the fight in March 1994, when the lev lost more than 40% of its value against the US dollar. This, combined with the price effects of the introduction of value-added tax, created 22% inflation in April alone.

This again was followed by reasonable stability, helped by the resumption of IMF assistance after the devaluation, but things started to go wrong again in the spring of 1996. Bulgaria was about to experience the most dramatic currency crisis yet seen in any transition country. The pace of devaluation accelerated throughout the rest of the year and, during the four months from the end of

October, the lev lost almost 90% of its value against the US dollar. This collapse in the external value of the lev of course generated massive domestic inflation, culminating in a rate of almost 250% during February 1997. In the three months from the end of November 1996, the domestic price level rose sixfold. The situation then calmed down, and the autumn of 1997 ushered in a period of the greatest exchange and price stability in Bulgaria since transition began.

Two questions arise: why did these crises, and especially that of 1996–97, occur, and why has stability been established?

First, Bulgaria has shared with other transition economies the experience of the long-term rate of nominal devaluation falling short of domestic inflation: that is, over the long run there has been real appreciation of the currency. Only during the short periods when there were huge nominal devaluations (the "big bang" of February 1991, the relatively brief crisis of spring 1994, and the longer crisis from the spring of 1996 to early 1997) has there been real depreciation. This provides a constant threat to the currency in countries where the difficulties of improving real international competitiveness through improvements in productivity have been central to the whole transition process. The BNB, along with other central banks, has been under constant pressure to intervene to prop up the currency, so as to limit the effects of devaluation on the domestic value of foreign debt obligations, and because of fear that any nominal devaluation would lead to a loss of confidence and subsequent collapse. But, in the face of long-term pressures, reserves eventually become insufficient and major devaluation becomes unavoidable.

A second long-term pressure on domestic inflation and the exchange rate has come from the difficulties of keeping the budget deficit, which can be financed only by creating money or borrowing abroad, under control. In Bulgaria, the crises of 1994 and 1996–97 were both preceded by significant increases in government borrowing.

Third, since these factors are apparent to the market, the immediate cause of currency crises is always a dramatic loss of confidence in the currency. Domestic holders of the lev deserted it (this was very obvious in 1996), and moved their liquid wealth into goods and, more importantly, into foreign currency, as there are now few restrictions on the holding of US dollar accounts in Bulgaria.

Fourth, international agencies such as the IMF and the World Bank in effect suspended dealings with the country because, despite repeated exhortations and threats, its governments had made inadequate progress with structural changes in the real economy, such as privatization. Thus, large potential capital inflows were denied to Bulgaria, and the very public criticisms of such agencies further eroded confidence.

Fifth, the currency crisis of 1996–97 was exacerbated by the simultaneous existence of a banking crisis. Several large banks, both state-owned and private, and together accounting for more than one fifth of total deposits, have gone into liquidation, primarily because of their imprudent lending policies. Since state deposit insurance has been rudimentary, many Bulgarians have lost large amounts of money, even when their accounts were in US dollars. The resultant collapse of confidence in the banks caused both households and firms to take their holdings right out of the banking system. The favorite strategy seems to have been to convert into US dollars, withdraw them, and keep them as cash or deposit them outside the country. This added to the other causes of a collapse in the domestic demand for the lev, fueling devaluation and inflation.

The situation was changed dramatically by the announcement in early 1997 that, with the support of the IMF, a currency board would be set up with effect from July 1, 1997. The essence of such an institution, which had been shown to be effective in Argentina since 1991, in Estonia since 1992, and in Lithuania since 1994, is that the nominal exchange rate is fixed with respect to a target currency. In Bulgaria, it was the Deutschmark until January 1, 1999, and has been the euro since then. The domestic money stock must be backed totally by foreign exchange reserves, and the central bank is forbidden to lend to the government. As a result, since July 1997 the only movements in the exchange rate between the lev and the

US dollar have been movements in the US dollar/Deutschmark rate, and domestic pressures on prices have been severely reduced by the limitation on creating money. Since expectations are so important in these matters, the impact of the currency board can be dated to the announcement of the policy. There was nominal appreciation in March and April 1997, then some devaluation, as the market attempted to predict the exchange rate that would be established, and complete stability after that.

The currency board has been by far the most successful exercise in Bulgarian economic policy since the transition began – some may say the only successful one. The resulting stability of exchange rates and prices has laid the ground for long-delayed improvements in the real economy.

## The Real Economy

Just as in the monetary respects reviewed above, Bulgaria's real performance reflected that of neighboring countries in the early years of transition, but with greater severity, and more recently it departed from that experience by reverting to a downward spiral in output, employment, and real income. In considering these matters, of course, one must constantly bear in mind the statistical problems of tracking economies in transition, especially the difficulties of measuring what is happening in the private sector. However, official figures are probably a reasonable guide to what has happened – at least qualitatively – even though the actual magnitudes may be unreliable.

The most significant events for economic activity in the formerly planned economies in Europe have been the collapse of Comecon and the liberalization of trade. These events exposed such economies to the full blast of international competition, at a time when real demand was collapsing throughout the region, in countries that had been major markets for each other. The impact was especially severe for Bulgaria, for which, as we have seen, Comecon was so important.

Primarily because of supply difficulties, real GDP turned down in 1990, before true transition began. Thereafter, the full effects of the decline in real demand in the region, and of the lack of competitiveness of Bulgarian industry, began to be felt, with real GDP falling by 12% in 1991, 7% in 1992, and 2% in 1993. Then, as was happening elsewhere, the depression bottomed out, but not after an overall decline in real GDP of 26% since 1989 – the deepest depression in the whole region. Tentative recovery during 1994 and 1995, with an increase in real GDP of 4% over those two years, was overtaken by the real effects of the monetary crisis of 1996 and 1997, when real GDP fell by 10 and 7% respectively. Over the whole period from 1989 to 1997, therefore, real GDP fell by 36%.

This was of course associated with a very significant increase in unemployment. However, this is particularly difficult to measure, because the only regular statistical series relates to those registering for unemployment compensation. Since compensation is available for a maximum of only nine months, there is little incentive for the long-term unemployed to register; yet this effect may be offset by the registration of those who have been made unemployed in the state sector but have jobs in the private sector, which is difficult to monitor. Movements in the official unemployment rate may therefore be reasonable indicators. Officially registered unemployment rose very rapidly, from 2% of the labor force at the beginning of 1991 to 11% by the end of that year, and to 16% by the end of 1993. As output recovered somewhat, unemployment declined to 11% by the end of 1995, turning upward, with the subsequent decline in output, to 14% by the end of 1997.

Because of the paucity of detailed information on the private sector, total employment is also difficult to track. However, one indication of the enormous structural changes that have been occurring is that employment in the state sector – government bodies, the military, and, especially, state-owned enterprises – fell from well over 3.3 million in early 1991 to less than 1.3 million in early 1998. In addition, by early 1998 the average real wage in the state sector was only 75% of what it had been in early 1991; and there was an even greater fall in the real value of pensions, which are an important source of household income in Bulgaria.

All these trends combined to produce a dramatic reduction in real living standards. On official figures, real household consumption in 1997 was barely 60% of its level in 1991. Official figures significantly overestimate the decline, but this factor is offset to a considerable extent by the fact that, while free social services such as education and health care, which do not appear in consumption statistics, were delivered primarily through one's employing enterprise under Communism, they are now delivered by a penurious government that cannot afford to maintain standards, especially as regards health care, above the most rudimentary level. This is a social catastrophe by any standards. Apart from a very small minority that has developed living standards above the median in developed economies, usually by methods of dubious legality and even more dubious morality, millions of people who had economically secure lives in an industrialized society have been reduced, in many cases, to growing their own food, and taking their own bedclothes to hospital. For pensioners, physical survival is achievable only through the support of their children. If nothing else, this state of affairs helps to explain the political instability referred to above. No government in a western democracy could hope to survive the electoral impact of even one tenth of the privations suffered by the mass of the Bulgarian people.

## International Trade

As has already been noted, under the planning regime Bulgaria's trade was dominated by Comecon, where aggregate demand collapsed in the early days of transition. Further, intra-Comecon trade, except in the case of primary energy, was dominated by "soft" goods – that is, goods of a quality that made them uncompetitive in world markets. Against this background, the liberalization of trade was expected to have two effects. First, both the origins and the destinations of trade would change, in the case of exports toward richer markets and, in the case of imports toward suppliers offering better combinations of price and quality. Second, the commodity composition of trade would change so as to reflect the relative sectoral efficiency of Bulgaria in international markets.

These expectations have been realized (see Table 5.2). On the export side, the share of the developed industrial countries in the OECD has risen from 8% to 58% and the EU alone now accounts for 43%. This increase is only marginally explicable by the fact that the five states in eastern Germany are now in the EU and not, in the form of the German Democratic Republic, in Comecon. Balancing this shift toward trade with the OECD is the dramatic decline in the significance of ex-Comecon countries, and especially of the former Soviet republics. The other members of Comecon took 82% of Bulgaria's exports in 1989, and the Soviet Union alone took 65%; in 1997, six years after Comecon's demise, the figures were 20% and 18% respectively. Similar though somewhat less dramatic changes occurred on the import side. In 1997, the OECD accounted for 46% of Bulgaria's imports, and the EU for 37%, as against 17% from the OECD, and 10% from the EU, in 1989. Over the same eight years, the import share of the Comecon group fell from 72% to 36%, and that of the Soviet Union and its successor states from 53% to 33%. The continuing importance of the former Soviet Union on the import side chiefly reflects the fact that almost all of Bulgaria's nonnuclear primary energy consists of oil and natural gas from Russia and other CIS countries.

Because of discontinuities in the statistics, it is not possible to be so precise as to what has happened to the commodity composition of trade, although qualitatively one's expectations have been confirmed. Engineering products are now much less important in total exports, which is to be expected, since such products were and are generally not of good quality by international standards, and the huge growth of this sector under the Communists was perhaps the greatest economic distortion of all. Exports of chemicals, on the other hand, have become relatively much more important, reflecting the generally good quality of chemical products from Bulgaria. The major disappointment concerns food and related products. Up to the beginning of central planning, Bulgaria was an almost totally agricultural country. However, two factors are at work here. First, quality is generally poor, or the output is of a type, as in the case of tobacco or many types of processed food, not to the taste of western consumers. Second, productive capacity and output in agriculture have declined markedly, primarily because of the effects of the land restitution policy (discussed below).

Overall, therefore, predictions regarding trading patterns have been fulfilled. With progress in restructuring to raise the general levels of international competitiveness, these trends can be expected to continue.

# Decollectivization and Privatization

## Land Restitution

Land reform is probably the most radical and certainly the most complex reorganization of economic activity yet attempted in Bulgaria. The driving force was less economic necessity than political opportunism. Although restoration of the land to its original owners could have been expected to be resisted, as it was, by the TKZS bureaucracy, the number of potential beneficiaries far exceeded the number of potential losers, which made the political implications of land restitution quite different from those of industrial privatization.

As a result, almost immediately after the fall of Zhivkov, and before the first free elections, the BSP government, recognizing the political advantages of being associated with land restitution, set in motion the process that led to the enactment, in 1991, of the law that still forms much of the foundation of policy, even though it has subsequently been amended. The essence of the scheme is that previous owners or their heirs have the right to be assigned, without charge, the land they owned before collectivization. Where this is not possible, because boundaries are ill-defined or the land has been built on, they may receive an equivalent area in the same district, or obtain financial compensation.

Few would contest that collective agriculture had failed, and that land privatization should have been a priority for policy. To that extent, therefore, the radicalism and urgency of the scheme are to be applauded. However, the political factors that generated this radicalism and urgency were allowed to overcome economic considerations.

The legal and administrative tasks involved with land restitution are daunting and, although considerable progress has been made, it has been much slower than was originally envisaged. One indication of the legal complexities is that, where original deeds of ownership or probate documents are not available, claims may be supported by an affidavit – yet the total area of land claimed under such affidavits added up to more than the total area of the country.

Regardless of the longer-term benefits of land privatization, the restitution program has, in the meantime, been inimical to improvements in agricultural production, especially because it has introduced huge uncertainty. At the fall of Communism, about one seventh of collectivized land was in fact being cultivated very efficiently on a personal basis, but users now have no long-term assurance of continuing occupation. More generally, the permanent ownership of much of the land has yet to be finalized, and investment incentives have more or less disappeared, since current users have no assurance that they will be able to reap the fruits of any investment. This has led to substantial disinvestment, resulting from rational risk aversion: equipment and buildings are not being maintained, and the size of herds and flocks has been run down.

There are other major problems in addition to this endemic uncertainty, notably the small size of the average holding per claimant, and the mismatch between eligible persons and those likely to wish to engage in agriculture. The small size of the average holding is susceptible to two solutions. Voluntary cooperatives could be developed, and they are indeed in evidence; or, as a response to the problem of size and to the problem of mismatch as well, an efficient market in land could be established. However, the uncertainty already noted also acts as an impediment to the development of land markets. Uncertainty of ownership, and of the enforceability of leasing contracts, seriously inhibits both the demand for land and the supply, and acts as a disincentive to

lessees to make expensive investments in land improvement. Further, such uncertainty makes the banks, which are in any case very weak, seriously averse to lending for land purchase, and even for working capital purposes. The whole situation was made worse by the policy of the BSP government of 1995–97, which restricted the legality of land sales.

## Privatization

The first attempts to dispose of state-owned businesses came very early in the transition process, in 1991, and involved small service establishments, such as gas stations. They were aborted, however, because of the ambiguous legal status of the entities to be sold. This status was clarified by the enactment, later in 1991, of a commercial code based on the ownership concepts familiar in market economies, including companies and partnerships. This was complemented by the enactment in January 1992 of the Foreign Investment Law. Legislation permitting foreign participation in joint ventures had been in existence throughout the 1980s, but had had little effect; the new Law was remarkably liberal, at least in its formal provisions, imposing few restrictions on foreign investment. It turned out to be less liberal in its implementation (a matter to which we return below). The most important step, a true Privatization Law, was not enacted until May 1992, and then had to be radically amended, in June 1994. Legal provision was also made for the restitution of small businesses to their former owners, a process that has led to most shops and other service activities now being in private hands.

Initially anyway, Bulgaria decided to follow the Hungarian rather than the Czech route to privatization: state assets were to be sold, not given away through mass (voucher) privatization. The stated justifications for this approach were that it is wrong to give away state assets; that bidders prepared to put up their own money have the best incentive to operate the enterprise efficiently; and that the state needs revenue. The only concession to non-market considerations was that employees could participate in the privatization of their firms on especially favorable terms.

The original Law provided for shares to be sold by open sale, by public auction, by public tender, or by direct negotiations with potential buyers. The last of these proved to be the most used method, especially for large enterprises.

Three types of entity have competence to effect privatization. In the case of large firms owned by the central government, the Privatization Agency, set up in 1992, takes charge, although the approval of the Council of Ministers is required for certain designated firms. Smaller firms are privatized by the relevant ministry, while the owning municipality is the competent body for disposing of municipally owned enterprises. An enterprise itself may initiate the privatization process, but the approval of the competent body is required.

Early experience revealed serious defects in the Law, but also, and more seriously, it showed how vulnerable the whole process was – as it still is – to subversion at both the political and the official levels, particularly in cases where there was significant foreign interest. The Council of Ministers repeatedly interfered where the Law gave it no special competence, and the legally competent bodies actually engaged in litigation against each other to frustrate individual privatizations. Potential foreign investors continually complained that ministry officials broke agreements and generally blocked progress.

The first problem is simply an ideological one. Ministerial officials are almost universally those who were in place under the old regime. They think of enterprises in their industries as "their" firms, and their unwillingness to see these assets ending up in foreign hands prompts them to use their regulatory power to set up roadblocks. More sinister, and prevalent throughout the region, is the corruption already referred to. The power of politicians and officials has been used to impede foreigners in the many cases where there is a significant domestic interest in a large enterprise with good prospects.

Under the Privatization Law of 1994, the most significant change was the introduction of rather vague provisions for mass privatization. These were consolidated in further legislation in 1995, which set up a new agency for the purpose, specified the procedures in detail, and provided for the establishment of mutual investment funds. All Bulgarian adults became entitled to receive, at a nominal fee, a book of vouchers that they could either use as currency in the auctions relating to enterprises nominated for mass privatization, or use to buy shares in a mutual fund, which would then participate in auctions. Vouchers were distributed during 1996 and the first auctions were held in the fall of that year. Slightly more than one half of those eligible took up their vouchers, and more than 80% of them where then invested in mutual funds. More than 1,000 firms were nominated for this process, which is typically combined with cash sales and employee privilege: the totality of shares in a nominated enterprise is divided among those sold through vouchers, those assigned free to employees, and those sold through one of the cash methods outlined above.

Significant progress has at last been made in a process that, in Bulgaria, had been noticeably sclerotic. Mass privatization has been quite successful and, importantly, has provided a fresh stimulus to cash sales. Even more fundamentally, early 1997 saw the arrival of a government that was committed to privatization, and had the strength in the Assembly to implement its policies. There has been a noticeable reduction in the informal impediments to "clean" privatization in general and to foreign participation in particular. Only time will finally tell but, at least when this was being written, a corner seems to have been turned.

## Conclusion

Bulgaria has to date been one of the less successful transition economies, for both exogenous and endogenous reasons. It had the worst initial conditions, most obviously in its former reliance on Comecon, the scale of the distorting effects of that institution on the domestic economic structure, and the large debts accumulated during the 1980s. It has also suffered, as an innocent third party, from the UN embargoes on Iraq and Yugoslavia (Serbia and Montenegro). The Iraqi authorities have admitted a debt to Bulgaria of US$2 billion, which was to be repaid with oil, but it cannot be repaid because of the embargo. Large losses have also resulted from the embargo on Yugoslavia, not only from trade but also from the inability to move goods by road through that country.

The main internal impediment to progress has been the lack of general political commitment that would enable hard choices to be made. The population has suffered grievously, and there has been no shortage of politicians willing to exploit that suffering. The wonder is that the political situation has not been even less stable than it has been. No government, until the present one, has had both the commitment, and the political and popular strength, to restrain the budget deficit and monetary expansion, and enforce real movement on structural changes through such devices as privatization. However, with the macroeconomic stability induced by the currency board, the favorable view of the present government among international agencies and businesses, that government's apparently genuine belief in reform, and the strength of its political and popular support, one can have, for the first time, a rational basis for optimism.

## Further Reading

Bell, John D., editor, *Bulgaria in Transition: Politics, Economics, Society and Culture after Communism*, Boulder, CO: Westview Press, 1998

A volume for readers whose Bulgarian interests are eclectic, since its subjects include political behavior, the treatment of minorities, literature, and foreign policy, as well as the economy

Bristow, John A., *The Bulgarian Economy in Transition*, Cheltenham and Brookfield, VT: Edward Elgar, 1996

One of the few book-length treatments in English of Bulgaria's experience of transition

Bulgarian National Bank, *Monthly Bulletin* and *Annual Report*, various dates

Crampton, Richard J., *A Short History of Modern Bulgaria*, Cambridge and New York: Cambridge University Press, 1987

One of the most accessible works on modern Bulgarian history up to the mid-1980s

Jones, Derek C., and Jeffrey Miller, editors, *The Bulgarian Economy: Lessons from Early Transition*, Aldershot and Brookfield, VT: Ashgate, 1997

A valuable set of essays on economic topics, especially useful for its reviews of banking, labor markets, privatization, and agriculture

Lampe, John R., *The Bulgarian Economy in the Twentieth Century*, London: Croom Helm, and New York: St Martin's Press, 1986

This book by the best-known western scholar of Balkan economic history is essential reading on the Bulgarian economy since independence and, especially, on the Communist era.

Pundeff, M., "Bulgaria," in Held, J., editor, *The Columbia History of Eastern Europe in the Twentieth Century*, New York: Columbia University Press, 1992

A thorough but readable review of recent history in a volume which, importantly, enables the reader to place Bulgaria in the context of the Balkans as a whole

Sjöberg, Örjan, and Michael L. Wyzan, editors, *Economic Change in the Balkan States: Albania, Bulgaria, Romania, and Yugoslavia*, London: Pinter, and New York: St Martin's Press, 1991

This early appraisal of the prospects for transition in southeastern Europe contains two useful chapters on the beginning of the process, along with equivalent surveys of Albania, Romania, and the former Yugoslavia.

Zloch-Christy, Iliana, editor, *Bulgaria in a Time of Change: Economic and Political Dimensions*, Aldershot and Brookfield, VT: Avebury, 1996

A collection of essays on a range of economic, political and legal topics, with particularly valuable contributions on macroeconomic issues, the debt problem, and international relations

## Internet Resources

Radio Free Europe/Radio Liberty, at www.rferl.org, provides a wide range of information on transition economies, including Bulgaria; daily news bulletins are available by e-mail.

---

*John Bristow* is a Professor in the Department of Economics at the University of Dublin (Trinity College) in the Irish Republic, specializing in public sector economics and the economics of transition. He has written extensively in these areas, and is the author of *The Bulgarian Economy in Transition* (cited above), the only comprehensive treatment yet published on the economy in transition. He is a regular consultant to the IMF and the World Bank, especially on tax reform in transition and developing countries.

**Table 5.1 Average Monthly Rates of Inflation and Devaluation in Bulgaria, 1991–98 (%)**

|  | *Inflation* | *Devaluation (BL/US$)* |
|---|---|---|
| January to June 1991 | 31.5 | 26.0 |
| July to December 1991 | 5.5 | 3.6 |
| January to June 1992 | 5.9 | 0.9 |
| July to December 1992 | 4.1 | 1.0 |
| January to June 1993 | 5.1 | 1.4 |
| July to December 1993 | 3.3 | 3.3 |
| January to June 1994 | 8.1 | 7.9 |
| July to December 1994 | 5.7 | 3.3 |
| January to June 1995 | 2.4 | 0.1 |
| July to December 1995 | 2.4 | 1.1 |
| January to June 1996 | 6.7 | 12.3 |
| July to December 1996 | 18.6 | 17.3 |
| January to June 1997 | 34.2 | 18.9 |
| July to December 1997 | 2.5 | 0.6 |
| January to June 1998 | 0.4 | 0.1 |

Source: Bulgarian National Bank

**Table 5.2 Bulgaria's Main Trading Partners, 1989 and 1997**

|  | *Exports 1989* | *Exports 1997* | *Imports 1989* | *Imports 1997* |
|---|---|---|---|---|
| Value (US$ billions) | 3.138 | 4.914 | 4.337 | 4.886 |
| Proportions of total (%) |  |  |  |  |
| EU | 6 | 43 | 10 | 37 |
| Other OECD | 3 | 14 | 7 | 9 |
| (Former) Soviet Union | 65 | 18 | 53 | 33 |
| Other (former) Comecon countries[1] | 17 | 2 | 19 | 3 |
| Others | 9 | 22 | 11 | 17 |

1 For 1989, this category includes the former German Democratic Republic; for both years, it excludes Romania, which is in "Others."

Source: Bulgarian National Bank

## Chapter Six

# Romania

## *David Turnock*

Although Romania has historically claimed to be part of "central Europe," its position on the Danube, and its close association with the Ottoman Empire as the suzerain power, also introduce a clear Balkan dimension. Despite the inevitable influence of external events in this turbulent part of Europe, Romania is traditionally a stable country, and this quality, maintained at present despite severe economic difficulties, merits recognition by the world community. Romanians are proud of their direct descent from the Romanized Dacian population of the classical period. They have developed a strong sense of nationhood, despite the ethnic minorities in their midst, and have succeeded in building what is now one of the largest states in central and eastern Europe. Romania also occupies a position of importance at the point of contact between Europe, on the one hand, and such areas as Central Asia and the Middle East on the other. The significance of this position can be seen, for example, in the planning of oil exports from the Caspian Sea region to Europe, which will start early in the 21st century. Romania's leading port, Constanţa, is poised to play a leading role and a pipeline to Trieste is under serious consideration.

## Development to 1989

Romania has struggled to modernize, despite becoming embroiled in the struggles among the Habsburg, Ottoman and Russian empires, and enjoyed considerable success in the late 19th and early 20th centuries, as a result of reforming governments and the development of staple exports of grain, oil and timber. These resources, along with uranium, were subsequently coveted by the Soviet Union, and its special interest in Romania was conceded under the "percentages agreement" between Churchill and Stalin at the end of World War II. Under the Communist regime of Nicolae Ceauşescu, Romania was well-known for its adherence to a Stalinist system of centralization. There was a single-minded drive for industrialization, supported by cheap energy, combined with a social policy to expand the urban proletariat. Instead of locating production with maximum profit in mind, economic planners were, in theory at least, seeking greater equality of opportunity. There was some justification for this view, because the differences between advanced and backward regions were actually reduced as investments were made in the fringe areas, making fuller use of their labor and raw materials. Differences in the extent of regular wage-earning by the active population and in the per-capita level of industrial production were made significantly narrower, although they were not eliminated entirely. Within regions, there were considerable variations in opportunity between the regional centers and the smaller towns, and between town and country generally.

The policy was helped by inputs delivered by the Soviet Union, such as steel for tube mills in Romania. This provided an economic justification for locations close to the eastern frontier, at Iaşi and Roman. Some distortion arose through subsidized energy and transport, and there was political interference by party chiefs in support of their home regions. Ceauşescu, for example, helped Oltenia, and especially his native village of Scornicesti, which was eventually made into a town. The industrial establishment was biased too strongly towards heavy industry, based increasingly on imported raw materials and the hoarding of labor. A new industrial geography was created, and output increased in line with plan targets, but productivity was low and exports were secured mainly because of low prices. The economic shortcomings were to some extent inevitable, but the whole idea of the central planning system was to override market forces in the interest of state security, ensuring as far as possible that each country – and the wider Communist bloc – would be adequately defended. The dominance of the military-industrial establishment was entrenched, and radical economic reforms were ruled out. Despite strikes in Brasov in 1987, and some discontent within the Communist Party preceding the 14th Party Congress in November 1989, the liberalizing trends in other countries in central and eastern Europe were consistently deplored.

## The First Transition Years

Romania's revolution excited western television viewers during Christmas 1989. There appeared to be elements of spontaneity in the initial demonstrations in Timişoara and Bucharest, yet part of the infrastructure may have already been in place, and the revolution has been described by one well-informed observer, Jonathan Eyal, as a "prime candidate for hijacking" (see Eyal). Ceauşescu and his wife were executed, and the National Salvation Front (NSF) took power. Under the leadership of the interim President, Ion Iliescu, a former high-ranking Communist official, and the Prime Minister, Petre Roman, who was relatively lacking in political experience, the NSF government quickly abolished many of the most unpopular Communist edicts, and promised a token piece of land for every rural inhabitant. The way was opened for political pluralism but, contrary to initial declarations, the NSF decided that it would remain in being as a political party and contest the elections called for 1990 (see Kligman). This caused considerable misgivings when it became apparent that many former Communists had

simply transferred their loyalties to the Front and then retained solidarity as alternative political parties came into existence. These included both parties with some basis in Romanian history, such as the National Liberal Party and the National Peasant Christian Democrat Party, and a large number of entirely new political organizations (see Verdery and Kligman). A measure of consolidation was eventually achieved through the formation of an effective center-right coalition, the Democratic Convention of Romania (DCR), which eventually gained power in 1996.

Given the size of the old Communist Party, and the extent of secret police surveillance of non-Communists, it was always going to be difficult for other new parties to gain immediate political credibility. Through its control of the levers of power, including the media, the NSF had a major propaganda advantage, and it came over to the conservative rural electorate as a progressive force in view of its association with early reforms, notably the restitution of land to former owners. Although the authorities may have found it disconcerting that many cooperative farms quickly fell apart, as peasant communities unilaterally reclaimed their historic landholdings, the government was astute enough to recognize the inevitability of this step. It legislated for restitution of holdings with a maximum size of 10 hectares arable equivalent. On the one hand, this would leave the vast majority of *de facto* restitutions on the right side of the law. On the other, it would allow a large section of the peasantry to own land, at the very least through symbolic 1 hectare plots (or one half of a hectare in the case of families who were not members of cooperative farms). When the opposition started to advocate more generous terms for former landowners, the NSF was able to invoke the specter of further expropriation of smallholders, or alternatively of bankruptcy in the face of radical market reforms. The NSF and its successors were thus able to control the rural areas, almost solidly in the provinces of Moldavia and Wallachia, and this was the key to their electoral successes up to 1996. However, the NSF was obliged to work with the nationalist groups that had emerged through regional movements such as Vatra

Românească in Transylvania, although the opposition parties, and some foreign observers, condemned such organizations as extremist (see Calinescu and Tismaneanu).

The liberalization of prices attracted protests, and in September 1991 misgivings over the brisk pace of reform led President Iliescu to replace Roman with the more cautious Theodor Stolojan, who had been Minister of Finance. The NSF subsequently split. Its reformist wing, led by Roman, retained the original name, while the President's supporters formed the Democratic National Salvation Front (DNSF) before metamorphosing into the present Party of Social Democracy of Romania (PSDR). Meanwhile, Stolojan's government prevented escalation of social tension during the winter months of 1991–92, and it won the elections in September 1992 on a platform of very gradual reform (see Shen). Iliescu was returned as President, with a reduced majority, while the DNSF became the largest party in the Chamber of Deputies, the lower house of Parliament. A new government, headed by Nicolae Văcăriou, was composed of DNSF politicians but was also supported by two nationalist parties, the Greater Romania Party and the Romanian National Unity Party (RNUP), which drew considerable support from Wallachia and Transylvania respectively (see Tismaneanu). The RNUP had developed out of the Vatra Românească movement, partly in response to the resentment felt against the indigenous Hungarian population of Transylvania by Romanian migrants from the province of Moldavia who could not qualify for land restitution.

The Hungarian minority generally supported its own ethnically based Democratic Union of Hungarians in Romania (DUHR), while the main opposition party, the DCR (already mentioned above), drew its support overwhelmingly from the cities, especially the capital, Bucharest, and such Transylvanian cities as Brasov and Timişoara. The DCR favored more rapid market reforms and cuts in subsidies, along with more generous provisions for restitution. It took a strong line over excesses in the Communist period, and made considerable progress in local elections in 1992,

although it made little headway in the rural areas. It refused to consider any links with the government as long as it continued to depend on the support of the nationalist parties, which were blamed for raising tensions in Transylvania, especially in Cluj-Napoca, where local government was controlled by Gheorghe Funar, the populist leader of the RNUP. Strong nationalist rhetoric emanated from Cluj, and tension was heightened by controversy over the memorial to King Matthias Corvinas of Hungary that stands in the main square in the city. Alteration of the inscription and the threat that it would be removed to make way for archaeological work were interpreted as hostile gestures by Hungarians, who were seeking cultural autonomy. However, the RNUP made it clear that it would not remain in the governing coalition if a treaty with Hungary gave the Hungarian minority a special status. Meanwhile, the DCR was forced to distance itself from the DUHR in order to win more votes from Romanians in Transylvania (see Fischer).

## Policies for Restructuring

Despite euphoria, there were serious economic difficulties, because the central planning system had, understandably, not made contingency plans for its own demise. Building new institutions was a particularly painful process, and the government sensed the electorate's preference for incremental change, even though this could not be a viable long-term policy (see Ronnas). Radical change was made all the more difficult because intellectuals lacked credibility. Although the DCR gradually increased its effectiveness in communicating its policies, its newspapers were difficult to find in rural areas, allegedly because of the action of the National Office for Press Distribution, an agency subordinate to the Ministry of Post and Telecommunications. The government found willing allies among the peasants, who, despite the trappings of landownership reflected in first provisional and then definitive titles to land, did not behave as businesspeople. The smallholders feared higher taxes and even lower net incomes, which raised the specter of landlessness. While people were happy with the idea of free competition, they did not want government control to be replaced by the vagaries of a society governed by market forces. Political parties seeking major economic reforms therefore found the going hard. The government bureaucracy and the large workforces maintained by the state-owned industries and utilities were bastions of conservatism. There seemed to be a distinct danger that a Latin American model would prevail, and that a small, rich and corrupt oligarchy would rule a poor nation.

One significant achievement was the creation of a modern central bank, the National Bank of Romania, headed by Mugur Isarescu. It tackled the problem of building reserves, despite delays in reaching agreement with the IMF and in returning to international capital markets. The Communist government had paid off around US$10 billion-worth of foreign debts during the 1980s, by boosting exports while cutting imports, and running down the gold and foreign exchange reserves, but it was evident that new borrowing would be necessary. An initial lack of tight credit control saw growth in the money supply reach 100% in 1991 and 133% in 1993. These rates contributed to the annual doubling or trebling in prices, while compensation in the form of wage increases was more limited, especially after the relaxation of price controls in May 1994. However, Romania has gained an international credit rating which has paved the way for the issue of its first post-Communist international bonds: a US$150 million loan was arranged in 1995 by Citibank for the National Bank of Romania, with the aim of improving foreign currency reserves (see Shen).

Major dislocations of Romania's international trade occurred in the early 1990s, following the unification of Germany, and the replacement of the Ostmark by the Deutschmark; the collapse of the Soviet Union, which brought many longstanding exchanges to an abrupt conclusion; and the disintegration of Yugoslavia, which led to the imposition of UN sanctions on Serbia and Montenegro. New trade relations developed gradually with EU member states and other countries, but production fell sharply in the meantime (see Teodorescu; and Table 6.1).

Romania's state-owned enterprises became autonomous in 1990, as joint stock limited liability companies, in advance of privatization. However, the state remained responsible for them and was obliged to cover their losses. The closure of the least efficient plants, and investments in the more viable units, were much discussed. Politicians believed that restructuring would incur heavy social costs and increase instability, but some economists thought that their fears were exaggerated. The result was a compromise, involving modest layoffs and retention of core establishments, sometimes with compulsory "vacations" taken in rotation. Further pressure on the workforce arose from postponements of wage rises, intended to keep them in line with inflation. Major strikes and demonstrations occurred from time to time as a result, for example in 1994 in the heavy industrial center of Resita, which many residents have been forced to leave in the face of redundancies and low living standards (see Van Frasum et al.).

Heavy industry was in great need of restructuring because productivity was low, especially in the country's large iron and steel industry, created under Communism to turn out ships and railway rolling stock for export at competitive prices. Some plants were able to expand through imports of cheap iron ore from countries formerly in the Soviet Union, which soon greatly outstripped the scale of the Romanian mines that had sustained the industry in its early years. Only a few bulk steel producers will be needed in the future, and the smaller and less well-located plants will have to reduce output and concentrate on quality products, using scrap in electric furnaces. In the case of the chemical industry, it is possible that significant capacity in oil-refining and petrochemicals will be needed when Caspian Sea supplies start flowing westwards (as discussed above), but in any case pollution problems must be addressed. There are heavy concentrations of dust, sulfur dioxide and other gases in the vicinity of the main industrial centers, and the extent of the damage over wider areas can be seen in the deterioration in the quality of river water and the health of the forests.

Reorganization must be supported by investment in modernization. Indeed, Romania has tried to create a favorable environment for investment and entrepreneurship, with low wages as a powerful incentive. A liberal foreign investment law, enacted in 1991, was followed by the "Daewoo Law" of July 1994, which was designed expressly to attract Daewoo of South Korea, a company well-known for its hard bargaining over tax incentives (see below). Yet foreign investment is at a very modest level, and there are few resources within the country to modernize the economy, as only a limited supply of money is available through the domestic banking system. Some foreign investment in industry has arisen through partnerships and joint ventures. Where enterprises supplied western markets before the collapse of Communism and, even more so, where joint ventures were established, there is a good basis for further progress today. Many other enterprises are trying to build up their overseas contacts from a much lower level, in the hope of finding partners that will invest capital to modernize production and then take a proportion of the output for marketing in the West through established channels, benefiting from the low wages paid to Romanian workers. Alternatively, a western company may be happy to take advantage of Romanian expertise in trading with central and eastern Europe, the CIS, and perhaps even the Middle East, and allow its products to be manufactured in the Balkans for sale in one or more of these regions.

Investment in the car industry has been one very positive element in recent development. Pride of place goes to the investment by Daewoo, involving more than US$150 million, in the former Oltcit factory in Craiova. The Dacia car works near Pitesti is also looking for a foreign partner. Other attractive investment targets include hydrocarbon exploration, which was opened up to foreign companies in 1990, through production-sharing agreements. Enterprise Oil of the United Kingdom has found gas in the Black Sea, while Shell has drilled for gas beneath a salt layer in Transylvania, at depths of 1,500 meters, which are beyond the capacity of the domestic corporation Romgaz. BP Amoco has also started prospecting onshore.

To stimulate new enterprises, the Ministry of Research and Technology has coordinated a program to provide low-cost spaces for fledgling businesses to develop new ideas, often by arrangement with universities and other institutions. New enterprises have also been assisted by scientific support from the EU's PHARE program, which has backed the Institute of Technology's Business Incubation Centers, and from similar initiatives by individual EU member states, such as the United Kingdom's Knowhow Fund. Technological centers with an educational and training role, and a remit to develop foreign contacts, have been supported by partners such as the University of Washington. Business has also been fostered by such new institutions as the Romanian Chamber of Commerce and the Romanian Development Agency.

The Agency has recognized a succession of waves of investment. The first, in 1990–91, involved small and medium-sized projects. It was followed in 1991–94 by large-scale projects involving transnational corporations, such as ABB, Alcatel, Amoco, Coca-Cola (with its network of bottling plants), Colgate-Palmolive, Shell, and Siemens. Finally, a third wave from 1995 has been characterized by strategic investments made by transnational firms in the context of an improved international environment. Investment continues to be highly uneven, as the bulk of the foreign capital goes to Bucharest and a handful of other urban centers. Transylvanian cities are among the most dynamic in the country, notably Cluj-Napoca, which has recovered from its association with the Caritas pyramid investment scandal. Cluj has a local development association and seeks to build on its successful industries, which include the privatized Ursus brewery, majority-owned by Brau und Brunnen of Germany, and Porcelaine Manufacturers, a Romanian-German joint venture that began production in 1990.

## Privatization

The launch of privatization was delayed for a number of reasons. The government was reluctant to sell to foreigners at low prices, and some political mileage was won from brave declarations against selling the national patrimony. It also desired to retain a large measure of control over the economy. In addition, there was a lack of domestic private resources for buying assets, and the public were unfamiliar with the concept of share ownership. A law was passed in 1991 to sell off 55% of state equity, including some direct sales to foreign buyers. At the same time the government saw a continuing role for autonomous state corporations (*regii autonome*) operating in strategic areas such as power supply, transportation and telecommunications (see Earle and Săpătoru). As late as 1996, a decree provided for full state control of the oil and petrochemical industries, including subsoil and submarine resources. Compania Romana de Petrol sought to integrate the petrochemical industry with pipeline operators, distributors, and fuel retailers. The opposition deplored such a return to gigantism and state intervention, including holdings of at least 51% in 62 companies, and the rule that foreign companies can buy into Compania Romania de Petrol only up to 49%.

In the selling of equity by the state, 30% was to be allocated to Romanian citizens, leaving the rest for foreign and domestic investors. A State Ownership Fund (SOF) was set up, on the model of the Treuhandanstalt that supervised privatization in eastern Germany, to sell one tenth of the equity of state-owned enterprises each year. The National Privatization Agency moved very slowly, despite assistance from PHARE in 1991. By the end of that year, no enterprise had been privatized, and no holding companies or private ownership funds (POFs) had been set up. Romanians registered for their 30% holdings in July 1992, each paying RL100 for a book of five vouchers, one for each of the new POFs. A market then developed for the voucher books, and prices rose, for example to RL100,000 in Timişoara, but to only RL4,000 in the province of Moldavia. The whole scheme was undermined by unintended speculation in voucher books, public apathy, and inflation, which prevented significant negotiation of shares. Meanwhile, foreign investors were being invited to bid by tender for substantial shareholdings in 40 companies selected for the purpose by the SOF, including the state airline, Tarom, and representative companies across the range of industries (see Ben-Ner and Montias).

In 1994–95, the government tried again to deliver a Mass Privatization Program under pressure from the World Bank. It was always questionable whether the public would take the plan seriously, and even with a downward revaluation of assets, to encourage buyouts by employees and managements, the process had failed to gain momentum by the end of 1994. The SOF eventually announced that 658 companies passed into private hands in 1995, less than half the target figure. A new program for 1995–96 covered 2,200 large and medium-sized enterprises, representing all branches of the economy and drawn from all parts of the country. This time, 60% of equity was made available for allocation through nontransferable vouchers worth US$464 million in total. After a great deal of initial confusion, more than 2.3 million citizens invested their coupons between October 1995 and the end of the year, using computers installed in post offices, in anticipation of share certificates being issued by the end of March 1996. More than 70% of citizens participated through investment funds, trust companies or citizens' associations. However, even in the companies that featured in the program, less than a fifth of the shares changed hands, and the state maintained majority holdings in almost all of them (see Earle and Telegdy).

## The 1996 Elections and After: A New Start?

It seemed to many observers in 1996 that the PSDR had a good chance of reelection, in view of its astute reading of the public mood of extreme caution over the DCR's more radical approach to reform. However, the campaign found the government undermined by bad economic news, largely resulting from the economic boom engineered in 1995, when heavy borrowing, capitalizing on the low debt levels of the early 1990s, led to inflation, devaluation, and industrial slowdown. In addition, an increase in bread prices embarrassed the Minister of Agriculture, Valeria Tabara, a member of the RNUP, after cereal stocks had been depleted by exports. Manufacturing output was down because of a lack of investment, foreign exchange, and energy. The energy crisis in the winter of 1995–96 reduced foreign exchange earnings at a time when reserves could secure only 70% of the oil and electricity needed. A decree issued in July 1996 required certain companies to sell foreign exchange earnings to the National Bank at the official exchange rate, and thus create a fund to pay for imported fuel. Around 100 major companies, the core of the PSDR's business support, were promised a guaranteed energy supply in return for compliance. At the same time, the value of the minimum wage continued to fall, and agriculture suffered a poor harvest after a difficult planting season beset with delayed provision of credit. The PSDR was also hit by scandal because of its links with the state-owned foreign trade bank Bancorex, where funds had been misused with respect to unsecured loans. Scandals affecting the Credit Bank and Dacia Felix Bank were not linked directly with the PSDR, but President Iliescu's bland confidence in the banking system seemed inappropriate.

Dissatisfaction with the government, and the DCR's own attractive program, helped its presidential candidate, Emil Constantinescu, to win a convincing victory in the second ballot, with strong support from Banat, Transylvania, and many of the towns in Moldavia and Wallachia, especially Bucharest. The DCR also became the largest party in the Chamber of Deputies, and secured a majority in coalition with two other groups: Petre Roman's party, then the Social Democratic Union but since renamed the Democratic Party; and the main Hungarian party, the DUHR. The challenge was to create a credible working government that would mobilize the coalition parties, and provide a credible practical strategy to follow the initial "200 day contract." Constantinescu launched his own programs for educational reform, cultural transformation and moral leadership, including a resolution of ethnic tensions.

There appears to be greater moderation in Romanian politics. Gheorghe Funar, the fiery leader of the RNUP, has been replaced by Valeria Tabara (referred to above), who would have the party project a social-liberal image to supersede the primitive nationalism of the past. Apparently, overtures have been made as to the possibility of the RNUP joining the DCR, even though it is in coalition with the DUHR. However, the moderate wing of the latter party appears to be in charge, since moderate Hungarians were able to deliver a satisfactory *modus vivendi* in 1996, for the first time since 1920, but there are still extremists pressing for more Hungarian autonomy in cultural matters.

The new government, led by Victor Ciorbea of the National Peasant Christian Democrat Party, made a positive impact by embracing reforms which many observers believed were long overdue (see de Neve). There was an initial growth in investment, linked with a more committed privatization program, which has seen the disposal of large state-owned companies at low cost to foreign companies prepared to undertake large investments. These include the Bucharest heavy engineering firm IMBG, which was sold to Kvaerner of Norway. Economic policy was modified to reduce extensive price controls and an over-valued exchange rate, which attracted imports while constraining exports. Unemployment increased following the closure of unprofitable mines, but redundancy packages were improved and the labor unions were pacified. Assistance to agriculture has become more equitable, through the issue of coupons to all farmers in proportion to farm size: these are exchangeable for necessities such as seeds, fertilizers and fuel for tractors. Following the liberalization of prices, processors have been paying market rates, which have stimulated farming. During 1996–97 a regional development strategy was drawn up. Romania's counties have been grouped into eight large regions for the coordination of funding from the central government and the EU. A campaign against corruption has made inroads into the banking mafia, and investigations have been launched into alleged undervaluation of assets in connection with privatization that could have benefited clients of the previous government.

Nevertheless, progress has been difficult. Despite the country's substantial resources, and its large potential market of 23 million people, investment is still very low in comparison with the Czech Republic, Hungary or Poland.

There are few takers for the former state-owned enterprises, and most of the money that foreign firms are prepared to pay is in the form of guaranteed investment, rather than payment for the assets as such. For example, 51% of the equity in the Mangalia 2 Mai shipyard was sold to Daewoo for US$51 million, but the deal really amounted to US$20 million in cash and the remainder in the form of components sent from South Korea to be assembled into ships by low-paid Romanian workers. The government has very little money to invest, partly because the black economy accounts for 35–38% of GDP. Tax revenues should be 70% higher than at present, yet with high taxes on incomes and profits there is every incentive to evade payment. Professional people are paid a proportion of their fees in cash, and factory workers labor on farms at weekends. There are also major smuggling rackets involving alcohol, cigarettes, coffee and cheap clothing.

The value of Romania's large home market is undermined by the low level of consumer spending. Despite substantial external assistance, a delicate balancing act is needed in order to satisfy both the IMF and other international institutions, on the one hand, and the electorate, on the other. Reform of former state-owned enterprises has often been delayed, and there has been dissension within the governing coalition over the speed of reform. The Democratic Party, which has tended to act as both a governing and an opposition force, was largely responsible for the resignation of Prime Minister Victor Ciorbea in 1998, and his replacement by Radu Vasile, while compromise and inconsistency characterize government action as a whole. One damaging incident in 1998 was the departure of Daniel Dianu, the cautious Minister of Finance, who insisted on financial rectitude over a major deal with the US company Bell to build and procure helicopters.

The government would like to take Romania into the EU and NATO as soon as possible. A "Europe agreement," bringing Romania into association with the EU, came into force in February 1995, and an application for full membership was submitted later the same year (see Phinnemore). However, while membership is formally open to all countries that have signed an association agreement, there are three sets of conditions – the Copenhagen criteria, drawn up in 1993 – relating to institutions to guarantee democracy, a functioning market economy, and capacity for progress in political, economic and monetary union. In July 1997, the EU Commission stated that Romania did not satisfy these criteria, and the most recent assessment, published in November 1998, described Romania as the most backward of all the candidate countries.

## Scope for Growth

It seems certain that 1998 will have been the second consecutive year of economic decline since Romania recovered from depression in 1993 (see Hunya; and Table 6.1). Even if the economy can be turned around in the next few years, GDP is likely to have reached only around 30% of the present EU average by 2010.

Yet Romania certainly has potential for rapid growth over the coming decade, given its resources, including Caspian oil on the horizon; its underlying ethnic harmony; and the absence of disputes with neighboring countries, aside from a relatively minor disagreement over whether Zmeinyy Island in the Black Sea is Romanian or Ukrainian territory. The country has a record of stability, and now supports a large, efficient and well-equipped private sector. Privatization and restructuring have made slow progress, and it is clear that, where investment is available to bring the quality of production up to international standards, Romanian goods can compete. However, the advantage of low wages can only be realized with higher productivity, good design, and short delivery times. Their absence is constraining progress in some major industries where Romania has advantages, through long experience, ample capacity, skilled labor and access to raw materials, such as the furniture industry. The high cost of importing raw materials and energy also places a burden on industry, while exports involve only limited value added. It will take time for a new generation of technically advanced industries to replace some of the older industries, which have only limited potential for growth.

Heavy investment in modernization is also needed in Romania's substantial tourism industry. In addition to climate, scenery and natural monuments, Romania has many cultural and historic sites to offer, but foreign investment has been slow to arrive, and the country still suffers from the poor image acquired in the closing years of the Communist regime. The rural landscapes of the coastal and mountain regions are frequently outstanding, and the extension of the government's conservation program to cover more reserves and national parks is likely to be entirely beneficial.

There is also potential for growth in agriculture. Farm production is increasing again after the years of drought and fertilizer shortage in the early 1990s, and some important new trade deals have been struck: for example, Fructexport sends tomato juice to Heinz's ketchup division in the United Kingdom. However, agricultural credit is in short supply, and many of the new owners who have benefited from the restitution of land lack the knowhow and technology to produce for the market. Private farmers often have to manage without fertilizers, and tend to concentrate on the fullest use of family labor, sometimes including inexperienced relatives from the cities.

Market production must compete with cheap imports: the market price of sugar, for example, may remove the incentive for some peasant farmers to produce sugar beet. Price controls imposed in the interest of consumers have been counterproductive, and in some cases they account for a quarter of industrial output, but private farmers will not sell to the processors when the fixed prices are below production costs. Many Romanian peasants therefore adopt a subsistence strategy, seeking greater output of maize by cutting down fruit trees on restituted land, and restricting off-farm sales to livestock, using either the state marketing system or direct sale to local abattoirs. Political pressure to break up state farms in order to meet restitution claims means that commercial farming will have to emerge, through consolidation of small plots and an extension of the farm associations that the NSF and its successors have always tried to encourage. A great deal of attention is being given to new schemes for cooperation, linked with more efficient wholesaling, especially in the Bucharest area, but there are many constraints on efficiency, including the lack of a land market in which ambitious farmers could make profits and invest in more land. Despite significant offers of help to modernize agriculture, the aid that can be given to individual farmers is not enough to make a real difference.

Romania's infrastructure is being overhauled as and when funding permits. Road improvements are in hand to cater for increasing freight traffic and the rapid growth in the number of private cars, including many used cars imported from Austria and Germany. By western European standards, traffic levels in Romania do not yet justify a national highway system, yet ordinary roads can only be negotiated at low speeds because of poor surfaces, difficult alignments, and congestion by agricultural and commercial traffic using horse-drawn carts or low-powered trucks. The Pitesti-Bucharest highway is being overhauled, and extended to both Constanţa and Giurgiu via a ring road around Bucharest, while the Trans-Europe Motorway and other international corridors being promoted by the EU will require additional bridges or ferries across the Danube. There has been increasing congestion at frontier crossing points, which are not yet sufficiently modernized, but there is a 10-year plan for transportation, under which Italian firms have formed joint ventures to improve border crossings and 1,000 kilometers of roads. This is part of a US$400 million program financed by the World Bank, the EBRD, and the EU's European Investment Bank.

Meanwhile, passenger train travel is increasing, particularly on international trains, where loadings were previously very light because of bureaucratic frontier controls. However, the speed and comfort of the trains require significant improvement, connections with the Euro-City network must be made, and there needs to be a major shift away from the tradition of long heavy trains toward the use of lighter railcar sets operating at frequent intervals. The modernization of airline fleets is also proceeding, in some cases with foreign collaboration. Tarom is buying Airbus A-310 and Boeing 737–300 aircraft, while the Romanian plane-maker Romaero has reached a deal with Boeing over the construction of wings for some of its aircraft. Priority also attaches to the improvement of airports both in Bucharest and in provincial cities. Inland water traffic, centered on the Danube, could be extended on to some of its tributaries, such as the Olt and Prut, while Romania's sea ports have established roles serving domestic markets, as well as the landlocked countries to the north. The flow of oil from Central Asia across the Black Sea could well enhance the importance of Constanța and justify the construction of a pipeline to Trieste.

Romania has a considerable fuel endowment, but much of its coal is low grade, while its hydrocarbons are to be reserved for use in the petrochemical industry. The first 700 megawatt unit at the Cernavodă nuclear power station, completed in 1996, should be very helpful in dealing with winter shortages. The decline in industrial output, and the modernization of plant and machinery, are reducing demand for power, but over the long term there will be further new demand, which nuclear reactors seem most likely to provide. There is substantial backup available through factories to process nuclear fuel and produce the heavy water needed by the Candu system installed at Cernavodă, but money is tight. A balance is therefore being struck: investment is kept under control, while work on the next unit is maintained at a low level, in order to avoid irreparable damage to the country's capacity to build and commission further nuclear power stations.

## Conclusion

Romania's transition from Communism has been painful and controversial. On the one hand, the country has frequently been viewed as a refuge for conservatives, where reforms have been restricted to relatively insignificant measures taken by a neo-Communist governing elite. According to this analysis, western help has been misappropriated in order to support the regime of subsidies to unviable state-owned enterprises. On the other hand, it

is undeniable that Romania faces massive problems in restructuring large firms, which were managed for so long without any concern for economic efficiency as it is generally defined in the West. Given the experience of the Ceaușescu years, it is understandable that Romania is wavering in the face of problems with the market economy. Even the reformist coalition returned in 1996, when the Romanian electorate made a clean break with the past, has found it difficult to maintain a radical program. Romanians have been accused of political apathy, yet clear preferences have been expressed for western democracy and, eventually, EU membership. Now that Romania is firmly on the escalator leading to European integration, conservative factions have little credibility, ethnic violence has subsided, and the terror tactics of the past, notably the interventions by "miners" in Bucharest, appear to have been consigned to history. The economic situation is difficult, for there is a limit to what indigenous business can do when domestic demand is modest and funding to support new enterprises is scarce. Foreign investment has not grown as rapidly as the new government expected, and concerns over the country's stability could generate self-fulfilling prophecies if lack of growth and rising social tensions encourage nationalist excesses and economic protectionism. However, Europe needs Romania, with its record of stability and its strategic position on the Lower Danube, especially as the Caspian oil trade will be expanding in the first years of the new century.

## Further Reading

Ben-Ner, A., and John Michael Montias, "Economic Systems, Reforms and Privatisation in Romania," in Saul Estrin, editor, *Privatisation in Central and Eastern Europe*, Harlow and New York: Longman, 1994

A detailed economic study of privatization (which, like others cited here, they spell in the British manner) by authors long familiar with the country

Calinescu, M., and Vladimir Tismaneanu, "The 1989 Revolution and Romania's Future," in *Problems of Communism*, Volume 40, numbers 1–2, 1991

A thorough examination of the 1989 revolution and the immediate prospects

Earle, John S., and D. Săpătoru, "Privatisation in a Hypercentralised Economy: The Case of Romania," in John S. Earle et al., editors, *Privatisation in the Transition to a Market Economy: Studies of Preconditions and Policies in Eastern Europe*, London: Pinter, and New York: St Martin's Press, 1993

This paper discusses the constraints affecting the privatization process.

Earle, John S., and Almos Telegdy, "The Results of Mass Privatisation in Romania: A First Empirical Study," in *Economics of Transition*, number 6, 1998

A critical review emphasizing the initial scope of the program

Eyal, Jonathan, "Romania," in Stephen Whitefield, editor, *The New Institutional Architecture of Eastern Europe*, London: Macmillan, and New York: St Martin's Press, 1993

Eyal provides plenty of detail on the progress made during the first transition years.

Fischer, Mary Ellen, "The New Leaders and the Opposition," in Daniel N. Nelson, editor, *Romania After Tyranny*, Boulder, CO: Westview Press, 1992

The author considers the leading personalities of the early transition years.

Hunya, Gabor, "Romania 1990–2002: Stop-go Transformation," in *Communist Economies and Economic Transformation*, number 10, 1998

A critical review of the economic record and the failure to achieve comprehensive reform

Kligman, Gail, "Reclaiming the Public: A Reflection on Creating Civil Society in Romania," in *East European Politics and Societies*, number 4, 1990

A thoughtful assessment of the prospects for civil society

de Neve, D., "Political Dimensions of Transformation in Romania," in Wilfried Heller, editor, *Romania: Migration, Socioeconomic Transformation and Perspectives of Regional Development*, Munich: Südosteuropa-Gesellschaft, 1998

A positive assessment of the government that came into office in 1996, but written before the coalition tensions of 1997–98 were fully apparent

Nicolaescu, T., "Privatisation in Romania: The Case for Financial Institutions," in D. E. Fair and R. J. Raymond, editors, *The New Europe:. Evolving Economic and Financial Systems in East and West*, Dordrecht and Boston: Kluwer, 1993

Nicolaescu provides useful insights into the public appetite for radical reform in the early transition years.

Phinnemore, David, "Romania and the EU: Prospects for Entry," in Duncan Light and Daniela Dumbraveanu-Andone, editors, *Anglo-Romanian Geographies: Proceedings of the Second Liverpool-Bucharest Geography Colloquium*, Liverpool: Liverpool Hope Press, 1997

A pessimistic assessment of Romania's prospects for EU membership

Ronnas, Per, "The Economic Legacy of Ceauşescu," in Örjan Sjöberg and Michael L. Wyzan, editors, *Economic Change in the Balkan States: Albania, Bulgaria, Romania, and Yugoslavia*, London: Pinter, and New York: St Martin's Press, 1991

An authoritative survey by an economist with personal experience of the Communist era

Shen, Raphael, *The Restructuring of Romania's Economy: A Paradigm of Flexibility and Adaptability*, Westport, CT: Praeger, 1997

A detailed study of the economic reforms of the Iliescu presidency, but with little consideration of the opposition's case

Teodorescu, A., "The Future of a Failure: The Romanian Economy," in Sjöberg and Wyzan, cited above under Ronnas

An examination of the limitations of the reform program

Tismaneanu, Vladimir, "The Quasi-revolution and Discontents: Emerging Political Pluralism in Post-Ceauşescu Romania," in *East European Politics and Societies*, number 7, 1993

An authoritative assessment of political pluralism

Van Frasum, Yves G., Ulrich Gehmann, and Jürgen Gross, "Market Economy and Economic Reform in Romania: Macroeconomic and Microeconomic Perspectives," in *Europe-Asia Studies*, number 46, 1994

A detailed academic analysis of the reform process

Verdery, Katherine, and Gail Kligman, "Romania After Ceauşescu: Post-Communist Communism," in I. Banac, editor, *Eastern Europe in Revolution*, Ithaca, NY: Cornell University Press, 1992

A useful political and sociological survey, identifying elements of continuity

*Dr David Turnock* is Reader in Geography at the University of Leicester in England.

**Table 6.1    Selected Macroeconomic Indicators for Romania, 1990–97**

|  | 1990 | 1991 | 1992 | 1993 | 1994 | 1995 | 1996 | 1997 |
|---|---|---|---|---|---|---|---|---|
| GDP (US$ billions) | 39.5 | 34.4 | 31.4 | 31.9 | 33.1 | 35.5 | 37.0 | 34.6 |
| GDP change (%) | −5.6 | −12.9 | −8.8 | 1.5 | 3.9 | 7.1 | 4.1 | −6.6 |
| Inflation (%) | 50.1 | 174.5 | 210.9 | 256.1 | 136.8 | 32.3 | 38.8 | 154.8 |
| Average exchange rate (RL/US$) | 22.4 | 76.4 | 307.9 | 760.1 | 1,655 | 2,033 | 3,085 | 7,168 |
| External debt (US$ billions) | 1.2 | 2.1 | 3.2 | 4.2 | 5.5 | 6.7 | 8.8 | 10.1 |
| Balance of trade (US$ billions) | −3.4 | −1.5 | −1.4 | −1.1 | −0.4 | −1.6 | −2.5 | −2.0 |

Source:   Economist Intelligence Unit

## Chapter Seven

# Communism in Yugoslavia and Albania

## *Will Bartlett*

Unlike most of the other countries in central and eastern Europe, Yugoslavia and Albania were liberated at the end of World War II mainly by their own indigenous partisan guerrilla resistance movements. Although the Soviet Army entered Belgrade toward the end of the war, the establishment of the Communist system had a popular legitimacy. Both the Yugoslav Communist Party and the Albanian Party of Labor, which led the partisan movements, were nevertheless ideologically aligned to Stalinism (see Djilas). In the final days of the war, the Albanian leadership sent troops into the province of Kosovo to assist the Yugoslav authorities in crushing a nationalist rebellion by the Kosovo Albanians, some of whom had collaborated with the Italian and German occupiers during the war (see Cviic). In the early postwar years, the two parties worked closely together on both political and economic agendas. Yugoslavia and Albania agreed a program of economic cooperation; in July 1946, the two countries signed a Treaty of Friendship, Cooperation and Mutual Aid; and Yugoslavia sent advisors to Tirana to assist in Albania's program of postwar reconstruction (Jelavich pp. 329–30).

However, this cooperation was not to last. In 1948, Stalin became anxious about the independence of the Yugoslav leadership and, after failing to bring them more closely into the Soviet orbit, he saw to their expulsion from Cominform, the organization of European Communist Parties, broke off diplomatic relations with the Yugoslav government, and withdrew Soviet advisors. Albania, under the leadership of Enver Hoxha, sided with Stalin, and simultaneously broke diplomatic relations with Yugoslavia, expelled the Yugoslav advisors, and sealed the border. Significant minorities of Albanians within Yugoslavia and of Yugoslav Macedonians within Albania were to be sources of friction within and between the countries throughout the postwar years. (A poignant reflection on the fate of the Yugoslav Macedonians living in Albania during this time is recounted in the Macedonian film *Across the Lake.*)

The subsequent evolution of the Communist system in the two countries could hardly have been more different. Albania became the most closed and centralized Communist economy in the world, with the possible exception of North Korea, while Yugoslavia developed a unique brand of relatively liberal market-based socialism, open to trade and movement of labor to both East and West. Under the leadership of President Tito, Yugoslavia became a leading member of the Movement of Non-Aligned Nations, and acted as a bridge between the opposing power blocs in the Cold War.

### Yugoslavia

Regional inequalities bedeviled Yugoslavia from its foundation in 1918. A persistent North/South division was inherited from the historical experience of subjugation under the Austro-Hungarian empire in the North and the Ottoman empire in the South. The more developed northern republics of Slovenia and Croatia, and the autonomous province of Vojvodina, had been parts of the Austro-Hungarian empire, while the southern republics of Serbia, Montenegro, and

Macedonia, and the autonomous province of Kosovo, had been ruled by the Ottoman empire. Bosnia-Herzegovina was a special case among the six republics in the federation. It had passed from rule by the Ottoman empire to become a protectorate of Austria-Hungary in the late 19th century.

Linked to these differences in the historical background of the different republics are differences in religion, language, and culture. The populations of Slovenia and Croatia are largely Catholic, but in Serbia, Montenegro, and Macedonia the eastern Orthodox version of Christianity is predominant. Bosnia-Herzegovina has a large population of Moslem faith as a result of religious conversion under Ottoman rule, although there remain large numbers of people who adhere to one or other variety of the Christian faith. The predominant Slavic language is Serbo-Croat, although since the breakup of Yugoslavia, what most linguists would still consider to be dialects of this single language have been officially redesignated as "Croatian" and "Serbian." Distinct Slavic languages are spoken in Slovenia and Macedonia. The large Albanian minority speak a non-Slavic language, as different from Serbo-Croat as Welsh is from English. Differences in culture also follow from these religious and linguistic mixtures.

With the historical development of its component parts conditioned by experience within two different traditions and under the domination of foreign empires, the Yugoslav state that emerged after World War I was already characterized by large variations in economic structure and levels of economic development, essentially on North/South lines (see Hamilton). Economic development between the two world wars did nothing to eradicate these differences. At the end of World War II, Yugoslavia's economy was still largely agricultural, and what little industrial infrastructure existed had been badly damaged.

Under the political hegemony of the Communist Party, broad national support existed for a program of rapid industrialization under state ownership and central planning. In particular, the Communists saw socialist planning as their main tool for rectifying the regional inequalities within Yugoslavia. However, the series of different approaches to economic policy by the Communist regime – central planning between 1946 and 1950, "administered self-management" between 1950 and 1964, "market self-management" between 1965 and 1973, and "self-management planning" between 1974 and 1989 – undermined progress toward reducing regional inequalities, which steadily increased between 1955 and 1989 (see Table 7.1). The ratio of output per capita between the most developed republic, Slovenia, and the least developed, Macedonia, increased from 2.5:1 to 3.2:1 between these years. The position of Kosovo was even worse, for it underwent a continuous relative decline throughout the period.

## Central Planning, 1946–50

One of the first acts of the new Communist government was the introduction of a land reform, which abolished the large estates and placed a limit of 35 hectares on holdings of arable land. A Federal Planning Commission, established in 1946, drew up the first Five-year Plan, which was to be implemented along the lines of the Soviet command economy. The commitment to building a classical "socialist" system continued for a while, even following the break with the Soviet Union. In 1948, nationalization was extended to the entire industrial sector, and the collectivization of peasant farmers into agricultural cooperatives was initiated. However, the collectivization was resisted by the peasant farmers: in Bihać in Bosnia-Herzegovina, for example, there was a "massive uprising" against collectivization (Lampe p. 27). The resistance of the peasants and the stagnation of agricultural output quickly led to the abandonment of the collectivization policy. Thereafter, Yugoslav agriculture was based upon a system of privately owned peasant smallholdings, the maximum size of which was reduced to 10 hectares in 1950, alongside agricultural cooperatives. There was also a residual sector of large state farms, which were concentrated in the flat Danube basin regions of Slavonia (in Croatia) and Vojvodina (in Serbia).

## Administered Self-management, 1950–65

The Yugoslav authorities soon recognized the need for a new approach to economic development that could distance their economic system from the Soviet model. In 1950, the centralized economic system began to be replaced with a more decentralized, market-driven approach. This was epitomized by the introduction of the system of "workers' self-management," which established workers' councils as the basic element of enterprise governance. Rereading Marx, the Yugoslav leadership fell upon the idea of "associations of producers" as an alternative to the state capitalism that they identified as the hallmark of the distorted Soviet variant of socialism. The idea of "returning factories to the workers" fitted well with the smallholder land reform which had "returned land to the tiller." The Marxist concept of the "withering away of the state" also provided an opportunity to resolve the nationalities question by permitting a gradual decentralization of economic power to the six republics and reducing the powers of the federal government, long viewed with suspicion by the non-Serbian republics as a bastion of Serbian hegemony.

The system of workers' self-management had three main elements. First, it gave greater autonomy to enterprises. In place of centralized state control, workers' councils elected enterprise managers. However, workers did not have complete sovereignty, as local committees, dominated by the local Party apparatus, had two votes in the selection of directors, compared to the single vote wielded by the workers' council (Lampe p. 253). Second, and perhaps more importantly, the new system of workers' self-management introduced some basic elements of a market economy, as a result of the free hand it gave enterprise directors to control managerial strategy. This sharply distinguished the Yugoslav economy from the economies of the Soviet bloc, and from the highly centralized model of Communism being developed in Albania. The third and weakest element of the system was its treatment of the ownership of company assets, which became amorphous "social property," owned neither by the state, the workers, nor any identifiable shareholders.

As a result of the introduction of a more flexible economic system, Yugoslavia experienced a long period of rapid economic growth and industrialization, which lasted up until the end of the 1970s. However, a key weakness of the system was that the self-managed enterprises did not face the prospect of bankruptcy, but rather enjoyed a "soft budget constraint," so that their investments were often financed by state subsidies and foreign borrowing (see Uvalić 1992). This gave local Party functionaries the opportunity to intervene in enterprise affairs and management, which was eventually to undermine the benefits of the move towards a market-based economy.

The self-management system evolved gradually over the following decades. In the early years of the new economic system, the planners retained central control over the allocation of investment funds. The Federal Investment Fund directed investment resources among the various republics, and Republican Investment Funds carried out the same function at the next level of government. The centralized determination of investments encouraged the growth of "political factories." These were often white elephants designed to bolster the prestige of local politicians in the various republics (see Singleton and Carter). Five-year Plans were retained, but these were indicative only, and bore no relation to the plans used in command economies. Industrial output increased at over 10% a year in the 1950s (see Moore), and GDP per capita increased at nearly 5% a year. The smallholding peasant farmers were encouraged to enter into marketing cooperatives, and agricultural output improved. Up until 1964, the economic positions of Slovenia, Serbia, and Vojvodina improved relative to the other republics (see Table 7.1).

The Yugoslav economy also benefited from its opening to western markets. Being outside the Soviet bloc, it traded equally with West and East, and Italy and Germany became major trading partners. Its independent line brought access to international financial institutions and to large inflows of US aid. One estimate suggests that US aid covered 60% of the current account deficit between 1950 and 1964

(Lampe p. 270). The open borders to the West also permitted an outflow of migrants to feed the labor demands of the expanding economies of western Europe. Many went to Germany to become *Gastarbeiter* ("guest workers"). By 1964, there were more than 100,000 Yugoslavs working abroad.

## Market Socialism, 1965–74

Liberal reforms received a further boost in the mid-1960s, following the introduction of a new Constitution in 1963. The centralized system of investment allocation was abandoned, and economic reforms introduced in 1965 deepened the market elements of the self-management system. Enterprises were able to keep and reinvest their own profits, and price controls were relaxed. The share of investment financed by enterprises increased from a pre-reform level of 32% to 46% in the year following the reforms. The effects of the reforms were mixed. Between 1965 and 1980, economic growth slowed down from its previous rapid rate of 7–8% a year, while the growth of GDP per capita fell to a still impressive 4–5% a year (see Madžar). With greater freedom over management decision-making, the self-managed enterprises restricted employment growth, and employment in the social ownership sector actually fell in the first two years following the reforms. School leavers found it more difficult to find work and unemployment increased (see Woodward). Migration abroad took off and by 1970 more than 500,000 Yugoslav workers were employed abroad, mainly in Germany. The more prosperous enterprises paid their workers higher wages and the dispersion of incomes for labor of equal skills increased (see Estrin). Household income inequality increased in the years immediately following the reforms (see Lydall 1984), although the overall level of inequality was still low by western standards (see Flakierski).

The development of self-management was closely connected with the decentralization of political power. These two processes were rooted in the ideological concern with the "withering away of the state," but had the primary effect of transferring powers away from the federal state to the six republics and the two autonomous provinces. Political liberalization was boosted by the dismissal of the hard-line secret police chief Alexander Ranković in 1966. This had a particular impact in Kosovo, where it heralded a growth of Albanian nationalism, since Ranković had orchestrated the repression of Albanian nationalist sentiment in the province (see Vickers pp. 162–168). Towards the end of the 1960s, pressure mounted for further decentralization. During the period 1965–74, only Slovenia, Croatia, and Vojvodina experienced relative improvement, while the southern republics fell further behind, with the exception of Macedonia, which recorded a small improvement (see Table 7.1). The Party leaders in Croatia insisted that their republic should be entitled to retain a greater share of foreign exchange earned by its coastal tourist industry. The "Croatian Spring" of 1971 saw the emergence of a nationalist movement led by the Croatian League of Communists, calling for greater regional autonomy. This movement was suppressed and the Croatian Party leaders were dismissed. The federal government turned its attention to ways of limiting the unequalizing effects of the market, while simultaneously accommodating the nationalist aspirations that the liberal policies of the 1960s had encouraged.

Notable among these policies was the establishment of a special program, the Federal Fund for the Development of the Less Developed Regions, which was financed by a 1.56% tax on incomes in the more developed regions. The Fund had little impact on the pattern of regional inequality, largely because of the focus on prestige investment projects designed to bolster the prestige of regional elites (see Bojičić). Only Vojvodina managed to cross the threshold from relative underdevelopment to above-average levels of output per capita, and it was not even a principal beneficiary of the Fund's resources. Kosovo, which was a principal beneficiary, experienced a continuous worsening of its economic performance. The investment funds were channeled into large prestige projects, such as the marbled University Library in Priština, and pollution-creating chemicals industries. A high rate of population growth among Kosovar Albanians, which at 3% a year was the highest in Europe, also reduced the meager gains in output per head. In broad terms, the normal unequalizing effects of marketization combined with poorly directed structural development assistance to exacerbate existing regional inequalities (see Plestina). This in turn fueled regional tensions and contributed, ultimately, to the growth of the nationalist movements in the Yugoslav republics.

## Self-management Planning, 1974–88

The upsurge of nationalism induced the Party to introduce a set of new measures, to rein in what were seen as the adverse effects of marketization. In an attempt to restore its control over the economy, the federal government sought to reintroduce elements of planning and to reduce the market freedoms of self-managed enterprises. The solution was found by introducing a system of "self-management planning," combining some elements of market and plan in a complicated system of bargaining between the various levels of political and economic power (see Lydall 1984, and Madžar). At the same time, however, nationalist aspirations were accommodated by further decentralization of powers from the federal level, still widely perceived as being dominated by Serbian interests, to the various republics. The perceived influence of Serbia in federal decision-making was reduced by giving far greater autonomy to the provinces of Kosovo and Vojvodina. In Kosovo, Albanian became an official language, and Albanian-language newspapers, radio stations and television stations were established. The 1974 Constitution enshrined these changes, which had already been partially introduced through constitutional amendments in 1971, and raised the status of the autonomous provinces to that of federal entities in their own right, with representation in federal institutions, including seats on the collective Federal Presidency.

The decentralization of power to the republics and the weakening of federal control over the economy were to have fatal consequences for Yugoslavia. The relative improvement in Slovenia came to a halt, and the differentials among the regions were virtually

frozen throughout the late 1970s and 1980s (see Table 7.1). Meanwhile, in the latter part of the 1970s, an enormous deficit in foreign trade had begun to open up, as each republic strove to promote its own economic interests through international borrowing aimed at stimulating consumption and initiating prestige investment projects (see Dyker 1990). Policy conflict also centered on the distribution of foreign exchange earnings. A new foreign exchange law, introduced in 1977, created federal and republican "self managed communities for foreign trade," which were responsible for allocating above-quota foreign exchange among regional importers at a premium above the official exchange rate, effectively bringing about a regionalization of foreign exchange earnings (see Bartlett). Between 1975 and 1980, the external debt of Yugoslavia increased from under US$6 billion to more than US$17 billion. The international debt crisis triggered by the second oil price shock, in 1979, hit Yugoslavia hard (see Dyker 1990). Increased interest rates on the debt and declining export markets brought about a crisis of debt repayments. Since federal control over the levers of economic policy had been weakened, the economy was unable to adjust in an appropriate way to the new economic climate.

Throughout the 1980s, the federal authorities strove to rein in domestic consumption, in order to bring expenditure on imports into line with export revenues. The currency, the dinar, was repeatedly devalued, price controls were reintroduced, and expenditure on social services was slashed. However, the main effects were to reduce imports of needed capital equipment and raw materials. Yugoslavs could easily evade controls on imports of consumer goods by the simple expedient of travelling abroad. The nearby Italian city of Trieste was a favorite destination for "shopping tourism." On a typical weekend, hundreds of shopping buses from Ljubljana and Zagreb could be seen parked on the Trieste quayside. Within Yugoslavia, soft budget constraints in the self-managed industries prevented loss-making companies from going bankrupt. The lack of managerial authority and the influence of the workers' councils allowed workers to push for wage increases to compensate for the inflation that resulted from the depreciation of the dinar, counteracting the beneficial effects of devaluation. Most seriously, the federal government lost control of the money supply. As a result of regional decentralization, each republic had its own national bank, and their main debtors, the self-managed enterprises, effectively controlled the commercial banks in each republic (see Lydall 1989). Politicians in the republics were unwilling to restrict the emission of money through their "own" banking systems. It was not in the interest of politicians in the republics to reign in inflationary pressures, since the inflationary impact of money creation in any one republic would be dispersed throughout the rest of the federation. Inflation therefore steadily increased through the 1980s.

The failures of economic policies in response to the changing international environment brought about what Harold Lydall has called "the Great Reversal" (Lydall 1989 p. 40). Between 1979 and 1985, real output per head fell by 10%, real incomes in the social sector fell by 25%, and real gross fixed investment fell by 37%. At the same time, employment steadily increased under the terms of self-management planning agreements laid down by republican authorities. In Serbia, and probably elsewhere too, the self-managed enterprises were required to take on new workers, even though, in many cases, their levels of output were falling. Overall, employment grew by 16%, leading to a disastrous decline in productivity, which further undermined the international competitiveness of the economy (see Lydall 1989). In the second half of the 1980s, the situation deteriorated further. Throughout this period, Yugoslavia was in receipt of loans and assistance from the IMF, and also received advice from the World Bank. However, all this was ineffective, as the standard monetarist approach of these international organizations was inappropriate to the circumstances of an economy in which the reins of economic power had been devolved to the republics, and in which self-managed enterprises faced soft budget constraints. What was really needed was structural reform, especially the removal of interference in the affairs of enterprises by local politicians, who had in some cases virtually created feudal fiefdoms,

and the opening of the economy to the entry and development of new private or cooperative businesses.

## The Marković Reform Program, 1989–91

In 1989, a final attempt was made to impose a federal solution to the economic crisis. A reformist Prime Minister, Ante Marković, introduced a series of measures at the federal level in an attempt to tackle some of the root causes of the crisis. A new Enterprise Law was introduced, permitting private ownership, and it stimulated the setting up of large numbers of new private firms. A privatization law allowed self-managed firms to carry out voluntary privatization ("ownership transformation"), through the sale of shares to managers and workers at substantial discounts (see Adamovich). Further measures, introduced in 1990, were designed to stabilize the economy through a temporary wage freeze, a fixed exchange rate, and tight monetary and fiscal policies. By the middle of 1990, the reform package had achieved some remarkable successes. Inflation was cut from 64% a month at the end of 1989 to virtually zero by April 1990; the foreign debt was reduced; and western financial institutions supported the reform package with new credits and loans (see Bartlett).

However, the federal reform program eventually ran into the same problem that had defeated earlier, less radical attempts to turn the economy around: the independent powers and self-interest of the republics. A year before the reforms, in 1987, the Serbian League of Communists had been swept by a rising tide of Serbian nationalism, and had backed Slobodan Milošević as party leader. The new Serbian leadership introduced a number of administrative measures to promote an increasingly populist Serbian nationalist program. In 1988, the Albanian leadership of the Party in Kosovo was purged and replaced by leaders more sympathetic to Belgrade, as a prelude to constitutional changes that gave Serbia control of the police and judiciary in the province. The changes were resisted by widespread strikes and protests by Albanians in

Kosovo, which were severely repressed by the police, now under Serbian control. In 1990, the Kosovo Assembly was suspended. A new Constitution of Serbia was introduced, which unilaterally changed the status of both Kosovo and Vojvodina from provinces to mere regions of Serbia. Nationalism also raised its head in Slovenia, where constitutional amendments introduced in 1989 promised multiparty elections and reasserted the republic's right to secede from the federation (Lampe p. 345).

In January 1990, the League of Communists, the only force, apart from the federal army, holding Yugoslavia together, broke up, and was replaced by separate republican parties with a variety of different names. The nationalist agenda soon degenerated into open economic warfare among the republics, as each attempted to evade the costs of adjustment implied by the federal stabilization program. To protect its own industries from competition from more efficient "imports" from the northern republics, Serbia introduced customs duties on Slovenian and Croatian goods. Slovenia and Croatia issued new money through their banking systems, in violation of federal monetary restrictions, and the other republics soon did the same (Lampe p. 349). In late 1990, the Marković reform program was given the *coup de grace* by Serbia, which "robbed" the National Bank of Yugoslavia of YD 18 billion (then around US$1.5 billion) to fund pay increases and pensions in advance of the first multiparty elections. Slovenia, Croatia and Macedonia announced their independence in June, heralding the wars of the Yugoslav succession which have bedeviled the Balkans throughout the ensuing decade; and Bosnia-Herzegovina declared independence in 1992 (see Chapters 8 and 9).

## Albania

World War II ended for Albania in November 1944, and the formation of a People's Republic was declared in January 1946 (see also Chapter 10). The guerrilla war was fought by the Albanian Communists, known as the Albanian Party of Labor, against Italian and German occupiers, as well as the anti-Communist National Front (Balli Kombëtar), which also

fought against Tito's Partisans in Kosovo. As in Yugoslavia, the war was won with little outside assistance, and resulted, uniquely, in the installation of the first Communist regime in a predominantly Moslem country (see Prifti). Religion, however, was soon abolished, and Albania proclaimed itself to be not only a Communist state but an atheist one.

In stark contrast to the Yugoslav experiment with market-led reforms and decentralization, the Albanian government persisted with its devotion to the Stalinist system of central planning and state ownership of property. While the Yugoslavs pursued the withering away of the state and progressively reduced the power of the federal government, in Albania the influence of the state was increasingly dominant in all aspects of life, extending well beyond the confines of economic management.

As one of the most backward countries in Europe, in which 80% of the population were illiterate and nearly 90% were engaged in agriculture, Albania began postwar reconstruction with assistance from Yugoslavia and the Soviet Union. It was not until the early 1950s that the first railway lines in Albanian history were constructed. The first university, in Tirana, was not established until 1957. One of the first steps taken by the new government was to nationalize all industry, and other sectors of the economy, and to draw the peasant farmers into agricultural collectives. However, this was a slow process: by 1955, the collectives still accounted for only 13% of agricultural production. The pace of collectivization speeded up in the late 1950s and was virtually complete by the time Albania broke off relations with the Soviet Union in December 1961. Thereafter, agriculture was further centralized on the model of the Chinese system of "people's communes," and the size of the collectives was increased. By 1970, the whole agricultural sector was organized into 643 huge collective farms (Prifti p. 67). As in Yugoslavia, peasants resisted the collectivization of their assets, notably by slaughtering their livestock. Collectivized agriculture was never efficient, and the country never achieved the proclaimed goal of self-sufficiency, that is, a capacity to feed the population without imports of food from abroad. Throughout the postwar period up to 1978, Albania ran a balance of payments deficit, and was effectively reliant on outside powers for aid in order to support its economy.

Between 1961 and 1978, Albania depended upon economic aid from China, but after breaking off relations with its last remaining ally in 1978, the government adopted a new Constitution that prohibited the receipt of loans and aid from other countries, as well as cooperation with foreign or multinational companies. In the 1980s, therefore, Albania was one of the most isolated countries in the world, pursuing a path of economic self-sufficiency. It was during this time that the excesses of Albanian Communism reached their peak. Even the private ownership of land and cattle was prohibited. Not surprisingly, international reserves of currency were soon depleted. Equipment became increasingly obsolescent, unemployment increased, and living standards declined. Throughout the 1980s, the economy stagnated. One careful study of the country's economic performance during these years concluded that real output per capita did not change at all between 1978 and 1988 (see Sandström and Sjöberg). The only surprise is that output does not appear to have actually fallen, as it did in Yugoslavia in the 1980s, although other studies indicate that agricultural output, the mainstay of the economy, decreased substantially, again when measured per capita (see Sjöberg).

It was not until the death of the dictator Enver Hoxha, in 1985, that a gradual opening to the outside world again became possible, initiated by the new party leader Ramiz Alia (see Vickers and Pettifer). Albania began to improve its trade links with other countries in central and eastern Europe, and participated in the Balkan Cooperation Conference held in Belgrade in 1988. In May 1990, the 10th Central Committee Plenum agreed on a program of limited economic reforms that were to be implemented in January 1991. These involved a relaxation of centralized supervision of enterprises, which were to be allowed to retain a part of profits for internal investment, and to control the use of up to one fifth of capacity to produce goods for the market independently of the planning targets (see Pashko).

This initiative was too little, and came too late, to produce any substantial improvement in economic conditions. The gradualist reforms permitted peasants to cultivate small private plots, but this only raised the expectations for more radical reforms. Albania was soon embroiled in mounting internal turmoil as food shortages resulted from bad harvests. Average wages were as low as US$20 a month and there was widespread poverty.

Eventually, pushed by a rising tide of protest and civil unrest, multiparty elections were organized in March 1991. In a desperate attempt to turn the tide of Albanians emigrating from the country, the international community organized an emergency aid package worth US$150 million, and 500 Italian soldiers were sent to Albania to distribute the aid. The final fall of Communism in Albania was heralded by the victory of the opposition Democratic Party, led by Salih Berisha, in March 1992.

## Conclusion

The Communist system was established simultaneously in Albania and Yugoslavia, and collapsed in both countries at the beginning of the 1990s. During the period of Communist rule, both left the Soviet bloc and pursued independent approaches to economic development. Despite these similarities, the contrasts between their chosen paths of economic development could hardly have been greater. Yugoslavia developed its own unique brand of market socialism, open to the outside world through trade links, labor migration and cultural contact, while Albania pursued a path of extreme Communist centralism. It also eventually isolated itself from the outside world and sought to secure complete self-sufficiency. Yet ultimately neither approach proved successful.

While it is not surprising that the Albanian variety of centralized planning under autarky should have proved a dismal failure, the explanation of the collapse of Yugoslavia, not only as an economic unit but also as a state, is more complex. A wide range of explanations has been put forward. Some emphasize the inefficiencies of the self-management system, which gave partial control over management decision-making to workers. It has been argued that this led to endemic wage pressure and permanent institutionalized inflation. This argument is often linked to the inadequacies of the banking system, which accommodated these cost-push pressures (see Lydall 1989). Another related explanation focuses, not on self-management as such, but on the system of property rights based on the concept of "social ownership." This essentially removed responsibility for the efficient management of enterprise assets from any single group of stakeholders. Productive assets were owned by no one, and everyone had incentives and opportunities to pillage the resources of the firms in which they worked (see Madžar, and Uvalić 1992). Both these approaches have a great deal of plausibility, but they do not explain the apparent success of the self-management system in the northern republics, especially Slovenia, where a relatively high level of prosperity was achieved and unemployment was consistently low, at around 2%, for most of the postwar period.

Other explanations focus on the existence and growth of regional inequalities. These increased over time and brought about political tensions among the republics, especially in the 1980s, when incomes and output were falling and the republics began to come into conflict over their shares of an ever-diminishing pie (see Hall, and Lampe). The many accounts of the breakup of Yugoslavia and the wars that followed also tend to follow this approach, partly because the political collapse was structured on republican lines (see Cohen, and Bennett). However, regional inequalities had been increasing throughout the postwar period, and were held in check in the 1980s under the system of self-management planning, which had been introduced partly in response to the rapid growth of inequalities experienced after the 1965 reforms.

A final set of explanations centers on the vulnerability of the Yugoslav economy to shocks emanating from the wider world economy, and, ultimately, on the failure of the system and its political leaders to respond effectively to the pressures of globalization. As an open economy, Yugoslavia was dependent on its export industries. The widening gap between imports and exports in the late 1970s led to an enormous buildup of foreign debt. The federal government, having lost control of the levers of economic power to the republics, was then unable to respond effectively to the international debt crisis of the early 1980s. Attempts to control imports through devaluation were unsuccessful, and only led to falling output and inflation, since the exporting industries failed to respond effectively to the challenge of improving their international competitiveness (see Woodward, and Dyker 1990). However, this explanation fails to account for the lack of appropriate policy responses, and the failure of the export industries to improve their performance on world markets.

All of these explanations of the collapse of the Communist system in Yugoslavia have a degree of validity. Taken together, they build up a picture of a system that was riven by fundamental inconsistencies, partly due to systemic failures, and partly due to the historical legacy of a state created from units with different levels of economic development, as well as differences in religion, language, and culture. In 1981, more than 60 years after the first form of the Yugoslav state was established, only a tiny proportion of respondents to the census regarded themselves as "Yugoslavs," while most people still referred to themselves as Slovenians, Croats, Serbs, or Albanians.

However, there was one similarity between Yugoslavia and Albania that was fundamental, the political dominance of the one-party state, albeit in Yugoslavia this soon became a collection of one-party republics. As elsewhere in central and eastern Europe, the level of opposition to the ruling ideology was limited and to various degrees suppressed. Ultimately, this created a rigidity in policy responses to whatever short-term difficulties arose, whether in enterprise management or in the international economic environment. This political culture was not eliminated overnight as a result of democratization, even in those of the successor states of Yugoslavia that have been most active in pursuit of structural reform and the transition to a market economy. The prospects for economic development and successful transition – in all the former Yugoslav republics, but also in Albania – depend on the extent to which genuine democratization and the development of civil society can replace a politics based on narrow nationalisms (see Radošević).

The Yugoslav idea was born in the late 19th century from the realization that Balkan states cannot prosper without a high degree of economic integration and cooperation. However, the postwar experiment in cooperation between Yugoslavia and Albania was as short-lived as other attempts to create Balkan "federations" and "associations," and at present the region is moving ever further away from such approaches. Consequently, the prospects for economic development and regeneration appear to be extremely bleak. Nevertheless, at some point in the future renewed efforts at regional cooperation will be required if the former Yugoslav republics and Albania, along with other parts of the Balkans, are not to remain a permanent backwater of Europe.

## Further Reading

Adamovich, Ljubiša S., "Economic Transformation in Former Yugoslavia, with Special Regard to Privatization," in Sabrina P. Ramet and Ljubiša S. Adamovich, editors, *Beyond Yugoslavia: Politics, Economics, and Culture in a Shattered Community*, Boulder, CO: Westview Press, 1995

A short account of privatization in Yugoslavia under the Marković government and the differences in its implementation in the different republics

Bartlett, Will (1991), "Economic Change in Yugoslavia: From Crisis to Reform," in Örjan Sjöberg and Michael L. Wyzan, editors, *Economic Change in the Balkan States: Albania, Bulgaria, Romania, and Yugoslavia*, London: Pinter, and New York: St Martin's Press, 1991

A brief account of the economic crisis of the 1980s and attempts to reform the economy, with an economic analysis of the foreign trade sector

Bennett, Christopher, *Yugoslavia's Bloody Collapse: Causes, Course and Consequences*, London: Hurst, and New York: New York University Press, 1995

A highly readable account by a journalist of the events leading up to the breakup of Yugoslavia and the war in Bosnia-Herzegovina

Bojičić, Vesna, "The Disintegration of Yugoslavia: Causes and Consequences of Dynamic Inefficiency in Semi-command Economies," in David Dyker and Ivan Vejvoda, editors, *Yugoslavia and After: A Study in Fragmentation, Despair and Rebirth*, Harlow and New York: Longman, 1996

A short study of the economic causes of the decline of the Yugoslav economy, with some useful information about regional differences and development trends

Cohen, L. J., *Broken Bonds: Yugoslavia's Disintegration and Balkan Politics in Transition*, Boulder, CO: Westview Press, 1995

Cohen covers the history of the political system of Yugoslavia, the transition to democracy, the first multiparty elections, and the breakup of the country. This is the best book on the subject.

Cviić, Christopher, *Remaking the Balkans*, London: Pinter, 1995

This paper from the Royal Institute of International Affairs in Britain presents an overview of the historical and political development of the Balkan region, and develops some scenarios for the future shape of the Balkans.

Djilas, Milovan, *Wartime*, New York: Harcourt Brace Jovanovich, 1977

A first-hand account of the Partisan struggle to liberate Yugoslavia from the Axis forces and of the civil war within Yugoslavia

Dyker, David, *Yugoslavia: Socialism, Development and Debt*, London and New York: Routledge, 1990

An in-depth analysis of the debt crisis that was a key element in the collapse of the Yugoslav economy in the 1980s

Dyker, David, "The Degeneration of the Yugoslav Communist Party as a Managing Elite – A Familiar East European Story?" in Dyker and Vejvoda, cited above under Bojičić

A short study of the political background to the breakup of Yugoslavia, and the role of the Communist and nationalist elites in the transition from socialism to nationalism

Estrin, Saul, *Self-Management: Economic Theory and Yugoslav Practice*, Cambridge and New York: Cambridge University Press, 1983

An economic analysis of the impact of the self-management system on the growth of income differentials in Yugoslavia

Flakierski, Henryk, *The Economic System and Income Distribution in Yugoslavia*, Armonk, NY: M. E. Sharpe, 1989

A short but comprehensive study of income inequality under Yugoslav socialism

Hall, Gregory O., "Ethnic Conflict, Economics, and the Fall of Yugoslavia," in *Mediterranean Quarterly*, Summer 1994

A short history of the collapse of Yugoslavia, emphasizing the economic roots of the crisis

Hamilton, F. E. Ian, *Yugoslavia: Patterns of Economic Activity*, London: Bell, and New York: Praeger, 1968

A classic study of the economic geography of Yugoslavia in the early postwar years

Jelavich, Barbara, *History of the Balkans: Twentieth Century*, Volume 2, Cambridge and New York: Cambridge University Press, 1983

A scholarly history of the Balkans that places postwar developments in context

Lampe, John, *Yugoslavia as History: Twice There Was a Country*, Cambridge and New York: Cambridge University Press, 1996

Probably the best historical account of Yugoslavia from its formation after the end of World War I to its demise at the beginning of the 1990s

Lydall, Harold, *Yugoslav Socialism: Theory and Practice*, Oxford: Clarendon Press, and New York: Oxford University Press, 1984

A clear and comprehensive economic history of the postwar Yugoslav socialist experiment

Lydall, Harold, *Yugoslavia in Crisis*, Oxford: Clarendon Press, and New York: Oxford University Press, 1989

An authoritative study of the development and causes of the economic crisis in Yugoslavia in the 1980s

Madžar, Ljubomir, "The Economy of Yugoslavia: Structure, Growth, Record and Institutional Framework," in John B. Allcock, John J. Horton, and Marko Milivojević, editors, *Yugoslavia in Transition: Choices and Constraints*, Oxford and New York: Berg, 1992

An insider's view of the successes and failures of the Yugoslav economic system, by one of its leading academic economists. He is particularly critical of the system of "social ownership."

Moore, John H., *Growth with Self-Management: Yugoslav Industrialization 1952–1975*, Stanford, CA: Hoover Institution Press, 1980

A detailed study of the rapid economic development of Yugoslavia up to the end of the 1970s, including a detailed examination of statistics on the growth of industrial output

Pashko, Gramoz, "The Albanian Economy at the Beginning of the 1990s," in Sjöberg and Wyzan, cited above under Bartlett

An insider's account of developments in the Albanian economy in the 1980s. The author was a leading member of the country's Democratic Party.

Plestina, D., *Regional Development in Communist Yugoslavia*, Boulder, CO: Westview Press, 1992

A useful study of regional development and regional inequalities in Yugoslavia

Prifti, Peter R., *Socialist Albania Since 1944: Domestic and Foreign Developments*, Cambridge, MA: MIT Press, 1978

This scholarly history of the politics and economy of Albania focuses on the early postwar period, but it also includes coverage of the struggle of the Albanian partisans during the war, as well as a chapter on the Kosovar Albanians.

Radošević, Slavo, "The Collapse of Yugoslavia – Between Chance and Necessity?" in Dyker and Vejvoda, cited above under Bojičić

A short account of the political and economic causes of the breakup of Yugoslavia, and the role of nationalist elites in that process

Sandström, Per, and Örjan Sjöberg, "Albanian Economic Performance: Stagnation in the 1980s," in *Soviet Studies*, 1991

An economic analysis of development trends in Albania in the 1980s

Singleton, Fred, and Bernard Carter, *The Economy of Yugoslavia*, London: Croom Helm, and New York: St Martin's Press, 1982

An economic history of Yugoslavia by two leading experts in the field

Sjöberg, Örjan, "The Albanian Economy in the 1980s: Coping with a Centralized System," in Sjöberg and Wyzan, cited above under Bartlett

A brief account of developments in the Albanian economy in the 1980s

Uvalić, Milica, *Investment and Property Rights in Yugoslavia – The Long Transition to a Market Economy*, Cambridge and New York: Cambridge University Press, 1992

This comprehensive study of the investment behavior of Yugoslav self-managed enterprises argues that the existence of "soft budget constraints" was a principal cause of inefficiency.

Uvalić, Milica, "Privatization in the Yugoslav Successor States: Converting Self-management into Property Rights," in Milica Uvalić and David Vaughan-Whitehead, editors, *Privatization Surprises in Transition Economies: Employee Ownership in Central and Eastern Europe*, Cheltenham and Lyme, NH: Edward Elgar, 1997

A detailed study of privatization legislation and its outcomes in the Yugoslav successor states in the first half of the 1990s

Vickers, Miranda, *Between Serb and Albanian: A History of Kosovo*, London: Hurst, and New York: New York University Press, 1998

An excellent historical account of the development of the crisis in the province

Vickers, Miranda, and James Pettifer, *Albania: From Anarchy to a Balkan Identity*, London: Hurst, and New York: New York University Press, 1997

A readable journalistic account of the tumultuous political and social events surrounding the collapse of Communism in Albania

Woodward, Susan, *Socialist Unemployment: the Political Economy of Yugoslavia 1945–1990*, Princeton, NJ: Princeton University Press, 1995

This in-depth study of the causes of unemployment in Yugoslavia traces the roots of differences in economic policy back to the ideas formed by different factions in the Partisan movement during World War II. Woodward argues that the collapse of the Yugoslav economy in the 1980s was largely brought about by problems of international trade and payments.

---

*Dr Will Bartlett* is Reader in Social Economics in the School for Policy Studies at the University of Bristol in England.

---

**Table 7.1    Relative Levels of Social Product per Capita in the Six Republics and Two Autonomous Provinces of the Former Yugoslavia, 1955 and 1989 (Yugoslavia = 100 at current prices)**

|  | *1955* | *1989* |
| --- | --- | --- |
| Bosnia-Herzegovina | 83 | 67 |
| Croatia | 122 | 126 |
| Macedonia | 71 | 66 |
| Montenegro | 77 | 74 |
| Serbia, excluding Kosovo and Vojvodina | 91 | 104 |
| Slovenia | 175 | 200 |
| Kosovo | 43 | 26 |
| Vojvodina | 94 | 119 |

Source:    Calculated from Table G7 in *Razvoj Republika Prethodne SFR Jugoslavije 1947–1990: Studije, Analize, Prikazi 132* [Development of the Republics of the Former Socialist Federal Republic of Yugoslavia, 1947–90: Studies, Analyses, Reviews 132], Belgrade: Savezni Zavod za Statistiku [Federal Office for Statistics], 1996

Chapter Eight

# Serbia and Montenegro

## *Will Bartlett*

The Socialist Federal Republic of Yugoslavia established after World War II consisted of six republics – Bosnia-Herzegovina, Croatia, Macedonia, Montenegro, Serbia, and Slovenia – and two autonomous provinces, Kosovo and Vojvodina, within Serbia. Economic development was rapid until the end of the 1970s, and, unlike other countries in central and eastern Europe, Yugoslavia was a "liberal market socialist" economy, with extensive trade relations with the West and freedom for its citizens to travel widely abroad. Despite the economic freedoms enjoyed by Yugoslav citizens, political power remained firmly in the hands of the Communist Party, known as the League of Communists since 1952. The last new Constitution of this federation, introduced in February 1974, decentralized political power to the individual republics and autonomous provinces, and thus weakened the federal government.

Extensive borrowing from international financial institutions and capital markets fueled economic growth in the 1970s, but led to a large buildup of foreign debt. The onset of the international debt crisis in the early 1980s, coupled with a lack of domestic economic adjustment, caused a slowdown in economic growth. The economic crisis gave rise to tensions over economic policy, with the northern republics of Slovenia and Croatia pressing for further development of the market economy, and the southern republics, especially Serbia, seeing the solution in increased state activity (see Woodward). These disputes eventually brought about irreconcilable differences among the republics and contributed to the breakup of the federation.

The new Federal Republic of Yugoslavia established in April 1992 was comprised of only two republics, Serbia and Montenegro, and was an unreformed Communist state (see Teokarević). The League of Communists of Serbia and the League of Communists of Montenegro changed their names – becoming the Socialist Party of Serbia (SPS) and the Democratic Party of Socialists of Montenegro (DPSCG) – but they did not change their basic orientation. Democratization has been shallow, despite the introduction of a formal multiparty system, and the absence of genuine market-oriented reform has inhibited any effective solution to the economic crisis. In late 1997, however, the DPSCG split in two, and reformist politicians have since gained the upper hand in Montenegro.

## The Breakup of Yugoslavia, 1987–92

Serbian politics has been dominated by the forceful leadership of Slobodan Milošević ever since September 1987, when he led a nationalist faction of the Serbian League of Communists to victory over the liberal reform faction at the eighth Plenum of the Central Committee in Belgrade. The nationalist tide in Serbian politics was directed above all at reversing the gains that the Kosovo Albanians had made when the province was given extensive autonomy within the Yugoslav federation in 1971. Milošević set about consolidating his power by launching the "antibureaucratic revolution" in October 1988. The Communist leadership in Kosovo was replaced by leaders loyal to Milošević, and the leaderships of

Vojvodina and Montenegro were also forced to resign (see Bennett). A new Serbian constitution, adopted in March 1990, reduced the powers of the provincial authorities in Vojvodina and Kosovo, and gave Serbia effective control over these provinces, as well as three votes within the collective Presidency of Yugoslavia. These, along with the pliable Montenegrin vote, gave Serbia, and therefore Milošević, control over half the eight votes within the Presidency. The new Constitution afforded a strong position to the President of Serbia, a position held by Milošević from December 1990 to July 1997, when he became President of Yugoslavia. The Kosovo Albanians protested against the constitutional changes through demonstrations and strikes, but these were put down by force. After holding an unofficial referendum, they declared an independent Republic of Kosovo in September 1991, with Ibrahim Rugova as President from May 1992. In the face of this incipient secession, the Serbian authorities occupied Kosovo by force and imposed their rule in the face of Albanian opposition.

The legislative elections held in Serbia in December 1990 were boycotted by the Kosovo Albanians, and for the first and only time the SPS won an outright majority. In Montenegro, the DPSCG also won a legislative majority at the same time. Elections at the federal level were far less important, as power was effectively held by the new President of Serbia, Slobodan Milošević.

## The Marković Reforms

While these changes were proceeding apace at the political level, the federal government, led by Prime Minister Ante Marković from March 1989, was attempting to introduce economic reforms that might pull the economy out of the economic crisis in which it had been mired since the early 1980s. The first elements of these reforms had been introduced even earlier, at the end of 1988, when a new Law on Enterprises permitted the formation of joint stock and limited liability companies, and other forms of private enterprise. Over the following two years thousands of new private enterprises were established. In addition, a Foreign Investment Law opened up Yugoslav enterprises to foreign investors.

In 1990, the reforms were extended by measures to create price stability, including a wage freeze and a restrictive monetary policy, and a privatization program was introduced in the second half of 1990. The federal law on privatization permitted enterprise management boards to initiate privatization in a variety of ways, but with an emphasis on "insider" privatization to workers and managers. Companies in Yugoslavia had operated under a system of "social ownership," under which assets were owned by society at large and company managers were elected by workers exercising "self-management." Thus, rather than talk of "privatization," the Yugoslav authorities preferred to use the term "property transformation" when referring to the process of changing social ownership into private ownership. Under the federal law, ownership shares could be offered to workers at a discount of up to 70%, depending on the length of service. The main difficulty was in the valuation of the social capital to be privatized, since there was no market for capital assets. The valuations were highly subjective and the process was open to abuse.

In any case, separate privatization laws in the individual republics soon replaced the federal law. Unlike in the other republics, however, the Serbian privatization law, adopted in 1991, did not seek to abolish "social property" (see Uvalić 1997a). Employees could buy shares at a discount, but these discounted sales could not exceed 30% of the total social capital in the enterprises. The Montenegrin privatization law, introduced in 1992, differed from that in Serbia, insofar as all unsold social capital was to be transferred to various republican funds.

By August 1991, around 1,200 enterprises in Serbia, or one third of all social sector enterprises, had begun the process of property transformation under the provisions of the federal law. After the Serbian law came into effect, the pace of privatization slowed, and only 173 more enterprises began privatization up to the end of 1992 (see Uvalić 1997a). It was mainly the more profitable enterprises that were privatized, since these were attractive to enterprise managers and employees, especially if it could be arranged that the assets were undervalued and high discounts made available.

## Disputes and Disintegration

In the absence of a consensus on reform among the different republics, the federal government was in a weak position to introduce economic reforms. While Slovenia and Croatia were broadly in favor of market-based reforms, Serbia, now under the control of the nationalist faction led by Milošević, was skeptical. The main problem was the vulnerability of relatively inefficient Serbian industry to the introduction of market forces, which would have exposed their underlying weakness and led inevitably to rising unemployment. The market reforms were therefore unpopular in Serbia.

Meanwhile, economic disputes between the republics were already tearing the federation apart. Serbia introduced customs duties on imports from Slovenia and Croatia, and in late 1990 it flouted the monetary restrictions imposed by the reform program by taking YD18 billion (then around US$1.5 billion) from the central bank to fund wage rises, pay pensions, and subsidize loss-making enterprises. The IMF, which had been supporting the Yugoslav economy on condition that it stuck to the reform program, promptly suspended its US$1 billion standby arrangement, which in turn led to the suspension of a further US$4 billion of western credits.

Elections held in Slovenia and Croatia in March and April 1990 had been won by anti-Communist parties, and in June 1991 these two republics declared independence from Yugoslavia; Macedonia followed suit in December 1991, and Bosnia-Herzegovina in April 1992 (see Chapter 9). In May 1991, however, Serbia had blocked the candidacy of Stipe Mesić for the rotating Yugoslav Presidency, effectively bringing the federation to an end.

The Federal Republic of Yugoslavia was created on April 27, 1992, through a new constitution that formally recognized the demise of the former Socialist Federal Republic of Yugoslavia. Disputes over the "succession issue" – the division of the debts and assets of the former state – have never been resolved, and this has provided a basis for the continuing exclusion of the new federation from international recognition and membership of international organizations.

## The Effects of Sanctions, 1992–95

The UN Security Council imposed economic sanctions on the new Yugoslavia in May 1992 on the grounds that it had failed to withdraw support from the Serb forces in Bosnia-Herzegovina. Exports from Serbia and Montenegro were prohibited, and all imports, except of food and medicines, were banned. The sanctions regime was tightened in November that year with a ban on the transit of selected goods through Yugoslavia and a blockade of the Montenegrin coast. In April 1993, financial assets held abroad were frozen and border monitors were put in place to ensure the effectiveness of the sanctions. The sanctions were highly effective in damaging the Yugoslav economy and in the middle of 1994 the Yugoslav authorities stopped the flow of aid to the Bosnian Serbs. This led to a partial easing of sanctions in September 1994, when international flights to and from Belgrade were permitted, as were cultural and sporting exchanges (see Teokarević).

Sanctions had a severe impact on the economy of Yugoslavia between 1992 and 1995. However, the lack of structural reform and the government's inflationary monetary policy were also responsible for the deteriorating economic situation. Both were closely linked to the lack of democratization. Structural economic reforms were no part of the agenda of the SPS or, at that time, of the DPSCG, while inflation was used as a tool to finance the war effort in Croatia and Bosnia-Herzegovina. Economic decline predated the imposition of sanctions, and a major stabilization policy was implemented while sanctions were at their height. At the same time, sanctions became a useful instrument for the ruling parties to deflect popular anger away from their own mismanagement of the economy.

## Hyperinflation

During 1993 and up to January 1994, Yugoslavia experienced one of the most dramatic episodes of hyperinflation in history. The inflation was brought about not only by the disruptive effect of sanctions but also by the government policy of printing money to finance its support for the war being waged in Bosnia-Herzegovina (see Petrović and Vujosević). By October 1993, inflation was so high that the value of individuals' savings in dinars was almost wiped out. Two pyramid banks that had attracted large amounts of foreign currency savings collapsed. Inflation reduced the value of the currency so much that people were reportedly using old dinars as scrap paper (see Lyon). Delays of a few days in paying wages or pensions reduced their value to near zero. By November 1993, the average pension was YD4.5 million, which would buy only a box of cookies (see Lyon). Conditions deteriorated in public hospitals, where there was a growing lack of medicines, heat, and food. Only the wealthiest in society, who could transfer their incomes into foreign currency through illegal financial transactions, could protect themselves from hyperinflation, while those on fixed incomes, such as pensioners, welfare recipients, and government employees, suffered most. By December 1993, the average monthly pension had increased to YD10 billion, but in reality this was worth less than DM1.00. At one point, the National Bank issued a bank note with a face value of YD500 billion. The dinar officially collapsed on January 6, 1994, when the Deutschmark became legal tender for the payment of all financial transactions. During January, daily inflation of over 100% was the norm, and the monthly rate of inflation reached an astronomical 313,000,000%. However, a stabilization program introduced at the end of the month brought inflation to an end virtually overnight, with the introduction of a new dinar pegged at a ratio of 1:1 against the Deutschmark. The Serbian government had officially ended its support for the Bosnian Serbs in late 1993, and could expect that its promise to stop printing money would be believed, and that inflationary expectations would be eliminated.

## The Slide into Poverty

Real GDP had been falling sharply since the end of 1989, due to the economic conflicts among the republics and then the breakup of Yugoslavia. The GDP of Serbia and Montenegro fell by 8% in 1990, and by a further 12% in 1991. A large part of the fall in output can be attributed to the breakup of Yugoslavia, and the loss of markets in Slovenia and Croatia, but the sharpest falls came after the imposition of sanctions. The GDP of the new federation fell by 28% in 1992 and by a further 30% in 1993. Thus, between 1989 and the end of 1993, GDP fell by three fifths, GDP per capita fell from the equivalent of US$3,000 to a mere US$1,000, and industrial output declined to only 35% of its previous level. Average real wages fell to only 15% of their previous level, and, owing to inflation, they had a purchasing power equivalent to only US$84 per month (see Pošarac).

There was an enormous increase in poverty as a result of the economic crisis. Household income surveys showed that by 1995 almost one third of the population, around 3 million people, were living below the minimum subsistence level, which represented a doubling of the numbers in poverty in comparison with 1990. A further one third were subsisting only marginally above the poverty line (see Pošarac). Pensioners and refugees were particularly badly affected. By the end of 1994, the average monthly pension was equivalent to only DM100 (see Popović).

Following the imposition of sanctions, layoffs in socially owned industries were prohibited. Nevertheless, the labor force fell as workers retired, left low-paid jobs to find better jobs in the private sector or went to work abroad. The policy of prohibiting layoffs led to the growth of hidden unemployment, in the form of surplus labor in social sector enterprises. Officially, unemployment reached 25% by 1996, but when surplus workers were added in the real level of unemployment was estimated at 50%. Many supposedly employed workers were put on "paid vacation" as there was no work to be carried out in their factories.

The population structure also changed radically as a result of the crisis. Many of the most able and educated people left the country to seek better lives abroad. At the same time, there was an enormous influx of refugees from Croatia and Bosnia-Herzegovina. The largest single influx, in 1995, followed the Croatian offensive to regain the Krajina region from the local Serb rebels: around 160,000 new refugees entered Yugoslavia in a single week, bringing the total number of refugees in the country to around 600,000. Most refugees stayed with relatives or other families, putting a further burden on their already low incomes, and around 100,000 lived in collective refugee centers. One third of the refugees settled in Belgrade, and many others went to Vojvodina and to central Serbia. Relatively few were settled in Kosovo (see Pošarac).

## Political Developments

As the economic position deteriorated during 1993, the ending of sanctions became the highest priority for the regime. Milošević urged the Bosnian Serb leaders to accept the Vance-Owen peace plan to end the war in Bosnia-Herzegovina, and when they refused, he officially ended Serbian support for them in the hope of getting sanctions lifted. The government was becoming increasingly unpopular. Milošević dissolved the Serbian Assembly, after breaking with his allies in the ultranationalist Serbian Radical Party, and called new elections in December 1993. The SPS lost its overall majority and won only 123 out of 250 seats; the United Opposition improved its position and won 45 seats; the opposition Democratic Party won 29 seats; and the Radicals won only 39 seats. These results indicated that the voters were disillusioned with the performance of the ruling party, which won 25% less support than the opposition, but the SPS was able to continue in power through a coalition with the small New Democracy party, the successor to the former Socialist Youth Organization.

## Privatization and the Gray Economy

The privatization process initiated under the reformist Yugoslav government of Ante Marković ground to a halt after the imposition of sanctions. Some companies were denationalized, notably in public utilities such as electricity, railways, airlines, oil, forestry, water supply, communications, radio, and television, but in other industries, such as steel, nonferrous metals, and electronics, enterprises were converted to "mixed ownership," in which the state had effective control (see Lazić and Sekelj). The banks, which often had a dominant shareholding, controlled many firms that were formally privatized, and the major banks in turn were controlled by the state. The other major shareholders were very often managers who had bought large shareholdings at heavily discounted prices, while "employees were unable to participate in the process because of their total pauperization" (Lazić and Sekelj p. 1,067). Further, under a law enacted in 1994 that aimed to revalue the assets of privatized companies, most of the previously privatized enterprises were effectively returned to state ownership as their nonprivatized "social capital" was increased in value. The imposition of sanctions and the heavy tax burden facing small firms led to the rapid growth of an extensive "gray" economy, which came to account for around one third of total output. This represented a huge loss of potential government revenue as more and more businesses sought shelter within it. The Institute of Economics in Belgrade estimated that 34% of the labor force – 1.2 million people – were working in the gray economy. In 1995, the Serbian government introduced a Program of Measures for the Suppression of the Gray Economy. This involved strengthening supervision and control, but also legalizing illegal buildings in towns. Nevertheless, private businesses still had to pay bribes to officials for the allocation of foreign exchange, for import and export permits, and for access to premises in urban areas. A large number of businesses used dual documentation to hide their real transactions. Part of the gray economy was a genuine parallel economy, which could in principle be formalized through a reduction of tax rates. Another part, however, was a criminal economy, which could not be formalized but was merely engaged in profitable but unproductive activities, including arms smuggling, drugs smuggling, and protection rackets.

## Macroeconomic Stabilization

In January 1994, a stabilization program devised by Dragoslav Avramović, the governor of the National Bank, pegged the dinar to the Deutschmark at a ratio of 1:1 (see Adamović). This effectively made the dinar into an ersatz version of the Deutschmark. The currency was made partially convertible, and the government was to cease the inflationary financing of its deficit following the implementation of a tight monetary policy. New money was printed only insofar as it was backed by foreign reserves. The stabilization policy produced immediate effects. In 1994, inflation was reduced to single digits, and real GDP increased by around 6%, although industrial production increased more slowly. Real wages rose sevenfold and real pensions ninefold over their disastrously low levels at the beginning of the year. However, the stabilization policy was not followed by serious structural reforms. There was no privatization of socially owned or state-owned enterprises, and there was no policy to promote the development of small businesses.

## Developments since the Dayton Agreement, 1996–99

At the end of 1995, sanctions against Yugoslavia were lifted following the implementation of the Dayton Agreement on Bosnia-Herzegovina. However, the economic recovery was still hampered by the "outer wall" of sanctions, which prohibited Yugoslavia from access to the international capital markets and financial institutions, in particular the IMF and the World Bank. Not surprisingly, the dinar was devalued at the end of 1995, to YD3.30 to DM1.00, and a further devaluation, to YD5.00 to DM1.00, took place in early 1997. Real GDP increased by 6% during 1995, and by 1997 the "social product" per capita had reached the equivalent of US$1,500. However, losses in socially owned industries continued to mount, and workers' wages remained at poverty levels.

Dragoslav Avramović, the architect of the successful stabilization program of 1994, put forward a new privatization program in 1996. This envisaged the complete abolition of social property (see Uvalić 1997b). However, the proposal was never discussed by the Yugoslav Federal Assembly, and in any case Avramović was forced to resign. The failure to implement Avramović's "Program II" has been called the "inner wall" of obstacles to economic regeneration (by Popović, p. 166). Instead, a new federal law was adopted, which permitted voluntary privatization by enterprises, and effectively preserved social property as the main form of property ownership in Serbia (see Uvalić 1997a). The government clearly had no intention of introducing a genuine economic reform. As a result, the opening up of foreign trade markets resulted only in the creation of an enormous trade deficit. The current account deficit was US$1.2 billion for 1996, and US$1.5 billion for 1997. Although output grew by 8.5% in 1997, the trade deficit widened to unsupportable levels, as imports increased faster than exports in order to support the renewed growth of the battered manufacturing sector.

The Yugoslav government based its development plans on the assumption that there would be an inflow of US$1.5 billion of foreign capital over the five years following the lifting of sanctions. However, the continuing imposition of the outer wall of sanctions meant that the Yugoslav government did not have access to foreign credits. It was entirely dependent upon inflows of foreign direct investment, and on the revenues raised from foreign investors through the privatization of industrial assets.

At the same time numerous administrative obstacles were placed in the way of developing independent small businesses in the formal economy. Imports and exports required extensive paperwork, and special permits were required to import or export any goods. Customs regulations, import duties of up to 41%, and complicated foreign currency transfers all inhibit small firms from becoming engaged in formal foreign trade. Imports are often brought into the country on a private basis, or smuggled through the gray economy, and foreign currency is usually exchanged on the black market. Article 128 of the Serbian Labor Relations Law, which requires that all enterprises should employ at least two workers, effectively discourages new business startups, even though unemployment is at least 26%. It has also given extra impetus to the development of the gray economy.

## Foreign Investment

During 1996 and 1997, following the ending of sanctions, there was a rapid inflow of western companies and investors interested in buying up Yugoslav companies offered for privatization. For example, in 1997 the London investment branch of the Banque Nationale de Paris bought 40% of a small Belgrade bank called International Genex Bank; Messer Greihein GmbH of Germany bought up 60% of the gas monopoly Tehnogas; and the TetraPak group of Sweden bought a Serbian packaging factory for DM24.5 million from the holding company Tipoplastika. Other forms of direct investment were also adopted. A business cooperation agreement was signed between the Yugoslav tire company Ruma Guma and Continental of Germany. The Austrian Creditanstalt Investment Bank opened offices in Belgrade in October 1997, and the British investment bank NatWest Markets also became deeply involved in the privatization program.

A new privatization law became effective in Serbia in November 1997. In the first round of privatization, free or discounted shares were to be given or sold to employees, pensioners, farmers, and citizens of ex-Yugoslavia. The money raised would go to the Serbian Development Fund (50%), the Republican Labor Market Fund (25%) and the Republican Pension and Invalid Insurance Fund (25%). The basic discount was set at 20% plus 1% per year of service, up to a limit of DM6,000. The privatization law covered 4,500 socially owned and state-owned companies in Serbia, and 3,000 companies in "mixed ownership" (see above). A further 75 large companies were put on a special list for privatization under government control. These comprised the large metal producers, such as the Sartid steel works and the Glagovac ferrous chrome companies. Other prominent companies on the special list included the Trepea lead and zinc mine in Kosovo, the Bor lead and zinc mine, various copper and aluminum smelters, and factories

in the defense industries. Some sales were concluded in late 1997. The Belgian beer producer Interbrew bought 60% of the beer and juice company Trebejsa for DM25 million. The Reynolds tobacco company was engaged in a bid to buy the Vranje tobacco company. By the end of the year it was estimated that more than 100 German companies had investment stakes in Yugoslav companies.

## A Shift to the Right

A coalition of four opposition parties, known as Zajedno ("Together"), won local elections in several cities in November 1996, but, after an initial attempt to falsify the results in the government's favor, Milošević nullified them. Mass protest demonstrations, initiated by students and supported by the citizens of Belgrade, were held in the center of the capital over several months. Eventually, Milošević accepted the election results, and it began to look as though his government was on its last legs. However, regrettably, Zajedno split in the summer of 1997, and one of its leading figures, Vuk Drasković, head of the nationalistic Serbian Renewal Movement (SPO), eventually accepted the post of Deputy Prime Minister of Serbia. In July 1997, Milošević ended his term as President of Serbia, only to become President of Yugoslavia instead.

One of the largest privatization deals that year was the purchase of 49% of the Serbian Telecom company by Italian and Greek investors, in June. The DM1.25 billion from the sale was partly used to increase public expenditure and salaries up to the Serbian Assembly elections in September. As a result, the money supply grew by 46% in the three months before they were held. This was not enough to boost the popularity of the government, which by then was supported by a coalition of the SPS, New Democracy, and the Yugoslav United Left, a small but influential group led by Milošević's wife, Mirjana Marković. The government lost its majority, but remained the largest bloc, with 110 seats, while Drasković's SPO won 45 seats and, in a dramatic turn to the right, the Radicals won 82 seats.

This rightward shift in politics put an end to hopes that a more liberal reformist economic policy would be pursued. Foreign investors who had expected to be actively involved in buying up profitable parts of Yugoslav industry became disappointed. Enterprise directors were free to choose whether to transform their companies through internal distribution of shares or through sales to foreign investors. Often, they opted to keep the companies under insider ownership. According to one prominent Yugoslav economist, Miodrag Zec, the government would postpone privatization as long as possible, and "instead it will sell some hot property once the boat starts to fill with water" (as quoted in *Business Yugoslavia*, January 1998). The privatization process was also slowed down by the need to make initial valuations of enterprise assets. This produced some frustration among foreign embassies, which were keen to see the sales that had been discussed by the various trade missions go to their own nationals. Western governments gave Yugoslavia until mid-1998 to start the transition process, and declared that they would withdraw their trade delegations if there was no progress. Some EU countries in particular were willing to invest large amounts of money in Yugoslav industry – some estimates suggest as much as US$10 billion of new capital – but only in the event of real structural and economic reforms, which presupposed genuine democratization.

By the end of 1998, the economic situation had once more deteriorated and international investment had dried up. Unemployment was up to 50% and the average monthly wage had sunk to less than US$100 (according to a report in the *Financial Times*, December 16, 1998). Avramović came out of semiretirement to bring the Democratic Party, led by Zoran Djindjić, together with the Civic Alliance, led by Vesna Pesić, in a new opposition coalition, Alliance for Change.

## The Succession Issue

Apart from the lack of reforms, the most serious problem facing the economy was the continuation of the outer wall of sanctions, which prevents Yugoslavia from borrowing money on the international capital markets to finance its trade deficit and the reconstruction

of its economy. The ostensible reasons for the maintenance of the outer wall of sanctions were the lack of progress on democratization and, later, the deteriorating situation in Kosovo (see below). However, a more serious issue was the stalemate on the proportions in which the international debts of the former Yugoslavia, amounting to nearly US$20 billion, were to be divided between the successor states. The debt had already been sold off at a discount to various banks and hedge funds that wanted to see a good return on their investment. Yugoslavia requested a discount on repaying the debt, claiming that it should only have to repay US$500 million, and wanted the four other successor states to shoulder what it saw as a fair share of the burden. The banks refused to accept such a heavy discount. There was also a dispute over the division of the assets of the former federal government, including US$2 billion-worth of international reserves and real estate, such as foreign embassies. Meetings with the London Club of bankers were held throughout 1997 to negotiate on this issue, and in November that year the Yugoslav Deputy Prime Minister, Danko Djunić, began to hold unofficial talks with the IMF and the World Bank. However, following the electoral gains by the Radicals in the Serbian Assembly elections, the influence of the reformists was weakened and the negotiations eventually broke down at the end of 1997.

## Montenegro Goes its Own Way

Montenegro introduced a mass privatization program in 1995. All employees received free shares, but only up to 10% of the value of enterprise assets; up to a further 30% of assets could be bought at a discount. The remaining 60% of shares were transferred to the three funds controlled by the republic: the Development Fund (36%), the Pension Fund (18%) and the Employment Fund (6%). Altogether, 299 companies worth DM4.5 billion were transformed, and DM2.6 billion, or around 58% of the total, went to the three Funds. Nearly 80% of enterprises underwent "ownership transformation" under this program, but critics argued that far from being a privatization, the transfer of nearly 60% of enterprise assets to various state funds represented a renationalization. The remaining 51 nonprivatized companies had assets worth DM3.5 billion.

A new privatization law was introduced in Montenegro in May 1997, under the reformist government led by Prime Minister Milo Djukanović. Many of the remaining nonprivatized companies were privatized or sold off to foreign investors. Prominent among these sales was the takeover of the indebted aluminum company Kombinat Aluminijuma Podgorica (KAP) by Glencore, which became controversial since it occurred under conditions of secrecy and without an open tender. The plant accounts for more than half of Montenegro's economy and foreign exchange earnings (according to a report in the *Financial Times*, December 8, 1998). It turned out that Glencore had acquired KAP's debt from the major creditor Vektra, which was owned by a businessman reportedly closely linked to Djukanović.

In the Montenegrin presidential election held in October 1997, Djukanović defeated the incumbent, Momir Bulatović, a close ally of Milošević, who promptly organized demonstrations in Podgorica, the capital of Montenegro, in protest against the result. Serbia then imposed an economic blockade on Montenegro, trucks were held up at the border for up to five days at a time, and Serbia began shifting imported goods through the Greek port of Thessaloniki rather than the Montenegrin port of Bar.

One of the legacies of sanctions was the persistence of smuggling. Around 17,000 tons of contraband cigarettes were being smuggled into Yugoslavia each year, threatening the viability of the four socially owned tobacco companies. Nebojsa Medejović, representative of the Montenegrin Agency for Restructuring the Economy claimed that this smuggling "couldn't have been realized without the support and protection from the authorities' most powerful men, especially the Federal Customs Administration" (as quoted in *Business Yugoslavia*, number 8, October 15, 1997). However, a campaign against smuggling, focused mainly on the trade through Montenegro, has been interpreted as a further action designed to destabilize the government of that republic.

## The Rekindling of the Kosovo Crisis

Kosovo had long been the poorest and most underdeveloped region in the former Yugoslavia. In 1989, measured income per capita in the province was only 25% of the average for the whole of Yugoslavia, and the rate of unemployment, which was above 30%, was much higher than in any of the other seven federal units. Many migrant workers in western Europe sent money back to their families in Kosovo, and actual income levels were probably higher than the officially recorded levels as a result, but poverty was undoubtedly widespread nonetheless. In addition, the Albanian population increased faster than the Serb population in the province, as a result both of a higher birth rate and of Serb outmigration. The government-controlled Serbian media blamed the outmigration on persecution by the Albanian majority, but a more realistic explanation was the poor living conditions in Kosovo. A policy of reverse discrimination adopted by the government of former Yugoslavia had led to a gradual Albanianization of political institutions and socially owned enterprises, which led to a more proportionate structure of employment than had existed in the past (see Bartlett). This threatened the position of Kosovo Serbs as the ruling elite of the province, and fueled the absurd claims that Albanians were forcing Serbs to leave the province.

The implementation of the new Constitution of Serbia in 1990 removed the province's autonomous status, many Albanians in leading positions in the province were dismissed from their posts, and a process of Serbianization of economic, political and cultural organizations was carried out (see Vickers). Schools and universities were no longer permitted to teach in Albanian, and Albanian-language newspapers were closed down. Not surprisingly, the majority of Kosovo Albanians were unwilling to accept these changes, and popular resistance was widespread. The Democratic League of Kosovo (LDK) led the resistance movement in Kosovo during most of the 1990s, under the leadership of Ibrahim Rugova (see Malcolm). Having established a parallel underground government in the province, the LDK won a majority in the unofficial elections to the assembly of the self-declared Republic of Kosovo in May 1992. Under Rugova's leadership, Kosovo Albanians boycotted official Serbian elections and adopted a policy of peaceful resistance, but as the repression of their parallel institutions intensified, many began to turn towards groups advocating more violent methods. The Kosovo Liberation Army (KLA, or UÇK) first admitted responsibility for killings in April 1996. The violence intensified over subsequent years, and broke out into open warfare between the KLA and the Serbian paramilitary police in late 1997 and throughout 1998. Following a negotiated truce in Kosovo in October 1998, the government also clamped down on the opposition movement in Serbia, and imposed harsh new restrictions on the independence of Belgrade University.

## Conclusion: Prospects for the Future

In response to the Kosovo crisis, the EU reintroduced a partial sanctions regime, banning foreign investment into Yugoslavia and grounding flights by the Yugoslav airline JAT. The outbreak of open war in the province, the failure to reach a peace settlement at the Rambouillet talks in February 1999, and the launching of NATO air strikes on Yugoslavia in March, convinced most foreign investors that Yugoslavia was still too risky a prospect. The signs of capital flight were apparent, as the black market value of the dinar fell to YD9.00 to DM1.00. The economic growth that had taken place since the introduction of the Avramović stabilization program, and especially since the lifting of UN sanctions, came to an abrupt halt. Industrial production fell by nearly 10% in January 1999 in comparison to January 1998, and a further fall of 5% was predicted for the first quarter of the year. The mutual indebtedness of enterprises exceeded YD26 billion, interest rates on corporate loans had risen above 100%, and 23,000 companies, employing a total of 425,000 workers, were technically bankrupt. Isolated from international capital markets by the outer wall of sanctions, Yugoslavia found its foreign exchange reserves depleted, while the government deficit had risen to 12% of GDP and

public expenditure accounted for 60% of GDP. Despite this high level of government expenditure, payments to pensioners and public sector workers were in arrears. The economy was once again heading on a downward path, propelled by the lack of any serious structural economic reform.

According to one economist, Stojan Stamenković (quoted in *Business Yugoslavia*, January 1998), "the current economic model cannot last more than three years. After that we will face the fate of North Korea." Yugoslavia is among the small number of post-Communist economies that have still not introduced significant structural reforms. The ruling elite is strongly attached to the continued operation of the current economic model, and would lose their privileged positions if significant reforms were introduced. At the same time, the repressive apparatus of the police force is well-paid and privileged, and is apparently capable of putting down all opposition protests and rebellions. It has been especially active in the repression of the movement for autonomy in Kosovo. The outer wall of sanctions will remain in place until economic reforms are introduced, yet it has been persuasively argued that the western policy of isolating Yugoslavia is itself preventing the development of a virtuous circle of economic improvement and political reform (see Popović). The perception that the West is threatening and bullying the Serbian people can easily be exploited to marginalize reform-minded groups within the ruling elite, and reformist parties outside it.

The Yugoslav economy has a potentially important role in the economic regeneration of the whole Balkan region, in view of its size and the legacy of its advanced industrial base, as well as its productive agricultural sector. However, the immediate outlook is one of further decline. This could well push Montenegro into secession from Yugoslavia. Economic reform and restructuring, as well as reintegration into the international economy, are preconditions for the economic regeneration of both Serbia and Montenegro, whatever their future relationship may be. The alternative is a bleak future for both, with damaging consequences for the entire region.

# Further Reading

Adamović, Svetlana, "Efforts towards Economic Recovery and Monetary Stabilization in FR Yugoslavia," in *Communist Economies and Economic Transformation*, Volume 7, number 4, 1995

An evaluation of the impact of sanctions and the main features of the stabilization policy of 1994

Bartlett, Will, "Labor Market Discrimination and Ethnic Tension in Yugoslavia: The Case of Kosovo," in M. L. Wyzan, editor, *The Political Economy of Ethnic Discrimination and Affirmative Action*, New York: Praeger, 1990

An economic analysis of the purported labor market discrimination against Serbs by Albanians in Kosovo in the 1980s, which concludes that the allegations were essentially unfounded

Bennett, Christopher, *Yugoslavia's Bloody Collapse: Causes, Course and Consequences*, London: Hurst, and New York: New York University Press, 1995

One of the best studies of the breakup of Yugoslavia, emphasizing manipulation by political interest groups. The author teaches at the School of Slavonic and East European Studies in the University of London.

Lazić, Mladen, and Laslo Sekelj, "Privatization in Yugoslavia (Serbia and Montenegro)," in *Europe-Asia Studies*, Volume 49, number 6, 1997

A study of the privatization process in both parts of the present Federal Republic of Yugoslavia

Lyon, James, "Yugoslavia's Hyperinflation, 1993–1994: A Social History," in *East European Politics and Societies*, Volume 10, number 2, 1996

A fascinating first-hand account of the daily course and impact of hyperinflation in Serbia in 1993. The article also provides a penetrating insight into the political and economic rationale that led the leadership of Yugoslavia to adopt an inflationary economic policy.

Malcolm, Noel, *Kosovo: A Short History*, London: Macmillan, and New York: New York University Press, 1998

An impressive scholarly history of the province, which is both informative and readable

Minić, Jelica, and Alexander Denda, editors, *How to Support SMEs in Yugoslavia*, Belgrade: European Movement for Serbia, Institute of Economic Sciences, Ekonomska politika, and Konrad Adenauer Stiftung, 1998

A collection of papers from a conference held in Zrenjanin in 1997

Petrović, Pavle, and Zorica Vujosević, "The Monetary Dynamics in the Yugoslav Hyperinflation of 1991–1993: The Cagan Money Demand," in *European Journal of Political Economy*, Volume 12, 1996

An econometric analysis of the phenomenon of hyperinflation

Popović, Danica, "Yugoslavia's Prospects for Sustained Growth," in Jelica Minić, editor, *EU Enlargement: Yugoslavia and the Balkans*, Belgrade: European Movement in Serbia, Institute of Economic Sciences, Ekonomska politika, and Friedrich Ebert Stiftung, 1997

A short but incisive account of the impact of sanctions, which argues that the lack of structural reform has been a major cause of the poor performance of the economy

Pošarac, Alexandra, "Yugoslav Economic Crisis and Its Social Consequences," in Minić, cited above under Popović

An account of the extensive pauperization brought about by the combination of sanctions, hyperinflation, and the lack of structural reforms

Teokarević, Jovan, "Neither War nor Peace: Serbia and Montenegro in the First Half of the 1990s," in David Dyker and Ivan Vejvoda, editors, *Yugoslavia and After: A Study in Fragmentation, Despair and Rebirth*, Harlow and New York: Longman, 1996

A useful overview of political and economic developments in the early 1990s

Uvalić, Milica (1997a), "Privatization in the Yugoslav Successor States: Converting Self-management into Property Rights," in Milica Uvalić and David Vaughan-Whitehead, editors, *Privatization Surprises in Transition Economies: Employee Ownership in Central and Eastern Europe*, Cheltenham and Lyme, NH: Edward Elgar, 1997

A detailed discussion of the privatization models adopted in Serbia, Montenegro, and the four other successor states

Uvalić, Milica (1997b), "Economic Reforms in the FR of Yugoslavia: Privatization Results and Current Debates," in Minić, cited above under Popović

A summary of the privatization models adopted in Yugoslavia and of the radical proposals that were put forward in 1996 by Dragoslav Avramović but never adopted by the government. The author was a member of the team that worked on the proposals.

Vickers, Miranda, *Between Serb and Albanian: A History of Kosovo*, London: Hurst, and New York: New York University Press, 1998

An excellent historical account of the development of the crisis in the province

Woodward, Susan, *Socialist Unemployment: The Political Economy of Yugoslavia 1945–1990*, Princeton, NJ: Princeton University Press, 1995

An economic analysis of the high levels of unemployment in the former Yugoslavia. The author argues that the country's exposure to international debt was a major factor in the economic crisis of the 1980s.

*Dr Will Bartlett* is Reader in Social Economics in the School for Policy Studies at the University of Bristol in England.

Chapter Nine

# Slovenia, Croatia, Bosnia-Herzegovina, and Macedonia

## *Gavin Gray*

The former Socialist Federal Republic of Yugoslavia certainly was not in "the West," if gauged by standard measures of freedom. It was also out of kilter with an otherwise fairly homogeneous East, even though it was almost invariably grouped with it. Perhaps the most striking differences between the former Yugoslavia and the rest of the region were in industrial and economic policy. Yugoslavia abandoned the collectivization of agriculture early on, and after nationalizing industry in the late 1940s, it changed policy radically in 1950, with the launch of "self-management." From then on, in contrast to other Communist countries, it gradually ceased to be a fully centrally planned economy. The state did not own manufacturing industry, nor did it always dictate what factories produced. Instead, much of the decision-making process was devolved to workers' collectives in each enterprise, which had considerable say in the appointment of the management, and in the day-to-day running of the plant. Of course, Yugoslavia was still a one-party state, and the governments at both federal and republican levels could and did intervene if any enterprise attempted anything too radical, but this rarely occurred. The hybrid system fostered ingenuity and imagination, and since any "profit" was distributed to workers through year-end bonuses, or used to build local infrastructure, enterprises were subject to some of the incentives that exist in market economies. By the 1980s, many factories, particularly in the northern part of the country, were exporting their products to western Europe, often dealing directly with

their customers, and therefore were beginning to learn how market economies work. Most Yugoslav factories also had a finance function, often using bank loans to finance investment. The banking system was decentralized, and from the 1960s commercial banks, set up and capitalized by the largest enterprises in each republic, acted in some senses as outsourced corporate treasuries.

These features of the economy partly explain why the former Yugoslavia achieved a better economic performance in the 1970s and 1980s than the rest of central and eastern Europe. They also help to explain the fact that by the mid-1980s living standards in its northern republics rivaled those in the poorer countries of western Europe, such as Spain or Portugal. However, Yugoslavia also exhibited vast regional inequalities in income, coupled with bouts of unemployment and inflation – three evils that, according to Communist ideologues, were peculiarities of capitalism.

## Achievements and Challenges in the 1990s

Yugoslavia's unique approach to socialism after World War II clearly made a considerable impact on all six of its constituent republics (see Chapter 7, and also Jelavich), and some important aspects of the development of Slovenia, Croatia, Bosnia-Herzegovina, and Macedonia before they became independent are discussed below. However, these countries should also be seen in the light of the wars that accompanied the breakup of the former federation, as well as the policies that each of the four has pursued since gaining independence. Indeed, the four are nearly as hard to categorize as the former Yugoslavia was. At the same time, it would be a mistake to assume that, since the breakup of the former Yugoslavia was accompanied by wars, all four are economic disaster zones, suffering hyperinflation and economic collapse.

Consider, first of all, inflation. In the early 1990s, all four countries suffered hyper-inflation, reaching, for example, 1,925% in Macedonia by the end of 1992, and 1,149% in Croatia by the end of 1993. However, they have also been among the most successful countries in central and eastern Europe at achieving monetary stability. Retail price inflation in Croatia was below 5% from 1993 to 1997, and edged above this level only in 1998. Slovenia and Macedonia have both recorded inflation rates consistently below 10% since 1995. At least four currencies have been in circulation in Bosnia-Herzegovina, making it impossible to quote a unified inflation rate for the entire country, but inflation appears to be under control nonetheless.

Since the head start that these four countries enjoyed over the rest of central and eastern Europe has been only partly offset by the effects of the wars, they are also much richer than many outside observers appreciate, although there is room for debate over just how rich they are. Official figures for GDP at market prices (the conventional measure) probably overstate the living standards in the four countries, in comparison with others in the region, because nontraded goods, such as housing and other services, are relatively expensive. GDP at purchasing power parity, which takes this factor into account, is a more accurate measure. There is also a great deal of evidence to suggest that the GDP figures officially reported in the early 1990s overstated the scale of initial economic downturn in all the transition economies (see, for example, Bartholdy, or Dobozi and Pohl).

Nevertheless, the clearest example of relative economic success is Slovenia, where the second war broke out in June 1991 (two months after fighting started in Croatia). This conflict lasted just 10 days, and, since Slovenia's territorial army, which was equipped with small arms,

succeeded in blockading its opponent, the Yugoslav federal army, into its bases, there was little fighting. Seven years on, Slovenia is the richest and most developed country in central and eastern Europe: its standard of living, as measured by GDP per capita at market prices, is more than double that of Hungary, the second richest. Slovenia is also the only country among the four that is a serious contender for membership of the EU. Following its inclusion in 1997 among the five countries from the region selected to enter negotiations on membership, Slovenia has embarked on administrative and economic reforms comparable to those in the other four early applicants (the Czech Republic, Estonia, Hungary, and Poland). Slovenia has been much less open to foreign direct investment than those others and its approach to reform has been more gradualist.

Croatia also largely escaped destruction. Skirmishing in the summer of 1990 degenerated into a bitter war, which started in April 1991 (before independence was declared) and lasted up to a UN-brokered truce in January 1992, but direct damage was concentrated in a handful of regions. Following macroeconomic stabilization in 1993, Croatia enjoyed strong economic growth between 1994 and 1997, when it was the fourth richest country in central and eastern Europe.

The other two countries have suffered worse fates. Both society and industry were destroyed in Bosnia-Herzegovina during the war in 1992–95, and have barely recovered since then. There was no war in Macedonia, but its first few years of independence were marred by the loss of subsidies from the former Yugoslav federal government, the effects of the UN's trade sanctions against Serbia and Montenegro, and the effects of the trade blockade imposed by Greece on Macedonia itself. However, wages in Bosnia-Herzegovina and Macedonia are relatively high by the standards of central and eastern Europe, at US$150 a month in the Moslem and Croat parts of Bosnia-Herzegovina, and US$182 in Macedonia, compared with around US$100 in Bulgaria and Romania. Slovenia and Croatia have the highest wage rates in the region, at US$920 and US$640 respectively, underlining the major challenge for policy-makers and industrialists in all four countries: how to create industries generating sufficient value added to justify such relatively high wages.

## Slovenia

Even before independence, Slovenia was the most developed Yugoslav republic, and the richest area in central and eastern Europe. Judged by broader, albeit more nebulous criteria of success, it probably also came the closest of the six republics to creating a society with a population that felt contented. This was chiefly because, at least from the 1960s, it had the most liberal Communist regime in Yugoslavia, which stretched the unwritten rules of the federal system to the limit. This would probably not have been possible if Slovenia had not been so isolated. Much of its terrain is mountainous; it was the furthest republic from Belgrade, the federal capital; and it was probably also isolated by language. All Slovenians learned Serbo-Croat, the *lingua franca* of Yugoslavia, but few outside Slovenia learned the Slovene language. The Communists in Slovenia therefore had some advantages when presenting what was happening, on their own terms and in their own native language. By giving the people some freedoms, the Communists averted popular discontent until June and July 1988, when the controversial trial of Janez Janša and three others accused of revealing military secrets in a Slovenian magazine provoked massive demonstrations (see Janša).

Slovenia's greatest achievements were economic. With the encouragement of the republic's leaders, local enterprises went the furthest in exploiting the freedoms offered under the Yugoslav system. The main channel through which this occurred was the signing of licensing agreements for technology transfer, which enabled enterprises to receive state-of-the-art knowhow as well as equipment. Car components became a particularly strong industry for special reasons. In order to develop industry and reduce hard-currency imports, Yugoslavia insisted that all imported cars be financed by barter transactions, in return for exports of car components of equal value. Most of the factories producing components were located in Slovenia, the most northerly republic, in order to reduce the cost of transporting the components to developed markets.

Thus, by the late 1980s, Slovenia had a well-developed and diversified manufacturing base, most of which was internationally competitive. This base included not only the car component factories, but also Gorenje, a producer of washing machines, refrigerators, and other white goods; Iskra, a diversified electrical engineering conglomerate; and two pharmaceuticals companies, Lek and Krka. Companies went a long way in building their links with the West. Adria Caravan, based in the southern city of Novo Mesto, opened facilities in Belgium to support the marketing of its exports; Elan, a maker of skis, opened a manufacturing plant in Austria and sponsored foreign skiers in order to build recognition of its brand name.

Slovenia's economic success was also at least partly due to the nature of its relationships with other Yugoslav republics. It received raw materials and semifinished goods from Serbia and Bosnia-Herzegovina, at below-market prices. Serbia and Bosnia-Herzegovina in turn represented important markets for goods from Slovenia, many of which were sold at above-market prices, as nationalists in Serbia frequently pointed out in the early 1990s, in support of their claim that they were being exploited by Slovenia. Privately, Slovenian industrialists have admitted that, even accounting for the costs of transportation, their profit margins were much higher on the domestic market than in exports. However, through a complex system of subsidies, Slovenia's budget was required to transfer funds to the southern republics for development projects, a practice that dismayed many in Slovenia.

Economic issues such as these came to the fore in the late 1980s and early 1990s, and provided a strong impetus for the independence movement. Indeed, when consumers in Serbia staged a boycott of goods from Slovenia in 1989, with the active encouragement of the Serbian government, many Slovenians decided that it was no longer possible for their republic to coexist with Serbia. Many people articulated their stirring national feelings by saying that they felt themselves to be "Europeans," and that, by remaining in Yugoslavia, Slovenia was artificially included in the Balkans; but baser forms of nationalism were less prevalent. An overwhelming majority of the population supported independence in a referendum held in December 1990, and independence was declared in June 1991.

## Politics and Society since 1991

Slovenia has probably experienced the smoothest political and social transition of any former Communist country, even though its declaration of independence was followed by war. However, while one can pinpoint a single day when Communism collapsed in Poland or Czechoslovakia, for example, it is harder in the case of Slovenia. Many Slovenian politicians refuse to acknowledge that the country was ever truly Communist anyway: they prefer to describe the transition as a seamless process that started in the 1970s, and to lay the blame for past woes on the other republics of the former Yugoslavia.

The transition has been so smooth in part because most of the people who were running Slovenia before independence are still active in politics. The last leader of the Communist Party, Milan Kučan, was elected President in 1992, and reelected for a second five-year term in December 1997. Lojze Peterle, Prime Minister from 1991 to 1992, still leads the Slovenian Christian Democratic Party; Janez Drnovšek, leader of the Liberal Democratic Party, has been Prime Minister since 1992; and Janez Janša still leads the Social Democratic Party. It could be argued that, in a country the size of Slovenia, personalities have a greater influence on politics than policies, and most political parties are vehicles of support for a handful of senior politicians.

The range of politicians in power began to alter after the most recent elections for the unicameral National Assembly, held in December 1996, which produced an inconclusive result. Drnovšek was able to form a new coalition only after lengthy negotiations, by accepting the support of two somewhat

unlikely partners: the Slovenian People's Party and Desus, a party representing pensioners. The People's Party, led by two brothers, Marjan and Janez Podobnik, derives much of its support from farmers and anti-Communists, and has competed with Drnovšek's Liberal Democrats for control of industry and public institutions, in a rivalry that has impeded structural reform. The presence of Desus in the coalition makes it unlikely that Slovenia will undertake the radical reform of its pension system, even though it needs to because of its low birth rate and its high dependency ratio (the number of dependents in relation to the number of working people).

## Economic Policy

Gradualism and consensus-building have been the chief characteristics of Slovenia's economic policy since independence. The authorities initially focused on building the institutions of state, while shrinking back from radical reform. Slovenia has done little to restrain government expenditure (including offbudget funds), which was the equivalent of 45% of GDP in 1997, greater than in most other states in central and eastern Europe. It has also discouraged foreign direct investment, the cornerstone of industrial development in Poland and Hungary.

The gradualist approach and the aversion to foreign investment reflect the nature of Slovenian society, but they also result from the country's economic performance in the 1990s. While living standards collapsed in much of central and eastern Europe, particularly in the rest of former Yugoslavia, because of the dislocation brought about by war, Slovenia suffered much less. If the EBRD is correct in its estimates, Slovenia's GDP (at constant prices) in 1997 stood at 99% of its level in 1989, and among the other transition economies only Poland performed better, with GDP at around 110% of its level in 1989. Slovenia is the only transition economy that has not suffered a double-digit decline in real GDP in the 1990s: its worst performance was in 1989, when GDP fell by 8.9%. This is partly because industry in Slovenia found it relatively easy to switch sales to export markets in the EU when they lost their markets in the rest of former Yugoslavia.

Success appears to have bred complacency. There has always been less support in Slovenia for structural adjustment than in other former Communist countries, where the notion that Communism had failed was taken as self-evident. Many Slovenian politicians maintain that the country needs fine-tuning, not radical reform. Accordingly, the privatization of manufacturing industry was seriously delayed, and the public debate on the issue focused on finding the fairest method, not on determining what would foster industrial development or encourage new investment. Slovenia selected a voucher system, in which every citizen received shares free of charge, although employees were granted particularly strong concessions, being allowed, for example, to buy additional shares on installments, and at a discount. Partly as a result, industrial restructuring has been piece-meal. Many factories have laid off workers, but little has been done, for example, to dispose of peripheral assets, such as holiday homes and other social facilities. Crucially, few Slovenian managers have acknowledged the importance of economies of scale, with the result that there are factories that were competitive in the past, but are simply too small to survive in the global economy.

By the end of 1998, the authorities had only just begun other reforms that had already taken place in many other countries in the region, or had even delayed them. The two largest banks, Nova Ljubljanska Banka and Nova Kreditna Banka Maribor, had been taken over by the state and successfully overhauled, but the more controversial issue of their eventual privatization has been stalled. Tax reform, particularly the introduction of value-added tax, has also been subject to several false starts. Yet these and other issues will have to be addressed, and soon, as part of the process of accession to the EU.

## Prospects

When it became an independent state in 1991, Slovenia had a substantial head start over the rest of central and eastern Europe in the race to create a modern, competitive economy. There have been some industrial successes, and the successive governments' ability to build

support for their policies has at least ensured that there have been few reversals in the reform process. Nevertheless, the country has surrendered much of its lead in the 1990s, because of its gradualist and inward-looking policies.

Slovenia's acceptance as one of the five front-runners for EU membership in central and eastern Europe will bring about profound changes in the early years of the 21st century. As we have seen, the government will have no option but to carry out several delayed reforms, notably bank privatization and tax reform, but also the removal of several rules that discriminate against foreign companies. Foreign banks will be allowed to open branches in Slovenia, and foreign portfolio investment will no longer be strictly limited. All this is likely to have a generally beneficial effect on Slovenia, particularly by supporting economic growth, which was 3.1% in 1996 and 3.8% in 1997, compared, for example, with the growth of between 5% and 7% achieved by Poland. EU membership will also give Slovenia greater international credibility, and could enhance its sovereignty, as it will have a greater role in European decision-making. Nevertheless, Slovenia is likely to stand somewhat apart from the EU mainstream, since, as in Denmark, Austria, or the United Kingdom, its people tend to be averse to anything that looks like cultural assimilation.

## Croatia

After World War II, the Yugoslav Communists strove to suppress the ethnic tensions that had undermined the state ever since it was formed, as the Kingdom of the Serbs, Croats, and Slovenes, in 1918. These concerns particularly shaped their policies in Croatia (as well as in Bosnia-Herzegovina – see below), for some of the worst wartime atrocities had been perpetrated by the "Independent State of Croatia" (*Nezavisna Država Hrvatske*, or NDH), which was allied to Nazi Germany. Thousands of Serbs and others had died at a concentration camp in Jasenovac, and Bosnia-Herzegovina had been subjected to severe repression. The Communists therefore banned Croatian national symbols, notably the red and white checkered device known as the *Šahovnica*, and installed a disproportionate number of ethnic Serbs in positions of power in Croatia, such as in the police force and in factory management. In 1971, when a cultural organization, Hrvatska Matica, began seeking to articulate national feeling, the Communist Party leadership was replaced, and the Matica was wound down.

Despite its uneasy relationship with the federal government in Belgrade, Croatia succeeded in developing the most diversified economy in Yugoslavia. Like Slovenia, it had a relatively well-developed manufacturing base, some of which was internationally competitive, and much of which was located around the capital, Zagreb. This included Pliva, a pharmaceutical company; Rade Končar, a sprawling electrical engineering conglomerate producing everything from household appliances to elevators and generators; Nikola Tesla, a manufacturer of telecommunications components; and Podravka, a food-processing concern, which was located in Koprivnica, near the border with Hungary. Other sections of manufacturing industry were less impressive. There was excess capacity in heavy industries, such as shipbuilding, the major steel mill at Sisak, oil refining, and petrochemicals. In addition, Croatia had a fairly strong agricultural sector, particularly in the region of Slavonia, bordering the Pannonian plain, where the soil and climate are suitable for grain production. Croatia also had oil, albeit not enough to give Yugoslavia self-sufficiency in energy. However, Croatia's largest single industry was tourism. From the 1960s, the Yugoslav regime decided to develop the Istrian Peninsula, as well as the Dalmatian coastline and islands, for foreign tourists, partly because these regions were unsuitable for industry, but also because visitors generated foreign exchange. By the 1980s, Yugoslavia rivaled Spain and Greece as a tourist destination.

Croatia's economic relationship with the other republics within Yugoslavia was similar to that of Slovenia, as it depended on them for raw materials, and for markets for its products. The terms of trade were also in its favor, so that it became the second richest republic, although this was partly offset by redistributive transfers. Nevertheless, a disproportionate number of ethnic Croats took advantage of treaties, agreed in the 1960s, that allowed Yugoslavs to work in western Europe. The number of ethnic Croats in Bavaria alone is estimated at 200,000, the equivalent of 5% of the population.

Against this background, the revival of national feeling in the late 1980s came to be combined with a growing belief that Croatian development was being impeded by the transfers it was making to other republics. Together, these attitudes provided impetus to the independence movement in the late 1980s and early 1990s.

## Politics and Society since 1991

Croatia held its first free multiparty elections in April 1990. They produced a convincing victory for a newly founded nationalist party, the Croatian Democratic Union (Hrvatska Demokratska Zajednica, or HDZ), led by Franjo Tudjman. Apart from Bosnia-Herzegovina, it was thus the only Yugoslav republic in which elections brought about a comprehensive transfer of power from the Communists to new parties.

Although Croatia and Slovenia found themselves united in the early 1990s in their disputes with the Yugoslav state, the independence movements that sprang up in the two republics were profoundly different. Practical considerations, and above all the consensus that Yugoslavia had failed, convinced the Slovenians that they should break away. The drive for Croatian independence, by contrast, was stirred more by national feelings, and began to resemble the national movements that led to the creation of nation-states in the 18th and 19th centuries. This reflected the heavy influence on Tudjman of expatriate nationalists, particularly in North and South America, many of whom had left Yugoslavia shortly after World War II. Accordingly, the new government set about removing many ethnic Serbs from jobs in enterprise management or the police, and it also reintroduced the national symbols that had been suppressed since 1945.

War broke out in Croatia in July 1991 between the new government's forces and rebel Serbs, who were backed up by the Yugoslav federal army. By early 1992, when a peace agreement was signed, the Serbs had gained control of broad swathes of territory along Croatia's border with Bosnia-Herzegovina, collectively called Krajina, along with Eastern Slavonia, on the border with Serbia. The Croatian army retook Krajina in two military assaults, in May and August 1995, while transfer of control of Eastern Slavonia occurred peacefully following an agreement in December 1995.

The nationalistic character of the Croatian state has consistently brought it into conflict with the major powers, particularly the EU and the United States. In June 1993, for example, Croatia supported a move by ethnic Croats in Bosnia-Herzegovina to create a state of their own, called Herceg-Bosna, and its uncomfortable relationship with the West has continued since the war in Bosnia-Herzegovina ended in 1995. This has mainly been due to continuing western concerns over Croatia's policy in Bosnia-Herzegovina, but it has also been due to western responses to the Croatian government's domestic policies. The HDZ controls the media, and power is largely exercised not through parliamentary institutions but through a series of committees and structures associated with the presidency. One result is that Croatia has been ruled out as a candidate for membership of the EU.

## The Economy and Economic Policy

Croatia was facing hyperinflation and economic collapse when it declared independence. Real GDP fell by 19.8% 1991, and by 11.1% in 1992, as the severing of links with suppliers and customers in other republics forced much of industry to shut down, while the outbreak of war meant that few tourists were willing to visit the country. Although industry sustained little direct damage during the fighting, which had died down by early 1992, the economy remained in limbo until late 1995, mainly because the rebel Serbs were able to obstruct transport and energy links. For example, Croatia's second city, Split, was subjected to power cuts in 1992 and 1993. Continued fighting in Bosnia-Herzegovina discouraged investors, while western governments blocked multilateral financing.

As a result, Croatia had no alternative but to undertake the first stages of economic reform without foreign assistance. It began the process in October 1993 by launching a counterinflation program under which an initial large devaluation was followed by a tightening of monetary policy, and the introduction of a strict incomes policy. It produced immediate results. The inflation rate (month on month) exceeded 35% in October 1993, but by 1994 prices were stable or falling, and the average level of prices fell by 3% in the course of that year (see Anusić et al.). The economic decline bottomed out, and real GDP grew by 5.9% in 1994, 6.8% in 1995, and 6% in 1996.

Structural reform took place faster in Croatia than in any other former Yugoslav republic, particularly between 1992 and 1995. The government was quick to cut back on nonessential expenditure, taking advantage of the fact that wartime conditions helped to minimize open dissent. The disadvantaged suffered greatly, particularly pensioners, since the level of pensions ran behind inflation, and they were often paid late.

Croatia initiated its privatization program in 1992 by ordering companies to arrange sales of shares to their employees through installment schemes. Unsold shares were transferred to two funds controlled by the state. The scheme was partly successful, perhaps its greatest achievement being that it was completed, unlike in several other countries in central and eastern Europe. However, existing managements remained in control, and there was little input of new capital or knowhow. In some cases, foreign investors were discouraged because local tycoons, many of them HDZ supporters, enjoyed preferential treatment. In 1998, the government made plans for a second stage of privatization, involving assets that were directly owned by the state. It announced that it would sell the national telecommunications operator Hrvatske Telekomunikacj, the national oil company INA, and several banks that had been taken into the hands of the state.

Economic growth slowed down sharply in 1998, and the government faced mounting social and economic turbulence. The slowdown was exacerbated early in the year by the introduction of value-added tax, which led to a fiscal squeeze, resulting in a decline in real growth in GDP to an estimated 3.5% for 1998, compared to more than 6% in previous years. With memories of the war beginning to fade, social groups that had suffered the most began to protest that they should receive more of the benefits of growth, and there were demonstrations by labor unions and pensioners.

## Prospects

Croatia's economic achievements in the 1990s were impressive, given that it was starved of foreign capital between 1991 and 1995, many transport links were ruptured, and the government had to divert much of its resources to defense. Perhaps it was precisely these constraints that meant it had no alternative but to control inflation and undertake privatization. With the passage of time since the end of the war, Croatia still needs to establish a more democratic approach to decision-making, if reform is to command public support and be sustainable. This is unlikely during the Tudjman presidency, which lasts until 2002, or while the HDZ is in government. Subsequent regimes will need to encourage faster industrial restructuring, close down large sections of heavy industry, and promote industries based on knowledge and knowhow that can generate greater value added.

## Bosnia-Herzegovina

Bosnia-Herzegovina was the most ethnically mixed of the six republics that made up the former Yugoslavia. The federal government installed a particularly hard-line regime there, to ensure no repetition of ethnically motivated fighting. By the 1970s and 1980s, Bosnia-Herzegovina appeared to be the most "Yugoslav" republic. In its major cities at least, its development had brought it closer than other parts of the country to the Communist leadership's dream of a homogeneous country, where people regarded themselves as Yugoslavs rather than defining themselves by ethnicity or religion. The number doing so in Bosnia-Herzegovina increased eightfold between the censuses of 1971 and 1981. In rural areas,

however, intermarriage was much rarer, and villages tended to be ethnically homogeneous.

The economy of the country was developed during the Communist period in ways that overwhelmingly favored heavy industry. This was partly for strategic reasons: lying at the center of Yugoslavia, it would be partly protected in the event of invasion, making it the preferred location for military production and for metal-processing factories supplying components. In any case, deposits of minerals, including coal, made it a good location for heavy industry. Accordingly, the leading enterprises in Bosnia-Herzegovina were the Zenica iron and steel mills, the largest anywhere in the Balkans, and the Sredna Bosna coalmines. Bosnia-Herzegovina was also a net exporter of electricity to the rest of Yugoslavia, mainly from coal-fired thermal plants. Yet Bosnia-Herzegovina had the poorest economic performance in Yugoslavia: its national income fell from 20% below the Yugoslav average in 1947 to 38% in 1967, and it had the lowest rate of literacy, and the highest rate of infant mortality, among the six republics (see Malcolm). As a result, the Bosnians were looked on by many in the rest of Yugoslavia, in a mostly affectionate but condescending way, as somewhat backward.

War broke out in Bosnia-Herzegovina in 1992, and raged on until late 1995. Much of industry and society was destroyed, and more than 1 million people were displaced from their homes. The war came to a halt in October 1995, because, for the first time since 1992, it was in the interests of all involved to stop fighting. The Bosnian Serbs were losing territory, and decided that this would be a good time for them to set about preserving their gains, while the Croat and Moslem forces were gaining territory but realized that they would lose western support if they pushed much further.

The peace agreement drawn up in Dayton, Ohio, in November 1995 and signed in Paris the following month divided Bosnia-Herzegovina into two "entities," the Republika Srpska, and the Federation of Bosnia and Herzegovina. These made up 49% and 51% of the country's territory respectively, and corresponded to the areas controlled at that time by the Bosnian Serbs, on the one hand, and the Moslem and Croat armies on the other. The Dayton Agreement placed a heavy emphasis on the right of refugees to return to their homes, partly to avert allegations that the main perpetrators of human rights abuses were being allowed to retain their gains from the war, but also because the western European countries that had received large numbers of refugees from Bosnia-Herzegovina wanted them to return as soon as possible. Although Bosnia-Herzegovina remained one state, central government was given only highly restricted areas of responsibility under the Agreement, principally foreign affairs, trade, and monetary policy. Most powers lay with the two entities, which were given the right to negotiate treaties with neighboring countries.

The Dayton Agreement also created one of the world's most complicated political systems. The central state was to have a three-person Presidency, with one representative each for the Moslems, Serbs, and Croats, as well as a bicameral Assembly. Each entity has its own president and legislature, unicameral in the Serb case but bicameral in the Federation. The Agreement has effectively forced the citizens of Bosnia-Herzegovina to vote on ethnic rather than ideological lines, thereby perpetuating the ethnic divide. As a result, the elections in September 1996 and September 1998 returned to power the parties and politicians that had won the first multiparty elections, and therefore bore considerable responsibility for the outbreak of the war. Another important feature of the Dayton Agreement was the creation of the post of High Representative, a foreign diplomat appointed to oversee the implementation of the civilian parts of the Agreement, such as the establishment of new government institutions and the launch of a reconstruction program costing US$5 billion, mainly in donations from foreign governments. A large number of foreign troops were also installed in Bosnia-Herzegovina to avert the outbreak of another war.

Although the Dayton Agreement cemented the end of the war in Bosnia-Herzegovina, by the spring of 1999 it had not brought about a sustainable peace. It appears unlikely that the country's politicians will be capable of managing affairs on their own for some years to come. The level of foreign involvement in government increased in 1998 after the powers of the High Representative were strengthened to allow him to impose legislation and to remove elected officials from office. This made Bosnia-Herzegovina resemble an international protectorate. In the short term the change helped to speed up the introduction of certain measures, such as the first privatizations, but it undermined the development of democracy and removed the incentive for politicians to act responsibly. Meanwhile, Bosnia-Herzegovina has barely begun the process of transition undertaken by most other countries in central and eastern Europe. The economy remains dominated by heavy industry, much of which is unlikely ever to become competitive. Registered unemployment was above 40% of the labor force at the end of 1998, and there was little new investment in manufacturing facilities that would create new jobs.

## Macedonia

Macedonia came into existence as a political entity in November 1943, with the proclamation of a new Yugoslav federation by the Communist-led Partisan resistance. The territory had often been referred to as "southern Serbia"; in any case, it occupies only that part of the historical land of Macedonia known as Vardar Macedonia for the Vardar river, which flows through the capital, Skopje. Macedonia had and still has much in common with its northern neighbor, Serbia: most notably, in both countries an Orthodox Christian and Slavic majority has historically lived alongside numerous ethnic and religious minorities. Macedonia and Serbia also had similar economies. Macedonian industry included a large number of heavy industrial plants or factories, producing raw and semifinished goods, such as a large iron and steel plant in Skopje, textiles factories in the West of the republic, and plants producing bulk chemicals and other products with low value added from oil derivatives. Agriculture represented a substantial proportion of the economy and employment. The most important products included tobacco, and fresh fruit and vegetables. Thus, Macedonia was dependent on the other republics for markets and the few Macedonian products exported beyond Yugoslavia were marketed by foreign trade organizations in Serbia, denying Macedonian executives the opportunity to meet customers abroad. A powerful earthquake in 1963 destroyed parts of Skopje, setting back the republic's economic development.

Macedonia received substantial subsidies through the federal system. This meant that, in the absence of ethnic tensions of the kind that emerged in Croatia and Bosnia-Herzegovina, Macedonia was one of the few republics where the population generally wanted to remain within Yugoslavia. However, by the middle of 1991 it was clear that the federation was collapsing. Accordingly, the regime organized a referendum on independence, which was held in September 1991. The country was recognized by the UN in 1993, albeit as the Former Yugoslav Republic of Macedonia (or FYROM), listed and seated under "F," not "M."

## Politics and International Relations since 1991

Macedonia was the only republic of Yugoslavia to declare independence without war breaking out, yet it has probably endured a tougher five years since independence than, for example, Croatia, where war raged for six months. Its economic problems (see below) were largely the result of political factors. The first blow came in May 1992, when the UN imposed trade sanctions on "rump" Yugoslavia, blocking the most important trade route for Macedonian goods. It suffered further the same year, when a bitter dispute broke out with Greece, and this escalated in March 1994 when Greece imposed a trade blockade. The dispute had three main strands. Greece objected to the use of the name "Macedonia," to clauses in the country's Constitution that it interpreted as making a claim on its own province of Macedonia, and to Macedonia's flag, which featured the 16-pointed star of Vergina, a symbol that Greeks hold dear.

The leader of the Communist Party, Kiro Gligorov, was elected President of Macedonia, and the party reinvented itself, changing its name to the Social Democratic Alliance of Macedonia (SDSM). After a short-lived coalition government left office, the SDSM came to power in 1992 and then won the elections for the unicameral Assembly in 1994. However, it was convincingly defeated in the next elections, in October and November 1998. The winners were two parties that contested the elections as a coalition for change: the Democratic Alternative (DA), and the Internal Macedonian Revolutionary Organization-Democratic Party for Macedonian National Unity (VMRO-DPMNE).

## The Economy

Although there was no war in Macedonia, it suffered the worst economic collapse in the former Yugoslavia, apart from Bosnia-Herzegovina, Serbia, and Montenegro. It lost substantial federal subsidies, much of its industry ceased production because it lost markets in the rest of Yugoslavia, and, crucially, the Greek trade blockade robbed it of its main potential replacement market. The blockade also complicated the supply of oil, which had been imported by tanker into the Greek port of Thessaloniki, and then sent on by rail. The country received some respite by breaking UN sanctions against Yugoslavia (Serbia and Montenegro), and acting as a conduit for illicit trade, but its economy nevertheless contracted sharply. Real GDP fell by 12.1% in 1991, 21.1% in 1992, and 8.4% in 1993, before bottoming out. Although a moderate economic recovery began in 1996, there was little immediate impact on unemployment, which stood at 45% in late 1997, according to official figures; and many of those who were in formal employment were being paid in arrears.

Macedonia began economic reform in earnest in September 1995, with the launch of a monetary stabilization program anchored by fixing the exchange rate at MD26.50 to DM1.00. As in Croatia, which had launched a monetary stabilization program in October 1993 (see above), this was an important achievement, as it generated confidence in the economy among a population that had recent experience of losing savings through hyperinflation. Industrial restructuring has been slower, however. Although most assets were sold off, principally to the workforce, and some workers have been dismissed, there has been little new investment. Foreign direct investment, which propelled economic recovery in much of central and eastern Europe, was particularly sparse in Macedonia until July 1998, when several deals were concluded in principle.

## Prospects

The elections for the Assembly in October and November 1998 gave Macedonia a second chance to begin the process of transition that had been held back for so long by the Greek blockade and the instability common to all the former Yugoslav republics. The new government has centered its foreign policy on improving relations with its neighbors, such as Greece and Bulgaria, and on persuading western Europe to cease treating it purely in terms of Balkan security, and instead to regard it as a potential candidate for eventual membership of the EU. The government's first step was to request negotiations on an association agreement, but EU officials initially reacted coolly to this proposal. The government's focus on improving foreign relations reflects its realization that, assuming instability has abated, political risk can be reduced, opening the way to greater foreign direct investment and commercial borrowing. It could also remove political obstacles to free trade agreements, improving the chances for exporters and cutting the cost of imports. Whether it achieves these goals in the early part of the 21st century will also have a strong influence on the government's chances of encouraging industrial restructuring, and the development of new industries to replace uncompetitive heavy manufacturing.

## Conclusion

At the end of the 1980s, Yugoslavia was the most unevenly developed country in central and eastern Europe. Intrinsic advantages and better political leadership made its two most northerly republics, Slovenia and Croatia, far richer and more developed than the other four

republics, including Bosnia-Herzegovina and Macedonia. This division widened in the 1990s, partly because Slovenia and Croatia were quicker to embrace the free market, but much more because the economy of Bosnia-Herzegovina was destroyed by war, while Macedonia was crippled by regional instability and trade blockades.

The four countries will probably continue to diverge. By the spring of 1999, Slovenia, the richest country in central and eastern Europe, was well on course for early membership of the EU, and is likely to rank at least among the middle tier of EU members once it has joined. Croatia could eventually follow Slovenia's lead, but is unlikely to do so until late in the first decade of the 21st century, or later still, because of its dubious record on human rights and democracy. This in turn will hold back the restructuring of its economy. The prospects for Bosnia-Herzegovina and Macedonia are even bleaker. Although the war in Bosnia-Herzegovina has come to an end, there has been little genuine progress on creating a society that can survive without massive international involvement and funding. The country's viability therefore hangs in the balance, while the process of restructuring has barely begun. Macedonia, the only former Yugoslav republic to achieve independence without bloodshed, faces a political and economic future as uncertain as Bosnia-Herzegovina's: industry has collapsed and there is unlikely to be a recovery until regional instability has been further reduced.

## Further Reading

Almond, Mark, *Europe's Backyard War*, London: Mandarin, 1994

   One of several readable books about the politics and history of the breakup of Yugoslavia

Anusić, Zoran, Zeljko Rohatinski, and Velimir Sonje, *A Road to Low Inflation: Croatia 1993/1994*, Zagreb: The Government of the Republic of Croatia, 1995

   A semiofficial account of Croatia's counterinflationary program

Bartholdy, Kasper, "Old and New Problems in the Estimation of National Accounts in Transition

Economies," in *The Economics of Transition*, Volume 5, number 1, 1997

Dobozi, Istvan, and Gerhard Pohl, "Forget GDP, Try Electricity," in *Transition Newsletter*, 1995

Drnovšek, Janez, *Escape from Hell: The Truth of a President*, Martigny: Editions Latour, 1996

Drnovšek, who has been Prime Minister of Slovenia since 1992, provides an insider's view of the breakup of Yugoslavia, albeit in his customary deadpan manner.

Glenny, Misha, *The Fall of Yugoslavia*, London: Penguin, and New York: Viking, 1996

Probably the most readable and evenhanded of the journalistic accounts of the war in Yugoslavia

Janša, Janez, *The Making of the Slovenian State, 1988–1992*, Ljubljana: Mladinska Knjiga Publishing House, 1994

An account by an eyewitness and prominent participant who was a journalist before Slovenia achieved independence. He has since become leader of the Social Democrats.

Jelavich, Barbara, *History of the Balkans: Twentieth Century*, in two volumes, Cambridge and New York: Cambridge University Press, 1983

The most comprehensive history of the Balkans, including Yugoslavia, although it provides little detail on Slovenia or Macedonia

Malcolm, Noel, *Bosnia: A Short History*, London: Macmillian, and New York: New York University Press, 1994

Silber, Laura, and Allan Little, *The Death of Yugoslavia*, London: Penguin and BBC Worldwide, and New York: Penguin, 1995

Along with Glenny's book cited above, probably the best journalistic account of the war, based on an unrivaled number of interviews with the main politicians involved

*Gavin Gray* is an analyst, covering transition economies, at the Economist Intelligence Unit in London. After completing Bachelor's and Master's degrees at the London School of Economics, he was a correspondent for the *Financial Times* in Slovenia and Croatia from 1994 to 1996. His publications include *Eastern Europe* (London: Euromoney, 1996).

**Table 9.1  Selected Macroeconomic Indicators for Slovenia, Croatia, Bosnia-Herzegovina, and Macedonia, 1997**

| | Bosnia-Herzegovina Moslem-Croat Federation | Republika Srpska | Croatia | Macedonia | Slovenia |
|---|---|---|---|---|---|
| Real GDP growth | 37 | 42 | 6.5 | 1.5 | 3.8 |
| Growth in industrial output | 30 | 34 | 6.8 | 3.4 | 4.7 |
| Retail price inflation (annual average) | 13.4 | −6.7 [1] | 3.6 | 1.3 | 8.4 |
| Current account balance (US$ millions) | n.a. | n.a. | −2,435 | −275 | 39 |
| (% of GDP) | n.a. | n.a. | −12.6 | −8.3 | 0.2 |
| GDP per capita (US$, market prices) | n.a. | n.a. | 4,267 | 1,663 | 9,101 |
| External debt at December 31 (US$ millions) | n.a. | n.a. | 6,660 | 1,141 | 4,176 |

1 Measured in Deutschmarks

Source: EBRD

## Chapter Ten

# Albania

## *Shinasi A. Rama*

Albania, which has a total area of 28,750 square kilometers, comprises three main geographical regions. A mountainous region to the East is dominated by three mountain ranges separated by deep valleys, notably those of the Rivers Vjosa, Osumi, Shkumbin and Mat, while the Albanian Alps in the North constitute a second region. The region of low-lying, flat land can be further divided into three subregions. One, in the West, extends from Koplik to Vlora: it accounts for 27% of the surface area, but it is inhabited by around 60% of Albania's population. This subregion is thus the heartland of the country's economy. In the East, there is a second subregion of flat land, known as the Fusha e Korçës (the Plain of Korça), and in the South lies a third subregion of flat land, the Fusha e Dropullit (the Dropulli Plain). More than 20% of the whole territory is covered by forest.

Albania's social, political, and economic development has been deeply affected by its geography and its climate. The hinterland is mostly mountains and hills, while the more thickly inhabited plains are all along the coast, where the climate is characteristically Mediterranean. Winters are cool, cloudy, and rainy, while summers are hot and dry. The mountainous region has much colder winters, with heavier snow, and alpine summers. The rugged, mountainous nature of the country has created considerable problems for transportation and communications. Indeed, for a relatively long period these physical barriers hindered the development of markets on a national scale.

## The Population

At least 95% of the total population of Albania, which was estimated at nearly 3.42 million in 1995, are ethnic Albanians; most of the remaining inhabitants are Greeks, but there are also around 34,000 Roma and around 4,000 people of ethnic Macedonian descent (see also Table 10.1). The official language is Albanian. There are four main religious denominations in Albania, although it is extremely difficult to determine the exact proportion of the population that can be described as fully active members of any of them. It is widely accepted, however, that around 72% of the population are Moslems, including the members of the widespread schismatic sect known as Bektashi, while 18% are Orthodox Christians and 11% are Catholics.

Albania underwent a process of rapid urbanization from 1944 up to the 1970s, and a second wave of urbanization, which began after the year 1991, is still continuing. As a result, at least two fifths of the population now live in cities and towns. The capital city, Tirana, is home to around 18% of the population, or 537,000 people (as estimated in 1996). Other major cities include Durrësi, which had around 100,450 inhabitants in 1996, Shkodra, with around 92,000, Elbasani, with around 87,000, Vlora, with around 71,000, and Korça, with around 70,500. Nevertheless, around 60% of the population continue to live in rural areas, making the country one of the least urbanized in Europe.

Between 1944 and 1990, when the Communist regime implemented programs to encourage a high birth rate and improved health services, thus reducing death rates, the population of Albania increased fourfold. Since 1991, however, the birth rate has dropped significantly. This reduction in what had been the main factor in population growth can be explained by reference to the considerable emphasis that governments have placed on birth control programs, to the relatively high general level of education, and, most notably, to the constant political turmoil and successive economic crises that have characterized Albania's transition to democracy since 1990.

Income distribution is highly unequal. In 1989, at least if the statistics compiled by government agencies for that year are reliable, the managers of state enterprises, who were the highest-paid individuals under the Communist system, received salaries that were around three times the average wages of manual workers. Ten years later, more than 55% of the population were living on incomes below the official poverty level. Besides having the youngest population structure of any country in Europe, Albania has around 500,000 retired people. Not surprisingly, the old and the young, who have the greatest dependence on government spending and the fewest opportunities to earn money for themselves, have sustained the greatest amount of suffering as a result of the economic reforms implemented in the 1990s, which have generated far-reaching changes in the distribution of incomes and wealth.

## From Independence to Communism, 1912–44

The Albanians are descendants of the ancient Illyrian people, and they take their modern name from one of the Illyrian tribes, the Albanët. Throughout the centuries up to the attainment of independence in 1912, Albania was subject to foreign domination, except for a relatively brief period from the 14th century until it finally became part of the Turkish Ottoman empire in the 16th century. Even when Albania became an independent state recognized by the great powers of Europe, its territory amounted to less than half of all the territories inhabited by ethnic Albanians.

It must be noted that from the beginning of the existence of an independent Albanian state,

the country's elites consciously sought to imitate the political practices of the leading countries of western Europe. As in those countries, stability and democracy were adversely affected by the experience of the First World War, but from 1919 to 1924 Albania consistently maintained a liberal democratic form of government. In 1928, however, Ahmet Zogu, then Prime Minister, had himself proclaimed King Zog I, and he ruled the country until 1939. During the years of his regime, a uniform state administration was firmly established, and the local warlords and *Bajraktar* (tribal leaders) were brought under the government's control. Even under King Zog, there was a functioning system of relatively competitive parties, taking part in regular elections that were manipulated by the regime but served to preserve the image of a constitutional monarchy. One of the great achievements of this period was the establishment of a judicial system that was fairly successful in harmonizing and domesticating the westernizing tendencies of the elites, as manifested in the adoption of a Civil and Penal Code, modeled on the French Code Napoléon, alongside the widespread persistence of common law practices. However, King Zog's Albania suffered from one fatal weakness: the economy remained at a generally low level of development and suffered, along with the rest of Europe, from the impact of the Great Depression of the 1930s. In consequence, the regime remained completely dependent on aid and support from the Fascist government of Italy.

In April 1939, Albania was annexed by Italy and after September 1943 it was occupied by Nazi Germany. During World War II, politically conscious and active Albanians came to be divided into two major camps. In the first camp were the nationalists, organized in the National Front (Balli Kombëtar), a resistance organization led by Mid'hat Frashëri. Balli Kombëtar advocated a policy of neutrality, the preservation of the integrity of Albania, and a general preference for an orientation toward the western sphere of influence. On the other side stood the Democratic Front, led by the Communist Party of Albania (formally known as the Albanian Party of Labor), which advocated the introduction of the Soviet model of government and economic activity, and the strengthening of ties with the Soviet Union. Albania was the only country anywhere in central and eastern Europe to be liberated from occupation exclusively by indigenous resistance forces (even the Partisans in Yugoslavia relied on external aid and support). The victory of the Democratic Front over both Nazi Germany and the non-Communist camp was sealed on November 29, 1944. The price that Albania had paid was high. An estimated 28,000 people had been killed in action, thousands more were declared "missing" and never traced, and more than 100,000 houses had been burned down or otherwise destroyed.

## The Communist Period, 1944–90

The Provisional Government established under the leadership of Enver Hoxha at Berat on October 22, 1944, was completely dominated by the Communist Party, although at that time it was still operating under the umbrella of the Democratic Front. In January 1945, this government agreed to restore the province of Kosovo (known to Albanians as Kosova) to Yugoslavia, from which it had been detached by the Italian occupation forces in 1941. The government also nationalized manufacturing industries, transportation services, and forests, and confiscated the property of the churches and of political opponents. It announced a sweeping agrarian reform under which around half of the arable land in the country was taken from the former landowners and redistributed to the working peasants. Albania was declared a "People's Republic" on January 11, 1946. It has been estimated that in the relatively unsettled period between 1944 and 1948, at least 8,000 opponents of the new Communist regime were killed, either in the course of military campaigns against the government, or as a result of "elimination" by the Communist-controlled judicial system. The country remained under heavy Yugoslav influence until the summer of 1948, when it cut virtually all ties with Yugoslavia, partly at the behest of the Soviet dictator Josef Stalin, and became a loyal satellite of the Soviet Union (although formal diplomatic relations were maintained with Tito's regime, despite its expulsion from the

Soviet bloc, up to May 1950). It is important to note that, at least initially, there was strong support for the Communist regime, especially among young people, peasants, and women, social groups that saw the establishment of a socialist system and the implementation of its political program as likely to be beneficial to their interests and to the interests of Albania as a whole.

After 1948, Albania, which had been a predominantly agrarian country, sought to industrialize rapidly and catch up with the modern world. Following the Soviet model, collectivization was introduced in agriculture, while ambitious plans for industrialization were drawn up, based on the assumption that the Soviet Union would continue to provide economic aid and technical advice. Large numbers of Albanian students were sent to study in the Soviet Union, and Albania rapidly became integrated into the Soviet bloc. It joined Comecon, the trading group dominated by the Soviet Union, in February 1949, and became a founder member of the Warsaw Pact in May 1955. As early as October 1954, however, Albania was signing its own bilateral agreements on cooperation and mutual assistance with the other major Communist power, the People's Republic of China.

The period of predominant Soviet influence lasted until December 1961, when Albania broke off all relations with the Soviet Union, denouncing the attempts of its leadership to eliminate some of the worst features of Stalinism. From January 1962 onward, Albania was excluded from meetings of the Warsaw Pact governments, and in September 1968, after its refusal to join in the invasion of Czechoslovakia, it was formally expelled from that organization. Meanwhile, its involvement in the Comecon system of trade and economic planning also effectively lapsed. Isolated within Europe, the government of Albania turned instead to enhance its alliance with China, although that relationship lasted only until 1978.

It has been estimated that, during the first 34 years of Communist rule, the Soviet Union and China together gave Albania a total of around US$6 billion (at the 1988 exchange rate) in the form of economic aid and credits.

Thanks, in large part, to this economic aid, the standard of living in Albania greatly improved. By 1970, most Albanians were living in relative comfort, at a level significantly beyond anything experienced in earlier periods, and the standard of living was probably comparable with conditions in Greece, Portugal, and Spain at that date. Clearly, the influence of the omnipresent police state, and the government's control of education and the media, must not be underestimated, yet this improvement in lifestyles also goes some way toward explaining the general acquiescence of the population in the drastic measures introduced by Enver Hoxha's regime in the 1960s and 1970s.

In February 1966, Hoxha's regime, imitating the Chinese Cultural Revolution, introduced a policy of extreme egalitarianism both in the payment of wages and in the organization of workplaces. In the following year, it incited a violent campaign to transform Albania into what was announced as the world's first atheist state. In the 1970s, a campaign of purges within the leadership of the Communist Party was initiated. By December 1981 – when one of Hoxha's longest-serving aides, the Prime Minister Mehmet Shehu, died in suspicious circumstances after being accused of spying for the West ever since the 1940s – more than four fifths of the Politburo membership of 1970 had been eliminated. Meanwhile, in line with its extreme isolation from neighboring countries and the rest of the world, the regime introduced an autarkic economic program that ended in abject failure. In particular, forced collectivization simply served to bring about the further impoverishment · of the rural areas of the country. By 1986, the Albanian economy was in deep crisis, and what had been a low but positive rate of growth had been superseded by contraction. A number of factors combined to cause this disaster, which effectively annihilated whatever past positive achievements could be credited to the regime: most notably, the unrelenting reign of terror, the tremendous pressure on resources from the quadrupling of the population in just 40 years, the long-term stagnation of the economy, the regime's fundamental lack of any social or political legitimacy, the intensifying ideological madness of Hoxha and his circle, and the

regime's total inability even to consider, let alone introduce, any of the measures that were necessary to improve the situation.

During the late 1970s and the 1980s, Hoxha's regime relied mainly on the secret police, the Sigurimi, to secure its hold over the population. Their activities placed a tremendous burden on Albanian society, which traditionally was based on the extended family, on the ideas of honor and loyalty to relatives, and on the cultivation of close family ties. On the one hand, the rapid urbanization that had followed in the wake of industrialization, the influence of rising levels of education, and the new social relations imposed from above by the regime, were already creating formidable pressures that the traditional society found it increasingly difficult to resist. On the other hand, the police system, which was a far more oppressive regime even than the postwar Soviet system, rapidly came to place a high priority on the deliberate destruction of the traditional family networks. The regime sought to inculcate loyalty to the Communist Party and its leader in the minds of the people, yet these constituted a very poor substitute for the still powerful traditional sources of legitimacy based on family ties. The replacement of family by "class" – defined by Hoxha – as the favored locus of loyalty had the terrible effect of dividing Albanian society into two hostile ideological groupings, whose interests were mutually irreconcilable by definition. The regime sought to draw its legitimacy from this division, which played off Albanians, even members of the same family, against each other. The effects of this policy would be understood in their entirety only after the democratic transition started in Albania, in 1990.

When the processes of transformation began in the Soviet Union in the late 1980s, the Albanian ruling elite discovered that Albania could not stay the course that had been designed for it by Enver Hoxha, who had died in 1985. Nevertheless, the close hold on power retained by Hoxha's family, along with the powerful clan of Hysni Kapo, remained unchallenged until June and July 1990. Protests against the regime during those months culminated in 6,000 protesters seeking refuge from the police in foreign embassies in Tirana, attracting the attention of the world and severely embarrassing those in the regime who were still capable of being embarrassed. Half-measures introduced after January 1990, aimed at improving economic and political conditions while leaving the Communist system unreformed, had too little impact and came much too late.

In October 1990, the defection to France of Ismail Kadare, a prominent writer, gave a clear signal that the regime was rapidly losing even the limited support it had enjoyed among the intelligentsia. On December 8, 1990, the students of the Enver Hoxha University in Tirana started mounting demonstrations to demand better living conditions, and their protests soon became the basis of a political upheaval. At a meeting with President Ramiz Alia, on December 11, 1990, the representatives of the student movement demanded the establishment of a multiparty political system. This was the one crucial reform, symbolized that month by the official recognition of the opposition Democratic Party, that broke the hold the Communist Party had exerted over the whole country for the previous 46 years.

## The Early Stages of the Transition, 1990–92

The Democratic Party, officially established on December 12, 1990, was led by a number of intellectuals who had begun that year to be active in public as dissidents. They included Salih Berisha, later President of Albania, Gramoz Pashko, and Aleksander Meksi, a future Prime Minister, as well as a strong representative group from the leadership of the university students' protest movement. The foundation of the Democratic Party was soon followed by the appearance of a large number of other opposition parties, notably the Republican Party, led by Sabri Godo, and the Social Democratic Party, led by Skender Gjinushi. It was also at this early stage that there was the beginning of the resurrection of the old monarchist and nationalist political formations that had ceased to exist after the Communists came to power.

In February 1991, university students in the capital, acting independently of any of these new parties, organized a well-prepared hunger strike that brought down the lingering cult of Enver Hoxha, initially by forcing the renaming of their institution as the University of Tirana, thus giving the death blow to the only remaining source of any legitimacy for the regime, and opening the door to the acceptance of Albania into the democratic family of nations. In the first democratic elections, held on March 31, 1991, the newly renamed Socialist Party, which was now trying to shake off its Communist past, won 169 seats in the People's Assembly (Kuvënd Popullóre), with 67.9% of the votes cast, while the Democratic Party won 70 seats (and 29.0% of the vote), the remainder being distributed among a number of minor parties. As might be expected, the turnout in the country's first free and fair elections since before World War II was extremely high: 98.92% of eligible voters participated.

Notwithstanding its victory, the Socialist Party, led by a young and inexperienced Prime Minister, Fatos Nano, was crippled by a series of widespread strikes and its ability to govern was proved to be almost nonexistent. Key sectors of the economy were completely paralyzed, there were serious shortages of many foodstuffs, and the country was in a condition of almost total anarchy. A "caretaker" government, mainly composed of technocrats, was formed by Ylli Bufi on June 4, 1991, but it lost its base in the legislature when the leadership of the Democratic Party, under vehement attack from the right-wing politicians among its own ranks, formally withdrew support from Bufi in December 1991. An agreement on the terms of cooperation among the parties was secretly brokered in Trieste, Italy, in late 1991. New elections were called for March 1992, while another technocrat, Vilson Ahmeti, served as Prime Minister until then.

## The Democratic Party in Power, 1992–97

The Democratic Party came out victorious in the elections held on March 22, 1992 (see Table 10.2). One of its founders, Aleksander Meksi, became Prime Minister, while another, Salih Berisha, was directly elected President, replacing the discredited former disciple of

Hoxha, Ramiz Alia. These changes coincided with one of the most difficult stages of the Albanian transition.

Crucially, the Trieste agreement referred to above was disregarded by all the various factions of the Albanian elites, as they fell to factional fighting not only between parties but also within them. The fragile consensus that had held the Democratic Party together during its first two years of existence broke down soon after it entered government, and a new splinter party, the Democratic Alliance, was formed by Gramoz Pashko, Preç Zogaj, Arben Imami, Arben Demeti, and others who had been leading figures but could no longer tolerate Berisha's autocratic style. (The Democratic Alliance is now one of the members of the governing coalition.) Similarly, the internal feuding among the powerful factions within the Socialist Party undermined the capacity of Ramiz Alia, who was still its leader, to influence its direction, still less that of the country. As a result, the Socialist Party, which attracted a varied range of supporters among the overwhelming majority of the people who had any experience of government or any technical skills, was completely frozen out of any influence on policy, and consequently assumed a highly combative and obstructive attitude to whatever the new government proposed.

On the other hand, President Berisha tried to preserve the populist coalition that had brought him to power by distributing official posts according to the degree of loyalty that individuals had demonstrated to Berisha himself as well as according to his assessment of their past record. In a sense, Berisha reversed the "class struggle" that had been waged so savagely by the Communists, but this time around it was the former Communists who became the targets of exclusion and what they saw as persecution. By concentrating all the power in his hands, rather than accepting a division of responsibilities among the presidency, the government, and the legislature, Berisha effectively undermined Albania's chances of being able, at long last, to build a state based on the rule of law and an effective bureaucracy.

In the economic sphere, Berisha and the Democratic Party set about removing all restraints on the freedom of the growing stratum of entrepreneurs, and seized every opportunity to proclaim that Albania's future lay in becoming a virtually tax-free haven for free enterprise. They failed – or, as their opponents claimed, refused – to acknowledge that there could be any connection between the development of an enduringly successful economy and the maintenance of reliable systems of education, health care, and infrastructure. The determination of Berisha, Meksi, and their colleagues to push through some radical economic reforms was, if anything, enhanced by their initial success. Faced with an economy that had more or less ground to a halt, the government managed to stabilize inflation, and encouraged the growth of small and medium-sized enterprises. However, its economic program was slowed down, on the one hand by its inability to channel the remittances from emigrants on which so many Albanians depended, and on the other by its unwillingness to exploit domestic resources efficiently rather than relying, as they preferred to do, on foreign credits and aid. One major defeat was inflicted on Berisha by the voters in a referendum held in November 1994, when they overwhelmingly rejected his plans to overhaul the Constitution and transform the country's fledgling parliamentary democracy into a presidential republic.

In the elections to the People's Assembly held on May 26, 1996, the Democratic Party won a landslide victory, but it very quickly became clear that the election process had been deeply flawed by government interference. The electoral law had been changed, gerrymandering had become the norm, and the leading opponents of the government had been excluded from running in the elections under a special law approved by the People's Assembly a few months earlier. The Democratic Party's activists used every possible means at their disposal to make sure that their party would win the elections. In response, all the opposition parties withdrew from cooperation with the government and refused to take part in the restaging of the elections in June, which predictably resulted in another victory for the Democratic Party. Meanwhile, many opponents of President Berisha's regime had been savagely beaten by police a few days after the May elections, and as they found increasing support in the West Berisha lost the approval of US and EU leaders, and influential international agencies, that he had enjoyed in the past.

The summer of 1996 was characterized by the explosion of pyramid (or Ponzi) schemes, which promised to make people incredibly rich incredibly quickly, as well as by heated political conflict, not only about domestic issues but also over the role that Albania should or could play in relation to Yugoslavia's increasing repression of the ethnic Albanian majority in the province of Kosovo. By the end of 1997, most of country's savings had been deposited in pyramid schemes, many of which were controlled by people with dubious past associations, either with the Communist regime, or with organized crime, or in some cases both. President Berisha's increasingly embattled government continued to support the schemes nevertheless. Sude became the first of the schemes to collapse, in September 1996, but the true scale of the disaster did not become clear until January 1997, when Gjallica, one of the largest of the schemes, declared bankruptcy, and rioting erupted in Vlora, the town where most of its victims lived. Berisha rashly promised to return all the money that the depositors had lost, only to find that he was legally and financially unable to do so. Other pyramid schemes failed in rapid succession and the situation got out of control. The state apparatus crumbled, army officers joined the rioters in towns and cities all over the country, arms depots were looted, and it seemed that Albania was disintegrating.

However, on March 9, 1997, an agreement signed by the Democratic Party and the opposition parties made it possible to form a "government of national unity," headed by Bashkim Fino. The agreement also provided for the holding of elections on June 30, 1997, and for the granting of an amnesty for political prisoners, including most notably Fatos Nano, the former Prime Minister who was now leader of the Socialist Party. The elections duly took place, in an extremely tense atmosphere (see Table 10.3). The climate of violence

surrounding them meant that they came nowhere near the recognized democratic standards for a "free and fair" voting process; nevertheless, they must be considered as a very important step towards the stabilization and normalization of political life in the country. In particular, it is striking that none of the explicitly nationalist Albanian ethnic parties managed to get more than 1% of the popular vote. This suggests that most Albanian voters now accept that the solution of their pressing domestic problems has priority over addressing the issue of ethnic Albanians living in the former Yugoslav republics. It is also noteworthy that, in a referendum held on the same day as the elections to decide whether Albania would remain a republic or become a kingdom under Zog I's son, Lek, 66.74% of those voting favored the continuation of the republic.

After the elections, the Socialist Party returned to power, but, crucially, was unable to form a government by itself. Fatos Nano was appointed Prime Minister once again, but at the head of a coalition government that included not only representatives of his own party, but also leading politicians from the Democratic Alliance, the Human Rights Union, the Social Democratic Party, and the Agrarian Party. President Berisha promptly resigned from office, and the transition from rule by the Democratic Party to the new coalition government appeared to be orderly. Prime Minister Nano began his second term in office by announcing an ambitious program of political and economic reforms that theoretically made sense, but were unrealizable in practical terms, given the depths of the economic and financial crisis facing the country. Law and order began to be restored, notably in and around Tirana, the security situation improved generally throughout the country, and the economy began to stabilize. Soon, however, the political conflict that had culminated in the elections but had not been ended by them was exacerbated. In particular, Berisha and his supporters embarked on a series of public meetings, hunger strikes, and provocative rallies that proved to be highly disruptive. Meanwhile, the ruling coalition began a thorough campaign of replacing officials appointed by Berisha with either nonparty professionals or people who were loyal to the Socialist Party and its coalition partners.

On February 22, 1998, Berisha's followers attempted to take over the town of Shkodra, but were defeated within one day. In September, another riot exploded when Azem Hajdari, one of the leaders of the student movement of 1990 who had become a prominent aide to Berisha, was killed by unknown gunmen. On September 14, angry supporters of Berisha took over government buildings, the television stations, and other institutions in Tirana. Their revolt was suppressed with relative ease by the police and the military, but Prime Minister Nano took responsibility for the events and resigned, to be replaced by Pandeli Majko.

In addition to these domestic sources of instability, the emergence of the Kosovo Liberation Army and the intensification of the violent conflict in Kosovo, where ethnic Albanians were fighting against the Serbian regime, brought about a situation in which the government of Albania found itself drawn against its will into an international crisis, which has deeply affected and conditioned all its activities, and yet has remained wholly outside its control. By March 1999, when the Serbian regime began accelerating its repression of Kosovo and NATO launched air strikes on Yugoslavia, Albania's political and economic situation was perhaps even more hazardous than at any time since the start of the transition away from Communism. The arrival of hundreds of thousands of individuals driven out of Kosovo has put enormous pressure on the central government, which was already facing internal unrest, and on the economy, which continues to be in very bad shape following the disastrous collapse of the pyramid schemes under the previous government. Even with aid and support from NATO, the UN, and the EU, Albania is finding it very hard to handle the problems created by this massive displacement of people. In such conditions of extreme humanitarian emergency, the government has had to postpone the reform measures with which it hopes to continue the transition process, in order to focus on the short term.

## Further Reading

Biberaj, Elez, *Albania: A Socialist Maverick*, Boulder, CO: Westview Press, 1990

A wide-ranging description of Albania under Communist rule

Biberaj, Elez, *Albania in Transition: the Rocky Road to Democracy*, Boulder, CO: Westview Press, 1998

A sequel to the previously cited book, taking the narrative and the analysis forward

Hall, Derek, *Albania and the Albanians*, London and New York: Pinter, 1994

A comprehensive overview of the development of Albanian society

Hoxha, Enver, *The Artful Albanian: The Memoirs of Enver Hoxha*, edited by Jon Halliday, London: Chatto and Windus, 1986

This extraordinary book reveals a great deal about Hoxha's view of the country he dominated for more than 40 years.

Pano, Nicholas C., "The Process of Democratization in Albania," in Karen Dawisha and Bruce Parrot, editors, *Politics, Power and the Struggle for Democracy in South-East Europe*, Cambridge and New York: Cambridge University Press, 1997

Rama, Shinasi A., "Transition, Elite Fragmentation, and the Parliamentary Elections of June 29, 1997," in *The International Journal of Albanian Studies*, Volume 1, number 1, Fall 1997

Vickers, Miranda, and James Pettifer, *Albania: From Anarchy to a Balkan Identity*, London: Hurst, and New York: New York University Press, 1997

A readable journalistic account of the tumultuous political and social events surrounding the collapse of Communism in Albania

Winnifrith, Tom, editor, *Perspectives on Albania*, London: Macmillan, and New York: St Martin's Press, 1992

A collection of essays on various aspects of the country, addressing both the Communist period and what went before it

*Shinasi A. Rama* is a doctoral candidate in the Department of Political Science at Columbia University, New York, and Editor in Chief of the *International Journal of Albanian Studies*.

**Table 10.1   Basic Statistics on Albania, 1995 and 1998**

*The Population, 1995*

| | |
|---|---|
| Estimated total population | 3,413,904 |
| Estimated rate of population growth (%) | 1.16 |
| Average life expectancy at birth (years) | |
|     Females | 76 |
|     Males | 70 |

*The Economy, 1998*

| | |
|---|---|
| Estimated GDP (US$ billions) | 2.88 |
| Estimated rate of GDP growth (%) | 10 |
| Estimated value of trade | |
|     Exports (US$ billions) | 0.34 |
|     Imports (US$ billions) | 1.06 |

Sources: *The World Factbook 1998*, Washington, DC: Central Intelligence Agency, 1998, and official publications of the Albanian Government

**Table 10.2   Results of Elections for the People's Assembly of Albania, March 22, 1992**

| | Votes cast | Proportion of votes cast (%) | Seats won | Proportion of seats won (%) |
|---|---|---|---|---|
| Democratic Party | 1,046,193 | 62.08 | 92 | 65.71 |
| Socialist Party | 433,602 | 25.70 | 38 | 27.41 |
| Social Democratic Party | 73,820 | 4.30 | 7 | 5.00 |
| Union for Human Rights | 48,923 | 2.90 | 2 | 1.43 |
| Republican Party | 52,477 | 3.11 | 1 | 0.71 |
| Other parties | 30,022 | 1.80 | 0 | 0.00 |
| | | | | |
| Totals | 1,685,037 | | 140 | |
| Turnout of voters (%) | | | | 90.35 |

Source: *Fletorja Zyrtare e Republikës së Shqipërisë*, number 2, May 1992

| Table 10.3 | Results of Elections for the People's Assembly of Albania, June 29 and July 6, 1997 | | |
|---|---|---|---|
| | *Seats won in direct voting for localities* | *Seats allocated by the national proportional system* | *Total seats* |
| Socialist Party | 79 | 22 | 101 |
| Democratic Party | 16 | 11 | 27 |
| Social Democratic Party | 7 | 1 | 8 |
| Human Rights Union | 3 | 1 | 4 |
| National Front (Balli Kombëtar) | 0 | 1 | 1 |
| Movement of Legality Party (Monarchists) | 0 | 2 | 2 |
| Republican Party | 1 | 1 | 2 |
| Unity of the Right | 2 | 0 | 2 |
| Democratic Alliance | 1 | 1 | 2 |
| Christian Democrats | 1 | 0 | 1 |
| National Unity Party | 1 | 0 | 1 |
| Agrarian Party | 1 | 0 | 1 |
| Independents | 3 | 0 | 3 |
| Totals | 115 | 40 | 155 |

Sources: "The Parliamentary Election Results," *ATA*, July 10, 1997; OSCE, "Albania's Parliamentary Elections of 1997," Washington, DC: Commission on Security and Cooperation in Europe, 1997; *The World Factbook 1998*, Washington, DC: Central Intelligence Agency, 1998

# Economic
# and
# Social Issues

Chapter Eleven

# Sources and Uses of Energy

## *Tamás Novák*

In all the countries of central and eastern Europe, producers and consumers of energy are still feeling the effects of the low prices, inadequate policies, and obsolete technologies imposed during the Communist period. These effects are perhaps especially severe in Estonia, Latvia, and Lithuania, with their experience of Soviet occupation. However, all the governments of the region followed very energy-intensive economic policies throughout the period, and it is still difficult to extricate their economies from the consequences. The main emphasis was placed on developing heavy manufacturing industries, and in most cases the energy for these industries was imported at favorable prices from the Soviet Union. Apart from making several countries in the region lastingly dependent on Russia, the Soviet Union's main successor state, for much of their energy supply, this policy had three results that increased energy intensity. First, the share of manufacturing in GDP became, and has generally remained, significantly higher than in most western countries, and manufacturing tends to consume more energy for each unit of output than other components of GDP (agriculture, extraction industries, or services). Second, most of these countries still have relatively high concentrations of manufacturing industries that are even more energy-intensive than manufacturing in general, such as the organic and inorganic chemical industries. Third, the technology used in manufacturing was generally much less energy-efficient than the technology now used in western countries, and the region is still facing difficulties in attempting to catch up with best practice in energy conservation.

Against this background, it is not surprising that the energy intensity of these countries – energy consumption as a proportion of GDP – is still much higher than in the EU, the region that central and eastern Europe is most appropriately compared with, and that most of the countries under discussion aspire to join. More specifically, electricity remains the energy form most heavily relied upon for both industrial applications and household heating, and it is still generally obtained from Soviet-designed power plants. Most of these plants cannot meet international standards for safety, environmental protection, and efficiency, and their installation has resulted in heavy dependence on fuel imports. Following the collapse of Communism in 1989–91, and a number of external shocks, this led to widespread energy shortages and unsustainably high import bills.

Overcoming the effects of the policies pursued under Communism will require continuing reform and growth, and energy supply is crucial to the whole process of economic restructuring. Every country in the region is already making some progress, at differing speeds, on liberalizing prices; restructuring and privatizing state-owned energy enterprises; adopting safer, more efficient and less polluting forms of energy; encouraging energy conservation; increasing and diversifying connections to international oil and natural gas pipelines, and electricity networks; and improving productivity in production and distribution. However, none of these reforms is a matter for the energy industries alone. For example, in every country in the region except Hungary, the prices charged to households for energy are still subsidized by the state to a greater or less extent, and do not fully cover costs, yet it is extremely difficult to eliminate such subsidies without causing significant social dislocation, with its attendant political consequences. To take another example, every country in the region is committed to improving the protection of the environment and to making attempts to clean up the areas ravaged by pollution in the past, yet the energy supplied or used by polluting plants must either be reduced, or be replaced from other sources, with important implications for the balance of trade, for energy efficiency, and for the restructuring of all the industries in question. In short, any realistic analysis of energy supply in central and eastern Europe must take account of the political and social circumstances in which the energy industries operate.

This task is not made any easier by the inadequacy or unavailability of accurate and complete information in some of these countries: hence the absence from this chapter of sections on Albania, Bosnia-Herzegovina, Macedonia, and Yugoslavia. The principal features of the energy balances of the remaining countries in the region are indicated in the tables that follow this chapter.

## Poland

Poland's energy supply is dominated by coal, wood, and other domestic solid fuels, which represent around 75% of the energy balance; oil supplies only 15% of energy demand. Poland is the world's seventh largest producer of hard coal, producing a quantity equivalent to the total output of the 15 EU states, and the production of lignite (brown coal), concentrated in central Poland, remains economically viable. Poland does not use nuclear power for the production of electricity. Energy efficiency is much lower than the EU average, and the polluting operations of the mining industry and oil refineries have serious environmental consequences. The energy market is protected from outside competition by limitations on licensing.

The restructuring of the energy industries was long delayed, in contrast to other sectors of the Polish economy. An overall energy policy was not adopted until 1996. Its major objectives are to introduce more competition into the supply of energy, to ensure the security of energy supplies, and to protect the environment. Market mechanisms are to be introduced and fully implemented, provided that their use is justified on grounds of energy security and economic effectiveness. In areas where market mechanisms must be limited, energy activities will continue to be regulated by the state through specialized agencies. The competition framework is rapidly approximating to that required under EU directives, which Poland is committed to implement in full as part of its process of accession to the EU. Plans for demonopolization and privatization are now being prepared, notably for the electricity industry, where it appears that the new structures will be based on privatized distribution. The privatization process for oil refineries is already well-advanced, however, and prices for oil and oil products were liberalized in 1997.

The prices of other forms of energy supply have been rising in recent years. The setting of prices continues to be closely linked with the progress of restructuring in the coal industry, which is aimed at ensuring that domestic coal will play an important role in the future, but will not be as dominant as in the past. In 1998, the government announced its latest program for reform of the industry, covering the period 1998–2002. This envisages some closures of mines, with consequent redundancies among miners. If all goes well, there will be an overall increase in productivity of around 25%, the remaining mines will return to profitability, and the government will be able not only to eliminate the remaining state subsidies, but also to initiate a program of debt repayment. However, some questions remain unanswered. In particular, it is not clear how financing will be secured for the environmental measures that are needed to remedy the severe problems related to the use of solid fuels. These measures include a planned reduction in sulfur dioxide emissions to 700,000 tons a year by 2010; the introduction of facilities to deal with the waste water in mines; and the transfer of ash and other wastes from electric power stations to storage in disused mines and eventual recycling.

The natural gas industry is being promoted as an alternative to coal. New foreign sources of supply are being sought, while the development of domestic production will require the extraction of methane from the coal beds. Priority construction projects agreed by the government and the natural gas industry include underground storage facilities, in order to build up strategic reserves and provide for varying demand throughout the year; and the Polish section of the transit pipeline from Russia to western Europe, in cooperation with the Russian company Gazprom.

## Hungary

Domestic energy production from oil, natural gas, nuclear power, low-calorific coal, and lignite meets only around half of Hungary's energy requirements. The Paks nuclear power plant alone produces 40% of the country's electricity. However, domestic resources of all fuels are shrinking and are generally of low quality. The extraction of solid fuels has declined significantly during the 1990s, while the production of uranium ceased altogether in 1997. The remaining energy need is met from oil imports. Since domestic oil production has passed its peak, dependence on oil imports is likely to rise when energy consumption rises. Hungary depends on Russia for all of this imported oil, as well as for supplies of natural gas and uranium.

The energy policy of the Hungarian government has four main aims: developing diverse energy supplies, allowing the country to cease being dependent on imports from the CIS; improving environmental protection; enhancing energy efficiency, chiefly by modernizing supply structures and rationalizing electricity consumption; and attracting foreign capital for investment in capital-intensive energy projects. The policy also provides for the gradual contraction of the coal industry by merging mines that supply coal to electricity companies.

Most of the elements in the competition framework that Hungary is required to introduce, as a prospective member of the EU, have already been put in place. Prices have been increasing and generally cover costs, while privatization, covering both production and distribution, has been extensive. The privatization

of electricity generation and distribution is practically complete, but details of proposed sales are still under discussion in respect of MVM Rt, which plays a dominant role in both parts of the electricity industry; the Paks nuclear power plant, which is owned by MVM Rt; and the National Grid Company.

The issues of energy efficiency and environmental protection are being addressed by the Energy Environmental Center, established in October 1997, which has begun preparations to set up regional energy centers. Some significant issues remain to be addressed, however, including the adjustment of monopolies, access to networks, energy pricing, and state intervention in the solid fuels industries.

## The Baltic States

Given their geographic location, and their history as subject territories of the Russian empire and, later, of the Soviet Union, it is not surprising that the three Baltic states are still closely bound up with Russia in energy supply as in other areas. All three countries remain linked to the Russian electricity system, and all three still largely depend on Russia for imports of oil, natural gas, and coal, equivalent to 35% of domestic demand in Estonia, 60% in Lithuania, and nearly 75% in Latvia, although Latvia also imports electricity from the other two Baltic states. Latvia and Lithuania are also strategic transit countries for Russia, the former in respect of its exports of natural gas and oil to western Europe, the latter in respect of its supplies to the Kaliningrad region, which has been governed by Russia since 1945 but is separated from it by Lithuanian territory.

In these circumstances, all three states continue to give priority to energy cooperation, not only among themselves, but also with other states that have shores on the Baltic Sea – including Russia – and with the EU. This cooperation has included the establishment of Baltrel, an association of electricity companies in the states around the Baltic, in preparation for eventual connection to the Nordic and EU electricity grids. In the longer term, a Baltic electricity ring could contribute to enhancing growth and efficiency throughout northwestern Europe.

## Estonia

Estonia's energy industries, particularly its production of electricity, are dominated by the use of indigenous oil shale, which represents 99% of domestic supplies of electricity and meets 60% of domestic demand. The mining and burning of oil shale are inefficient, and the high levels of pollutants emitted present considerable environmental problems. Reducing dependence on oil shale will involve a major restructuring program and present a major challenge in the making of appropriate regional and sectoral policies. Meanwhile, alternative sources of energy are being sought. The exploitation of domestic peat, wood, and wind is increasing, and now accounts for 5% of the country's energy balance. Nuclear power is not generated in Estonia.

The inefficiency of energy supply in Estonia is indicated by the fact that the country's energy intensity (energy as a percentage of GDP) is two to four times higher than in EU countries. The district heating systems in Estonia's urban areas were designed and built during the period of Soviet occupation, when conditions of energy supply differed greatly from the situation prevailing today. However, there has recently been some development toward the wider use of alternative energy resources in local heating schemes, and towards the use of combined heat and power plants, which optimize the use of fuel, and also keep investment costs and running costs low. Natural gas is also more widely used today.

Estonia has adopted a long-term national development plan for fuel and energy, which is to be revised every second year. It provides specific targets and forecasts up to 2005 and general guidelines up to 2018. Under this plan, a new Energy Law entered into force on January 1, 1998. It covers fuel networks and deals with issues such as the liberalization of energy markets and the distribution of electricity and natural gas. Apart from trade in oil and coal, the energy industries in Estonia are generally still dominated by state-owned monopolies. Privatization of some large energy companies has begun, however, and energy prices have been considerably increased.

## Latvia

Latvia's high level of dependence on energy imports (see above) accounts for a large component of the country's foreign trade deficit. Domestic resources such as water, peat and woodchip are being used, but they represent only 20% of the country's energy balance. Overall energy efficiency is two to three times lower than the EU average.

A law providing for a "super regulator," covering energy, telecommunications, and other utilities, was enacted in 1998, but its establishment will take some time. In 1999, the Latvian government announced a new comprehensive program for energy, covering the period up to 2020. The program focuses on restructuring according to market principles, energy security and efficiency, environmental protection, and cooperation with the EU and with other states on the Baltic Sea. The largest energy companies, with a few exceptions, are state-owned monopolies, but preparations have begun for further privatizations. The prices of imported oil, natural gas, and coal have been liberalized; electricity prices are gradually rising closer to a level that will allow full recovery of costs; and a more flexible system of charges to industrial users of natural gas was introduced in 1998.

## Lithuania

Lithuania has only limited indigenous energy resources. Its two nuclear reactors, which produce 85% of its electricity and export electricity to neighboring countries, depend on nuclear fuel imported in manufactured form from Russia, partly in exchange for the electricity exported to Russia. Attempts to diversify sources of nuclear fuel supplies have not been successful to date. The Ignalina plant, the single largest source of energy in Lithuania, is to be kept open to the limit of its planned lifetime, but safety measures are to be improved. No plans have yet been made for prolonging the operation of the two reactors or for replacing the energy that they produce. The country also has excess capacity in electricity generation and oil refining, which should allow its export earnings to increase. Energy supply is at least three times less efficient than the EU average.

The energy industries are still dominated by state-owned monopolies. Oil exploration and production licenses have been issued to foreign companies, which are also active in retailing oil products and importing natural gas. The implementation of price liberalization and decentralization has enhanced the prospects for the restructuring of energy supply.

## The Czech Republic

The energy situation in the Czech Republic is dominated by domestic solid fuels, which amounted to 60% of the energy balance as of 1996. The country is dependent on external sources, particularly Russia, for its supplies of oil and natural gas. Energy use is two to three times less efficient than the EU average.

Several mines have been closed in the 1990s, resulting in a decrease in output of hard coal from more than 22 million tons in 1990 to less than 15 million tons in 1997. Lignite production has suffered an even greater decline. The labor force in the mining industry has been reduced by around 60%, to a total of around 75,000. However, the changes have not yet come to an end. According to the latest draft version of the Czech energy policy, the government intends to focus on harmonizing standards in the Czech energy industries with those prevailing in the EU, as part of its drive toward eventual EU membership. Accordingly, dependence on coal, wood, and other solid fuels as primary energy sources is to be reduced to around 50% by 2000 and to 40% by 2005. Coal will also gradually be replaced as a source of household heating, or will be increasingly used to generate electricity in combination with other fuels. Spending on the restructuring of the mining industry, which is to continue beyond 2000, is running at around CzK3 billion a year, most of which is spent on measures to address the social impact of the changes.

The Czech Republic's Energy Regulatory Administration, established in 1998, is to be transformed into an independent regulator. Privatization has started in some areas of energy supply, but the state retains ownership of the major monopolies and has a dominant position in the production and distribution of electricity, in uranium production, and in the transportation of oil and natural gas through pipelines. There have been substantial increases in charges for natural gas and electricity, and the cost level of prices is expected to be reached by 2000. Improvements are also planned in legislation, business conditions, and statistical and reporting standards, again as part of the process of preparation for EU membership.

## Slovakia

Slovakia is extremely dependent on external energy resources. It imports around 89% of its needs, particularly in the form of supplies from Russia. These account for 99% of its oil, 95% of its natural gas, and all of its nuclear fuel elements, although uranium is entirely imported from the Czech Republic. The only important domestic fossil fuel is coal, but Slovakia's coal industry is heavily dependent on state subsidies, and its brown coal is of decreasing quality. This has severe consequences for the environment, since the increasing amounts of sulfur in the brown coal cause extremely high emissions of sulfur dioxide, nitrous oxide, and carbon dioxide. Nevertheless, the intention is to continue mining brown coal at current production levels until 2005, if not later. Black coal is being imported, mostly from the Czech Republic, but there are few other available alternatives. Slovakia has water resources with a technical energy potential of 7,361 gigawatt hours, but substantial improvements in water quality are required, as around 75% of all the river water in the country is considered to be extremely polluted.

The main goals of Slovak energy policy were laid down in an energy strategy covering the period up to 2005, which was approved by the government in 1993. This strategy does not include a clear policy line on energy pricing, or make any reference to the prospect of changes in the present system, which, as elsewhere in the region, is not related to cost and depends on cross-subsidies. The Energy Law, which entered into force in July 1998, was an important step toward harmonizing Slovak policy with EU directives, but important decisions on opening the energy markets have been postponed. Hence, the electricity and natural gas monopolies, the transportation of crude oil, and parts of the lignite industry are still owned and protected by the state, and the majority of Slovakia's energy output is controlled, directly or indirectly, through the state-owned National Property Fund. The government aims to maintain controlling interests in these companies, at least in the medium term. The electricity industry is organized as one production company, which owns the high-voltage transmission grid, and controls electricity imports and trade, and three regional distribution companies, which are protected from competition by being allocated monopolies in designated geographic areas. They buy most of their supplies from producers under long-term contracts. Nevertheless, a measure of liberalization and privatization has begun in relation to oil and coal.

Slovakia is a strategic transit country for Russian exports of natural gas to other countries in central and eastern Europe, as well as to the EU. Transit and storage capacities are being enlarged, and a new pipeline is being laid.

## Bulgaria

Bulgaria is around 70% dependent on external energy resources. Oil, natural gas, and nuclear fuels are mainly imported from Russia. Domestic sources of solid fuels, especially low-quality lignite, are extracted in an inefficient and uneconomical way, and mining is an important source of environment pollution. The only nuclear plant in Bulgaria, at Kozloduy, produces around 40% of the country's electricity, and has been extensively modernized since 1990. Bulgaria has no facilities for enriching uranium or making nuclear fuels, and must continue to depend on Russia for these resources as it once depended on the Soviet Union. As is the case with nuclear power plants around the world, there are concerns over the safety of the Kozloduy plant, and the problem of how to dispose of its radioactive waste has become increasingly urgent. Hydroelectricity plays no significant role in Bulgaria, and the mining of uranium ceased

in 1990. The energy sector accounts for 12–13% of GDP.

The initial response of Bulgarian governments to the energy crisis that followed the collapse of Communism was to implement a partial liberalization of petroleum fuel prices, along with sharp increases in the prices of other energy items. They also began preparing a "least cost" program for restructuring the energy industries, as well as a number of studies on the rehabilitation of the electricity system and improvements in its safety record. Much of the work recommended by these studies has now been carried out.

The most important companies in energy production, transmission and distribution are state-owned, vertically integrated monopolies, although the government has announced that it intends to privatize the energy industries. Energy prices have again been increased, and the government has adopted a strategy for the development of energy supplies up to 2010, based on a projection of continuous growth in energy production.

Bulgaria is an important transit country for gas supplies. The regional role played by Bulgaria may become even more important in the future as oil imports through the port city of Burgas increase, and also if imports of natural gas from Central Asia and Iran get under way.

## Romania

In 1990, the Romanian energy industries were reorganized by establishing two types of autonomous state-owned enterprises: holding companies for activities that the government regarded as strategic, including the production and supply of electricity, oil, natural gas, lignite, and coal; and commercial companies, with joint stock structures, for support services and activities. This enabled the government to separate policy-making and regulation, which are now the responsibility of the Ministry for Industries, from operational functions; to clarify issues of accountability; and to introduce commercial practices. In 1997, the restructuring of the coal industry was begun, based on a planned halving of the labor force as a result of mine closures. The severance payments being offered are relatively generous, but the plans have aroused considerable opposition from the miners' union, led by Miron Cozma, which has frequently clashed with successive governments over economic reforms. Substantial investments will be required to complete the closure of unprofitable mines and to mitigate the social and economic impact on the Jiu Valley and other regions. In July 1998, the government took some further important steps in the reform of energy supply by restructuring two of the holding companies established in 1990. The electricity holding company Renel was split into two national companies and one holding company, which produces heavy water for nuclear power plants and undertakes research, while the natural gas utility Romgaz was reorganized but remained intact. Some oil refineries have already been privatized, and parts of the electricity industry are to be privatized and opened up to competition following the restructuring of Renel. The framework has been put in place for the establishment of privately owned power plants.

In line with its restructuring plans, the government has started to raise energy prices and to phase out the cross-subsidies that have favored households since the Communist period. This process is due to be completed by the end of 1999. A new regulatory authority for the energy industries, independent of the Ministry for Industries, has also been established. A strategy for energy efficiency, approved in 1997, envisages the use of financial incentives to promote a reduction in energy intensity by 22% by 2005.

## Croatia

Croatia imports 36% of the energy it consumes. Total consumption remains significantly below the levels seen in 1990 and 1991, although there has been a rising trend since 1993, with increases of 2–3% every year. Since domestic energy production can be expected to remain steady, Croatia's dependence on imported energy could increase to 60% by 2010. Energy consumption per capita is very low in comparison to other European countries. Only Portugal consumes less, while Greece consumes 32% more and Luxembourg six times as much. Energy is used relatively inefficiently in Croatia. Its energy intensity is around 40% worse than in western Europe, although it is better than in most other countries in central and eastern Europe.

The use of natural gas to generate electricity is expected to increase. However, while the northern and northeastern regions of the country are well-supplied, there are no gas mains in the western and southern regions, where bottled propane and butane are supplied to a limited extent. Another potentially important route to improved supply is offered by various schemes for combined heat and power generation, which achieves better energy efficiency and hence saves fuel. It is also expected that several small hydroelectric power plants will be constructed, and the use of solar energy would be particularly practical along the coast of Dalmatia and on the islands nearby. There are confirmed geothermal gradients in the Northeast that are greater than the European average and in some places they could prove to be sufficient for cost-effective generation of electricity.

## Slovenia

Slovenia's energy supplies comprise conventional thermal sources (43%), hydroelectricity (31%), and nuclear power (26%). Energy efficiency is about half the EU average. The country's main indigenous resources are lignite, which causes serious environmental pollution, and low-quality sub-bituminous coal. Mining is expected to continue in the future, for strategic reasons, but production has already decreased sharply over the past few years. It now provides 20% of Slovenia's energy balance. Use is also made of domestic resources of hydroelectricity, biomass, and uranium, although extraction ceased in 1990 and decommissioning is being undertaken. Nuclear power is still being provided by a plant at Krsko, which is jointly operated with Croatia: it supplies 20% of Slovenia's electricity needs, while half of its output is taken by Croatia. Nevertheless, the country has to rely on imports for more than 70% of its energy requirements, particularly oil and natural gas.

Fortunately, this dependence on external sources is manageable, given that their geographic origins are diversified and there are reliable network connections. Oil and natural gas are imported from Russia but also from other sources. The oil industry is dominated by two large companies in which the state retains majority ownership, and competition has not yet developed. Demand for vehicle fuel has surged in recent years, mainly because of the continuing growth in incomes, but also because Slovenia's relatively low taxes on vehicle fuel have brought about an increase in crossborder purchases by drivers from Austria, Italy, and Croatia.

Energy supply is the responsibility of the Ministry of Economic Affairs and two autonomous agencies attached to it, the Agency for Efficient Use of Energy, and the Inspectorate for Energy, Mining, and Construction. The government's strategy for energy use and supply, adopted in 1996 is notable for its focus on disengaging and decommissioning nuclear power production, increasing the use of natural gas and renewable energy, and maintaining the rate of use of domestic coal. The government has reorganized the coal industry and plans to reduce the capacity of those mines that are still unprofitable. It also aims to increase energy prices by 7% each year (in real terms), so that they will be around 80% of average EU prices by 2000. The energy companies are generally state-owned monopolies, but there are some small independent power producers. Slovenia, one of the countries on the "fast track" to eventual EU membership, has made considerable progress on overhauling laws and regulations on energy and the environment.

## Further Reading

Antalóczy, Katalin, *Az Energiaárak és a Gazdasági Fejlödés Összefüggései* [Energy Prices and Economic Development], Budapest: AXON.EC, 1995

The author argues that changing conditions for enterprises make the economic transformation even more difficult, and that well-targeted reforms of energy prices may help enterprises to adjust.

EBRD, *Transition Report*, London: EBRD, annual publication

This extremely useful and informative publication, which appears every October or November, combines authoritative analyses of the post-Communist economies with comprehensive statistics and forecasts. A general *Update* is published every April, and there are also annual *Country Profiles* on each economy.

European Commission, *Agenda 2000: Commission Opinions on Applications for Membership of the EU*, Brussels: European Commission, 1998

These are official assessments by the EU's executive body of the extent to which Bulgaria, the Czech Republic, Estonia, Hungary, Latvia, Lithuania, Poland, Romania, Slovakia, and Slovenia have adapted their economies, and their systems of economic management, to meet the requirements of membership.

Gros, Daniel, *Energy Price Reform in Russia*, London: Center for Economic Policy Studies, 1996

This working paper analyzes the problems of reforming energy price systems in post-Communist countries.

International Energy Agency, *Energy Statistics and Balances of Non-OECD Countries*, 1995–1996, Paris: OECD, 1998

This statistical publication covers all aspects of energy-related issues in non-OECD countries.

Kiss, Károly, and Ferenc Glatz, *Termelés, Piac, Természeti Környezet* [Production, Market, Environment], Budapest: Hungarian Academy of Sciences, 1998

This stimulating study argues that production, markets, and the environment are closely connected with each other, and that the environment in particular must be taken into consideration when formulating the future direction of economic development.

Vértes, András, *A Kapitalizmus Alapjainak a Lerakása Magyarországon, 1990–2002* [Laying the Foundations for Capitalism in Hungary, 1990–2002], Budapest: Economic Research Institute, 1998

This publication combines a study of the reshaping of the whole economic structure up to 1998 with an analysis of the measures still to be taken, notably the elimination of subsidies and other market-distorting mechanisms.

---

*Dr Tamás Novák* is a Research Fellow at the Institute for World Economics of the Hungarian Academy of Sciences in Budapest.

**Table 11.1 Imports of Hard Coal into 11 Countries in Central and Eastern Europe, 1990–96 (thousands of metric tons)**

|                | 1990  | 1991  | 1992  | 1993  | 1994  | 1995  | 1996  |
|----------------|-------|-------|-------|-------|-------|-------|-------|
| Bulgaria       | 5,790 | 4,528 | 3,674 | 4,235 | 3,361 | 3,453 | 3,713 |
| Croatia        | –     | 583   | 759   | 633   | 377   | 106   | 106   |
| Czech Republic | 2,282 | 1,716 | 1,917 | 1,939 | 1,716 | 2,690 | 3,211 |
| Estonia        | 475   | 428   | 258   | 52    | 148   | 137   | 172   |
| Hungary        | 1,500 | 2,560 | 729   | 385   | 482   | 384   | 503   |
| Latvia         | 980   | 795   | 813   | 552   | 466   | 242   | 267   |
| Lithuania      | 1,584 | 1,457 | 919   | 304   | 514   | 259   | 414   |
| Poland         | 560   | 54    | 126   | 129   | 1,044 | 1,497 | 1,976 |
| Romania        | 4,981 | 2,971 | 5,786 | 2,666 | 4,035 | 4,705 | 4,005 |
| Slovakia       | 5,866 | 5,160 | 4,945 | 5,124 | 5,171 | 4,932 | 5,510 |
| Slovenia       | 23    | 15    | 14    | 21    | 23    | 20    | 22    |

Source:  International Energy Agency, *Energy Statistics and Balances of Non-OECD Countries, 1995–1996*, Paris: OECD, 1998

**Table 11.2 Production of Crude Oil by Eight Countries in Central and Eastern Europe, 1990–96 (millions of metric tons)**

|                | 1990 | 1991 | 1992 | 1993 | 1994 | 1995 | 1996 |
|----------------|------|------|------|------|------|------|------|
| Bulgaria       | 0.06 | 0.06 | 0.05 | 0.04 | 0.04 | 0.04 | 0.03 |
| Croatia        | 2.08 | 2.38 | 2.11 | 2.13 | 1.82 | 1.76 | 1.53 |
| Czech Republic | 0.05 | 0.07 | 0.18 | 0.15 | 0.26 | 0.28 | 0.25 |
| Hungary        | 2.30 | 2.21 | 2.15 | 2.04 | 1.96 | 2.30 | 2.12 |
| Lithuania      | –    | –    | 0.06 | 0.07 | 0.09 | 0.13 | 0.16 |
| Poland         | 0.18 | 0.17 | 0.22 | 0.26 | 0.33 | 0.37 | 0.39 |
| Romania        | 7.93 | 6.79 | 6.83 | 6.93 | 6.97 | 7.04 | 6.97 |
| Slovakia       | 0.08 | 0.12 | 0.09 | 0.07 | 0.07 | 0.08 | 0.07 |

Source:  International Energy Agency, *Energy Statistics and Balances of Non-OECD Countries, 1995–1996*, Paris: OECD, 1998

**Table 11.3  Imports of Crude Oil into Nine Countries in Central and Eastern Europe, 1990–96 (millions of metric tons)**

|                | 1990  | 1991  | 1992  | 1993  | 1994  | 1995  | 1996  |
|----------------|-------|-------|-------|-------|-------|-------|-------|
| Bulgaria       | 8.20  | 4.43  | 2.22  | 5.74  | 6.94  | 7.97  | 7.00  |
| Croatia        | –     | 2.90  | 2.73  | 3.66  | 3.80  | 4.21  | 3.42  |
| Czech Republic | 7.19  | 6.30  | 6.62  | 6.07  | 6.92  | 7.05  | 7.56  |
| Hungary        | 6.42  | 5.28  | 5.70  | 6.03  | 5.52  | 5.87  | 5.24  |
| Lithuania      | 9.51  | 11.72 | 4.07  | 5.16  | 3.59  | 3.18  | 3.74  |
| Poland         | 10.61 | 9.65  | 11.24 | 10.95 | 13.45 | 12.85 | 11.45 |
| Romania        | 16.06 | 8.40  | 6.57  | 7.58  | 8.12  | 8.66  | 7.16  |
| Slovakia       | 6.17  | 4.92  | 4.30  | 4.51  | 4.76  | 5.39  | 5.34  |
| Slovenia       | 0.54  | 0.53  | 0.50  | 0.48  | 0.34  | 0.50  | 0.46  |

Source:   International Energy Agency, *Energy Statistics and Balances of Non-OECD Countries, 1995–1996*, Paris: OECD, 1998


**Table 11.4  Exports of Electricity from 11 Countries in Central and Eastern Europe, 1990–96 (gigawatt hours)**

|                | 1990   | 1991   | 1992   | 1993  | 1994  | 1995  | 1996  |
|----------------|--------|--------|--------|-------|-------|-------|-------|
| Bulgaria       | 1,597  | 959    | 784    | 1,520 | 1,245 | 2,121 | 2,252 |
| Croatia        | 844    | 1,215  | 632    | 1,257 | 982   | 886   | 842   |
| Czech Republic | 8,871  | 9,724  | 9,192  | 8,056 | 5,860 | 6,304 | 8,814 |
| Estonia        | 8,477  | 6,993  | 3,492  | 1,596 | 1,506 | 1,005 | 1,100 |
| Hungary        | 2,152  | 1,059  | 1,521  | 1,619 | 920   | 805   | 1,276 |
| Latvia         | 3,555  | 2,829  | 3,396  | 170   | 830   | 391   | 211   |
| Lithuania      | 16,513 | 26,475 | 10,641 | 8,467 | 6,015 | 7,948 | 9,341 |
| Poland         | 11,478 | 9,326  | 9,066  | 8,011 | 7,242 | 7,157 | 7,925 |
| Romania        | –      | –      | 218    | 1,118 | 1,065 | 456   | 1,435 |
| Slovakia       | 2,059  | 1,723  | 2,527  | 1,896 | 2,379 | 2,065 | 698   |
| Slovenia       | 2,704  | 3,157  | 2,142  | 2,124 | 2,382 | 2,392 | 2,516 |

Source:   International Energy Agency, *Energy Statistics and Balances of Non-OECD Countries, 1995–1996*, Paris: OECD, 1998

## Table 11.5 Imports of Electricity into 11 Countries in Central and Eastern Europe, 1990–96 (gigawatt hours)

|  | *1990* | *1991* | *1992* | *1993* | *1994* | *1995* | *1996* |
|---|---|---|---|---|---|---|---|
| Bulgaria | 5,387 | 3,083 | 3,489 | 1,630 | 1,173 | 1,961 | 1,803 |
| Croatia | 7,543 | 6,068 | 3,419 | 3,583 | 4,547 | 4,382 | 3,371 |
| Czech Republic | 8,179 | 7,194 | 6,156 | 5,952 | 5,415 | 6,722 | 8,811 |
| Estonia | 1,475 | 2,222 | 254 | – | 315 | 245 | 240 |
| Hungary | 13,299 | 8,410 | 4,988 | 4,093 | 2,954 | 3,210 | 3,473 |
| Latvia | 7,138 | 7,054 | 7,473 | 2,672 | 2,648 | 2,647 | 3,438 |
| Lithuania | 4,539 | 3,725 | 5,338 | 5,736 | 7,159 | 5,270 | 4,182 |
| Poland | 10,437 | 6,708 | 5,034 | 5,600 | 4,563 | 4,356 | 4,801 |
| Romania | 9,476 | 7,047 | 4,421 | 2,991 | 1,790 | 755 | 2,242 |
| Slovakia | 7,255 | 6,061 | 5,995 | 4,009 | 2,817 | 3,448 | 4,220 |
| Slovenia | 1,716 | 1,138 | 329 | 706 | 448 | 740 | 855 |

Source: International Energy Agency, *Energy Statistics and Balances of Non-OECD Countries, 1995–1996*, Paris: OECD, 1998

Chapter Twelve

# Agriculture

## Andrew H. Dawson

The agricultural potential of central and eastern Europe is not being realized. Although the region includes extensive areas of fertile and easily cultivable land, some with a long growing season, the organization of farming, and of food-processing, militates against the effective use of much of their resources. Farming was subject to very considerable change after the establishment of Communist governments in the 1940s, and has found itself in turbulent circumstances again since the fall of those regimes in 1989. However, in many countries, such changes as have been made in the 1990s have not yet dealt adequately with some enduring weaknesses.

## Natural Resources

The countries of central and eastern Europe included in this book cover around 1,374,000 square kilometers (see Table 12.1). Around 60% of this area is in agricultural use, and a further 30% is forested. These are substantial resources in relation to the population of around 130 million, when compared with the EU, for example, but they are somewhat less per capita than those in Russia, Belarus, and Ukraine. Put another way, while there are only around 0.4 hectares of agricultural land per capita in the EU, there are around 0.6 hectares per capita in central and eastern Europe, and 1.3 hectares further to the East.

However, the quality of land in central and eastern Europe varies widely. That on the North European Plain (in the three Baltic states and Poland) and in the Danube basin (in Hungary, Serbia, Romania, and Bulgaria) is gently sloping, and thus is favorable to large-scale mechanized cultivation. In contrast, in the Carpathian Mountains and the uplands of the Balkans and Bohemia land is much steeper and more difficult of access. Much has remained under forest, some is used for pasture, and a little has been cultivated through the use of terraces, but arable plots are small. Albania, Bosnia-Herzegovina, and Croatia include much land of this type, and so do Bulgaria, the Czech Republic, Romania, and Slovakia. Agriculture in such areas is often confined to intermontane basins and valleys.

There is also a marked climatic contrast within the region. In the far North, along the Baltic coast, a short growing season restricts cultivation to hardy cereals, pasture crops, and roots, and obliges farmers to feed stock indoors during long winters, when the ground is frozen and there is often snow. Further South, in contrast, the growing season is longer, and summer temperatures are higher, permitting the growth of maize and fruits, including the vine. However, summer precipitation declines towards the South of the region, rendering the provision of pasture problematic, and placing a premium on irrigation.

Similarly, there is a wide variation in the quality of soil (see Figure 12.1). Some upland areas, especially in the Balkan peninsula, have suffered erosion over many years as a result of the clearance of forest, and are now useless for any except the most traditional and simple of pastoral enterprises, such as the herding of goats and sheep, and the keeping of bees. In lowland areas, on the other hand, fertility is closely related to the history of glaciation and subsequent melting of ice sheets. At its most extensive, the Scandinavian ice sheet covered the whole of what are now the three Baltic states, and northern and central Poland. Much of this area is covered by boulder clay, deposited directly from the ice. In the North of Poland and the Baltic states, from which ice disappeared only around 12,000 years ago, soils are often stony and heavy. They do not drain easily, and they warm up only slowly. Most difficult of all are those that have developed along the margins of the former ice sheets, where coarse sands and gravels were washed out of the ice. The resulting soils are thin, stony, acidic, and infertile. Many have never been cultivated. However, some of the older deposits of boulder clay, in central Poland, which were not covered by the last of the advances of the ice, offer better-quality soils.

The best soils are to be found in areas that escaped glaciation and, in particular, where loess was deposited. These include large parts of southern Poland, and the basin of the Danube and its tributaries, in Hungary, northern Serbia, southern and eastern Romania, and northern and central Bulgaria. They also include some smaller areas in Croatia and Slovakia, and some intermontane basins in the Czech Republic and Transylvania. During the Ice Age, small, airborne particles were deposited in some of these areas to a depth of several meters, creating a parent material that is stoneless and freely draining, and which warms up quickly in spring. As the postglacial climate improved, much of this land was rapidly afforested, although, in the Danube lowlands, with its more seasonal precipitation and frequent fires, a plagioclimax of steppe grass developed. Nevertheless, in all such areas, climate, vegetation, and parent material combined to create soils with high natural fertility and the potential for easy cultivation. Despite several centuries of use in some places, they remain among the best of the natural environments for agriculture in central and eastern Europe.

## Agricultural Policy and Farm Structure

The use of these natural resources has not been as effective as it might. The roots of this failure stretch back at least to the 19th century, being grounded in the region's political and economic history. However, they are also to be found in the more recent past, and in particular in the policies that were adopted by governments after World War II.

The chief difference between the Communist restructuring of agriculture in the Soviet Union and the equivalent process in central and eastern Europe was a matter of timing. By 1939, collectivization in the Soviet Union was largely complete, but agriculture in all the countries in this survey was in private hands. The structure of land ownership and farm enterprise varied considerably. For example, in East Prussia (then in Germany, now split between Russia and Poland), and in Pomerania (split between Germany and Poland), much land was in large, commercially oriented estates. In Lower Silesia (in Poland), and in Bohemia (in the Czech lands), medium-sized family farms also operated, principally to produce for sale. In Hungary, large estates employed many landless laborers. In much of the rest of the region, peasants cultivated scattered parcels using primitive means, with the primary intention of feeding their own families. By the 1960s, however, several million holdings had been consolidated into around 25,000 state or collective farms, which accounted for more than 90% of the farmland in Albania, Bulgaria, Czechoslovakia, Hungary, and Romania. There were also a few such farms in Poland and Yugoslavia. These were amongst the largest holdings anywhere in Europe, usually covering between 3,000 and 6,000 hectares, but averaging 17,000 hectares in Bulgaria. Many were eventually equipped with machinery and buildings suited to very large-scale cultivation and livestock operations.

This system suffered from a number of disadvantages. In particular, where commercially minded proprietors had been replaced by Party nominees, both knowledge of the best way to make use of particular pieces of land, and the incentive to do so, were reduced significantly. A system of massive food subsidies meant that there were few accurate signals as to what to grow where, and quantity of output was pursued without much thought for the most appropriate use of land. Much investment was poorly directed, and large areas were polluted through the inappropriate use of chemicals, or damaged by cultivation that encouraged erosion (see Meurs et al., and Unwin). In addition, difficulties in the centrally planned collection, processing, and distribution of farm products led to waste on a large scale, the range and quantity of food in the region's shops were small, and their quality was low (see Cook).

However, rural areas did benefit from heavy investment in manufacturing and mining, which provided considerable opportunities for people to leave the land. Before 1939 a large proportion of the working population, and in some countries the majority, were engaged in farming, but by 1989 that proportion had been reduced considerably. Nevertheless, it was much higher than in many more advanced economies, and labor productivity, at least on state and collective farms, remained low.

On private plots, in contrast, labor productivity was much higher. As in the Soviet Union, many of those who remained on the land were allowed to retain private plots, of not more than one hectare, on which they were allowed to grow fruit and vegetables, and rear small numbers of livestock. Some of this was eaten by those who produced it; most of the rest was sold in local, free markets. In the mid-1980s, each hectare of private gardens in Hungary was producing around four times as much as collectivized land (see Central Statistical Office). Private plots made a crucial contribution to the feeding of the whole region under central planning.

In Poland and Yugoslavia, however, the situation was very different. Land reform in Poland in the late 1940s broke up many of the larger holdings that had survived interwar attempts at redistribution, giving them to those with little or no land. By 1948, there were almost no farms of more than 20 hectares, except for the former German estates in the North and West of the country, which had been seized by the authorities as their owners fled in 1945. Similarly, in Yugoslavia, many holdings were small and fragmented, not least because of the mountainous topography in the West and South of the country, which offers few large areas of cultivable land. Nevertheless, collectivization was attempted in both countries in the late 1940s, only to be abandoned

in the 1950s in the face of peasant opposition and other difficulties. However, strict limits were placed on the size of privately owned farms, the enlargement of even the smallest was discouraged by the authorities, and private farmers were subject to special taxes, and to charges for some services that were free to other members of the public. After 1970, Polish farmers were no longer obliged to make compulsory deliveries of products to the state at low prices, and some specialist producers of fruit and flowers flourished, selling their products largely in free markets. Nevertheless, the Polish government never gave up its efforts to expand the state sector, persuading many elderly farmers to relinquish their land in return for pensions, and the private sector never enjoyed subsidies similar to those lavished on state farms. Indeed, farmers complained that the prices charged by the monopoly state suppliers of fertilizer and other materials were artificially high, and that the food processors, which were also in state ownership, operated as monopsonists against them. Farms in both countries, in consequence, continued to be very small, with little working capital or incentive to improve the quality of their products. Many provided no more than part-time employment for their owners, who often held factory or office jobs as well, while others were run by the elderly or widows. Methods of production were backward, and yields tended to be low. Such surpluses as were generated on Polish farms after 1970 were used as much to build large new farmhouses as to intensify production (see World Bank). Some of the best soils were subject to widespread erosion (see Kozłowski).

By the 1980s, the region as a whole was producing large quantities of cereals, potatoes, meat, milk, fruit, and wine, but was doing so much less effectively than some other parts of the continent. In general, agricultural yields in Denmark, northern France, the Netherlands, Sweden, the United Kingdom, and West Germany were much higher than in the three Baltic states, Poland, Czechoslovakia, or Hungary, while Albania and Yugoslavia performed less well than most other Mediterranean countries. Productivity was also low in Bulgaria and Romania. For example, the annual output of milk ranged from around 3.4 tons for each cow in central and eastern Europe, to 3.8 tons in the European Community (now the EU) and 4.8 tons in the countries that then belonged to the European Free Trade Association (EFTA). Albania, Romania, and Yugoslavia, along with Greece, performed worst. Across the Baltic Sea from Estonia, Latvia, Lithuania and Poland, areas of similar climate and soils in Sweden had double the yield that they achieved. By the 1980s, central and eastern Europe had become a substantial net importer of cereals from both western Europe and further afield (see Dawson).

The collapse of central planning in 1989 provided an opportunity to remedy these problems. In particular, it offered the countries of central and eastern Europe a chance to reorganize their farming and food-processing industries, and to choose between their former subservience to the Communist bloc and some closer association with western Europe. It was a tall order. Some farmers whose land had been collectivized were still alive, and they sought restitution. In other cases, relatives demanded the return of holdings that no longer existed in any functional sense. Small fields had been consolidated into vast, prairie-like units, individual steadings had been replaced by large centralized machine stations and processing plants, and large tractors had taken the place of individual peasants' horses. Reestablishing family farms required the undoing of many of the changes of the previous 40 years. In the economic turmoil that followed the collapse of central planning, few resources were available. Many of those who had been dispossessed in the 1940s and 1950s had lost all contact with farming, and were ill-prepared or simply unwilling to abandon urban employment and city life.

The links between farms and the market also required reform. Collectives and state farms bought most of their equipment, fuel, fertilizers, and seed from, and sold most of their products to, state-owned organizations. The establishment of an effective market required the privatization of these enterprises, as part of the creation of a range of competing suppliers and processors, capable of ensuring much higher standards of efficiency and hygiene. Meanwhile, in the early 1990s, the prospect for the export of many of the region's staple products was bleak. Trading arrangements in central and eastern Europe, which had been orchestrated through Comecon, had collapsed, and the EU showed little willingness to relax its barriers to imports of farm products.

There has been much change since 1989. Many state and collective farms have been broken up, or have collapsed. Much land has been returned to its previous owners, but farm output and incomes have fallen in all the countries in the region. Progress on the restructuring of the food-processing industry has been slow. In the most extreme cases, the fall of the Communist dictatorships has been followed by civil unrest and fighting, involving the destruction of agricultural infrastructure and ethnic conflicts, which have driven people off the land or killed them. However, there have been marked differences across the region. We shall examine Poland, the largest country in the region (see Table 12.2), before looking more briefly at some of the other countries.

## Change since 1989: Poland

Shortly after the fall of the Communists, Poland adopted one of the most far-reaching and rapid programs of economic reform in the region: it was known in Poland as "shock therapy." This program included the abolition of most price controls and state subsidies to industry, and the restoration of the right of individuals to operate businesses and conduct trade. Between 1990 and 1991, the country operated the most liberal tariff system on agricultural and food imports in Europe (see Adamowicz). There was a brief period of rapid economic decline, and much hardship, in which farmers were particularly badly affected. However, the economy began to grow again in 1993, and has since outpaced most others in the region.

The difficulties affecting Polish agriculture after the collapse of central planning were several. There was a sharp fall in the demand for many domestically produced farm goods, in part as a result of imports of higher quality, often subsidized by foreign governments. The

Polish government was obliged to alleviate the consequent distress among farmers, introducing guaranteed prices and imposing import tariffs. An Agricultural Market Agency was established, to stabilize the prices of rye, wheat, sugar, potato starch, beef, butter, milk, and pork, through purchases and stockpiling for later sale at home or abroad, after the manner of the EU's Common Agricultural Policy. It also offered credit to farmers to assist their marketing activities, and subsidized exports of butter, skimmed milk, and sugar. Nevertheless, subsidies to agriculture as a whole were halved, to levels well below the average in OECD countries, and less than half of those in the EU, while subsidies to state farms were withdrawn. Many state farms collapsed, and the proportion of agricultural land in state and cooperative farms fell from 23% in the late 1980s to 9% in 1996. The public sector's contribution to farm output was reduced by two thirds. There were sharp rises in the price of fertilizers and farm equipment, purchases of which fell markedly. Yields of all the major field crops were also lower in the 1990s than in the late 1980s. Large areas of land, much of which was on the poorer soils, fell idle (see Gorz and Kurek). Unemployment rose rapidly in almost all parts of the country, thus curtailing opportunities for farmers to leave the land.

Not surprisingly in these circumstances, the restructuring and reequipment of Polish agriculture have made little progress. The number of private farms, which had fallen from 2,390,000 in 1980 to 2,143,000 by 1989, declined further, but only to 2,041,000, by 1996. The average size of private holdings, which grew from 6.5 hectares to 7.2 hectares in the 1980s, rose, but only to 7.9 hectares. What is more, while the proportion of farms of more than 15 hectares continued to grow, that of the smallest farms – those between 1 and 2 hectares – increased to a similar extent. In 1996, only 11% of farmland was in holdings of 50 hectares or more, and 36% in those of more than 15 hectares. Although there was a marked increase in the number of tractors in the mid-1990s, there were still only two for every three farms. A majority of farms were still not connected to mains water supply, almost none was linked to mains sewers,

and the density of telephones in rural areas remained low (see Główny Urząd Statystyczny 1997).

The restructuring of Poland's food-processing industry has also been slow. Little attempt was made to privatize the largest enterprises, which continued employing excess numbers of workers, losing money, and failing to produce either on the scale or to the quality required for successful competition with rivals in western Europe. For example, it was not until 1996 that the creditors of Hortex, one of the country's chief fruit and vegetable processors, took charge of the enterprise, after seven years in which it made no profits. Only then was a start made on streamlining its activities, offering long-term contracts to those larger farms that could guarantee adequate supplies of produce of the requisite quality, and expanding sales to countries where the firm's name was already known – Russia, Ukraine, and Belarus (see _Business Central Europe_ 1998a).

Poland's international trade in farm products and food has also been problematic. Although its value has almost kept pace with the upsurge in the value of Poland's trade as a whole during the 1990s, there has been a marked deterioration in its balance. Exports of food and farm goods were worth more than twice the value of imports in 1990, but by 1996 imports had increased fourfold, while exports had grown by only a quarter: Poland had become a net importer. By 1996, around half of the trade was with the EU, while other important links were with Russia and other former Communist countries (see Główny Urząd Statystyczny 1998). However, this trade deficit was not entirely a consequence of the low quality of Polish products: it has been persuasively blamed on the conditions imposed by the EU in the Association Agreement with Poland signed in 1992 (see Adamowicz). That Agreement laid down a complex set of arrangements for the gradual easing of trade restrictions, but it was not generous. The European Commission, the executive body of the EU, suggested in 1998 that Poland may find it difficult to establish the necessary administrative machinery to enable it to implement milk production quotas and other EU systems. It also expressed concern about veterinary and phytosanitary standards in Poland's farming and food-processing industries. These comments indicated that the Commission does not foresee free trade in farm products between the EU and Poland in the near future (see European Commission). Meanwhile, increasing economic instability in Russia and Ukraine in the late 1990s has undermined trade with those countries.

## Change since 1989: Other Countries

Somewhat similar problems to Poland's have affected all the countries of central and eastern Europe. Some have reacted less effectively than the Poles, but others have done better. In particular, the Czech Republic, Hungary, and Slovakia have all achieved substantial changes in their farm structures, and achieved some of the highest yields in the region (see Table 12.2).

Almost all farmland in these three countries was in cooperative or state farms in 1989, but in 1997 less than 50% in the Czech Republic and only around 25% in Hungary was still in the public sector. In both these countries, around one sixth of farmland was in the hands of joint stock enterprises; their properties are known as "company" farms, as distinct from "private" farms. In Slovakia, the government of Vladimír Mečiar, in power from 1993 to 1998, was loath to pursue economic reform, and many farm managers and others were unwilling to adopt a more commercial approach (see Karasek). Nevertheless, by the mid-1990s around one tenth of farmland was in the hands of "company" farms and two thirds in those of "transformed" cooperatives (see European Commission). As a result, farms in these countries are generally much larger than in Poland, more commercially oriented, and more productive. In the Czech Republic in 1996, the average farm was 132 hectares in extent, and even among individual farms, which accounted for almost 90% of the total, the average size was 34 hectares (see Bičik and Gotz). Following the disruption occasioned by economic transition and the loss of some important markets in other post-Communist countries, there was a sharp fall in output in the early 1990s. However, government support

in both the Czech Republic and Hungary is at levels considerably below that in Poland, and even further below those in the EU, while support in Slovakia is also well below EU levels (see European Commission). In short, it would appear that farming in all three countries is relatively well-prepared to compete with the EU, if it should ever be allowed to do so. However, as in Poland, much further restructuring is required in the food-processing industry, if that potential is to be exploited to the full (see *Business Central Europe* 1998b, and European Commission).

Progress in Bulgaria has been slower. During the early and mid-1990s, the government failed to adopt a clear and vigorous policy of adjustment, thus exacerbating the problems that had arisen from the collapse of central planning. Much farmland has fallen out of use, and there has been a greater decline in livestock numbers, in output, and in crop yields than in Poland. Many of the giant farm enterprises were broken up during the mid-1990s, and much land passed into the hands of private owners (see Carter). However, these changes have not resulted in a return to the prewar pattern of very small, fragmented holdings, similar to that in Poland. Rather, they may yet prove to be the precursor of the establishment of a more successful medium-scale and large-scale commercial agriculture, for many farmers have chosen to remain within cooperatives, reconstituting them in forms more suited to their needs (see Yarnaul).

Changes in Romania have been less promising. The breakup of collective farms has led to the redistribution of more than 75% of the land to private farmers, but the demand for land has been such that the consequent holdings are very small, averaging only around 5 hectares in the lowland areas favorable to large-scale cultivation and less than 3 hectares in the mountains. By 1996, less than 20% of farmers remained within formal cooperatives, and although a similar proportion were participating in less formal "family associations," the majority of farmers were operating individually (see Turnock). In other words, there has been a return to something very similar to the prewar structure of very large numbers of tiny holdings, when land hunger was associated with primitive farming methods, low productivity, and considerable rural poverty. The Romanian Federation of Associated Privatized Farmers has suggested that the country should be developing cereal farms with a minimum area of 1,000 hectares, orchards of at least 200 hectares, vineyards of 100 hectares or more, and market gardens with a minimum area of 50 hectares. However, David Turnock has calculated that such a change would render 2.5 million people redundant. As in Poland, far too many people still depend upon farming, but unlike in that country, growth within the rest of the economy, and thus the prospect of finding employment outside farming, has been slight. These structural problems have been exacerbated by sharp rises in the prices of fertilizer and equipment since 1989, while those of many farm products have failed to keep up, resulting in a decline in both the yield and the quality of many crops. Further, the country's food-processing industry is in need of substantial improvement. Under the Communists, much investment was undertaken, but not all of it was appropriate. Much of the plant is now obsolete. Finally, the Romanian government's failure to pursue economic reform with vigor has discouraged foreign investors who might have redeveloped the industry (see European Commission). Notwithstanding the very substantial agricultural resources of the country, exports of Romanian farm produce in the 1990s have been low.

The position in much of the Balkans, other than in relatively tiny Slovenia, is even worse. In Yugoslavia (Serbia and Montenegro), the regime of Slobodan Milošević has spent little time on economic reform, but has embarked on a series of wars that has led the international community to impose an economic blockade on the country. Civil strife and military action have destroyed much of the farming infrastructure of Bosnia-Herzegovina, Kosovo, and the eastern regions of Croatia. Agriculture in Albania, which had been the most backward in the region even under central planning, suffered a double blow: the restitution of land reestablished the mass of tiny prewar individual holdings (see Hall), while the country as a whole spent much of the 1990s in anarchy. In Macedonia, government has been paralyzed by intercommunal tensions.

Mention should also be made of the Baltic states, and in particular Estonia, where agriculture has also suffered from post-Communist adjustment, yet a remarkable change has occurred in the relationship between it and the state. Land redistribution has restored many of the family farms in all three countries since 1991, reconstituting the prewar pattern of very small holdings in Lithuania, similar to that in neighboring Poland, but much larger units, with an average size of 23 hectares, in Estonia and Latvia (see European Commission). Under the Soviet occupation, agriculture in these three countries was closely geared to the needs of the huge Soviet market. It specialized in dairy products and meat, using large quantities of fodder crops from other parts of the Soviet Union and achieving levels of productivity that were among the highest in that country. The regaining of independence was followed by the imposition of high trade barriers by Russia, which had the effect of confining Baltic farmers to their tiny domestic markets. There they faced much increased prices for fodder crops and other agricultural supplies, and found themselves competing against subsidized imports from western Europe. Farm output declined sharply, and some state farms collapsed. However, farmers in Estonia now receive almost no support from the state, and the market for farm products, both within the country and in relation to the rest of the world, is open and free. In other words, the country has quickly established itself as a model of what European agriculture might look like, in the absence of both the failed policies of the Communists, and the controversially high levels of farm intervention and subsidy associated with the EU and EFTA.

## Conclusion

Comparisons between countries in the region and, for example, EU countries indicate that there is considerable scope for further improvement (see Table 12.2). Only in a minority of countries is the role of farming in employment comparable to that in most of northern and western Europe. Elsewhere, and especially in the two countries with the largest agricultural sectors, Poland and Romania, further structural change is still required to get people off the land. Similarly, there are both wide variations in yields across the region, and generally much lower levels of productivity than in northwest Europe, only part of which can be explained by climate. Given these differences, it is a measure of the extent to which the opportunities offered by agriculture in central and eastern Europe have gone begging, but also the extent of agriculture's problems, that little of the foreign direct investment that has flowed into the region since 1989 has been directed to food-processing and almost none to farming itself. By the mid- and late 1990s, some farmers, especially in the region's more rapidly recovering economies, had begun to reap the first meager rewards for their earlier privations. However, those in countries where the commitment to reform has been slight, or in which there has been civil unrest and bloodshed, have been much less well-placed to make something of the fall of Communism. Some farmers are themselves largely responsible, being unwilling to adopt a more innovative and commercial approach. However, the restructuring of agriculture in the region has also been hampered by the refusal of some governments to pursue well-founded and energetic programs of reform, the incompetence and brutality of a few regimes, and the meanness of the EU in failing to open its markets more widely to producers in central and eastern Europe. Thus, the full potential of the region's agriculture has yet to be realized.

## Further Reading

Adamowicz, M., "Evolution of Agricultural Market Regulations in the Process of Integration with the EU," in G. Eraktan and J. Gudowski, editors, *Transforming the Rural Sector to the Requirements of the Market Economy: Examples from Turkey, Poland, and Ukraine*, Warsaw: Dialog, 1997

An account of the changes in Polish government support for agriculture since 1989

Bičik, Ivan, and Antonin Gotz, "Czech Republic," in David Turnock, editor, *Privatization in Rural Eastern Europe: The Process of Restitution and Restructuring*, Cheltenham and Northampton, MA: Edward Elgar, 1998

An account of recent changes in the structure of Czech farming

*Business Central Europe* (1998a), "Fruitless Delay," September 1998; (1998b), "Czech Stereotype," December 1998/January 1999

Assessments of progress in the restructuring of the Polish and Czech food-processing industries

Carter, Frank W., "Bulgaria," in Turnock, cited above under Bičik and Gotz

An account of recent changes in the structure of Bulgarian farming

Central Statistical Office, *Statisztikai Evkönyv 1986*, Budapest: Central Statistical Office, 1987

One of the annual reports issued by the Hungarian government's statistical agency

Cook, E. C., "Agriculture's Role in the Soviet Economic Crisis," in M. Ellman and V. Kontorovich, editors, *The Disintegration of the Soviet Economic System*, London and New York: Routledge, 1992

An assessment of the role of agriculture in the economic problems of the declining Soviet Union

Dawson, Andrew H., *A Geography of European Integration*, London: Belhaven, and New York: Halsted Press, 1993

An assessment of the likely effects of economic reform and closer integration between western Europe and the post-Communist countries

European Commission, *Agenda 2000: Commission Opinions on Applications for Membership of the EU*, Brussels: European Commission, 1998

These are official assessments by the EU's executive body of the extent to which Bulgaria, the Czech Republic, Estonia, Hungary, Latvia, Lithuania, Poland, Romania, Slovakia, and Slovenia have adapted their economies, and their systems of economic management, to meet the requirements of membership.

Główny Urząd Statystyczny (1997), *Rocznik Statystyczny 1997* [Statistical Yearbook]; (1998), *Rocznik Statystyczny Handlu Zagraniczego 1998* [Statistical Yearbook of International Trade], Warsaw: Główny Urząd Statystyczny, 1997 and 1998

Two of the annual reports issued by Poland's Chief Statistical Office

Gorz, Bronislaw, and Wlodzimierz Kurek, "Poland," in Turnock, cited above under Bičik and Gotz

An account of recent changes in the structure of Polish farming

Hall, Derek, "Albania," in Turnock, cited above under Bičik and Gotz

An account of recent changes in the structure of Albanian farming

Karasek, E. H., "The Transformation of Agricultural Cooperatives in Slovakia," in Unwin, T., editor, *A European Geography*, Harlow and New York: Longman, 1998

A brief note on recent agricultural restructuring

Kozłowski, S., editor, "Obszary Funckjonalne w Ekologicznym Warancie Rozwoju Kraju" [Ecological Variety and the Economic Development of the Country] in *Biuletyn KPZK PAN*, number 148, Warsaw, 1990

An assessment of the ecological problems in Poland occasioned by Communist economic development

Meurs, Mieke, Monique Morrissey, and Robert Begg, "Village to State to Market: Agricultural Ecology and Transformation – The Bulgarian Experience," in Krassimira Paskaleva, Philip Shapira, John Pickles, and Boian Koulov, editors, *Bulgaria in Transition: Environmental Consequences of Political and Economic Transformation*, Aldershot and Brookfield, VT: Ashgate, 1998

An assessment of the ecological problems in Bulgarian agriculture occasioned by Communist economic development

Turnock, David, "Romania," in Turnock, cited above under Bičik and Gotz

An account of recent changes in the structure of Romanian farming

UN Food and Agriculture Organization, *FAO Yearbook: Production 1997*, Rome: UN Food and Agriculture Organization, 1998

One of the annual reports issued by this UN agency

Unwin, T., "Agricultural Change and Rural Stress in the New Democracies," in D. Pinder, editor, *The New Europe: Economy, Society and Environment*, Chichester and New York: John Wiley, 1998

A general overview of agricultural reform in central and eastern Europe

Varga, Zsuzsanna, "Hungary," in Turnock, cited above under Bičik and Gotz

An account of recent changes in the structure of Hungarian farming

Vriser, Igor, "Slovenia," in Turnock, cited above under Bičik and Gotz

An account of recent changes in the structure of Slovenian farming

World Bank, *An Agricultural Strategy for Poland*, Washington, DC: World Bank, 1990

An assessment of Polish agriculture at the end of the Communist period

Yarnaul, Brent, "The Land-use Impacts of Bulgarian Decollectivization," in Paskaleva et al., cited above under Meurs

An account of the effects of the breakup of collective farms in Bulgaria

*Dr Andrew H. Dawson* is Senior Lecturer in Geography at the University of St Andrews in Scotland.

**Table 12.1   Land and Agriculture in the Major Regions of Europe, 1998**

|                                          | Central and Eastern Europe | EU    | Russia,[1] Belarus, and Ukraine |
|------------------------------------------|----------------------------|-------|---------------------------------|
| Area (thousands of square kilometers)    | 1,374                      | 3,240 | 17,890                          |
| Proportion in agriculture (%)            | 60                         | 44    | 15                              |
| Agricultural land per capita (hectares)  | 0.6                        | 0.4   | 1.3                             |

1 Including non-European Russia

Source:   UN Food and Agriculture Organization, *FAO Yearbook: Production 1997*, Rome: UN Food and Agriculture Organization, 1998

**Table 12.2  Agriculture in Central and Eastern Europe, and in Selected Countries in the EU, 1995–97**

|                     | Farmland (thousands of hectares), 1996 | Proportion of labor force in agriculture (%), 1997 | Yields of wheat (tons per hectare), 1995–97 | Yields of milk (tons per cow), 1995–97 |
|---------------------|----------------------------------------|----------------------------------------------------|---------------------------------------------|----------------------------------------|
| Albania             | 702                                    | 50                                                 | 2.6                                         | 1.7                                    |
| Bosnia-Herzegovina  | 650                                    | n.a.                                               | 2.6                                         | 1.2                                    |
| Bulgaria            | 4,402                                  | 22                                                 | 2.7                                         | 3.1                                    |
| Croatia             | 1,362                                  | 10                                                 | 3.9                                         | 2.0                                    |
| Czech Republic      | 3,334                                  | 6                                                  | 4.6                                         | 4.4                                    |
| Estonia             | 1,143                                  | 7                                                  | 2.1                                         | 3.8                                    |
| Hungary             | 5,036                                  | 8                                                  | 3.9                                         | 5.3                                    |
| Latvia              | 1,726                                  | 18                                                 | 2.3                                         | 3.1                                    |
| Lithuania           | 3,007                                  | 24                                                 | 3.0                                         | 3.0                                    |
| Macedonia           | 658                                    | 15                                                 | 2.5                                         | 1.5                                    |
| Poland              | 14,452                                 | 27                                                 | 3.5                                         | 3.3                                    |
| Romania             | 9,882                                  | 34                                                 | 2.6                                         | 2.7                                    |
| Slovakia            | 1,608                                  | 8                                                  | 4.4                                         | 3.3                                    |
| Slovenia            | 285                                    | 7                                                  | 4.1                                         | 2.8                                    |
| Yugoslavia          | 4,061                                  | 23                                                 | 3.3                                         | 1.9                                    |
| France              | 19,461                                 | 4                                                  | 6.8                                         | 5.4                                    |
| Germany             | 12,064                                 | 3                                                  | 7.2                                         | 5.5                                    |
| Italy               | 10,768                                 | 6                                                  | 3.1                                         | 5.1                                    |
| Spain               | 20,129                                 | 9                                                  | 2.3                                         | 4.7                                    |
| Sweden              | 2,812                                  | 4                                                  | 6.1                                         | 6.9                                    |
| United Kingdom      | 6,133                                  | 2                                                  | 7.8                                         | 5.1                                    |

Sources:  European Commission, *Agenda 2000: Commission Opinions on Applications for Membership of the EU*, Brussels: European Commission, 1998; UN Food and Agriculture Organization, *FAO Yearbook: Production 1997*, Rome: UN Food and Agriculture Organization, 1998

**Figure 12.1 Soils in Central and Eastern Europe**

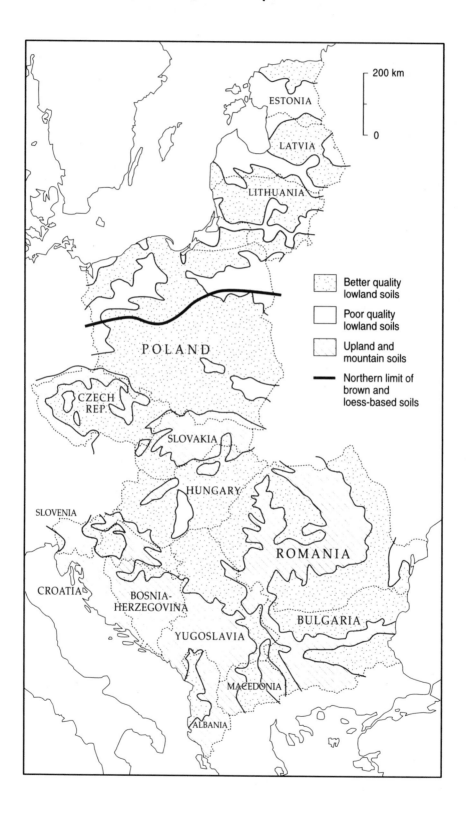

## Chapter Thirteen

# The Transformation of Manufacturing

## *Tamás Novák and Csaba Novák*

In analyzing the transformation of manufacturing in the transition economies of central and eastern Europe, it is useful to distinguish between two main periods of transition. In most countries in the region, there was an initial period of "shallow" restructuring. The enterprises established during the Communist period, exposed to the true costs of production for the first time, responded by shedding surplus labor. Hardly any investment took place, and markets were either static or contracting. In contrast, during the subsequent period of "deep" restructuring, which is still continuing, unemployment has continued to rise in most countries, but investment has recommenced or even accelerated. Patterns of ownership have shifted decisively from state domination of the economy to increasing reliance on the private sector, and manufacturing has undergone some degree of modernization. However, it has also begun to take second place to services as the main source of value added.

Apart from this general pattern of two-stage transition, the countries of central and eastern Europe display other common features. For example, their capital stock is still strikingly low by comparison to the more advanced market economies of western Europe, and the low level of personal incomes continues to present major problems. More specifically, the composition of the manufacturing sector in all these countries is undergoing a more or less rapid evolution away from the traditional industries that were the mainstays of their economies, toward more advanced and sophisticated activities. Thus, for example, all the countries in the region have textiles and clothing industries characterized

by very low wages and minimal growth in labor productivity. Since real appreciation of exchange rates has become the rule across the region, textiles and clothing from all these countries are being priced out of their markets, and production is being shifted further to the East. Similarly, while food production has risen overall, the types of food being produced have changed, as consumers have become more accustomed to processed products. There has also been a decline in the output of basic metals across the region.

Nevertheless, it would be wrong to assume that the experience of the transition in these 15 countries (let alone in all the transition economies of the world) has been uniform in every important respect. The variations among them, particularly the differences in the speed and scope of transition, are at least as significant as the characteristics they have in common. This chapter examines developments in the manufacturing industries of eight of the transition economies in central and eastern Europe (Poland, Hungary, the Czech Republic, Slovakia, Bulgaria, Romania, Croatia, and Slovenia). While general comparisons among these eight countries would be highly desirable, they have not been attempted here, because the commensurate and complete data that would make such comparisons valid is not available (see, however, Table 13.1 on unemployment). The economies of Albania, Bosnia-Herzegovina, Macedonia, and Yugoslavia are not so amenable to detailed analysis, again for lack of reliable statistical information, but also because these economies have undergone extreme disruption (see Chapters 8 and 9). Those of the three Baltic states, which have moved on from decades of direct control by the Soviet Union to become among the most successful in the region, also constitute a special case (see Chapter 3).

## Poland

The macroeconomic background of the transformation of Polish manufacturing has two important distinguishing features compared, for example, to the Czech and Hungarian cases discussed below. First, in 1989–90 Poland still had a huge foreign debt to renegotiate, and there was no realistic hope of a rapid inflow of foreign direct investment until it started to pay the debt back. The Czech Republic had no initial debt problem, while Hungary, which was less indebted than Poland, showed greater determination in repayment. Poland's insolvency meant that adopting the Hungarian technique of privatization by direct sales to foreign investors was out of question. Second, Poland's radical "shock therapy" program of economic reform, introduced in January 1990 (see Chapter 1), liberalized international trade, cut government transfers to firms, and secured a reasonable level of macroeconomic stability. Devaluation of the national currency, the złoty, made an exchange rate "cushion" available against external shocks, at least until the government introduced a "crawling peg" policy, but the traded sector of the economy, in which manufacturing still plays a leading role, was still badly hit by the reforms.

Nevertheless, the program was so successful that, after the initial shock had been sustained, Poland became the first transition economy to achieve renewed growth in GDP in 1992. One of the driving forces in this recovery was manufacturing. The fall in investment during the early 1990s was slower than the fall in output, unlike in Hungary: in other words, there was an unambiguously strong supply side reaction to the shock therapy program. The relatively vigorous pace of investment meant that restructuring reached the second, deep stage relatively smoothly and rapidly in Poland.

The dominant technique of privatization in Poland, unlike in the Czech Republic or Hungary, was to allow the management and employees of an enterprise to buy it jointly, not for cash but on credit. There was some anxiety that this combination of owners would prevent restructuring and postpone the injection of fresh capital into the enterprises concerned, but this has not generally turned out to be the case. Even before privatization began, managers in many enterprises had initiated some shallow restructuring (as defined above), and unemployment had risen very fast, especially in manufacturing. Surprisingly, perhaps, Poland began to accumulate capital quite fast and the low level of incomes among most of the new shareholders did not prevent dynamic investment activity.

Labor productivity has also increased. The branches of manufacturing that have shown the highest rate of increase in labor productivity are exactly the same as in Hungary or the Czech Republic: electronic equipment, transportation equipment, and machinery. However, the levels of wages in these industries (as measured in US dollars) place them only in the middle of the Polish scale for average wages in manufacturing. As in Hungary, the chemicals industries pay the highest average wages. Otherwise, the range of manufacturing industries has not changed drastically in the second half of the 1990s, following the enormous changes brought about by shock therapy.

In the second half of the 1990s, significant foreign direct investment has begun to flow into Polish manufacturing, attracted by the country's large and dynamic markets, its geographic proximity to Germany and other economies in western Europe, its macroeconomic policies, and the successful renegotiation of its foreign debts. Major investors include General Motors of the United States, FIAT of Italy, and Daewoo of South Korea in transportation equipment, and Sony of Japan in electrical equipment.

## Hungary

Hungary has been perhaps the classic model for the distinction between shallow and deep restructuring outlined above. The shedding of surplus labor was on a massive scale at the beginning of the 1990s, but expanding investment and output have characterized the second half of the decade.

The early period of transition in Hungary can be summarized as combining a relatively lax macroeconomic policy with a quite radical microeconomic approach to reform. Both trends directly influenced the performance of manufacturing. The traded goods sector, most of which still comprises manufactured goods, was among the worst hit by the abrupt liberalization of trade in 1989–90. As there was no abrupt depreciation of the currency, the forint, at this stage, there was no exchange rate cushion for the traded goods sector to alleviate the pain of restructuring. Instead, the real appreciation in the value of the forint started right from the beginning of the transition. On the microeconomic side, one should mention the enactment in 1993 of an extremely tough law on liquidation of enterprises, which remains one of the strictest in the region even after some of its provisions were later relaxed. Its application has had a major impact in helping to select healthy and viable enterprises, and in making the budget constraints on companies effective. Hungarian enterprises are now among the healthiest anywhere in central and eastern Europe, alongside those of Poland. The growth of the traded sector was also helped by the massive cleanup of debts at state banks and their subsequent privatization. Hardly any financial institution remains in the hands of the state, with the result that reserve requirements do not constrain the growth of lending to manufacturing to the extent that they did before.

Fiscal policy was quite expansive up to 1995, but from then on, in the wake of a stabilization package recommended by the IMF, there was a fiscal tightening, coupled with a fairly aggressive depreciation of the forint through a crawling peg system. This helped the manufacturing sector to regain at least some of its relative cost competitiveness. The simultaneous fall in aggregate demand led to a stagnation in the growth of manufacturing, as measured by output per capita and value added, during 1996, but growth has since picked up. However, even with the increases in manufacturing output and productivity in the late 1990s, the share of manufacturing in employment and value added is the lowest, or the lowest after Poland, in the region.

In fact, increases in labor productivity were significant right from the beginning of the transition. In the early 1990s, this tended to be mainly a statistical side effect of the massive shedding of surplus labor, but from 1993 onward the rising trend was more and more due to increases in capital stock and total factor productivity, that is, improving efficiency. Labor productivity has increased most dynamically in electrical equipment, transportation equipment, and machinery, with investment by the automotive and electronic equipment industries being key factors. As in Poland, manufacturing wages are highest in chemicals, even though in Hungary the growth of productivity in this area has been far less spectacular than in electrical equipment or transportation equipment. The most likely explanation of these relatively high wages is that pharmaceuticals and oil processing were already in better shape, or more monopolistic, than the rest of manufacturing before 1989–90, and restructuring did not need to be as drastic as elsewhere.

The rapid restructuring of Hungarian manufacturing was also supported by rapid privatization. Unlike the other countries of the region, Hungary privatized most of its domestic market leaders through direct sales to foreign companies. In the short term, the restructuring carried out by the new owners made a large contribution to the overall rise in unemployment, but in the long term it has brought overall expansion and higher wages. The most dynamic manufacturing industries have been those where shallow restructuring was carried out rapidly by the new owners, whether foreign or domestic, and the expansion of production could begin with the continuing support of the knowledge and skills accumulated before the transition. Thus, for example, the electronics industry is still geographically concentrated in those areas where it was already prominent during the Communist period. "Greenfield" investments were also encouraged by the local availability of skills inherited from the past. This is not to say that the accumulated stock of skills was the single most important aspect of investment decisions, but in most cases it was a necessary condition for their success. The leading foreign investment projects that have benefited in this way include investments by Audi, General Motors, and Ford in the automobile industry, and by Philips and Nokia in electronics.

## The Czech Republic

Before World War II, the Czech lands in what· was then the unitary state of Czechoslovakia contained one of the most advanced manufacturing bases of Europe. The economy was dominated by the production of coal, steel, machinery, textiles, and clothing, with high levels of technology and productivity that helped to make the Czech lands comparable to countries in western Europe, rather than to their neighbors in central and eastern Europe. The basic pattern of the economy continued in place during the Communist period, although it became much less internationally competitive than it had been between the wars.

After the collapse of Communism in Czechoslovakia in 1989, the lack of competitiveness of Czech manufacturing did not show itself immediately. The most important macroeconomic measure implemented early in the transition was the drastic devaluation of the currency, the Czechoslovak koruna, in 1990. This cushioned the transition to the market for domestic producers. Hence, unlike in some other transition economies, such as Hungary, the liberalization of trade did not have a devastating impact in the short term. Partly as a result, very little restructuring of industry took place, and not much labor was shed. As a consequence, unemployment remained very low (see Table 13.1).

There were two important microeconomic factors that also helped to prevent rapid restructuring. One was the technique adopted for privatization. Czechoslovakia preferred to issue vouchers to the general public, which then used them to buy shares either directly or through investment funds, rather than sell enterprises to foreign investors or other large single buyers. The end result is that much of Czech manufacturing is effectively owned by mainly state-owned commercial banks, by way of the leading investment funds, and that many companies still owe large debts to those banks. The other factor was the effective suspension of the law

on bankruptcy for several years, which allowed companies that were extremely indebted or inefficient to continue in operation longer than they would otherwise have been able to.

Despite the exchange rate cushion, the loss of value added and output was greater in manufacturing than in other sectors of the economy. This is indicated by the fact that, up to 1993, the share of manufacturing in total output and value added was sharply declining. The decline stopped, but overall it appears that the share of manufacturing in GDP has not returned to the level that it had reached before the transition began. To a large extent, this can probably be best explained by reference to the Communist assumption that services were nonproductive activities, which led to their being hugely neglected. As a consequence, particularly at the initial stage of the transition, services, particularly business services, telecommunications and trade, grew much faster than manufacturing, which declined by around 5% between 1992 and 1993 alone. This fall was generally much less marked in other countries in central and eastern Europe. The fall in the share of manufacturing in total employment also declined between 1990 and 1994, by almost 3%, but this was less than the fall in its share of total output.

After the depreciation of the Czechoslovak koruna in 1990, it began slowly to appreciate, as the deficit in the balance of payments remained small and the surplus in the government budget rose. Thus, wage rates became relatively high in industries such as textiles and clothing, and the decline from 1990 in the share of machinery, textiles, and clothing in total output was spectacular. This may come as something of a surprise, as the comparative advantage of Czech manufacturing traditionally lay in precisely these industries. The best that could happen was either to liquidate the enterprises affected by this phenomenon, or to shift output further to the East. The industries that have been on the rise in the 1990s include transportation equipment, electrical and electronic equipment, and, most impressively, chemicals, while the contribution of the basic metals industries to output has hardly changed. In these more dynamic industries, foreign direct investment played a leading role in boosting output. The most celebrated project in any of these industries is perhaps the revival and transformation of the Škoda automobile company following its purchase by Volkswagen of Germany.

However, all was not plain sailing even in these industries. As the fall in output in the Czech Republic exceeded the fall in employment in the early 1990s, growth in labor productivity stagnated. This effect was enhanced by the speedy scrapping of the capital goods that were kept at very high book values: hence, stagnant labor productivity can be attributed to the decline in the capital stock per capita as well. Fortunately, since 1994 the most important manufacturing industries, as measured by initial output, have typically shown strong positive growth in labor productivity. Interestingly, wages measured in current US dollars give a quite different picture. From this perspective the fastest growth in labor productivity has been in industries such as chemicals and basic metals. Nevertheless, whether measured in Czech koruna or in US dollars, the picture is very similar across the range of industries, except in the troubled textile and apparel industries, where wage rates now lag behind the general level of wages in the country.

## Slovakia

When Slovakia and the Czech Republic separated, at the beginning of 1993, both countries inherited favorable macroeconomic conditions. The level and structure of foreign debts were very low, so the currency risk attached to the new Czech koruna and Slovak koruna was small; the balance of payments and the government budget were either balanced or in surplus; and the first wave of voucher privatizations had already been implemented. Accordingly, both showed vigorous growth up to 1997, when the Czech Republic slowed down; Slovakia has begun to do so in late 1998 and early 1999.

However, even in 1993 the labor markets were already showing signs that the two countries would be taking different paths. While unemployment had not become an acute problem in the Czech Republic, in Slovakia it had begun rising with the start of the transition

back in 1990. The usual shallow restructuring had started before the privatization program, notably in the arms industry, which was concentrated in Slovakia, accounting for a large proportion of its output and exports. Hence, its collapse in the wake of disappearing demand caused serious and lasting problems.

Privatization also developed differently than in the Czech Republic. Having rejected the Hungarian method of selling enterprises to foreigners for cash, and the Polish method of privatizing to managers and employees, Slovakia then abandoned its attempt to continue with the voucher scheme following a change of government in 1994. Instead, privatization came to be one of the means by which Vladimír Mečiar, the populist Prime Minister of Slovakia, built up and maintained his political and economic base. Nevertheless, the result, following Mečiar's defeat in elections in 1998, is that the most important enterprises in manufacturing and other sectors have now passed into the private sector.

The traditional heavy industries still play important roles in the economy. The massive Košice steel plant alone accounted for close to 20% of all manufacturing output, and its relative weight has only began to decline with the rapid expansion of the transportation equipment industry, mainly due, as in the Czech Republic, to investments by Volkswagen. Most of the remaining heavy industries are still linked to arms production and sustained by government credits. The weakness of this stagnating structure of manufacturing is shown by the fact that the growth in labor productivity in basic metals is meager compared to what is happening in transportation equipment, electrical equipment, and other "new" industries. However, despite these differences in respect of productivity, the growth in wages has so far run more or less parallel across Slovak manufacturing, with the basic metals industries still paying significantly higher wages.

## Bulgaria

The economic transition in Bulgaria was accompanied by a highly unstable macroeconomic environment, the loss of traditional markets, and increased competition. Between

1990 and 1997, attempts to stabilize the economy were derailed by a combination of large losses in state-owned enterprises and the weakness of the banking industry, but the introduction of a currency board in 1997 led rapidly to a degree of financial stability.

Against this background, Bulgarian manufacturing continues to be characterized by a significant degree of state ownership, under-utilization of capacity, large losses and debts, declining investment and production, and overall lack of international competitiveness. Energy pricing also remains a problem, in that the charges to industries and households alike still do not cover costs. At the same time, the bad debt situation restricts the capacity of the banking system to provide capital, yet it is lack of investment capital that is the major impediment to restructuring and diversification.

Bulgaria's relatively weak competitive position is largely the result of its retention of an industrial base that is too narrow, with exports concentrated in a small number of basic industries. Most of the main export branches lack long-term viability and sustainable competitiveness. The industries facing significant problems in adapting to market conditions include textiles, clothing, machinery and metal processing, mining, electrical engineering, electronics and shipbuilding. The textiles and clothing industries have been among the worst hit parts of the manufacturing base during the transition. They are now experiencing strong competition from producers in Asia, but their combination of low labor costs, skilled workers, and high-quality products could be attractive to foreign investors. The mechanical engineering and machine industries were geared toward production for the member states of Comecon, and suffered greatly from the collapse of that organization. As a result, many enterprises in these industries remain among the heaviest loss-makers in Bulgaria. On the other hand, there are some strengths, such as a highly skilled labor force and, in certain specializations, high-quality capital stocks, which have attracted some foreign direct investment. In ferrous metallurgy there has been a relative stabilization of steel output, and the steel industry is medium-sized for a country in central and eastern Europe. Its problems

are the results of weak domestic and export demand, and variations in the quality of its output. The industry is undergoing a slow process of structural change, and the largest single steel producer, Kremikovci, is to embark on a program of major financial restructuring. Nonferrous metallurgy, where most exports are destined for the immediate region, the EU, and the Middle East, faces some similar difficulties. The situation in electrical and electronic engineering is also critical, since these industries have all but lost the market that once took almost all their output, the countries of the former Soviet Union. A few enterprises had already developed positions in western markets before 1989, but most companies in these industries have not yet managed to adapt to new conditions.

At the same time, the chemicals and oil-refining industries have been notably less affected by the economic decline, since they have been able to increase their exports to Bulgaria's traditional international markets in Russia and other CIS countries. The production of pharmaceuticals and certain other chemicals has remained profitable independently of the crisis. Bulgaria retains its traditionally strong agricultural sector, notably in fruit and vegetables, and it is logical for the country to seek to build up its food-processing industry, which has already attracted some foreign investors keen to develop its export potential and exploit its relatively low production costs.

In 1997, the government launched a complex program of structural reforms, aimed at substantial privatization and restructuring in most industrial sectors, in accordance with a strict schedule agreed with – or, as its opponents would claim, imposed by – international financial institutions. The goal is to complete the privatization of all state-owned enterprises, as well as a substantial proportion of utilities, by the end of 1999. However, it is likely that the privatization of heavy industry, which is very energy-intensive, might well lead, at least at first, to a contraction of output.

## Romania

Industrial development was among the highest priorities of the Communist regime in

Romania, resulting in huge companies and a high level of industrial concentration. Today, the majority of the manufacturing industries are characterized by obsolete production technologies, products that are not competitive in a market environment, low rates of capacity utilization, low levels of managerial skills, and very heavy losses. Industrial investment has decreased since 1990, and the inconsistent and unstable economic policies pursued since 1990 have left manufacturing at the early stages of adaptation. The heavy industries built up on indigenous coal, other sources of energy, and raw materials waste less energy than in some of the other countries formerly in the Soviet bloc, since Romania could not rely on cheap supplies from the Soviet Union as they could. Yet it is not a clear advantage for the future, since the costs of sourcing raw materials domestically are increasing and Romanian deposits are close to being exhausted. Overall, the ability of Romanian manufacturers to make significant changes is hindered by a number of factors, including infrastructure deficiencies, delays in installing modern information technology, weaknesses in corporate governance, lack of financial resources, and inflationary pressures.

Some manufacturing activities in Romania have survived into the 1990s by relying on supplying traditional basic goods to domestic and neighboring markets. The food industry is one of the most important in the economy, but it has low levels of productivity and capacity utilization, and its exports, which are of relatively low quality, are increasingly less competitive, even in the other countries of central and eastern Europe that are its main markets. The textiles and clothing industries comprise a large number of small companies alongside a small number of large enterprises, mostly state-owned companies with massive problems and heavy losses. It is expected that the low levels of productivity in the long-established leather and shoe industry, and in the furniture industry, which is one of the most important in the region, will be alleviated by a policy of encouraging investments and exports. There is a long tradition of shipbuilding, but investment has been delayed in recent years.

Other industries represent the legacy of the Communist drive for rapid, state-led industrialization. Mechanical engineering, the second largest manufacturing industry in Romania, lacks the capacity, specialization, labor productivity and technology that it needs in order to compete internationally. A large part of the installed production capacity will have to be dismantled in the coming years. On the other hand, the industry can probably continue to rely heavily on paying its workers relatively low wages, which may help to save some production of simple machinery, and other components requiring high labor inputs, largely for export. The fabricated metal products industry is also undergoing a deep crisis, and its scope for competitive upgrading is limited, because production is dispersed and labor productivity is low. The steel industry too is characterized by huge, obsolete facilities, and it has a high concentration in products that provide low added value and have a high sensitivity to the markets. The chemicals industry, the third largest manufacturing industry in Romania, is also dominated by obsolete equipment and has not attracted much foreign capital; the pharmaceuticals companies in particular are highly dependent on imported raw materials, making the industry very price-sensitive.

Finally, some of the industries started up toward the end of the Communist period have displayed more promise. There are three car producers and two manufacturers of commercial vehicles. About one third of production is exported, mostly to price-sensitive markets and other countries in the region. A joint venture between Daewoo and the government represented the first really large foreign investment in the country. The information technology industry started to develop in the early 1970s, based on importing licenses, and the growth achieved since then has been mainly the result of important research and development work. The pharmaceuticals industry is relatively small in comparison to its rivals elsewhere in the region, and production is mainly intended for domestic consumption.

State ownership of enterprises is still the predominant form of control in Romanian manufacturing. Of the 2.7 million people employed in 1998, around 2 million were in the public sector, and only around one fifth of industrial output was generated by the private sector. Privatization has proceeded slowly, despite the adoption of a comprehensive mass privatization program in 1995, while foreign investment in manufacturing remains sporadic.

## Croatia

The development of the Croatian economy was affected markedly by the political instability connected with the disintegration of the former Yugoslavia. Up to 1994, significant macroeconomic imbalances had a damaging influence on the microeconomic restructuring of manufacturing. Since stabilization was achieved at the end of 1993, serious structural problems have evolved.

The government has used monetary and exchange rate policies to protect domestic industries from foreign competition, helping them to survive even though large parts of the sector would not be viable under conditions of real market competition. As the currency, the kuna, has consistently been overvalued, exports cannot be increased and there is a large deficit on the balance of trade. In spite of the exclusion of foreign competition by way of the exchange rate policy, the rate of unemployment is close to 20%, mainly because of stagnating exports. Production is expensive and domestic demand is not sufficient to consume all that is produced, while the overvalued kuna makes imports very cheap. At the same time, the strict measures taken to control inflation, which have constituted the highest priority in the government's economic policy, have made it impossible to accumulate adequate amounts of investment capital.

Other major problems have arisen in the course of privatization. A significant proportion of manufacturing enterprises has been put in the hands of entrepreneurs who have close relations with the political leadership, and who prefer to focus on short-term profit targets rather than long-term restructuring. One consequence has been that the level of arrears on payments between companies is soaring, although other factors have contributed to this alarming trend. By 1998, the total amount of overdue debts was close to US$11 billion, or around 50% of GDP.

There are some success stories in manufacturing, especially in pharmaceuticals, perhaps the most successful industry in Croatia, and the only one to attract much foreign direct investment. However, as the role of the state is still dominant and there is a lack of fresh capital, other successful industries are difficult to find. The shipbuilding industry, for example, has traditionally been central to the Croatian economy and the government has proclaimed its determination to revitalize it, yet it still has to face the same problems as the rest of the manufacturing sector.

## Slovenia

Slovenia has successfully built on its favorable position as the most sophisticated manufacturing center of the former Yugoslavia, specializing in processing raw materials and semimanufactured goods from the southern republics. Since independence was achieved in 1991, manufacturing has become more export-oriented and a liberal import regime has been introduced. Slovenian industry started from a level of productivity that was much higher than in the other countries of central and eastern Europe, but over the past few years further progress has been slow, due to a moderate investment rate and slow privatization. Foreign direct investment has been limited and has so far financed only about 5% of all investment, one of the lowest rates in the region. While transformation of ownership has been completed for the majority of companies, restructuring has been slow for a variety of reasons, but above all because of the lack of sufficient financial resources. Undercapitalization is mainly the result of the prevailing pattern of management buyouts, combined with the impact of high real interest rates, which are aimed at avoiding large current account deficits and keeping inflation under control, but restrict enterprise investment.

Industrial production slowed down in 1995 and 1996, due to weak demand in some key export markets, the high level of the Slovene currency, the tolar, and reduced competitiveness in respect of labor costs. The industries that were particularly badly affected were paper, textiles and clothing, leather, food products, iron and steel, and printing. While these industries have not entirely recovered, electrical engineering, nonferrous metal processing, chemicals, and wood products have continued to operate relatively successfully.

These and other industries make up Slovenia's small but relatively well-developed manufacturing base, comprising more than 8,000 enterprises, of which 90% are privately owned. The degree of concentration is extremely high: 570 companies account for 80% of manufacturing employment, turnover, and exports. The most important industries are chemicals, electrical and mechanical engineering, automotive products, textiles and clothing, and paper and wood products. The chemicals industry does not include any major petrochemical activities, but there is an important tire production facility established as a joint venture between Sava and Goodyear. The pharmaceutical industry is one of the largest in the region, with production concentrated in three companies, and around 75% of output is exported, mainly to the rest of central and eastern Europe. The majority of the companies in the textiles and clothing industries are small and medium-sized enterprises, but production is concentrated in a few major companies, and wage costs are among the highest in central and eastern Europe, although still lower than in the EU. Foreign direct investment is focusing on introducing new technologies and modernizing equipment. Slovenia's very competitive forest-based industries, such as pulp, paper, and printing, enjoy high levels of inward investment, especially from companies based in the EU. Slovenia can be viewed as an emerging rival to EU countries in some niche markets in the paper industry, where the high level of privatization has played an important role.

Other industries have also been making significant contributions to Slovenia's prosperity. The steel industry is very small, but Slovenia has a relatively high degree of specialization and strong export capacity in nonferrous metals, notably aluminum. The information technology industry is small but in good shape, having originally been developed under the

program for long-term technological development implemented in the former Yugoslavia, which placed a high priority on electronics. Finally, Slovenia has a remarkable tradition in electrical and electronic consumer products, both "brown" and "white," and has been successful in maintaining a substantial level of exports to EU countries. Production is mainly based on licenses from major multinationals.

## Further Reading

Balcerowicz, Eva, editor, *The Enterprise Exit Process in Transition*, Budapest: Central European University, 1998

A collection of theoretical and empirical studies of the various exit mechanisms affecting manufacturing industry in central and eastern Europe

EBRD, *Transition Report*, London: EBRD, annual publication

This extremely useful and informative publication, which appears every October or November, combines authoritative analyses of the post-Communist economies with comprehensive statistics and forecasts. A general *Update* is published every April, and there are also annual *Country Profiles* on each economy.

Estrin, Saul, and John S. Earle, *After Voucher Privatization*, London: Centre for Economic Policy Research, 1997

This paper deals with the consequences of this particular method of privatization, which was applied in several countries, and concludes that in most cases it did not improve the performance of enterprises.

European Commission, *Agenda 2000: Commission Opinions on Applications for Membership of the EU*, Brussels: European Commission, 1998

These are official assessments by the EU's executive body of the extent to which Bulgaria, the Czech Republic, Estonia, Hungary, Latvia, Lithuania, Poland, Romania, Slovakia, and Slovenia have adapted their economies, and their systems of economic management, to meet the requirements of membership.

Havlik, Peter, *CEEC Export Competitiveness in Manufacturing Industry*, Vienna: Wiener Institut für Internationale Wirtschaftsvergleiche [Vienna Institute for International Economic Studies] – WIIW, 1996

This is one of numerous useful publications on the economies of central and eastern Europe issued by the Institute. It offers a description and evaluation of the many factors that determine export competitiveness.

Hunya, Gábor, *Large Privatization, Restructuring, and Foreign Direct Investment*, reprinted edition, Vienna: Wiener Institut für Internationale Wirtschaftsvergleiche [Vienna Institute for International Economic Studies] – WIIW, 1997

Hunya examines the ways in which the experiences of different countries in the region demonstrate the role of foreign direct investment as a major vehicle for restructuring of industries.

Hunya, Gábor, *FDI Penetration in Central European Manufacturing Industry*, Vienna: Wiener Institut für Internationale Wirtschaftsvergleiche [Vienna Institute for International Economic Studies] – WIIW, 1998

Hunya explores the key role played by foreign direct investment in the economic transformation of countries in central and eastern Europe, focusing on its interaction with increasing competitiveness in manufacturing.

Hunya, Gábor, *Integration of CEEC Manufacturing into European Corporate Structures*, Vienna: Wiener Institut für Internationale Wirtschaftsvergleiche [Vienna Institute for International Economic Studies] – WIIW, 1998

Here, Hunya examines the difficulties and rewards of building market economies and integrating these countries into the long-established division of labor in western Europe.

*Dr Tamás Novák* and *Dr Csaba Novák* are Research Fellows at the Institute for World Economics of the Hungarian Academy of Sciences in Budapest.

**Table 13.1 Official Unemployment Rates in Eight Countries in Central and Eastern Europe, 1990 and 1994–97 (% of registered labor force)**

|  | *1990* | *1994* | *1995* | *1996* | *1997* |
|---|---|---|---|---|---|
| Bulgaria | 1.7 | 12.8 | 11.1 | 12.5 | 13.7 |
| Croatia | n.a. | 14.8 | 15.1 | 15.9 | 17.6 |
| Czech Republic | 0.8 | 3.2 | 2.9 | 3.5 | 5.2 |
| Hungary | 1.9 | 11.4 | 11.1 | 10.7 | 10.4 |
| Poland | 6.3 | 16.0 | 14.9 | 13.2 | 10.5 |
| Romania | n.a. | 10.9 | 9.5 | 6.6 | 8.8 |
| Slovakia | 1.6 | 14.8 | 13.1 | 12.8 | 12.5 |
| Slovenia | 5.8 | 14.2 | 14.5 | 14.4 | 14.8 |

Sources: EBRD, *Transition Report*, London: EBRD, 1995–98

Chapter Fourteen

# Banking and Other Financial Services

## *Łukasz Konopielko*

When the transformation process started in central and eastern Europe, it was obvious that one of the most important elements of reform had to be structural changes in the financial system. In order to overcome their macroeconomic difficulties, these countries have applied mostly heterodox policies, as they simultaneously dealt with price liberalization, the establishment of property rights, and macroeconomic stabilization. In spite of the macroeconomic imbalances, microeconomic distortions have often been neglected, although they may well be more important in this region than in less developed countries. Price liberalization, the opening up of trade, and rapid privatization did not necessarily eliminate these distortions, but even strengthened some of them. Even if the domestic financial markets have been formally liberalized, inherited institutional structures will determine the structure of financial systems for a certain amount of time (see Buch 1996a). The crucial role of the financial system was recognized from the beginning of the transition, but the methods applied have differed from country to country. Not surprisingly, after less than 10 years, the results achieved are also far from being uniform (see Table 14.1).

The ultimate goals to be achieved by the financial sectors of central and eastern Europe can be defined by reference to the main features of banking in market economies. They are to become integrated into the world economy, financially sound, and privately owned; while the allocation of their resources is to be governed by the price system, and supported by an appropriate legal framework to enforce and complement contracts. However, views differ substantially on the necessary and sufficient conditions for reaching these goals.

## The Financial System in Centrally Planned Economies

Most of the countries in central and eastern Europe had significant financial sectors before World War II (see Cecco, and Cottrell), but the restricted and dwarfed financial systems in the planned economies developed along the same contradictory lines as the economies that they formed parts of (see Zwass). In each country, the financial system was regulated and directed by the Ministry of Finance and the National Bank. In general, the system comprised a "monobank," in which commercial and central bank functions were combined, and a few state-owned insurance firms; there were no securities, money or foreign exchange markets.

The separation between real flows and monetary flows under central planning resulted in a significant underdevelopment of the banking system. Banks were not treated as a special kind of institution, but were regarded as one of the instruments of administrative economic control. In this system, all enterprises had an account with the National Bank, which in turn ran these accounts in accordance with the administrative plans. Enterprises were obliged to keep their accounts, clear their business transactions, and obtain loans only through whichever branch of the monobank (or, in some countries, other state-owned bank) was designated for their use. However, these banks did not direct money and credit flows: since management of financial flows was a centrally administered task, banks functioned only as relatively insignificant accounting institutions. The same was true of the insurance institutions, which conducted risk-taking activities only with respect to domestic assets held abroad and foreign assets held within the country.

As private ownership was excluded from banking – with the exception of a number of cooperative banks – short-term credit and clearing operations in the production sphere, and control over the circulation of money, were conducted by the National Banks. They were banks of issue, but they also performed commercial functions, running the accounts of enterprises and allocating funds in accordance with the central plan. In order to service foreign trade, some banks from the pre-Communist period, such as Bank Handlowy in Poland or Živnostenská Banka in Czechoslovakia, did not cease operations in centrally planned economies, but were transferred to state ownership. Such banks were almost completely subordinated to the National Banks, and were generally not exposed to any type of profit-motivated activity. Thus, they became bureaucratic institutions, without any business skills related to credit appraisal, product marketing, and so on (see Slay). Only a small proportion of their staffs, especially in foreign transactions departments, possessed some market-related skills in, for example, foreign exchange oversight, or asset and liability management.

Money played a more significant role for households, although to a certain extent it was limited by the shortages of products in the retail sector. Savings banks were in some cases formally separated from the National Banks (such as PKO bp in Poland or OTP Bank in Hungary), but concentrated their activities almost exclusively on accumulating cash deposits from the population in domestic or convertible currencies. Deposits placed in these savings banks were implicitly guaranteed by the state. They were also able to grant loans to individuals, within strict limits. However, consumption of goods was more restricted by shortages of real products than by households' insufficient monetary balances. Most individual transactions were settled by cash

and the use of more sophisticated cash substitutes was limited.

No significant changes occurred in the institutional frameworks of the region's banking systems before the mid-1980s, when some reforms were undertaken. For example, in 1985, Poland institutionally separated its savings bank, PKO bp, from the National Bank of Poland, and in 1987 Hungary created a restricted two-tier system. In fact, in all the countries of the region, real reforms of the banking system started in the late 1980s, with the disaggregation of the centrally planned monobanking system.

## Banking in the 1990s

The banks in central and eastern Europe can be roughly divided into two main groups. First, several were created on the basis of the former monobanks. The monobanks transferred assets to the newly created banks along the lines of their established branch networks These banks started their commercial activities with these inherited portfolios, and in most cases were still fully owned by the state. For example, in Poland nine regional banks were created from the former National Bank, while in Hungary only three banks emerged, their assets being assigned by specialization in industrial sectors. Later, these banks started to diversify their portfolios, and enter into new activities, and in most cases they were subjected to privatization.

Second, a wave of new entries occurred, led by private capital, both domestic and foreign. Foreign (mostly European) capital is particularly visible in Hungary, where, by the end of 1997, more than 50% of banking capital was held by foreign owners. However, this large proportion of foreign capital was achieved through the privatization of major state-owned banks by way of sales to strategic foreign investors. In other countries in the region, the proportion of foreign capital is lower, ranging from 15% to 25%.

Whatever their origins, most banks in the region remain small in comparison with their western counterparts (see Table 14.2). As of 1997, Komerčni Banka in the Czech Republic, the largest single bank in central and eastern Europe, was the 289th largest bank in the world, as measured by capitalization, and the 358th largest as measured by size of assets (see *The Banker*).

Against this background, in the late 1980s and early 1990s banking in the region was still characterized by structural underdevelopment; a high level of monopolization, especially on the regional level; and institutional over-banking. Smaller banks were undercapitalized, and there was little supervision of their activities, leading to a number of scandals and liquidity disturbances. There was also a high potential for future competition among the banks, because of the fragmentation of the former monobank networks (see Slay).

Above all, however, banks were trapped by the inherited stock of troublesome bad debts and nonperforming loans on their balance sheets (see Table 14.3). A number of explanations have been put forward for the persistence of this problem, involving the overall deterioration of the economies in the region; the rises in interest rates; the banks' inherited lending criteria; and the weakness of accounting and information systems (see Buch 1996b). Bank recapitalization is closely linked with the problem of bad loans, and, given implicit deposit insurance, bad loans plague the governments and taxpayers of these countries too. Large proportions of these debts were caused by the fact that under Communism loans were not allocated on a commercial basis. Thus it is hardly surprising that in the new commercial environment many of these loans should turn out to be unrecoverable. Further, bank staff, having had no experience of allocating loans commercially, may well continue to misallocate credit for a significant period after market constraints have been imposed.

The countries of the region have applied various policies to tackle these problems. In the Czech Republic, a special "consolidation bank" was created to extract nonperforming loans from banks' portfolios. In Hungary, the state conducted a series of debt buyouts. In Poland, banks received Treasury securities in proportion to the volume of individual debt workouts performed by special divisions within the banks.

Another aspect of the segmentation of financial systems in the 1990s was that corporate and household finances were separated. A few large state savings banks (or in some countries just one bank) handled deposits and credits for the household sector, while other banks operated only with clients from the corporate sector. This counteracted the aim of promoting competition for household deposits, and consequently lowered the level of savings, as banking services were not widely accessible. In addition, several legislative measures contributed to the maintenance of "walls" within the financial systems of these countries. Depending on the degree of trade liberalization, which differed from country to country, not every bank was allowed by law to be involved in foreign trade and deal in foreign currencies. This had the adverse effect of concentrating highly skilled staff in those institutions that did handle foreign exchange, while other banks badly needed these skills. Concentration of portfolios meant that, in the case of Hungary for example, in 1993 the largest bank held one third of the assets of the entire corporate sector.

Because of segmentation of services and concentration of portfolios, the fate of the banks depended on that of a few of their clients: the bankruptcy of one or two enterprises could result in the bankruptcy of a bank. Most of the banks were still state-owned, their managements had distorted incentives, and the banks were still undercapitalized, with the result that the banks continued to lend to the enterprises with which they had established connections. On the other hand, close links between newly created banks and their owners in the corporate sector resulted in analogous problems of insider lending. Legislation often did not require the creation of provisions for bad debts from pretax profits, and did not enable banks to do this in Hungary, for example, until 1992, or in Poland until 1994. Some banks reported extremely high profits in comparison to international banks, mainly because of their neglect of doubtful loans. This also distorted the relative creditworthiness of banks, and caused valuation problems in the course of privatization (see Kormendi and Snyder).

Ownership of banks by the state created additional problems. The relative abundance of assets in state banks exposed them to the pressures of special interest groups, and some "spontaneous" forms of privatization occurred, leading to insider takeovers on very generous conditions. Some cases, such as the privatization of Bank Śląski in Poland, or takeovers by Motoinvest in the Czech Republic, were judged to have taken the form of criminal offenses, which were subsequently prosecuted. Yet prosecution was very difficult, because regulations were unclear and the political circumstances were changing rapidly. Another problem was that state-owned banks were characterized by negative net worth, while their inherent franchise value was positive (see Kormendi and Snyder). Once again, this caused the valuation process to be very difficult and complicated, creating incentives for rapid privatization based on low net value, with annexed provisions for writing off nonperforming debts at the public expense.

Yet another issue that significantly affected the development of financial services in central and eastern Europe was the inefficiency of payment systems. Insufficient or obsolete computer networks, and underdevelopment of telecommunication services, lengthened check-clearing and other money transmission services. This, in turn, affected the absolute level of liquidity provision. It also allowed operations that could undermine the stability of a whole system, as in the Art-B case in Poland (see Rostowski).

In a number of countries in the region, all these factors contributed to a significant banking crisis, as in Estonia in 1992, and in Latvia and Lithuania in 1995. In Poland, a wave of smaller bank failures took place over the period 1992–94, while the same happened in the Czech Republic and Bulgaria in 1996. These crises provided powerful support for the argument that the development of supervisory institutions and proper regulatory structures is crucial to the transformation process.

## Banking Reforms in Poland, Hungary, and the Czech Republic

In order to illustrate the characteristic features of the reforms implemented to address these problems, the banking systems of Poland,

Hungary, and the Czech Republic will be briefly analyzed. All three entered the transition period with a number of similarities (see Table 14.4). However, each of these countries has taken its own course in reforming banking, in respect of the five main factors in play: the treatment of new entrants, particularly foreign banks; methods for dealing with the bad debt problem; the speed and method of bank privatization; reform of the regulatory environment; and the overall level of financial intermediation.

Poland adopted a relatively liberal attitude towards new entrants (especially in the period 1990–92), privatized a number of state-owned banks, with a significant use of the stock market, and applied moderate measures toward foreign competition. Its method of dealing with bad debt problems, through individual workouts by banks and other debtors, supported by state-backed bonds, appeared to be relatively successful, reducing the burden of bad debts to 10% by 1997. Some efforts have also been made to consolidate the fragmented banking industry, with both state-owned banks (such as PeKaO SA) and private sector banks (such as Kredyt Bank and BIG Bank) becoming leaders in mergers and acquisitions of other banks (see Konopielko).

Hungary experienced a long period of bad debt bailout financed from budgetary funds, but then decided to privatize its banks, mostly by sales to strategic foreign investors without recourse to the stock market. As has been mentioned, this led to the highest proportion of foreign capital in any banking system in the region, as well as to an overall improvement in the capital adequacy ratio.

At the other extreme, the Czech Republic floated only minority shareholdings in its banks in the stock market, while the state retained control. Foreign entry was allowed mostly through the establishment of branches of foreign banks, while the level of concentration remains high.

The approach to privatization significantly affected the outcome of the financial restructuring of bad debt. Hungary generally overcame these difficulties by passing the remaining debts to new owners. In Poland, restructured banks were sold in most cases, while in the

Czech Republic bad debt problems still persist. It therefore appears that the most efficient sequence would be to restructure banks and then sell them as quickly as possible, in order to avoid further bailouts. Such rapid sales would also achieve some additional objectives, such as establishing a strong presence for domestic investors. In contrast, prolonged restructuring under state ownership does not allow for domestic private capital formation in banking, thus leaving banks open to takeover by foreign investors. In such a process, the role of the stock market remains crucial: it is not only a useful tool in the valuation of banks, but it also allows banks to adopt more flexible approaches to investment negotiations.

Only in the case of the Czech Republic does the ratio of banking assets to GDP appear to be on a par with EU standards. Once again, this underlines the magnitude of the bad debt problems in the Czech case, but it also provides an idea of the possibilities for expansion through further investment in other countries in the region. As the Hungarian banking system is perceived to be already equally well-developed in all respects, future investment may be expected from all types of banks. In the Polish case, however, there appears to be an imbalance between the quality and level of corporate services, and the quality and level of retail services. Substantial further development in retail banking in Poland should therefore be expected.

This brief survey of three countries in the region permits some general conclusions to be drawn. In particular, it is likely that the main factors in achieving improvements in the performance of the banking systems in all 15 countries must include an overall improvement in the economic situation; successful financial restructuring and a clearing out of bad debts; the privatization and consolidation of banks; and the gradual admission of foreign entrants into banking.

## The Insurance Industry

The situation of the insurance industry in central and eastern Europe is quite similar to that of banking. In particular, many insurance firms carry a burden of old policies that has an impact analogous to that of the bad debt burden on banking. One important difference, however, is that the insurance industry tends to be even more concentrated. In most countries in the region, large state-owned companies, or recently privatized firms, are still the market leaders. Thus, as of 1997 the market share of the three largest nonlife companies varied from more than 80% in Poland to around 40% in Estonia, and the market shares for the largest life companies were generally higher still. Nevertheless, these large, well-established firms are slowly losing market share to private insurers, particularly foreign-owned companies.

The usage of insurance services is very low by western standards, whether measured by insurance density, which is the volume of premiums per capita, or by insurance penetration, the ratio of the volume of premiums to GDP (see Table 14.5). Around 75% of all insurance business is nonlife, almost all of which is motor insurance, reflecting the prevalence of obligatory and regulated liability policies in most countries in the region, as well as the increasing number of new car registrations. Demand for life insurance is increasing, both because of new tax incentives, and because of the increasing availability of policies supported by intensified marketing activities, especially on the part of foreign-owned firms. Such "organic" growth will also be supported by reforms of pension systems, which in most countries have included (as in Hungary and Poland), or are expected to include, the introduction of obligatory reliance on the private sector. Whether as substitutes for state-operated "pay as you go" pension schemes, or, more usually, as supplements to them, these new schemes will redirect a significant proportion of pension contributions to fully funded capital pension funds (see Charlton et al.). It is also likely that increases in real incomes, and growing awareness of the different types of insurance policies, will benefit insurance firms more generally, across the region.

## Capital Markets

In general, capital markets, including securities and financial institutions other than banks, remain the least developed financial services in central and eastern Europe. On the eve of the collapse of Communism and the start of the transition, banking and insurance institutions did exist throughout the region, albeit, as we have seen, in more or less rudimentary forms, but capital markets had not existed for more than 40 years. During the 1990s, in contrast, capital markets have not only provided alternatives to reliance on banks for financing, but, crucially, they have also allowed clear attribution of ownership rights, which in turn has encouraged foreign investors and helped to accelerate the overall process of restructuring.

The new governments across the region encouraged the development of securities markets in particular, because they regarded this as an indispensable element of reconstruction. Most of the newly established stock exchanges now possess relatively modern and transparent regulatory structures. Those in Warsaw and Budapest are generally perceived as the most advanced, although, like others in the region, the volumes traded are relatively low in comparison to exchanges in more mature markets. Nevertheless, stock exchanges have played important roles in the privatization of large state-owned firms, both as sources of valuation and as venues capable of accommodating significant portions of the shares offered to the public. In Poland, for example, all the major privatizations in 1998, such as the sales of the country's largest bank, PeKaO SA, or of the former state telecommunication monopoly, Telekomunikacja Polska SA, were combined with their listing on the Warsaw Stock Exchange.

Corporate securities from the region are also increasingly traded abroad, in the form of American or global depositary receipts, which simplify investment for foreign-based entities. For example, shares in Telekomunikacja Polska SA are now quoted in the form of global depositary receipts on the stock exchanges in London, Frankfurt, Berlin, and Munich.

Another capital market that developed comparatively quickly in most countries in the region was the market for financing public debt. Treasury bills and similar instruments are increasingly popular instruments, replacing direct lending from national banks in the financing of budget deficits and the restructuring of foreign debts. As deficits and debts alike are widespread across the region, state debt instruments provide relatively high yields with perceived low levels of risk, and therefore attract foreign institutions and individuals as well as domestic investors. Most countries in the region have started to use such sovereign debt instruments as Eurobonds and global bonds. It has been estimated that in 1997 the 27 post-Communist countries (15 in central and eastern Europe, and 12 in the CIS) together accounted for 17% of the worldwide total of US$88 billion-worth of sovereign bond issuance (see Merrill Lynch).

Meanwhile, several other capital market activities that have become familiar in the West remain either in a nascent phase, or all but unknown, in central and eastern Europe. As a result, it is likely that in the near future there will be several opportunities for introducing and developing corporate bonds, derivatives, and other modern financial instruments.

## The Outlook

After the banking crises of the early and mid-1990s, discussed above, the financial systems of most countries in central and eastern Europe became more secure. The majority of large banks are now trustworthy, and several have been given comparatively good credit ratings, in some cases equal to sovereign grades, by the main international rating agencies. However, the banking systems of the region still display several features that create serious problems, especially in relation to preparations for membership of the EU. The pace of regulatory adjustment to EU standards is generally slow; banks still have low levels of capital adequacy, linked to low levels of capitalization; they tend to be significantly less efficient, and less developed technologically, than in the West; and most still lack a client-oriented approach to their operations.

Central and eastern Europe offers a potentially huge market for financial technology. There are still relatively few automated teller machines, computer systems, and other advanced technologies in use, and those that are in place are often obsolete. This contributes to high employment costs, as many standard procedures are still performed manually. Enhanced use of advanced technologies is severely restricted by the lag in telecommunications and other industries. Clearing systems have been reformed, but the number of transactions served by electronic systems is relatively small. As a result, foreign banks have been able to attract significant numbers of corporate customers by offering them rapid and efficient payment services associated with online banking systems. Technological underdevelopment is also a major obstacle to the introduction of credit and payment card services on a large scale. For example, in Poland the number of cards issued by the end of 1998 was less than 2 million, although it was growing very fast.

Sales and customer relations were neglected during the Communist period, and, as in all other branches of industry, marketing and sales skills were virtually nonexistent. In many state-owned banks and insurance firms, customers were treated as supplicants, not as the most important sources of revenue. Foreign institutions have thus been able to gain significant advantages because of their skill in dealing with customers, and their marketing activities have attracted corporate customers by offering them individually tailored services. Across the region, most of the more innovative instruments, such as futures contracts and new forms of financing, have been introduced by foreign banks, such as ING, Citibank, or Creditanstalt in Poland, and only later adopted by the leading domestic banks. Domestic banks have also taken some steps toward improving their relations with clients, as a means of improving their competitiveness.

The reconstruction and transformation of the financial systems of central and eastern Europe are still far from complete, and the density and quality of financial services, although much improved during the past few years, are still a long way behind the standards taken for granted in the West. In particular, retail financial services have been neglected. In 1997, for example, a survey conducted in Poland, one of the more advanced countries in the region, found that, while an estimated 50% of households maintained savings, only

25% had current accounts at banks; only 6% were engaged in credit transactions; only around 1% had credit or debit cards; and 36.7% of those questioned had never used a bank (see Miklaszewska). These figures, and similar survey results in other countries, point to the high potential for growth in banking and other financial services, especially if the underdevelopment of noncash payment systems, and the often low density of branch networks, are also taken into account. Other interesting fields for further expansion, in line with higher economic growth and continuing restructuring of industry, include investment banking and mortgage financing. There may well be many more opportunities in the insurance industry and in capital markets, but in many cases clear regulations are either lacking or still pending. Finally, the presence of foreign banks and foreign capital in central and eastern Europe is in itself a clear indication of market-based economic normalization. All these changes are making the financial systems of the region more open, more competitive, and better prepared for future EU membership, as well as for the challenges of the global economy.

## Further Reading

*Banker, The, The Top 1,000 World Banks*, London: FT Finance, 1998

  A listing of the world's largest banks, with basic data on each

Buch, Claudia (1996a), *Opening up for Foreign Banks*, Kiel: Kiel Institute for World Economics, 1996

  A brief discussion of foreign entrants into the banking systems of central and eastern Europe

Buch, Claudia (1996b), *Creating Efficient Banking Systems: Theory and Evidence from Eastern Europe*, Tübingen: J. C. B. Mohr, 1996

  A broad description of the early stages of the transition in banking

Cecco, Marcello de, *Central Banking in Central and Eastern Europe: Lessons from the Interwar Years' Experience*, Washington, DC: IMF, 1994

  A comparison of banking in central and eastern Europe between the world wars with the system in the 1990s

Charlton, Roger, Roddy McKinnon, and Łukasz Konopielko, "Pension Reform, Privatization and Restructuring in the Transition: Unfinished Business or Inappropriate Agendas?" in *Europe-Asia Studies*, Volume 50, number 8, 1998

A review of reforms in the pension systems of central and eastern Europe

Cottrell, Philip L., editor, *Rebuilding the Financial System in Central and Eastern Europe, 1918–1994*, Aldershot: Scolar Press, and Brookfield, VT: Ashgate, 1997

A collection of essays on various aspects of the region's financial systems

EBRD, *Transition Report 1998*, London: EBRD, 1998

An excellent review of major economic issues in the post-Communist states, with a special section devoted to financial services

Keuschnigg, Mirela, "Banking in Central and Eastern Europe," in *Moct-Most*, number 7, 1997

A cross-country analysis of data on monetary and banking reform

Konopielko, Łukasz, "A Note on Polish Bank Consolidation," in *Journal of Comparative Economics*, Volume 25, number 3, 1997

An analysis of mergers and acquisitions in the Polish banking industry

Kormendi, Roger, and Edward Snyder, *Bank Privatization in Transitional Economies*, Davidson Institute, 1996

A working paper that addresses major issues in bank privatization in post-Communist economies

Merrill Lynch, *Emerging Markets Debt Strategy*, January 1998

An appraisal of various issues of debt instruments by countries in central and eastern Europe

Miklaszewska, Ewa, editor, *Global Tendencies and Changes in East European Banking*, Kraków: Jagiellonian University, 1998

Papers from an international conference on banking in the region

Rostowski, Jacek, editor, *Banking Reform in Central Europe and the Former Soviet Union*, Budapest: Central European University, 1995

An assessment of the lessons from reforms of financial services, and their impact on the macroeconomic situation

Slay, Ben, "Polish Banks on the Road to Recovery," in *Post-Soviet Geography and Economics*, Volume 37, number 8, 1996

An overview of major issues in the Polish banking system

Swiss Re, *Sigma*, number 7, Zürich: Swiss Re, 1998

A special issue devoted to the insurance industry in central and eastern Europe

Zwass, Adam, *Money, Banking and Credit in the Soviet Union and Eastern Europe*, London: Macmillan, and White Plains, NY: M. E. Sharpe, 1979

An in-depth analysis of centrally planned banking systems

*Dr Łukasz Konopielko* is a Fellow of the Central and East European Economic Research Center in the Department of Economics at the University of Warsaw in Poland.

## Table 14.1 Progress on Reform of Financial Systems in Central and Eastern Europe (except Yugoslavia), as Assessed by the EBRD, 1998

| | Banking and interest rates | Securities markets and nonbank institutions |
|---|---|---|
| Albania | 2 | 2– |
| Bosnia-Herzegovina | 2 | 1 |
| Bulgaria | 3– | 2 |
| Croatia | 3– | 2+ |
| Czech Republic | 3 | 3 |
| Estonia | 3+ | 3 |
| Hungary | 4 | 3+ |
| Latvia | 3– | 2+ |
| Lithuania | 3 | 2+ |
| Macedonia | 3 | 2– |
| Poland | 3+ | 3+ |
| Romania | 2+ | 2 |
| Slovakia | 3– | 2+ |
| Slovenia | 3 | 3 |

*Key*

Banking and interest rates

1 Little progress beyond the establishment of a two-tier banking system
2 Significant liberalization of interest rates and credit allocation; limited use of directed credit or interest rate ceilings
3 Substantial progress on establishing bank solvency, and a framework for prudential supervision and regulation; full liberalization of interest rates, with little preferential access to cheap refinancing; significant lending to private enterprises; significant presence of private banking
4 Significant movement of banking laws and regulations towards the standards set by the Bank for International Settlements; well-functioning banking competition; effective prudential supervision; significant term lending to private enterprises; substantial financial deepening

Securities markets and nonbank institutions

1 Little progress
2 Formation of securities exchanges, market-makers and brokers; some trading in government paper and/or securities; rudimentary legal and regulatory framework for the issuance and trading of securities
3 Substantial issuance of securities by private enterprises; establishment of independent share registries; secure clearance and settlement procedures, and some protection of minority shareholders; emergence of nonbank institutions, such as investment funds, private insurance companies, pension funds, and leasing companies, and of the associated regulatory framework
4 Securities laws and regulations approaching the standards set by the International Organization of Securities Commissions; substantial market liquidity and capitalization; well-functioning nonbank institutions and effective regulation

Source: EBRD, *Transition Report 1998*

**Table 14.2  The 12 Largest Banks in Central and Eastern Europe, 1998 (US$ millions)**

|                          | Country        | Capital | Assets | Pretax profits |
|--------------------------|----------------|---------|--------|----------------|
| Komerčni Banka           | Czech Republic | 970     | 13,573 | 11             |
| Bank PeKaO SA            | Poland         | 900     | 14,188 | 352            |
| Bank Handlowy            | Poland         | 718     | 4,711  | 218            |
| Česká Spořitelna         | Czech Republic | 631     | 11,145 | 41             |
| BGZ                      | Poland         | 609     | 4,183  | 173            |
| PKO bp                   | Poland         | 503     | 13,307 | 220            |
| Obchodní Banka           | Czech Republic | 437     | 6,681  | 116            |
| Beogradska Banka         | Yugoslavia     | 358     | 7,088  | −3             |
| Banca Comerciala Romana  | Romania        | 338     | 2,249  | 182            |
| Vseobecná úverová banka  | Slovakia       | 337     | 4,458  | −1             |
| Zagrebacka Banka         | Croatia        | 330     | 3,669  | 71             |
| OTP Bank                 | Hungary        | 317     | 7,058  | 121            |

Source: *Banker, The, The Top 1,000 World Banks*, London: FT Finance, 1998

**Table 14.3  Nonperforming Loans as Proportions of Total Loans in 11 Countries in Central and Eastern Europe, 1991–97 (%)**

|                | 1991 | 1995 | 1997 |
|----------------|------|------|------|
| Albania        | n.a. | 40   | 49   |
| Bulgaria       | 40   | 13   | 13   |
| Czech Republic | 2.4  | 39   | 29   |
| Estonia        | n.a. | 3    | 1    |
| Hungary        | 10   | 19   | 4    |
| Latvia         | n.a. | 19   | 10   |
| Lithuania      | n.a. | 17   | 28   |
| Poland         | 15   | 21   | 10   |
| Romania        | n.a. | 30   | 57   |
| Slovakia       | n.a. | 42   | 33   |
| Slovenia       | n.a. | 13   | 12   |

Sources: Keuschnigg, M., "Banking in Central and Eastern Europe," in *Moct-Most*, number 7, 1997; EBRD, *Transition Report 1998*

**Table 14.4  The Banking Systems of Poland, Hungary, and the Czech Republic, as at December 31, 1996**

|  | Poland | Hungary | Czech Republic |
|---|---|---|---|
| Number of commercial banks[1] | 79 | 41 | 53 |
| Foreign capital (% of total) | 27.7 | 49.22 | 24.12 |
| State capital (% of total) | 49.3 | 33.17 | 31[2] |
| Branches of foreign banks | 3 | 0 | 9 |
| Average capital adequacy ratio (%) | n.a. | 15.18 | 10.32 |
| Assets of three largest banks, 1993 (% of total) | 42.4 | 46.4 | 65.1 |
| Assets of three largest banks, 1995 (% of total) | 39.3 | 36.9 | 50.8 |
| Banks listed on stock exchange, 1996 | 13 | 2 | 4 |
| Total assets, 1994 (US$ billions) | 49.8 | 27.3 | 53.7 |
| Total assets, 1995 (% of GDP) | 57 | 54 | 69 |

1  Excluding cooperative banks
2  Excluding indirect ownership

Sources:  Data supplied by the central banks of the three countries

**Table 14.5  The Insurance Industry in 12 Countries in Central and Eastern Europe, 1997**

|  | Total premiums (US$ millions) | Premiums per capita (US$) | Premiums (% of GDP) |
|---|---|---|---|
| Albania | 8 | 2.2 | 0.32 |
| Bulgaria | 161 | 19.6 | 1.59 |
| Croatia | 574 | 126.8 | 2.94 |
| Czech Republic | 1,513 | 146.8 | 2.91 |
| Estonia | 128 | 54.3 | 1.68 |
| Hungary | 1,043 | 102.8 | 2.34 |
| Latvia | 115 | 46.5 | 2.09 |
| Lithuania | 63 | 17.1 | 0.66 |
| Poland | 3,753 | 97.1 | 2.77 |
| Romania | 193 | 8.6 | 0.55 |
| Slovakia | 505 | 93.8 | 2.59 |
| Slovenia | 678 | 341.3 | 3.73 |

Source:   Swiss Re, *Sigma*, number 7, Zürich: Swiss Re, 1998

Chapter Fifteen

# Economic Relations with Russia

## *Kalman Dezseri*

Each country in central and eastern Europe has always had to balance considerations of its own interests and ambitions with the necessity to respond to the influence and intervention of external powers. Together, these countries form a region in which the interests of Germany, Austria, and other western European powers have frequently collided with those of Russia (or, for a time, the Soviet Union) over the centuries. Relations with Russia in particular have gone through a series of historical phases characterized by shifts in orientation, sometimes in Russia's favor and sometimes in opposition to it. Nevertheless, the traditional orientation of the region has generally been toward western Europe, whether expressed through economic interests, cultural identity, or political links. This orientation is being reinforced in our own time by the processes of NATO and EU enlargement.

It should also be emphasized that since the early years of the 19th century the economic and political orientation of Russia in its relations with the rest of Europe has been a subject of continual debate, both within Russia and outside it. The intensity of this debate has varied substantially in different periods, but it has repeatedly reverted to a focus on two contested concepts: Russia as a "western," or at least westernizing, country; and Russia as a special case, a "Eurasian" power distinct from West and East alike. For obvious reasons, this debate intensified once again after the collapse of the Communist regimes in central and eastern Europe in 1989–90 and the disintegration of the Soviet Union itself in 1991.

In the post-Soviet era, Russian foreign policy has given unambiguous priority to relations with the newly independent states that seceded from the Soviet Union, which are known to Russian policy-makers as "the near abroad" and which share membership of the CIS with Russia. Accordingly, the economic and political importance to Russia of the former allies of the Soviet Union in central and eastern Europe has undergone some reevaluation. Russian policy no longer treats these countries, or any group of them, as a single bloc, but pursues relations with them country by country. Thus, from the point of view of political and security relations, the Czech Republic and Hungary have generally been considered to be among the less important countries of the region for Russian policy-makers. In contrast, Bulgaria, Poland, Romania, and Slovakia have received more attention, for a variety of reasons. However, the issue of NATO membership has already modified the situation, initially in respect of Poland, which has now joined the alliance, and then in relation to other countries that have declared their intention of joining it. Russia also has varying priorities and preferences in its economic relations with the countries of central and eastern Europe, which are significantly influenced by the varying orientations of those countries toward the EU.

## Trade Relations

For more than four decades up to the end of the 1980s, central and eastern Europe and the Soviet Union were each other's most important trading partner. In 1989 and 1990, central and eastern Europe received more than 23% of Soviet exports and provided around 40% of Soviet imports; while the Soviet Union accounted for 35–40% of the region's exports and 30–35% of its imports. Mutual trade was directed within the framework of the Council for Mutual Economic Assistance (Comecon), which differed significantly from the security framework of the Warsaw Pact in that it included Albania for much of the Communist period and accorded associate membership to Yugoslavia from 1964. However, Comecon ceased to function effectively after the collapse of the Communist regimes in the region and was formally dissolved in June 1991.

No longer compelled to submit their economic policy-making to Soviet interests, the countries of the region began a profound reorientation of their economic and commercial relations toward closer integration with the EU. There was a rapid decline in the turnover of trade between these countries, on the one hand, and the Soviet Union and its successor states, on the other, which reached its lowest level in 1993 and 1994. The sharp decline in trade turnover resulted from the deep economic recession both in Russia and in central and eastern Europe, and the rapid rupturing of economic ties further aggravated the industrial recession. Between 1991 and 1995, GDP decreased by 30–40% in central and eastern Europe, and by more than 50% in the CIS countries. However, despite these serious difficulties, the turnover of trade between Russia and the countries of central and eastern Europe remained relatively more significant than the mutual trade turnover within the CIS, which was reduced by more than 60% between 1991 and 1995.

As soon as the economic situation had become relatively stable, particularly in central and eastern Europe, the decline in trade turnover stopped. Exports to Russia began to increase slowly in 1994, while exports from Russia started growing in 1995. Both upward trends have been unstable and uneven, however. Russian exports to the region have gradually increased overall, while the region's exports to Russia declined again in 1996 and began to increase again in 1997.

As a result of these trends, while Russia's total exports have increased continuously since 1992, the share of central and eastern Europe within that total has decreased. It fell from more than 23% in 1992 to less than 12% in 1994, as Russian supplies to these countries declined even in nominal terms; but then rose to around 15% because the region's imports from Russia grew faster than total Russian exports. Meanwhile, the region's share in Russia's total imports from the rest of the world has also fluctuated, although broadly in line with the fluctuations across the range of imports into Russia. The fact that imports into Russia have been pursuing a less dynamic course than its exports may be explained largely by reference to the financial and foreign exchange constraints that Russia has faced throughout the 1990s.

There have been similar changes in the relative importance of trade with Russia in the exports and imports of central and eastern Europe. Trade with Russia shrank continuously from 17.7% of the region's total trade in 1991 to around 8% in 1992 and to 5.6% in 1997. However, while the nominal value of exports to Russia also decreased at first, after 1993 it began to grow, indicating that the value of the region's total exports was increasing more substantially than that of its exports to Russia. As for Russia's share in the region's total imports, it stood at around 18.8% in 1991 but then fell, to remain in a range between 9.6% and 12.4% for the rest of the decade. There have been significant fluctuations within these ranges, both in respect of various commodities and in relation to the different countries of the region, but the steady flow of fuel supplies from Russia to most of these countries has provided some underlying stability.

## Geographic Distribution of Trade

In general, trade linkages with Russia are more important for the Baltic states (Estonia, Latvia, and Lithuania), the countries of southeastern Europe, or, indeed, the other 11 countries that share CIS membership with Russia than they are for Poland, Hungary, the Czech Republic, and Slovakia. (In passing, it should be mentioned that many publications still refer to these four countries as the "Visegrád Four," even though since 1996 Slovenia has also been a member of the Central European Free Trade Association formed in that city in 1992.)

Indeed, Russia's share in the total trade of Poland, Hungary, the Czech Republic, and Slovakia decreased almost continuously, from 7.5% in 1992 to less than 5% in 1995, before beginning to rise once more. This improvement, which has been on a relatively small scale, almost entirely reflects the improved export performance of Polish goods. Russia's share of the total imports of these four countries declined from 18% in 1991 to 8% in 1997.

Nevertheless, Poland shares with Bulgaria the distinction of having the highest exposure to Russia of any of the countries of central and eastern Europe. Both these countries supply around 8–10% of their total exports to Russia, while Russia's share of the total imports of Bulgaria remains in a range between 25% and 30%. It is, however, important to note that in Poland there is additional substantial cross-border trade that is not captured by trade statistics.

The relative importance of Russia in the trade relations of all three Baltic states has fallen sharply since they regained their independence. Russia's share in total imports into Estonia and Latvia, which had stood at 17% and 28% respectively in 1993, fell to around 15% for both countries by 1997. In the case of Lithuania, however, Russia's share of imports remained quite high, exceeding 24% throughout the 1990s, and in some years by a substantial margin. In contrast, the importance of the Baltic states in the total exports and imports of Russia doubled between 1992 and 1997, from 1.7% to 3.7% in the case of exports and from 0.9% to 1.9% in the case of imports. However, these official figures should be treated with some caution, particularly those for the first years of independence, since it is unlikely that they captured the full range of trade between Russia and these three countries.

Even greater caution must be observed in handling aggregate statistics for the group of Balkan states (Albania, Bosnia-Herzegovina, Bulgaria, Croatia, Macedonia, Romania, Slovenia, and "rump" Yugoslavia), which are rendered unreliable above all because of the wars in the former Yugoslavia. However, in broad terms it seems clear that the share of these eight countries in the total exports and

imports of Russia decreased significantly between 1992 and 1997, by around 50% in those countries with relatively reliable statistics (Romania, Bulgaria, and Slovenia) and by perhaps as much as 60% in the other five. The share of Russia in the total foreign trade of these Balkan countries developed somewhat differently. Its share of their total exports decreased from 7.1% to 3.9% between 1992 and 1997, while its share of their total imports fluctuated between 6.5% and 10%, indicating that Russia is more important to the Balkans as a supplier than as a market.

In addition to direct trade between Russia and central and eastern Europe, indirect trade links exist through intermediary, "third country" markets. For example, the exposure of Hungary and Macedonia to indirect trade was recently estimated at 20–30% of their total exports. Similar figures can reasonably be expected in the case of other countries in the region. This implies that commercial relations between Russia and the region may well be more significant than official statistics on bilateral trade are capable of showing.

## The Balance of Trade

The total balance of trade of the Soviet Union and then of its successor states was in significant deficit until 1992, but since then Russia in particular has achieved increasing surpluses, both in total trade and in its trade with the countries of central and eastern Europe. Russia exports more to the region – mainly oil – than it imports from them. As a result, in 1992 Russia's trade surplus in relation to the region accounted for around 75% of its total trade surplus. However, this declined to 14% in subsequent years and, although it began rising once more, by 1997 it was still only 25%.

Russia has also continuously run a trade surplus in respect of the three groups of countries discussed above: Poland, Hungary, the Czech Republic, and Slovakia; the Baltic states; and the eight Balkan states included in the region. Among these three groups, the Russian trade surplus with the first four named was by far the largest, accounting for around 60–65% of Russia's trade surplus with the whole region.

## The Commodity Structure of Trade

As has been mentioned, after the collapse and dissolution of Comecon the countries of central and eastern Europe had to find new markets, mainly in the EU. This did not simply mean selling old products at any price. Instead, it was a task of developing new or improved products to fit the new opportunities that could be obtained. In some countries in the region, up to 60% of exports to the EU are effectively new products. This has had important implications for the new Russian market. Nevertheless, the commodity structure of trade between Russia and the region has not changed very significantly during the 1990s. Russia continues to supply mainly fuel and raw materials, and certain types of consumer goods. The contraction or growth in the value of Russia's imports (in US dollars) can be largely explained by the falls or increases in the prices of fuels and raw materials, which generally account for nearly 75% of the region's purchases from Russia. On this basis, it can be concluded that the dynamic of trade between the region and Russia remains largely a function of the international prices of fuels and raw materials.

As for the commodity structure of the region's exports to Russia, these still comprise chiefly engineering products, vehicles, consumer goods, food products, and medicines, but the respective shares of these groups of commodities in total exports have changed remarkably over the 10 years since Communism began to collapse. Heavy industrial products are no longer the most important items in the commodity lists. For example, only around 25% of Hungary's sales to Russia now consist of engineering and mechanical equipment, compared to around 50% in 1990. A similar reduction in machinery exports can be seen in the case of Poland, even though its economy is still relatively more dominated by heavy industry than Hungary's now is. Food and agricultural products are now the most important commodity group in the region's exports to Russia.

Some of this shift stemmed from the impact of EU barriers to agricultural exports and changes in patterns of spending in Russia, both of which are likely to be eliminated in the longer term. The demand for food imports increased in Russia because domestic suppliers could no longer meet all the demand from consumers, while investment in machinery declined. Another factor in this changing pattern was the increasing import demand in the EU, which was accompanied by sinking prices in the world commodity markets. Exports and imports of machinery and transport equipment between the region and the EU rose considerably in value, and strongly influenced the aggregate level of export revenues for most countries in central and eastern Europe. In contrast, the share of mineral fuels from Russia shrank as a result of the steep decline in energy prices. Nevertheless, despite falling world prices for other commodities, the rising value of imports of raw materials other than energy made these the second fastest growing commodity group in the trade of central and eastern Europe.

Meanwhile, Russia's imports of intermediate goods and those of food, beverages, and other agricultural products all rose steadily. These increases were in response to gradually rising demand in the region for imported industrial inputs, particularly for the exporting industries, and to buoyant private consumption in some of the countries in the region. Between 1994 and 1997, food, beverages, and other agricultural products accounted for as much as 40–44% of exports to Russia from Hungary and Poland, often followed in importance by exports of chemical products and other industrial inputs, which, for example, made up 47–56% of Slovenia's exports to Russia and 27–36% of Slovakia's. Fuels, the commodities most affected by the falls in world prices, were important only in Lithuania's exports to Russia. Machinery and transport equipment accounted for 25–30% of Russian purchases from most countries in the region, while manufactured consumer goods made up another 10–15% on average.

## Capital Flows

The capital flows between Russia and the countries of central and eastern Europe have intensified during the 1990s, in both directions. Under the systems of central planning imposed during the Communist period, such flows were relatively limited and were strictly controlled by planning agencies and government ministries. Since the beginning of the transition to the market, capital transactions have been gradually liberalized, although to varying degrees in different ex-Communist states.

In addition to trade-related transfers, there have been capital flows of substantial amounts of uncertain origin, generally from Russia to central and eastern Europe. The aim of these unrecorded and uncontrolled flows has been to legalize the status of capital earned in dubious ways inside Russia. The amounts involved can only be estimated, but it is likely that they have decreased since most countries in the region signed international agreements to monitor and combat money-laundering.

Direct investment, meanwhile, has been the main form of capital flow, most often in response to privatization both in Russia and in central and eastern Europe, but the importance of such flows between the region and Russia in particular has been limited: most direct investment comes from outside the transition economies. It is only relatively recently that large enterprises in Russia have begun to try to establish a presence in central and eastern Europe, and their motive has usually been to use the region as a springboard to activities in western Europe, which offers a far larger market. In particular, the leading Russian companies engaged in producing and exporting oil and natural gas have acquired several trading and banking outlets in the region. Similarly, few of the larger companies of central and eastern Europe have yet established significant subsidiary operations within the vast Russian market, although many would clearly like to do so. For example, the Czech engineering giant Škoda Plzeň is planning to launch a joint venture company with two Russian truck-makers; the Hungarian pharmaceutical company Richter plans to open a packaging company in Russia; and the Czech car-maker VW-Škoda aims to set up production in Russia too.

## The Impact of Russian Crises

### Problems in Exporting

The adverse effects of Russia's economic crises in the 1990s appeared first of all in the export performance of the countries of central and eastern Europe. Although their reliance on Russian supplies has weakened considerably since the transition process began, as outlined above, Russia is still the single largest market for some of the exports from the region. For example, in 1997 Russia accounted for around half of all exports of food, beverages, and agricultural products from the Baltic states, for more than 15% of such exports from the Czech Republic and Hungary, and for around 30% in the case of Poland.

After each economic crisis in Russia, its trade with the region plummeted, as successive devaluations of the ruble considerably increased the costs of imports into Russia and led to difficulties for exporters in obtaining payment for their supplies to Russian partners. In 1998, for example, Romanian exports to Russia practically collapsed, and exports from Latvia, Slovakia, and Bulgaria all declined very significantly. However, exporters in central and eastern Europe are often hard-pressed to find alternative buyers, given the very competitive and sometimes protected markets (such as for agricultural products) in western Europe and North America. Nevertheless, there is evidence that many exporters in the region have withdrawn from Russia altogether after encountering difficulties in assuring payments for their shipments.

This issue of payment arrears for exports underlines the problems of export credits and insurance facilities in commercial relations with Russia. Export credits and insurance are both still in their infancy in central and eastern Europe. Cover is rarely available for exports to Russia, which is perceived as highly risky, with the result that arrears or defaults in payments can lead directly to shortages of working capital, hampering the activities of exporters. The situation is most severe in those countries, such as Romania and Bulgaria, where domestic credit resources are still relatively undeveloped. Partly in response to domestic pressures – exporters in politically sensitive labor-intensive industries, such as food and light manufacturing, tend to be hardest hit – governments in the region have resorted to barter or arranged export sales from government to government, by means of collateral loans guaranteed by the Russian government or another reliable institution.

## Effects on Financial Markets

Every time Russia has experienced a financial crisis, there has been "contagion" to the financial markets of central and eastern Europe. This phenomenon is partly a reflection of perceptions rather than realities. Large numbers of western investors still handle their dealings with the transition economies as if they constitute a single bloc, disregarding the differences, both in macroeconomic fundamentals and in progress toward reform, between central and eastern Europe, on the one hand, and Russia and other CIS countries, on the other.

Russian financial crises, both in 1998–99 and earlier, have had some serious and damaging effects on the economies of central and eastern Europe. Whenever such a crisis deepens, foreign investors withdraw their money from all the transition economies. In consequence, the prices of stocks in companies with heavy Russian exposure fall significantly and then the flight of foreign capital makes domestic investors pessimistic, leading to a general fall in share prices. (Much the same process followed the outbreak of the crisis in East Asia in 1997–98, when many foreign investors withdrew from central and eastern Europe, not because of developments in the region itself, but in order to cover their losses thousands of miles away.) In the wake of Russia's financial crisis in 1998–99, for example, general levels of share prices, as measured by stock market indices, dropped by 44% in Hungary, around 25% in Poland and the Czech Republic, and around 5% in Slovakia.

In addition, however, the heavy exposure of many of the region's banks to the Russian economy has meant that capital losses from exchange rate movements and falls in asset prices have precipitated banking crises within the region itself. For example, some Latvian banks have participated in the market for Russian GKOs (a type of government bond) to such an extent that the exposure of Latvia's banking sector to Russia has occasionally been as high as 10% of that sector's total assets. The collapse of Latvia's largest bank, Baltija Banka, in May 1995 was at least partly due to its involvement in Russia.

Ironically, the latest financial crisis in Russia, which erupted in the second half of 1998, could actually help some of the countries of central and eastern Europe over the longer term. Before the crisis began, concern was growing over the large amounts of "hot money" flowing into the region, which were driving up the value of currencies. Some of these currencies were being traded near the top of their official trading bands. Exporters feared that overvaluation would choke off economic growth, while the monetary authorities feared that they would have to cut interest rates prematurely, thus jeopardizing the fight against inflation. The Russian crisis has changed the situation entirely. So much "hot money" has left the region that the Polish złoty, the Hungarian forint, and other currencies that were under pressure were being traded comfortably in the center of their rolling trading bands in the spring of 1999. It has become possible once again to cut interest rates without driving up inflation.

## The Impact of Closer Links to the EU

In contrast to the enlargement of NATO, which a large body of opinion in Russia distrusts, proposals for future EU membership on the part of countries in central and eastern Europe have not aroused any strong objections. Indeed, the accession of such countries to the EU might well be in Russia's long-term interests, if it helps to accelerate their economic development, increase their national wealth, and underpin their political stability. The enlargement of the EU to the East may also help to solve some of Russia's financial problems, by enhancing credit possibilities and export credit insurance, for example.

There may, however, be disadvantages for Russia, especially in the short term. Experience with the impact of the "Europe agreements," signed by the EU and several countries in the region during the late 1990s, suggests that Russia may be placed in a less competitive position within enlarged EU markets (see also Appendix 3). Russia's exports of machinery and manufactured goods, and of certain raw materials, especially energy, are already facing increasing barriers, as free trade within the EU, and between the EU and associated countries, is matched by protection of those markets. Russian exporters are more seriously affected by certain types of trade barrier, such as anti-dumping taxes or product certification requirements, than exporters in central and eastern Europe are. If the EU maintains this approach in its dealings with the next wave of entrants, then Russia will doubtless demand special compensation for the inevitable loss of its present markets in western Europe. This might take the form of a free trade agreement with the EU, at least for industrial products, if the political circumstances are right.

The root of the problem for Russian policy-makers is that producers in central and eastern Europe are among Russia's most important competitors in EU markets. For example, the Czech Republic and Poland compete on timber and wood products, fertilizers, and iron and steel products; Latvia is also an important source of timber and wood products; Bulgaria's fertilizer producers have become highly competitive; Slovakia and Romania are joining in the competition to supply iron and steel products to the EU; and Hungarian products compete with Russian products in most EU markets. Russia has tried several times to conclude free trade agreements with these and other countries in the region, but only Slovakia has responded positively. The other countries have held back from such agreements because Russia's own partnership and cooperation agreement with the EU is much more limited than their Europe agreements. If they open their markets to Russia just as the EU is opening its markets to them, they could run the risk of being perceived as helping Russia into the EU by a back door. In the meantime, the new round of talks on free trade within the framework of the World Trade Organization (WTO) could eventually improve Russia's access to EU markets, regardless of any specific agreements in Europe itself. For this reason, among others, Russia is endeavoring to become a full member of the WTO before any countries in central and eastern Europe achieve full membership of the EU. It will have to liberalize its trade regulations in order to achieve this.

## Prospects for Improvement

The Russian economy is still uncertain and fragile, as becomes particularly clear during each of its successive economic and financial crises. Under such conditions, there are severe constraints on the possibilities of strengthening economic relations between Russia and central and eastern Europe.

### Trade Dilemmas

In every country where the Russian market accounts for a significant proportion of exports, that country's growth prospects are placed in jeopardy every time there is a Russian crisis. In addition to the obvious effects on production and employment, listed companies perceived as the most exposed to Russia see their projected profits downgraded and their share prices plummet even faster than the stock market indices in general. Food-processing and pharmaceuticals firms have been particularly badly hit in 1998–99, as investors have fled from these and other industries that are heavily dependent on Russian trade. Such industries are compelled to resolve a fundamental dilemma: whether to continue activities in the Russian market, which will certainly hold risks for years to come; or redirect their activities elsewhere, losing their footholds in Russia, perhaps as it begins to take off, and also risking price wars in other markets. This is not an easy dilemma to resolve, given the uncertainties about the future of the Russian market, but it becomes more complicated when it is considered in the context of the continuing problems faced by the countries of central and eastern Europe in penetrating world markets. Just as after the collapse of Comecon, it seems likely once again that many firms will survive and mitigate these problems only by exerting all their reserves of flexibility, entrepreneurship, and sheer desperation.

Access to the EU's markets is still restricted by import quotas and quality standards; the Europe agreements with the EU (already referred to above) only partially opened up the EU's agriculture market to products from central and eastern Europe. Faced with these barriers, the countries of the region have tended to see Russia as offering potentially lucrative alternative markets in which conditions of entry are not too onerous. The products sold to Russia have tended to be of lower quality than consumers in the EU would accept, but this is not a strategy that can be maintained for much longer as standards rise in Russia too. Firms exporting from central and eastern Europe into Russia have also tended to benefit, at least to some extent, whenever western exporters have been frightened out of Russia.

Various other factors continue to hamper trade between central and eastern Europe and Russia, most notably the trade policy measures introduced by the Russian government whenever the economic situation worsens. These have included temporary import surcharges, increases in import duties, and the withdrawal of tax concessions on tolling arrangements (mainly affecting aluminum smelters). All these measures have reduced the competitiveness of the region's exporters in Russian markets. Similar effects have flowed from each devaluation of the ruble.

## Potential for Growth

Despite all these present difficulties, there is significant potential for a considerable increase in trade turnover. Every positive trend toward the stabilization of Russia's economy helps its trading partners. In 1997, for example, imports into Russia grew by 17%, outstripping import growth in any other market. Yet among the countries of central and eastern Europe, only Poland, Hungary, the Czech Republic, and Slovakia were in a position to benefit from this surge. For the future, it is often argued that trade relations can be improved on the basis of technological compatibility of production: the relatively low productivity of producers in central and eastern Europe, and the relatively low quality of their products, could correspond better to Russian demand than more sophisticated western producers and their products. However, all the transition economies, including Russia, have developed new markets and new expectations, with the result that the technological compatibility inherited from the Comecon years may not last for very much longer. As the transition economies diverge

further from each other, with some becoming increasingly integrated with the West and others falling further behind, simply relying on established contacts in Russia may not be enough to maintain trade with that fast-changing market, let alone to improve it.

Indeed, shifts in consumption and investment patterns in Russia make it difficult to predict what producers in central and eastern Europe will be able to sell to Russia in the opening years of the 21st century. As consumer spending has been rising, food products are likely to maintain their shares, while imports of other consumer goods may well also grow, in value, in volume, and in variety. However, there is likely to be intense competition in Russian markets. Trade statistics reveal that the older heavy manufacturing companies in central and eastern Europe are already losing ground, and that small and medium-sized companies have been benefiting most from trade with Russia. One of the problems that such small and medium-sized companies face in Russian markets is their lack of adequate and reliable distribution networks. The old networks remaining from the Comecon years are not always reliable and in many cases they have been replaced by unstable private entrepreneurs who have only recently started to develop into reputable, legitimate businesses. Larger companies from central and eastern Europe have already had to undertake complete reorganization of their distribution networks in Russia; small and medium-sized companies will have to wait until these new networks have developed further and, crucially, begun to penetrate beyond the competitive Moscow region into the provinces.

After nearly 10 years of determined economic restructuring, most of the countries in central and eastern Europe are already remarkably disconnected from Russia's troubled economy, to a greater extent than many in western Europe and North America have realized. The leading economies in the region have entered upon phases of healthy growth, while Russia has remained stagnant. Poland, Hungary, and the Czech Republic, for example, now send two thirds of their exports to the EU, while exports to Russia account for less than 2% of their GDP. The rest of the region is almost certain to follow their lead over the longer term, although the temptation remains, especially when Russia is not in extreme crisis, to focus on the more accessible and familiar markets there. Bulgarian wine-makers, Czech engineering firms, Polish food-producers, Hungarian pharmaceuticals companies, and many others may continue to prefer trading with Russia, despite all the risks, as long as the EU maintains barriers against their products and they remain unable to increase either their productivity or the quality of their goods. It is still very much an open question whether such companies can acquire and maintain the determination, the capital, and the market access to continue shifting their focus westward, or whether they must go on waiting for the Russian economy to revive.

## Further Reading

Brocka-Palacz, Bogumila, "Die Polnisch-Russichen Wirtschaftsbeziehungen: Aktueller Stand und Entwicklungsmöglichkeiten" [Polish-Russian Economic Relations: The Current Situation and Possibilities for Development], in Deutsches Institut für Wirtschaftsforschung, *Polen und die Osterweitung der Europäischen Union* [Poland and the Eastward Expansion of the EU], Berlin: Deutsches Institut für Wirtschaftsforschung, 1996

Buch, Claudia-Maria, *Währungsreformen im Vergleich: Monetäre Strategien in Russland, Weissrussland, Estland und der Ukraine* [Currency Reforms Compared: Monetary Strategies in Russia, Belarus, Estonia, and Ukraine], Tübingen: J. C. B. Mohr, 1995

Csaki, György, editor, *Transition and Modernization: Russian-Hungarian Round Table Conference, Babol-Budapest*, Budapest: Hungarian Academy of Sciences Institute for World Economics, 1997

Dobroczynski, Michał, "Vnutrennie i Mezdunarodnye Obuslovlennosti Polsko-Rossiikikh Economitsekikh Otnosenii" [External and International Conditions of Polish-Russian Economic Relations], in *Vestnik Moskovskogo Universiteta* [Moscow University Bulletin], Serija 6, *Ekonomika* [Series 6, Economics], 1997

European Parliament, *Russia and the Enlargement of the EU*, Brussels: European Parliament, 1999

Fodor, Peter, "Russian Economic Relations with the Czech Republic and Slovakia," in Csaki, cited above

Hahl, Jarmo, and Urpo Kivikari, "Problems and Possibilities of Economic Cooperation and Trade around the Gulf of Finland: The Case of Finland, Estonia, and Russia," in Tampere Peace Research Institute, *Dimensions of Conflict and Cooperation in the Baltic Sea Rim*, Tampere: Tampere Peace Research Institute, 1994

Janusauskas, Ramunas, "Russia's Interests in and Policies towards the Baltics: Socioeconomic and Military Aspects," in *Perspectives*, Summer 1994

Kotyk, Václav, "Czech-Russian Relations in the Context of Russia's European Policy," in *Perspectives*, Summer 1997

Polkowski, Andreas, "Wirtschaftliche Entwicklung und Integration der Osteuropäischen Ostseeanrainerstaaten in die Weltwirtschaft am Beispiel Russlands und der Drei Baltischen Länder" [The Economic Development and Integration of the Eastern European and Baltic Sea States into the World Economy, with Special Reference to Russia and the Three Baltic States], in Karl-Heinz Breitzmann and Helmut Dora, editors, *Wirtschaft und Verkehr im Ostseeraum* [Economy and Interchange in the Baltic Sea Area], Rostock: Universität Rostock, 1997

Rethi, Sandor, "On the Trade Relations between Hungary and Russia," in Csaki, cited above

Šurubovič, Aleksei, "Die Wirtschaftsbeziehungen Russlands mit den Ländern Mittel- und Osteuropas 1992–1995" [Russia's Economic Relations with the Countries of Central and Eastern Europe, 1992–95], in *Berichte des Bundesinstituts für Ostwissenschaftliche und Internationale Studien*, number 13, 1998

Weyrauch, Peter M., *Aussenhandel als Entwicklungsfaktor im Ostseeraum* [Foreign Trade as a Factor in the Development of the Baltic Sea Area], Lübeck: Ostsee-Jahrbuch, 1994

## Periodicals and Reports

Aside from the items cited above, there has been surprisingly little serious research on the issues addressed in this chapter. However, a large amount of useful and reliable information on the transition economies discussed here can be found in special-ized periodicals, notably the journals *Perspectives* (cited above), *East European Politics and Societies*, *Economics of Transition*, *Business Central Europe*, and the *Central European Economic Review*.

The occasional publications of the following organizations, most of which are available in

English, are generally of a high standard: the UN Economic Commission for Europe; the EBRD; the EU Commission (and its PHARE and NIS/TACIS services); the Centre for Economic Policy Research, London; the Economist Intelligence Unit, London; the Vienna Institute for International Economic Studies (the WIIW); the Institute for World Economics of the Hungarian Academy of Sciences in Budapest; and the Central and East European Economic Research Center of the University of Warsaw.

*Dr Kalman Dezseri* is a Research Fellow at the Institute for World Economics of the Hungarian Academy of Sciences in Budapest.

## Chapter Sixteen

# Regional Development

## David Turnock

While perfect equality is unattainable, it is widely regarded as a responsibility of governments to work to reduce variations in prosperity within countries. As parts of western Europe's "periphery," the countries of central and eastern Europe have long formed a relatively backward region, a distortion that the Communist system was determined to resolve. However, there are also major disparities within the region, related to the relatively early start to modernization in the Habsburg and Prussian empires, and the relatively poor coal and iron ore resources of the Balkans. Growth policies were of great strategic concern to all the states in the region as they gained independence, although resources available for central planning were modest until the Communist system was introduced. In addition, the transition years are seeing a new approach to familiar problems as central and eastern Europe prepares for the enlargement of the EU, in which regional policy is a prominent concern (see Alden and Boland 1996).

## The Communist Period

Under Communism there was a clear north/south contrast: the economies of Czechoslovakia, East Germany, Hungary and, to a lesser extent, Poland were relatively strong, with a concentration of industry in the Halle-Łódź-Budapest triangle, in contrast to those of the Balkans (see Hamilton). Despite ambitious planning in the latter area, supported by Comecon, the more advanced economies retained their superiority (see Kende and Strmiska). By 1989, there were no great differences in employment in industry, but there

were relatively high levels of employment in agriculture in the Balkans and in Poland, and there were also significant variations between regions within each country (see Table 16.1). To cite the extremes, one region of Poland had only 6.0% of its active population in agriculture while another had 61.3%; the comparable figures for industry in the same country were 12.0% and 60.9%, and those for services in Hungary were 37.8% and 83.6%. All regional centers tended to grow rapidly, because they benefited from disproportionate shares of the capital invested. Nevertheless, there were clear contrasts between relatively advanced urban regions (where the regional center was a large city, with a population of perhaps 500,000 or more, and there was a high level of urbanization) and more backward rural regions.

Despite government intervention, rural regions typically lost population through migration to stronger regions. For example, in Poland there was a net loss of population to Warsaw from the surrounding regions of Lomza, Plock, Siedlce and Radom; also to Poznań from Gniezno, Konin and Pila. Governments showed some ambivalence over regional equality. The equity principle attracted support for rural regions, and, as Dostal and Hampl put it, there was "an extraordinary suppression of any important selective tendencies at the interregional level." Yet such factors as economies of scale and strong linkages in export-oriented industries, along with the "political clout" of the advanced regions, tended to limit decentralization. Despite controls on internal migration, especially where there were perceived congestion costs and severe housing shortages, and some relocation of manufacturing, especially for polluting and labor-intensive industries, vested interests continued to press for growth in the stronger regions. Regional development was therefore essentially the haphazard outcome of various sectoral decisions taken by ministries (see Enyedi). Capital allocation was obviously based on surveys of resources which planners exploited as they saw them; but the regions were largely passive and had little opportunity to initiate programs on an autonomous basis (see Tomasek).

## Aspects of the Transition

The transition has seen a collapse of production, followed by a gradual recovery. Such a drastic adjustment was not foreseen but proved inevitable. This was partly the result of the collapse of the Soviet Union, which had taken the lion's share of the region's exports, but it also reflected the delay in making either alternative trading arrangements in western Europe and elsewhere, or the many qualitative improvements that would be necessary in the process. Leo J. Paul has also referred to "a cynical paradox" in the international treatment of central and eastern Europe. While the international community sought to integrate the region into the capitalist world economy, western countries provided only limited market opportunities, yet they opposed even limited forms of protection within the countries of the region (see Paul). Only Poland registered positive growth in 1992. While the majority of the countries of central and eastern Europe have grown since 1994, the rates in the Czech Republic and Poland have been consistently good, but the Balkan countries have shown a propensity for collapse, as in Bulgaria in 1996–97 and Albania in 1997 (see Table 16.2).

Government allocations of capital have been drastically reduced, and they now take the form of contributions to local government budgets, rather than directives over specific projects. As a result, each local authority must compete for the attentions of "global" investors. Regions will need to modernize and develop new linkages, diversifying formerly closed economies that are no longer organized from the center (see Grabher). Ideally, regional

economies should seek a balance between "disembedded" networks, which imply dependence on external capital, and "embedded" networks, which are locally integrated and supported by regional policies geared to the encouragement of small and medium-sized enterprises (SMEs), in order to maintain indigenous growth. "Overembedded" networks are clearly undesirable, because state-owned enterprises may be grounded in an old Communist environment that can only be perpetuated through backward-looking defensive measures, and that may well be unfavorable for new enterprises. In this situation, the regions that were relatively advanced during the Communist period may well become even more important, despite the stronger emphasis on the tertiary sector (see Barta 1992), because they have superior resources and many have existing links with foreign capital.

However, while progress will be linked with the present economic structure, much will depend on the acceptance of reorganization for state-owned companies, along with the adaptability and skills of the population, which in turn are partly a function of the quality of education and training. Regions with large "gateway" cities are likely to increase their influence, and their potential will be enhanced by high-quality infrastructure, including transportation, telecommunications, and environment. (Structural funding from the EU has already been of great assistance to the eastern states of Germany in these respects.) Preferential axes will emerge where investment is concentrated on the modernization of links between major cities, such as Vienna, Budapest and Belgrade. The climate for investment will depend on national policies in each country, including the perceived stability of government, and on wider global considerations, but there is also the critical factor of local government, given the transfer of powers away from the center. Under Communism the lower tiers of administration had virtually no autonomy, and sectoral interests prevailed over local needs, but since 1990 the principle of local self-government has been reasserted. In the political vacuum created by decentralization, local government and the new private sector compete for influence. It seems likely that regional contrasts will increase (see Gorzelak). If Poland, or any other country in the region, is increasingly polarized between areas that are relatively prosperous and others that have high levels of unemployment, the antagonism between rich and poor may well result in what has been called the "Poland A/Poland B" syndrome (see Kortus).

## Regional Economic Structure

Despite some unemployment related to industrial monostructure, the leading manufacturing regions have done much better than remote underdeveloped areas with predominantly agricultural profiles (especially where large socialist farms have enjoyed the benefits of high subsidies). For example, the city and district (voivodship) of Łódź in Poland suffered badly though the loss of eastern markets, but there has been some recovery through the formation of SMEs and the development of a new identity (Walker 1993). Negative images of Łódź as a polluted industrial city are being complemented by links with culture and the arts, education and science, and creativity in industrial production is being promoted by a forward-looking local government. Even in the car industry, where a great deal of new investment has been undertaken, factories are generally rooted in existing large enterprises, or on sites with important infrastructural advantages relating to the former Communist military-industrial complex. General Motors are developing in an enterprise zone at Gliwice with 100% relief from corporation tax for 10 years and 50% relief for a further 10. Other subzones are located at Dabrowa Górnica, where the French glassmaker Saint Gobain is operating; Tychy; and Zory, site of an ABB tube factory. The expansion of the tertiary sector includes financial services in Katowice, a sign of the region's changing image.

Growth may also occur in the more fertile agricultural regions that reassert their comparative advantage – for example, richer areas, such as Czech Silesia, where small peasant farms persisted under Communism, partly because they were too small for the owners to be branded as *kulaks* (rich peasants). Meanwhile, although the reassertion of the principle of comparative advantage will create difficulty for farmers in poorer regions at a time of reduced subsidies, there is potential for tourism in highland regions where the successes of western mountaineering could be repeated. Otherwise, the poor rural regions, lacking good trading infrastructure, may depend on a "bazaar economy" and short-term speculative business. Rural Bulgaria shows the persistence of traditional installations, such as blanket factories working up local wool for local customers, along with small clothing factories for export, and trading companies that deal in cheap manufactures picked up in Istanbul and Thessaloniki. Such structures have limited potential for growth.

## Population Resources and Settlement

The adaptability of the population will be important in efforts to demonstrate and improve local competitiveness (see Chalupa). The labor markets of central and eastern Europe offer attractive levels of skill and motivation, as well as relatively low costs, but some communities may well be ambivalent towards the reform process in general, and foreign economic penetration in particular. Ethnicity can have a bearing on regional potential, and sensitivity over ethnic and cultural issues, such as the question of autonomy for Moravia within the Czech Republic, is to be expected (see Vaisher). Stability can also be compromised by the high levels of crime that may arise from organized smuggling and drug trafficking, as well as irregular privatization and the "mobsterization" arising from such irregularities.

It is an important question for the future how far the further decline of employment in agriculture will precipitate mass migration towards capital cities and regional centers. The alternative is for services and employment to become more widely available in larger nucleated villages or small urban centers, allowing for resettlement at a more local level. More even urban networks could achieve better regional balances: continuing progress in education and growth in the tertiary sector both encourage a more even distribution of population, as dependence on purely local resources decreases (see Nagy). However, at present some of the smaller towns may lack adequate services, especially those that were expanded by government decisions under Communism (see Csatari). For example, although no village in Hungary is more than a half-hour journey from the nearest town, there are variations in the quality of transportation and services within the hinterland of each small town (of up to 30,000 people).

## Central Government and Regional Policy

The national level of government remains of decisive importance throughout central and eastern Europe, despite some hollowing out through the redistribution of state power to the supranational and subnational levels. There is, however, diversity in respect of subnational development policies and institutions.

In the former Czechoslovakia, for example, almost all regions qualified for at least one category of assistance between 1989 and 1992, and this led to excessive dispersal of funds (see Pavlinek 1992). After 1992 the right-wing coalition government decided to concentrate on the development of SMEs in areas of high unemployment. Meanwhile, Hungary provides substantial subsidies for its northeastern counties, amounting to F300 million in 1997 alone. There are tax incentives for exporters and for improvements in infrastructure that are export-oriented, stimulating the customs depot and industrial park at Zahony, which will also benefit from the extension of the highway. Interspan of Switzerland has ventured into this area, while Michelin of France has acquired the tire company in Nyiregyhaza. Daewoo of South Korea has arrived in Debrecen and TDK of Japan in Salgotarjan. The problem is that other rural areas that are only slightly less poor are losing out: the Tolna area, for example, is cut off from the main transit corridors.

Investment may be attracted to specific areas on the basis of incentives available in special zones. These may involve areas of high unemployment, places with particular economic potential where inward investment needs to be stimulated in the first place, such as ports in Croatia, Montenegro and Romania. Designation may be linked with land reclamation, or with the availability of infrastructure arising from former use of land by the military or by large state-owned industries, where diversification is now needed. Poland's first "special economic zone" was established on a 575 hectare site at Mielec in the Southwest, based on a large transportation equipment factory, the local airport, and railway facilities available for both standard and broad gauges, the latter allowing shipment to the Russian Far East. Elsewhere in Poland, a Mazovian Economic Development Zone, established around a former military airfield at Modlin, 40 kilometers Northwest of Warsaw, will focus on the food industry, electronics and transportation services, with the aim of helping the economy in the provinces of Ciechanow and Plock. Another of Poland's enterprise zones involves a site at Zarnowiec, near Gdańsk, which was originally prepared in the Communist period for a nuclear power station.

Central governments must also take a leading role in deciding the form of regional system that may be needed to replace those inherited from Communism. Large regions are frequently preferred, although choices are by no means straightforward. Reform in Bulgaria has produced nine large regions, with a lower tier of 275 small counties, and large regions are also advocated for Hungary, based on the cities of Debrecen, Győr, Kecskemét, Miskolcs, Pécs, Székesfehervár and Szeged (see Toth). In the Czech Republic, however, where the issue remains unresolved, the former Prime Minister Václav Klaus wanted larger regions, while the President, Václav Havel, preferred 13 smaller regions that would allow people to participate more fully in government. However, small regions can be controversial where regional autonomy is an issue. In 1992, Croatia introduced a new system of 20 counties alongside the capital city, Zagreb (see Klemenčić). This has some advantages for Istria, where a regional party, the Istrian Democratic Alliance, represents an ethnically mixed population including Albanians, Italians, Serbs and Slovenes as well as Croats. Despite a political culture of tolerance, the party seeks a federal system that would allow more tax revenues to accrue to the regions and, in the process, allow Istria to keep much more of its revenue from tourism (see Markotich). However, at the same time there has been opposition from the Dalmatia Action Party to the high level of centralization in Zagreb, and to the division of Dalmatia into four counties (Dubrovnik-Neretva; Šibenik; Split-Dalmatia and Zadar-Knin).

## Local Government

Much greater importance attaches to local authorities in market economies than under the former state-directed industrialization programs, in which urbanization was linked to the development of large state-owned enterprises. Post-Communist decentralization has been driven by reformed Communist parties that have both experience of government and an appreciation of limited resources. However, decentralization makes for wider disparities between regions. It can also frustrate the planning of large cities when there are small district councils – such as the 22 in Budapest – reflecting the central government's desire to avoid strong regional challenges. Hungary has the most highly decentralized system, with 3,200 municipalities and settlements at the lower level of its two-tier system (see Surazska et al.). The capacity of local authorities to influence regional development depends primarily on their powers and finances, and powers tend to increase faster than financial capabilities. Thus, for example, although local authorities in Hungary have considerable powers over taxation and development initiatives, few of them engage directly in economic activity because their resources are very limited.

Local authorities are developing management skills, often through twinning with western European cities, and many important initiatives have been taken to increase income and employment. Even in the more successful regions, however, local corporatism is developing only slowly, and it is not at all clear where power really lies. In Wrocław in Poland, for example, the local Chamber of Commerce and Industry does not attract the support of the managements of the local state-owned enterprises, a very powerful group that may sell land

for industrial and commercial development without reference to any local plan. Most incoming investment has also bypassed both the district and city authorities, because industrial plants on "brownfield" (fully developed) sites are acquired through negotiation with the Ministry of Privatization or the Ministry of Foreign Investment. When dealings with local networks are necessary, it may be that rapid settlement of land deals will determine location, rather than the quality of local government services or other factors such as labor costs, local infrastructure or environment.

However, the district authorities in Łódź, for example, are actively stimulating the development of the economy, supporting entrepreneurship and attracting foreign capital. Meanwhile, the city government in Łódź itself has its own departments for municipal investment and property management, as well as a department of city strategy, responsible for transforming the structure of ownership, modernizing infrastructure, and attracting foreign capital. It issues municipal bonds to generate private capital for urban development, and has established a regional investment fund, as a joint stock company, to stimulate business. In addition, the regional development agency has supported promising companies and ensured adequate liquidity by purchasing their invoices and discounting them with local banks. To take another example, Plzeň in the Czech Republic benefits from a clever land deal struck in 1993, when former army barracks at Borska Polje were turned into an industrial park, offering facilities for foreign investors at attractive prices. The site is close to the Škoda car works, and to university departments involved in technological and business innovation. Matsushita of Japan is producing Panasonic television sets there; Carrefour of France has opened the country's largest hypermarket; and German firms such as Siemens and MEA Meisinger have led "greenfield" investment (on completely new sites) in the city.

## Gateway Cities

There is particular optimism over the future prospects of capital and provincial cities, since they usually offer a wide range of facilities, including relevant institutions, incubation centers, industrial parks, technology transfer centers and regional advice centers (see Farkas et al.). Although it may be difficult for all the larger cities to prosper, there are several that are already playing effective roles as "gateways." Kraków in Poland could be regarded as a gateway city on the grounds of its size, its range of functions and its integration with its hinterland. Its environmental attractions are enhanced not only by its historic center, designated a World Heritage Site by Unesco in 1978, but by the resort of Zakopane in the Tatra Mountains, and the Biesczady national forest on the border with Ukraine. Improvements are being made through investment in major roads running east and west, and in the enlargement of the regional airport of Balice so that larger jets can be accommodated. Careful management of the Tatra Mountains National Park is also being given a high priority (see Hardy and Rainnie).

The national capitals have the greatest potential. Redevelopment is being undertaken in Budapest, for example, to provide better services and create office accommodation for foreign firms (see Barta 1993). The building of the southeastern segment of the orbital road around the city is an important achievement, linking most of the country's provincial highways. Since Budapest is divided into separate districts (as mentioned above), there is an element of competition, and differences in development strategy result in some striking contrasts along the district boundaries. However, foreign capital is being drawn not only to Budapest and its suburbs but to a wider area extending over the Northwest of the country. The growth of the vehicle assembly and components industries has affected such places as Esztergom and Székesfehervár, and the latter is coming to be regarded as Hungary's equivalent of Silicon Valley. Ford Hungaria exports car parts from Székesfehervár to other countries in Europe and to North America. In addition, Philips Video International is active in the city; Alcoa produces aluminum and IBM makes disk drives there; Matsushita makes Panasonic mini hi-fi systems, CD players, and video recorders (partly in cooperation with Videoton); and

Nokia of Finland makes loudspeakers for export. Most companies have found locations on a former Soviet military base, now run by a US firm, the Loranger Industrial Development Company. The city now wants to attract SMEs with high levels of technology, especially where it is also environmentally friendly. Györ also has a history of industrial success, linked with the Raba truck plant, and it has longstanding cultural links with the West.

One test for dynamic cities will be their ability to spread growth into more backward rural regions as more space is needed for industrial estates, residential developments and recreation facilities. Some wealthy middle-class families may be encouraged to exchange their city apartments for upmarket housing on the urban-rural fringe, for example at Mysiadlo, 15 kilometers from the center of Warsaw, where homes are being individually designed by Canadian and Polish architects. Central Slovakia, to take another example, has a polycentric character, covering the Vah Valley (Povazie) and the Hron Valley (Pohronie), but there is a perceived need for greater coherence, with an emphasis on Banská Bystrica-Zvolen as a center for regional transformation. The Slovak government is supporting new university faculties and economic growth related to banking, foreign trade, and telecommunications. Similarly, an important feature of the Kraków region in Poland is the establishment of a development agency to implement a consistent policy of economic restructuring and development throughout the region, with particular attention being paid to improving infrastructure in small towns and rural areas.

## Infrastructure

Modern communications will reduce isolation by enhancing access to western European "core" areas and urban agglomerations. Much of the region's industry was developed on the basis of rail access through dedicated sidings. At the beginning of the 1990s, more than half the passenger and freight traffic in what was then Communist eastern Europe was carried by train. However, the use of roads will become more compelling with the completion of a new generation of factories for light industries.

There is also a growing volume of international road traffic, both freight and passenger, and this should increase further with more stream-lined border formalities and additional crossing points. There has already been considerable privatization of road haulage and bus services, especially in the northern countries, and further upheaval has occurred through price increases arising from reductions in subsidies and higher energy costs. Some of the countries in central and eastern Europe are making plans to extend their networks of highways. For example, Slovenia wants to develop links between Austria and Croatia, as well as between Italy and Hungary. The Transport Corridors designated by the EU are attracting most investment. The EU's program includes completion of the Trans-Europe Motorway, initially devised in the 1960s following agreement among 10 countries under UN auspices.

Airports are also in need of modernization, as in Prague, where British and North American companies are involved in building and operating a new terminal. The site, on a former Soviet airfield at Milovice, 30 kilometers Northeast of the city, will be linked to Prague by a "maglev" (magnetic levitation) train service. With a capacity of 4.8 million passengers a year, the new airport will be in a strong position to aim at a new status as a hub for air travel throughout central and eastern Europe. Further competition will also arise among sea ports, although there is the possibility of coordinated development along the shores of the Black Sea. Inland waterways will be included in this picture, especially the Danube, which is connected with western Europe by the Rhine-Main-Danube Canal. Constanţa in Romania should have a particularly bright future in connection with the flow of oil from around the Caspian Sea, which could be handled through a pipeline to Trieste in northeastern Italy. Finally, the poor state of telecommunications has been widely seen as a bottleneck to economic development, and massive improvements are now under way, with particularly rapid growth in cellular systems. National telephone companies are being separated from post office managements, and there is a trend towards privatization in order to increase foreign investment.

As well as influencing regional selection by boosting the prospects of the most accessible areas, new lines of communication will influence local siting. Within the preferred regions of central and eastern Europe where substantial investment is taking place, road access is increasingly important. Growth may be expected at Strykow near Łódź, for example, where the Polish section of the Trans-Europe Motorway will intersect with the highway from Swiecko to Terespol via Warsaw. Meanwhile, the highway from Szczecin in northwestern Poland to Prague, crossing the frontier at Lubawka, is destined to intersect with the Zgorzelec-Medyka highway at Kobierzyce, to the south of Wrocław. Here the local authority is already attracting distribution enterprises, starting with a huge Makro cash and carry warehouse, and the UK chocolate-maker Cadbury is now distributing its products throughout Poland. Ikea of Sweden is to build Poland's largest shopping center, including a furniture store and a supermarket, at this site, and there is cooperation with Wrocław on planning for an agricultural wholesale market. A starch and gluten factory operated by the US food processor Cargill will yield various foods, pharmaceuticals and cosmetics. Annual income to the commune will go towards a new health center, a church and a school, as well as improved supply of water, gas, telephone, and sewage services.

## The Environment

The prospects for regional development in central and eastern Europe are compromised by its generally poor environment. It is unfortunate that many of the larger cities have been blighted by high levels of air and water pollution, while the surrounding landscapes are sometimes disfigured by the activities of extractive industries, as well as by waste tips (see Carter and Turnock). Despite polluting industries, however, Warsaw has derived some benefit from the Kampinos National Park, a former royal hunting forest that is the second largest national park in Poland. Neglect of such conservation measures involves very high costs, in damage to landscapes, ill health, and water shortages (see Knight 1995), as well as wasted energy (see Kats). Despite ideological change and financial stringency, the region needs effective systems of rehabilitation.

Energy-efficient generating equipment will reduce pressure to bring new capacity on stream. Poland, for example, has energy guidelines in place (up to 2010) that involve diversification in favor of natural gas and liquid fuels. It is proposed that gas will be brought through a pipeline from the Yamal Peninsula in the Russian Arctic, but in the interests of energy security Poland may try to increase gas production from the Baltic Sea, and further links with western European distribution networks would also be desirable. Nevertheless, coal, the source of much of the pollution, will still account for 60% of all electricity in Poland in 2000, despite the need for modernization in the mines.

Another way of reducing coal consumption is to use nuclear power, despite the continuing controversy over its possible effects on health and safety. Romania opened its first nuclear power unit, at Cernavodă, in 1996, but Poland has decided to abandon its Zarnowiec project in Gdańsk, which had been dubbed "Zarnobyl" by Poles fearing a repetition of the Chernobyl´ disaster. However, despite public unease, it is not easy to close down generating plant that is in good working order (see Pavlinek et al. 1994).

Efforts are also being made to curb pollution in heavy industries. Many of the countries in central and eastern Europe have established conservation objectives in order to safeguard urban fringes for recreational purposes, while increasing use is being made of "green corridor" systems through larger grassland, woodland and water surfaces. Burgas in Bulgaria, for example, has its own director of ecology, who lays downs more demanding standards than apply nationally for implementation by a local ecological police service. Each enterprise has to report its inputs and outputs of energy and materials (see Yarnal). The present director also chairs a local environmental group, Ecoglasnost, which, like similar organizations across the region, has been effective in projecting public opinion and securing higher environmental standards (see Frankland).

Comprehensive rebuilding is needed in some badly damaged areas. Management of the Karkonosze Mountains in the Czech Republic is being improved through greater dispersal of industry, in contrast to the heavy concentration involved to the declining coalmining economy of Wałbrzych in Poland. Improvements in housing and services will be complemented by an expansion of forestry, which is already occurring spontaneously on abandoned farmland, linked with action to reduce pollution damage by power plants to the west. Organic farming and tourism are particularly evident in the vicinity of Karpacz and Sklarska Poręba, which attract many visitors from Germany. International cooperation has been established in the management of the Karkonoski National Park and more generally across the blighted "Black Triangle," the border zone where Poland, Germany and the Czech Republic meet, and pollution is at an extremely high level. Poland also cooperates with neighboring countries in the "Green Lungs of Europe" project, which helps to coordinate activities in national parks and other protected areas.

## Crossborder Cooperation

Regional development should not be seen as a purely domestic issue. There is a great deal of western expertise available to the countries of central and eastern Europe, for example through the EU's PHARE program. Growth axes linking capital cities are likely to assume special importance, and some commentators have therefore identified zones where more rapid expansion may be expected. There is also the special problem of isolated border regions where benefits could arise from crossborder cooperation.

These areas are sometimes less cohesive than is usual for social reasons. In the Czech Republic, for example, there is an ethnically mixed population in the northern and western borderlands from which the Germans were expelled after World War II. Levels of adherence to religion are low, which indicates, at least to some observers, that social control is inadequate, and there are relatively high levels of crime, divorce, suicide, and illegitimacy. Such problems may be alleviated by crossborder cooperation to overcome isolation. The opening of borders has often led to a growth of commerce, which may support half the population in some areas (see Stryjakiewicz), and as a result lobbies of small private commercial and service businesses have become politically powerful. Many SMEs have been started in Poland's western border region, where labor is cheap and German markets are close at hand.

Cooperation may be formalized through special arrangements. For example, even during the Communist era the Tatra Mountains region saw cooperation between Poland and Slovakia, and the Alps-Adria Working Community linked parts of the former Yugoslavia with Austria, Italy, Germany and Hungary (see Horvath). Since 1989, eight "Euroregions" have been established, under the auspices of the EU, along almost the entire length of Germany's borders with Poland and the Czech Republic. The Neisse Euroregion, for example, links the Zittau area of Germany with Liberec in the Czech Republic and Bogatynia in Poland: its administrative center moves around the three countries in rotation. After contacts were first made at Zittau in 1991, new border crossings were opened and EU support was provided for ecological studies of the Black Triangle (see above). As German investment moves across the borders to take advantage of cheap labor, there will be particular advantages for the Liberec area, where modernization of the industrial structure was constrained by the preference of Communist governments in the former Czechoslovakia for expanding the manufacturing base in Slovakia. There are similar crossborder arrangements elsewhere, although several are still only at the planning stage. For example, the Union of Municipalities of Upper Silesia and Northern Moravia promotes cooperation across the Czech-Polish border. In addition, private funding is being used to support a Carpathian "Euroregion," bringing together the frontier districts of Hungary, Poland, Romania, Slovakia and Ukraine (see Corrigan et al.).

However, historic problems remain, no matter what frontier regimes are in force. For example, most Hungarians still resent the borders imposed on their country by the Treaty of Trianon (1920), which removed 70% of its territory and 60% of its population, although

any improvements will always be welcomed as a means of closer social and cultural contact. Other border communities lacking close family ties with people on the other side may be fearful of the intrusions that might follow any opening, with the risk of increased noise, pollution and (perhaps) criminality. In any case, the permeability of frontiers is improving only slowly, and the bad working habits of customs officials can mean heavy losses for truck firms when their vehicles face long delays at borders. Meanwhile, developments on the German border are inevitably overshadowed by the outstanding issue of property rights for the Germans expelled from what is now the Czech Republic. There is also understandable concern that a government's scope for making and enforcing its own economic policies could be compromised where stronger neighbors gain disproportionate influence in border territories. While German investment is welcome, the economic links with Germany being developed in the border territories of the Czech Republic and Poland create some unease. Finally, there is also a danger of deepening regional antagonisms if some border regions are seen to be prospering on a much grander scale than overall national fortunes seem to warrant.

## Conclusion

Regional contrasts are likely to increase, following the efforts at equalization in the Communist period, and this trend creates a tension between advocates of efficiency, on the one hand, and those who favor regional protection, on the other. Some argue that areas with potential for growth should be strengthened, while others emphasize welfare, including effective policies to deliver education and other social services. Resources are limited, however, and the pursuit of efficiency is likely to predominate in the short term.

Against this background, the growth of multidisciplinary regional research institutes, such as the Transdanubian Research Institute at Pécs in Hungary, is a welcome trend. The EU also has a role to play. Research is being commissioned and the PHARE program could support enhanced crossborder cooperation. In this way, the differences between richer and poorer regions may be kept within manageable limits. However, the success of the more dynamic regions is by no means assured, and some commentators take a gloomy view of prospects for higher incomes. At the very least, there will be losers as well as winners from central and eastern Europe's flirtation with globalization.

## Further Reading

Alden, Jeremy, and Philip Boland, *Regional Development Strategies: A European Perspective*, London and Bristol, PA: Jessica Kingsley, 1996

The authors provide a broader dimension for understanding regional development in central and eastern Europe.

Bachtler, John, "Regional Problems and Policies in Central and Eastern Europe," in *Regional Studies*, number 26, 1992

A comprehensive review of the issues in the light of the enlargement of the EU

Barta, Gyorgyi (1992), "The Changing Role of Industry in Regional Development and Regional Development Policy in Hungary," in *Tijdschrift voor Economische en Sociale Geografie*, number 58, 1992

This article explains why industry is less significant for the transition than it was under central planning.

Barta, Gyorgyi (1993), *Budapest: a Central European Metropolis in 2005*, Budapest: Center for Regional Studies, 1993

Barta demonstrates the potential of Budapest as a gateway for foreign direct investment.

Carter, F. W., and D. Turnock, editors, *Environmental Problems in Eastern Europe*, London and New York: Routledge, 1993

A study, country by country, of the problematic inheritance from Communism

Chalupa, P. "Synergetic Conceptions of Regional Population and Social-democratic Processes Taking Place in the Czech Republic," in *GeoJournal*, number 31, 1993

Chalupa stresses the importance of human resources for regional development.

Corrigan, James, Istvan Suli-Zakar, and Csaba Beres, "The Carpathian Euroregion: An Example of Cross-border Cooperation," in *European Spatial Research and Policy*, Volume 4, 1997

A case study of the only Euroregion located entirely within central and eastern Europe

Csatari, B, "Crisis Signs of the Hungarian Small Towns," in A. Duro, editor, *Spatial Research and the Social-political Changes*, Pécs: Center for Regional Research, 1995

This paper examines in full the problems facing small towns that lack the resources to attract inward investment.

Dostal, Petr, and Martin Hampl, "Development of an Urban System," in Max Barlow et al., editors, *Territory, Society and Administration: The Czech Republic and the Industrial Region of Liberec*, Amsterdam: University of Amsterdam, Prague: Charles University, and Prague: Czech Academy of Sciences, 1994

The authors demonstrate the importance of the urban system for the transmission of inward investment to all regions.

Enyedi, Gyorgy, "Private Economic Activity and Regional Development in Hungary," in *Geographia Polonica*, number 57, 1990

An early assessment of the role of the private sector, and the tendency to exaggerate differences among regions

Farkas, Janos, Andras Kremer, Sandor Matyasi, Pal Tamas, and Gabor Varnal, "Innovational Perspectives: Contributions to the National Conception for Regional Development in Hungary," in *European Spatial Research and Policy*, Volume 3, number 2, 1996

The authors deal with the technological factor in regional development, stressing the need for innovation at all levels.

Frankland, E. Gene, "Green Revolutions: The Role of Green Parties in Eastern Europe's Transition 1989–1994," in *East European Quarterly*, number 29, 1995

A study of the effectiveness of political activity by environmental groups

Gorzelak, Grzegorz, *The Regional Dimension of Transformation in Central Europe*, London and Bristol, PA: Jessica Kingsley, 1995

A Polish geographer's assessment of the prospects for regional development

Grabher, Gernot, "The Disembedded Regional Economy: The Transformation of East German Industrial Complexes into Western Enclaves," in A. Amin and N. Thrift, editors, *Globalization, Institutions and Regional Development in Europe*, Oxford and New York: Oxford University Press, 1994

Grabher shows how some areas are developing strong links with the West, at the expense of local coordination.

Hamilton, F. E. I., "Changes in the Industrial Geography of Eastern Europe since 1940," in *Tijdschrift voor Economische en Sociale Geografie*, number 61, 1970

This article remains of great interest, as it shows the persistence of inequality in the spread of industry during the Communist period.

Hardy, Jane, and A. Rainnie, *Restructuring Krakow: Desperately Seeking Capitalism*, London and New York: Mansell, 1996

A pessimistic assessment of the prospects for job creation in the city, now that it is influenced by global industrial forces

Horvath, Gyula, editor, *Development Strategies for the Alpine-Adriatic Region*, Pécs: Center for Regional Studies, Hungarian Academy of Sciences, 1993

A collection of papers showing the scope for regional development on an international scale

Kats, Gregory H., "Energy Options for Hungary," in *Energy Policy*, number 19, 1991

A concise review of the choices available in view of the transition

Kende, Pierre, and Zdenek Strmiska, *Equality and Inequality in Eastern Europe*, Leamington Spa: Berg, 1987

A study of the persistence of inequality under Communism

Klemenčić, Mladen, "Administrative-territorial Division of Croatia," in *GeoJournal*, number 35, 1995

A case study of the spatial aspects of administrative reform

Knight, Gregory C., "The Emerging Water Crisis in Bulgaria," in *GeoJournal*, number 35, 1995

A timely demonstration of the need for conservation of water resources

Kortus, Bronislaw, "Poland in Transition: Geopolitical and Geoeconomic Transformations," in Zbigniew Taylor, editor, *Geographical Issues of Social and Economic Transformation of Contemporary Japan and Poland*, Warsaw: Polish Academy of Sciences Institute of Geography and Spatial Organization, 1992

Kortus underlines the variations in industrial development, and considers the prospects for the weaker regions.

Markotich, S., "Croatia's Istrian Democratic Alliance," in *Radio Free Europe/Radio Liberty Research*, Volume 3, number 33, 1994

A case study of the different approaches to administrative regions by central and local interests

Nagy, Jozsef Nemes, "Regional Disparities in Hungary During the Period of Transition to a Market Economy," in *GeoJournal*, number 32, 1994

An overview of regional problems in a major transition economy

Paul, Leo J., "Regional Development in Central and Eastern Europe: The Role of Inherited Structures, External Forces and Local Initiatives," in *European Spatial Research and Policy*, Volume 2, number 2, 1995

A discussion of the Communist legacy in relation to the interplay of global and local forces

Pavlinek, Petr, "Regional Transformation in Czechoslovakia: Towards a Market Economy," in *Tijdschrift voor Economische en Sociale Geografie*, number 83, 1992

A concise overview of the potential of different regions in the transition

Pavlinek, Petr, et al., "Demonopolization, Economic Restructuring and the Environment in Bulgaria and the Czech Republic," in Peter Jordan and E. Tomasi, editors, *Zustand und Perspektiven der Umwelt im östlichen Europa*, Vienna: Peter Lang Europäischer Verlag der Wissenschaften and Wiener Osteuropa Studien, 1994

A comparative study of environmental policy, focusing on two countries at different levels of development

Stryjakiewicz, Tadeusz, "The Changing Role of Border Zones in the Transforming Economies of East-Central Europe," in *GeoJournal*, number 44, 1998

An examination of the effects of expanding international trade and crossborder cooperation

Surazska, W., et al., "Towards Regional Government in Central Europe: Territorial Restructuring of Post-Communist Regimes," in *Environment and Planning C: Government and Policy*, number 15, 1997

A study of the restructuring of local government, and the prospects for larger regional units of administration

Tomasek, P., "Activities Supporting Regional Development in the CSFR," in T. Vasko, editor, *Problems of Economic Transition: Regional Development in Central and Eastern Europe*, Aldershot: Avebury, and Brookfield, VT: Ashgate, 1992

Tomasek presents examples of early initiatives in regional development in the former Czechoslovakia.

Toth, J., "Urbanization and Spatial Structure in Hungary," in *GeoJournal*, number 32, 1994

An examination of the problems that arise from the great variations in size between the capital city and the leading provincial centers

Vaishar, A., "Ethnic Structure of the Czech Republic in the Census of 1991 and its Connections," in *Geographica Slovenica*, number 23, 1992

A study of the implications of ethnic differences for regional planning

Walker, Antony R., "Łódź: The Problems Associated with Restructuring the Urban Economy of Poland's Textile Metropolis in the 1990s," in *Urban Studies*, number 30, 1993

A useful case study of the response to the transition in one industrial city

Williams, Richard H., *Blue Bananas, Grapes and Golden Triangles: Spatial Planning for an Integrated Europe*, Department of Town and Country Planning, University of Newcastle upon Tyne, 1993

A discussion of growth areas in Europe, and related issues in regional planning

Yarnal, B, "Bulgaria at a Crossroads: Environmental Impacts of Socioeconomic Change," in *Environment*, Volume 37, number 10, 1995

A paper on the environmental problems associated with metallurgical and other industries facing new conditions

*Dr David Turnock* is Reader in Geography at the University of Leicester in England.

**Table 16.1  Regional Disparities in Employment, by Sector, in Six Countries in Central and Eastern Europe, 1989 (%)**

| | Industry[1] | | | Agriculture | | | Services | | |
|---|---|---|---|---|---|---|---|---|---|
| | A | B | C | A | B | C | A | B | C |
| Bulgaria | 46.3 | 51.8 | 41.6 | 19.3 | 26.2 | 1.8 | 34.9 | 53.0 | 28.2 |
| Czechoslovakia[2] | 46.1 | 55.0 | 35.3 | 13.7 | 21.1 | 2.0 | 40.2 | 62.1 | 35.3 |
| Hungary | 38.6 | 47.8 | 28.2 | 16.0 | 32.3 | 0.7 | 45.5 | 83.6 | 37.8 |
| Poland | 36.4 | 60.9 | 12.0 | 28.9 | 61.3 | 6.0 | 34.2 | 46.6 | 22.7 |
| Romania | 40.2 | 61.4 | 25.8 | 27.9 | 48.1 | 3.8 | 27.0 | 43.1 | 16.8 |
| Yugoslavia[3] | 33.1 | 43.1 | 28.8 | 30.7 | 38.4 | 14.6 | 35.1 | 49.1 | 31.2 |

A Average proportion of national workforce employed in sector
B Highest proportion of a regional workforce employed in sector
C Lowest proportion of a regional workforce employed in sector

1 Manufacturing, mining and energy
2 Divided into the Czech Republic and Slovakia since 1993
3 Then comprising Bosnia-Herzegovina, Croatia, Macedonia, Montenegro, Serbia, and Slovenia

Source:   Bachtler, John, "Regional Problems and Policies in Central and Eastern Europe," in *Regional Studies*, number 26, 1992

**Table 16.2   Annual Changes in GDP[1] in 12 Countries in Central and Eastern Europe, 1989–97 (%)**

|  | 1989 | 1990 | 1991 | 1992 | 1993 | 1994 | 1995 | 1996 | 1997 |
|---|---|---|---|---|---|---|---|---|---|
| Albania | 9.8 | −10.0 | −27.1 | −7.2 | 9.5 | 9.4 | 8.9 | 9.1 | −7.0 |
| Bosnia-Herzegovina | n.a. | n.a. | n.a. | n.a. | n.a. | n.a. | 33.0 | 28.0 | 15.0 |
| Bulgaria | −0.6 | −9.3 | −11.7 | −7.3 | −1.5 | 1.8 | 2.1 | −10.9 | −6.9 |
| Croatia | −1.9 | −8.5 | −20.9 | −11.1 | −8.0 | 5.9 | 6.8 | 6.0 | 6.5 |
| Czech Republic | 1.4 | −1.2 | −14.2 | −6.4 | 0.5 | 3.4 | 6.4 | 3.9 | 1.0 |
| Hungary | 0.7 | −3.5 | −11.9 | −3.1 | −0.6 | 2.9 | 1.5 | 1.3 | 4.4 |
| Macedonia | n.a. | −9.9 | −10.7 | −7.9 | −9.1 | −1.8 | −1.2 | 0.8 | 1.5 |
| Poland | 0.2 | −12.1 | −7.0 | 2.6 | 3.8 | 5.3 | 7.0 | 6.1 | 6.9 |
| Romania | −5.8 | −5.6 | −12.9 | −8.8 | 1.5 | 3.9 | 7.1 | 4.1 | −6.6 |
| Slovakia | 1.1 | −2.5 | −14.6 | −5.4 | −1.9 | 4.9 | 6.8 | 6.9 | 3.4 |
| Slovenia | −2.7 | −4.7 | −8.1 | −5.5 | 2.8 | 5.3 | 4.1 | 3.1 | 3.8 |
| Yugoslavia | n.a. | −8.4 | 14.2 | −26.2 | −30.8 | 2.5 | 6.1 | 3.5 | 7.4 |

1 "Gross Social Product" in the cases of Macedonia and Yugoslavia

Source:   Economist Intelligence Unit

Chapter Seventeen

# Minorities, States, and Conflict

## *Boian Koulov*

**A**mong geographers, central and eastern Europe is often referred to as a "shatter belt," a zone of perpetual political instability and fragmentation. The period since the end of the Cold War has confirmed the region's reputation in this respect. In the early 1990s, the post-Communist countries of the region embarked on a unique political and economic reorientation, directed toward integration with the EU and NATO. Indeed, many geographers have suggested that, in the course of this process, the region itself has expanded significantly to the East, and should now be seen as incorporating some of the Soviet successor states that lie within Europe, namely Belarus, Moldova, and Ukraine (see, for example, De Blij and Muller). However, whether the region is defined as containing 12 countries (excluding the Baltic states), 15 (including them), or up to 18, one common factor is the process of political fragmentation that has accompanied their fundamental transformations. This is particularly striking against the background of the increasing cohesion of most of the countries in western Europe.

The devolution of power has had its most conspicuous effects on the former federal states. Czechoslovakia, Yugoslavia, and the Soviet Union, three federations organized largely on ethnic principles between the world wars, all fell apart, again largely along ethnic lines. The violent dissolution of the former Yugoslavia and Czechoslovakia's "velvet divorce" increased the number of states in the region by five. Only two federal structures still remain: Yugoslavia, which at present consists only of Serbia and Montenegro, and confederated Bosnia-Herzegovina. In both cases, conflicts, including threats of secession, mar the prospects of the last

federations in central and eastern Europe. Constituent republics and internal administrative borders have served as vehicles of political mobilization and legitimization for the new states in the region. These functions become particularly salient when administrative territorial units coincide, completely or partially, with historic regions containing cultural minorities. Nationalist elites tend to use ethnic, religious, and linguistic differences to further their own political and economic interests, while the lack of local autonomy adds to economic inequalities and political instability, enhancing the potential for such areas to generate conflicts.

Minorities in central and eastern Europe are geographically distributed, whether in concentrated or dispersed fashion, within their respective states. This chapter examines those minority groups that are territorially concentrated in certain historic, ethnocultural regions, and identifies specific social, economic, and political conditions that prompt particular localities to display high levels of active or potential conflict, including secession movements. It therefore excludes consideration of those minorities, such as the Jews or the Roma, that are usually relatively dispersed among local and national populations. It should also be noted that the Russian minorities in the Baltic states are not examined here (they form one of the topics of Chapter 3).

## States with Regionally Concentrated Minorities

Classifying the countries of central and eastern Europe according to the distribution pattern and relative share of ethnocultural minorities in specific areas produces two clusters of states. The first cluster encompasses those states that include regionally concentrated minorities. In this study, a minority qualifies as regionally concentrated if it amounts to more than 50% of the population of a given region.

The minority groups in this first cluster account for a much larger share of the population compared to the rest of the states in the region. Most troublesome for state nationalists is the very low rate of natural increase of the majority population in central and eastern Europe, compared to some of the ethnic minorities. In many cases, governments deal with this perceived problem by underreporting minority populations. For this reason, as well as in reflection of ethnic conflict and war, the statistics for the states in this cluster are the least reliable.

Governments generally view areas where minorities are concentrated as actual or potential destabilizing factors, especially when the "mother country" of a minority, or a foreign institution, shows interest and support for the minority population. Seven countries in central and eastern Europe fall into this category, which may partially explain the region's political instability. Further, all seven of these states, except Slovakia, are situated in the southeastern part of the continent, the Balkans, as if to prove the dictionary definition of "balkanization."

This first cluster can be further subdivided into two groups of states, according to the share of the largest minority in the total population of the respective country. The first group consists of the former Yugoslav republics, except Slovenia. These new states – Bosnia-Herzegovina, Croatia, and Macedonia – possess the highest share of a single minority and, at the same time, have demonstrated the highest potential for generating intercultural violence in central and eastern Europe. As of 1991, Bosnia-Herzegovina led the group, with a 31% Serb minority; Macedonia followed, with at least 22% of its population being Albanian; 14% of the population of Serbia and Montenegro were also Albanians; while Croatia had a Serb minority that was around 12% of its total population (see Seymore).

The respective majority populations in these four states are the smallest in central and eastern Europe: as of 1991, they ranged between 44% in Bosnia-Herzegovina and 78% in Croatia. The significant geographic congruence between the ethnic and religious affiliations of the population presents an additional problem in these four states. Thus, the majority of Albanians belong to the largest religious minority, the Moslems (30% in Macedonia and 19% in Yugoslavia), while the Serbs are predominantly Orthodox (31% in Bosnia and 11% in Croatia).

## Bosnia-Herzegovina

The former Socialist Federal Republic of Yugoslavia had certainly the most complex ethnic and historic geography in central and eastern Europe; among its six constituent republics, Bosnia-Herzegovina was certainly the most diverse. The two regions that the state is named for have had a common political, economic, and cultural history since they were conquered by the Ottoman Turks in the 15th century. Populated mainly by ethnic Serbs and Croats, Bosnia-Herzegovina remained under Ottoman rule until 1878, longer than either Serbia or Croatia. Uniquely in the former Yugoslavia, a very large section of the population converted to Islam during the period of Ottoman domination – a period that also gave rise to the traditional Islamophobia that still strongly influences ethnic politics in the Balkans. Accordingly, the status of Bosnia-Herzegovina was a profoundly divisive issue even at the high point of Serb-Croat amity, at the beginning of the 20th century (see Prelec).

After World War II, Bosnia-Herzegovina avoided being made into a province of Serbia, as some in the Communist government proposed, and received an equal status as a constituent republic of the Yugoslav federation. It was at this time that many Moslems in the republic began to redefine themselves as a nation (see Prelec). This development was in line with the attempts by the Communist regime led by Josip Broz Tito to balance the distribution of power as between the two major ethnic groups in the federation, the Serbs and the Croats. To the same end, in 1971 President Tito and his aides devised and instituted a "Moslem" ethnicity, which automatically became the largest single group in Bosnia-Herzegovina. Twenty years later, the fragmentation of Yugoslavia and the rise of competing nationalisms prompted the Moslem-led government of Bosnia-Herzegovina to declare sovereignty and then to separate from "rump" Yugoslavia.

Bosnia-Herzegovina's characteristics, however, differed significantly from those of any other former Yugoslavia member state. First, it was the only one of the six republics without a clear ethnic or religious majority. The largest group, the Moslems, made up around 44% of the population, and many areas in the republic had no explicit ethnic or religious majorities. The two sizable ethnic minorities, the predominantly Orthodox Serbs (31% of the total population) and the mainly Catholic Croats (17%), were concentrated in certain areas, most of which were situated across the borders from their respective "mother" states. Large numbers of Serbs and Croats indicated that their loyalties were not to a sovereign Bosnia-Herzegovina, and demonstrated ample determination and capacity to pursue their choice. Second, Bosnia-Herzegovina was poorer than either Croatia or Serbia. Its agriculture has been mostly private, but the republic has traditionally been a net importer of food and was able to satisfy less than 50% of the food requirements of its population. Third, the state is strongly dependent on its neighbors for access to the rest of the world, since it is practically landlocked. Its 20-kilometer coastline on the Adriatic Sea is surrounded on both sides by Croatian territory and lacks port facilities or direct transportation links to the rest of Bosnia-Herzegovina.

Despite these special circumstances, Moslem and Croat deputies in the Assembly of Bosnia-Herzegovina declared independence in October 1991, in the face of a walkout by most of the Serb representatives. Both sides attempted to create the appearance of democracy by carrying out referendums to legitimize their actions. Notwithstanding the violent conflict that ensued, the European Community (now the EU) and the UN recognized the sovereignty of Bosnia-Herzegovina in April 1992. It was predictable that the conflict would continue, and that it would turn each of the

three groups against the other two; there was also fighting within each group. Three years of war cost an estimated 250,000 lives, large-scale "ethnic cleansing," the worst refugee problem in Europe since World War II, and the destruction of much of Bosnia-Herzegovina's infrastructure. Tens of thousands of UN troops continue to police the US-brokered peace agreement, four years after it was signed in December 1995, and Bosnia-Herzegovina still relies on substantial international aid. The authors of the agreement hoped to avoid future violence by creating a complex and controversial political structure, which consists of a Serb Republic linked to a Moslem-Croat Federation. Nevertheless, there are still abundant possibilities for further hostilities. In particular, the conflict between the western part of the Serb Republic, centered on the city of Banja Luka, and the eastern part, ruled from Pale, remains a source of dangerous antagonism.

At the same time, most of the displaced citizens have not returned to their homes, and the shares of the different ethnic and religious groups in the population have changed significantly. According to some estimates, in 1998 around 40% of the population nominally adhered to Islam, but the Serbs were the largest ethnic group (40%); Moslems, as an ethnic group, were estimated at 38% of the population and Croats at 22%. The devolution of power, the new interethnic boundaries, and the apparent Serb plurality are likely to have profound implications for the cohesiveness of the state, if the adverse relations among the different communities persist.

## Macedonia

Albanians constitute the largest ethnic minority in Macedonia, being at least 22% of the total population. They occupy the only area where a national minority forms a local majority, across the border from Albania and the province of Kosovo, which historically has also had an Albanian majority. Religious differences make the ethnogeographic divide even wider, as the mostly Moslem Albanians, together with the other Moslem minorities – Turks, Roma, and Slavs – make up around 30% of the total population. There is also an ethnic

Serb minority area, situated in the northern part of Macedonia. Problems persist over the delineation of the border between the two states, and Yugoslav troops have encroached on the area (see Brown). Both sides, however, prefer to suppress these tensions, in order to focus on what they see as more compelling issues concerning their Albanian minorities.

Many Macedonians perceive the much higher natural rate of increase of the Albanians and other Moslems as a threat to the unitary organization of the country, and perhaps to its very survival. Relations between Albanians and Macedonians have been strained since the very emergence of the Yugoslav Republic of Macedonia, in the wake of World War II. President Tito encouraged a distinct Macedonian identity, mainly to undermine any loyalty to Bulgaria, which shares Macedonia's linguistic, cultural, and historic roots. At this time, the more numerous Albanians began yearning for greater autonomy. The mounting political instability in Yugoslavia in the late 1980s intensified ethnic insecurities and led to an upsurge of Macedonian nationalism. The republic's Constitution, adopted in November 1991, declares Macedonia a "nation state," largely excluding ethnic minorities. The disadvantaged Albanians boycotted the referendum on independence, conducted in September 1991, and followed the example of their ethnic kin in Serbia and Montenegro by boycotting the census held that year. Albanian representatives in both Macedonia and "rump" Yugoslavia complain that government officials significantly underreport their numbers, and have claimed discrimination in education, access to public sector jobs, and representation in the government. Confrontation over the illegal establishment of an Albanian-language university in Tetovo, in February 1995, which provoked clashes with the police, is often cited as an example of continuing interethnic tensions.

The similarities in the behavior of the Albanians in Yugoslavia and Macedonia, the contiguous character of the areas that they occupy, and their proximity to the state of Albania, have raised concerns about the possibility of a "spillover" of the conflict in Kosovo into Macedonia. If Kosovo ever regains autonomous status or even gains independence

– after the negotiations at Rambouillet in February 1999 and the NATO air strikes from March to June – there will be a significant impact on interethnic relations in Macedonia, enhancing the likelihood of a change to a federal structure. Temporary solutions that rely totally on outside intervention are not likely to create the internal conditions for lasting social peace.

Macedonia's political scene is also divided along minority lines. Most ethnic and even some religious groups have their own political parties, such as the Party of Yugoslavs in Macedonia, the Democratic Party of Serbs, the Democratic Party of Turks, or the Party for Democratic Action, which represents Slavic Moslems. The ethnic Albanian parties initially tried to dissuade the EU from recognizing Macedonia, on the grounds that their human and civil rights were being violated. Since then, however, they have participated in coalition governments that have testified to the possibilities of interethnic cooperation.

As measured by the UN's standard criteria, Macedonia is a "middle to upper middle income" state (see World Bank). Macedonia's poor economic performance creates significant additional challenges to social peace. It was the poorest of the republics in the Yugoslav federation, and, if the estimate of GNP per capita at US$1,090 is accurate, then it lags behind all the other countries in the region except Albania (see World Bank). Macedonia's food and energy resources are sufficient to meet the basic needs of its population, but it is a landlocked country, entirely dependent on outside sources for oil, natural gas, modern machinery, and industrial supplies. Its economy suffered serious losses when Greece imposed a blockade (1992–95) and when the UN imposed sanctions on "rump" Yugoslavia. Remittances from Macedonians working in the EU represent a significant share of GNP. Meanwhile, Macedonia's security is put in question by the reported violations of its airspace by Greek fighter planes (see Brown). Maintaining internal sociopolitical stability and cooperative international relations, especially with its neighbors, are therefore vital for overcoming Macedonia's geographic isolation, and for the future wellbeing of its economy and society.

## Yugoslavia (Serbia and Montenegro)

The Federal Republic of Yugoslavia comes second, after Bosnia-Herzegovina, in the number and size of areas in which minorities are geographically concentrated. Political problems plague the relations between its two constituent republics, Serbia, which has a population of around 10.4 million, and Montenegro, which, with a population of only around 600,000, is considerably smaller. Montenegro has one majority-Albanian area, in its Southwest, and shares with Serbia the Sanjak region, where Slavic Moslems form the largest single ethnic group (equivalent to around 54% of the total population of the Sanjak in the 1991 census).

The largest area of Yugoslavia with a concentrated minority population has been the province of Kosovo, inside Serbia, which has long been characterized by its significant Albanian majority. The 1991 census, the last to be held by the former Yugoslavia before its disintegration, was boycotted by most Albanians, but it was officially estimated that their share of the province's population was around 82%. Albanians have also exhibited a relatively high rate of population growth, at around 1.9% a year, while the annual growth rate for Serbia as a whole is around –0.1%. This contrast in demographic characteristics has been widely exploited by Serb nationalists.

For historical reasons, the third largest ethnic minority in "rump" Yugoslavia, the Montenegrins, who are around 6% of the total population, have their own constituent republic, as well as representation equal to that of the whole of Serbia in the Chamber of the Republics, the upper house of the Federal Assembly. In March 1989, however, the Albanians, the second largest minority at 14% of the total, lost even the autonomous status that Kosovo used to have. The past and present political and geographic context of Kosovo is of particular importance for understanding its drive for greater autonomy, which was transformed into an armed struggle for independence from 1997 onward.

Both Albanians and Serbs present historical claims to the province. Albanians lived in Kosovo centuries before any Slavs settled there, but the province later acquired unparalleled significance for Serb nation-building, especially because it contains the site of the Battle of Kosovo Polje, where the medieval kingdom of Serbia was decisively defeated by the invading Ottoman Turks in 1389. Kosovo remained within the Ottoman Empire as late as 1912, somewhat longer than Serbia, which gained independence in 1878. During the Italian occupation, from 1941 to 1943, it was once again separated from Serbia and joined to Albania, but in 1944 the new Communist regime in that country returned it to Yugoslav control. Kosovo enjoyed an autonomous status within Serbia from 1946.

Interethnic tensions increased in parallel with the deteriorating economic situation and the political uncertainty following the death of President Tito in 1980. Both sides traded claims of repression. In 1981, Albanian students demonstrated against Serbian control of education and demanded a wider use of the Albanian language in educational institutions, and separate Albanian schools and colleges were established in private homes. Meanwhile, the Serb minority within Kosovo dwindled further as many departed for Serbia proper. It has been estimated that around 10% of the Serb population of the province have left since 1981.

Tensions in Kosovo escalated further as a result of the political crisis in Yugoslavia in the late 1980s, and the wars that followed the dissolution of the Federation of six republics in 1991. In February 1990, Serbia imposed martial law on Kosovo, and in July it took full control of the provincial government and media. Large Serb nationalist rallies were organized in response to mass antigovernment demonstrations, more than 100,000 Albanians were dismissed from their jobs in state agencies and enterprises, and the Albanian Human Rights Council accused the (exclusively Serbian) police of causing wrongful deaths and committing widespread abuses of human rights (see Seymore).

In September 1991, the Albanian Democratic League of Kosovo (LDK), held an unofficial referendum that showed overwhelming support for independence. In October, the members of the provincial Assembly, which had been dominated by the LDK, met to declare independence; and in May 1992, the LDK's Chairman, Ibrahim Rugova, was elected President. The UN and other international organizations did not (and do not) support the Albanian claim to independence, but they have frequently condemned Serbian repression, and deplored the use of violence by both sides in the conflict. The OSCE stationed human rights monitors in Kosovo, the Sanjak, and another province, Vojvodina (see below), but in November 1997 the Albanian guerillas of the Kosovo Liberation Army mounted their first public display of weapons and insignia, and the province descended into violent conflict in February 1998. At least 2,000 people were killed and tens of thousands were driven out of their homes over the months up to the cease-fire in October 1998. Further killings and displacements followed the breakdown of that ceasefire, and continued through the inconclusive peace talks in Rambouillet, France. Armed intervention by NATO followed: it had just ended when this book went to press.

The political and geographic situation of Kosovo provides access to both Albania and the majority-Albanian region in neighboring Macedonia, while the Sanjak is situated immediately to the North of the province. Albania itself strongly supports its ethnic kin. In October 1991, for example, it unilaterally recognized Kosovo as an independent state several days after the provincial Assembly made its declaration. Albania reportedly also serves as a source of widespread arms smuggling into Kosovo. Nevertheless, even after the start of NATO action against Yugoslavia in March 1999, predictions of a "Balkan tinderbox," in which the armed conflict in Kosovo would directly involve Albania, Macedonia, and other Balkan states, have not materialized. In general, despite the frequent media portrayal of violence in the region as "Balkan," it remains confined strictly to the former Yugoslavia.

Serbia has two more areas of minority concentration, in these cases involving Hungarians and Slovaks, in its northern province of Vojvodina, although no single ethnic group amounts to more than 50% of the population in the western and northern peripheries of the province. Vojvodina includes the Yugoslav part of the historic region of Banat, where the boundaries of Yugoslavia, Hungary, and Romania meet. Banat was settled and ruled by Slavs from the sixth century onward, but by Hungarians from the ninth century, and Hungary reclaimed the region from the Ottoman empire in 1779. However, Hungary was on the losing side in World War I and, under the Treaty of Trianon (1920), it lost the larger part of Banat to Romania and Yugoslavia. In 1946, Yugoslav Banat was combined with the Bachka and Srem districts, populated mainly by Serbs, to form Vojvodina, which, like Kosovo, had a special autonomous status up to 1989. The majority-Hungarian area is much larger than the majority-Slovak one, and is situated across the border from Hungary and the Hungarian minority in Romania. Both the languages and the religious affiliations of the predominantly Catholic Hungarians and Slovaks separate them from the Orthodox Serb majority.

As in Kosovo, interethnic conflict in Vojvodina began after the death of President Tito. Minority organizations emerged, including the Democratic Community of Vojvodina Hungarians (DZVM), to defend the freedoms and rights of ethnic minorities. During the wars in Croatia and Bosnia-Herzegovina, draft evasion was widespread in Vojvodina, where 5–7% of the population were Croats. The other minorities – the Hungarians (20%) and the Slovaks (3%), but also the Romanians (2%) – complained of being disproportionately drafted to fight for a new Yugoslavia that offered them little protection (see Seymore). The government of Serbia, on the other hand, interpreted the protests against the draft as disloyalty and treason. Its decision to resettle more than 500,000 Serbs from Bosnia-Herzegovina and Croatia created additional problems for ethnic peace in Vojvodina. The Serbian authorities occasionally conceded that abuses of human rights were taking place, but they rarely took action sufficient to protect or reassure the minorities, who experienced discrimination, robbery, terror techniques, and eviction at gunpoint, all directed towards relocating them. Violence was targeted especially at Croats, because of their association with the country that many Serbs regard as their major rival. Ethnic persecution, coupled with economic hardship that was made worse by UN sanctions, induced at least 25,000 ethnic Hungarians to leave Vojvodina between 1990 and 1993 (see Seymore).

Finally, eastern Serbia includes the Dimitrovgrad and Tsaribrod areas, which are populated mainly by Bulgarians. Serbia acquired these areas, situated across the border with Bulgaria, under the Treaty of Neuilly (1919), which penalized Bulgaria for having sided with Germany in World War I. Human rights organizations have reported cases of police torturing prisoners, and of cultural and political discrimination against the Bulgarian minority (see *Monitor Daily*). Bulgaria has begun to take a much greater interest in the situation in what Bulgarians call the "western outlands."

## Croatia

The separate history of Croatia, which was long part of the Habsburg empire, has combined with the different political, ethnic, and religious affiliations of most Croats to widen the rift with the neighboring Serbs. The only area of Croatia with a concentrated minority population is the Krajina, which is occupied mostly by Serbs, the country's largest minority. The region is relatively far from Serbia itself, but it is situated across the border from the Serb Republic in Bosnia-Herzegovina. The oil-rich region of Eastern Slavonia, which does border Serbia, also has some Serb minority areas, but Serbs are less than 50% of its population.

In September 1990, Croatia declared its sovereignty; in March 1991 some of the Serb areas declared themselves independent, and Serb militia fought alongside the Yugoslav federal army against Croat forces. That war is now over, but the Serb National Party and numerous other groups still claim to represent and lead minority discontent, while the authoritarian and nationalistic style of Croatia's government, and its continuing violations of human rights, inhibit the elimination of Serb-Croat frictions. On the other hand, the country's economic characteristics generally discourage minority conflict. According to

World Bank estimates, it is the third most prosperous state in central and eastern Europe, and on most of the standard World Bank indicators it qualified as an "upper middle income" country in 1997: its GNP per capita was US$4,610. This is an impressive achievement, given the recent devastation caused by the war, the large numbers of displaced persons, and the disruption of economic ties that resulted from the fragmentation of the former Yugoslavia.

## Slovakia, Bulgaria, and Romania

The second group of states in the first cluster comprises Slovakia, Bulgaria, and Romania. Comparisons with the former Yugoslav republics confirm the broad correlation between the share of geographically concentrated minorities and the level of social conflict. The Hungarian minorities in Slovakia and Romania, and the Turkish minority in Bulgaria, range between 9% and 11% of the respective populations of these countries, while the majority populations of these relatively stable states vary between 86% and 89% of the totals.

These minorities form local majorities in some districts, which are often situated across the border with the "mother" country. The "historic memories" of the majority populations in Slovakia and Romania include discrimination at the hands of the Hungarians who once ruled over them, while many Bulgarians harbor similar attitudes towards the Turks. Except in Slovakia, religious differences – Catholic/Orthodox and Christian/Moslem – further widen the rifts between the ethnic groups, and present additional opportunities for their political exploitation. However, relations between religiously different communities that belong to the same ethnicity are much more sympathetic. For example, ethnological and sociological studies of the ethnic-Bulgarian Moslem community in Bulgaria (around 3% of the total population), who live predominantly in the highest areas of the Western Rodopi mountains, point to a high level of religious tolerance (see Zhelyazkova). Religious affiliation *per se* exhibits almost negligible potential to cause serious social tensions.

Both Slovakia and Romania also have Ukrainian minority areas in the region known historically as Ruthenia. (Some consider Ruthenians, or Rusyns, to be a linguistic minority distinct from Ukrainians.) It is notable that Slovakia has resisted proposals from this minority for the establishment of a Carpathian "Euroregion" (see Liebich; and also Chapter 16). In addition, Romania incorporates several German minority areas in its provinces of Transylvania and Banat. However, none of these groups constitutes more than 1% of the total population in either of these countries.

The social and demographic indicators of the countries in this group place them among "upper middle income" states, according to World Bank criteria. Slovakia, Bulgaria, and Romania did not initially share in the pursuit of "shock therapy" reforms and rapid privatization that swept across central and eastern Europe in the 1990s. Nevertheless, Slovakia still qualified as a "middle to upper middle income" country – its GNP per capita was US$3,700 – while Romania and Bulgaria were "low middle income" economies with GNPs per capita of US$1,420 and US$1,140 respectively. The severe economic crises and social deprivation that have accompanied the transition to market economies in these countries have the potential to become significant factors for intercultural discord. Nevertheless, it should be emphasized that measures of economic activity and quality of life cannot be directly correlated with potential for social conflict. Among these three countries, conflict over minority rights has perhaps been most bitter in Slovakia, where a law was enacted in November 1995 to make Slovak the sole official language and restrict the use of Hungarian and other minority languages.

Ethnic political parties provide an important vehicle for the channeling of ethnic claims. All three states in this group permit the existence of ethnic parties in practice, although the post-Communist Constitution of Bulgaria, which came into force in July 1991, formally prohibits parties based on ethnic, racial, or religious identities. In Slovakia, a coalition of three Hungarian parties – the Hungarian Christian Democrats, the Hungarian Civic Party, and Coexistence, took more than 10% of the votes cast in legislative elections in 1994. In Bulgaria, the ethnic Turkish party, the Movement for Rights and Freedoms, alone or in coalition, regularly accounts for 5–8% of the votes in the National Assembly. In Romania, the Democratic Union of Hungarians has been part of the governing coalition since 1996.

## States without Regionally Concentrated Minorities

Among the five states in the second cluster – Albania, Hungary, the Czech Republic, Poland, and Slovenia – only Slovenia does not have cultural minority areas, although it does have minorities nonetheless. The other four states do have such areas, but the respective minority constitutes less than 50% of the total population in each area it inhabits. These are generally ethnically homogeneous states, in which the majority ethnicity varies between 90%, in Hungary, and 98%, in Poland.

The religious situation in these countries is quite diverse, except in Poland, which is 95% Catholic. Significant religious minorities exist in Hungary, where 68% of the population are Catholics, as well as in Albania, where around 70% are Moslems. Around 20% of Hungarians are Calvinists, while 20% of Albanians adhere to the Orthodox Church and 10% to the Catholic Church. The share of the minority population, however, is often disproportionate to the seriousness of the problems with and for the state. The confrontations between radical Catholics and Jews at the site of the former Nazi extermination camp of Auschwitz in Poland, in April 1998, provide a good example of the internal and external complications that can accompany minority politics in central and eastern Europe.

Unusually, the Czech Republic shows a significant secular/clerical divide: 40% of the population are not actively religious, while 39% are Catholics. Statistical comparability in this respect is quite problematic, since, among all the states in the region, only the Czech Republic and Slovakia allow their citizens to indicate that they are "secular" in censuses and other surveys. However, social groups in central and eastern Europe have not generally demonstrated intractable differences on issues of religion and secularism that might be expected to cause concern for the social order.

Most of the minority areas in the states in this cluster involve ethnic groups that originated from outside central and eastern Europe (as the region has been defined in this book). Germans inhabit the largest minority areas in Hungary (1.9% of the total population) and Poland (1.3–2%). The Czech Republic also contains a German minority area, in the Sudetenland. Other such minorities include the Ukrainians in the Polish part of Ruthenia (less than 1% of the total population), and the Greeks in the southern region of Albania that Greeks call Northern Epirus (3%). Large numbers of ethnic Greeks have emigrated to Greece, but they often return to Albania to exercise their voting rights, thus influencing the political scene (see *Cosmos*).

In the Czech Republic, however, there are prominent minority areas of intraregional origin. Slovaks, who make up 3% of the country's total population, reside mainly in Silesia and Sudetenland, while Poles live in its easternmost corner near the Polish border. Hungary also has a small Slovak minority area, but Slovaks are less than 1% of its total population. Hungary's Roma and Serb minorities are larger, at 4.8% and 2% of the total respectively, but they have more uniform geographic distributions.

Parties based on ethnic minorities constitute an important factor in the preservation of social peace. For example, four seats in the Sejm, the lower house of the Polish National Assembly, are constitutionally assigned to ethnic German parties. Probably more important, however, are the state of the economy and the quality of life of the populations in this cluster of countries. On average, the level of prosperity is significantly higher than in the first cluster states, except in Albania. The most important social and demographic indicators for the Czech Republic, Hungary, and Poland classify them in the "upper middle income" group, making them comparable to countries in western Europe. Their literacy rates are among the highest in the world, their life expectancy is among the highest in their region, and only their levels of urbanization are lower than the average for Europe as a whole.

The Czech Republic is the cluster's most economically advanced state, with strikingly low unemployment, no debts to the IMF, and GNP per capita of US$5,200 as of 1997. Hungary's GNP per capita is US$4,430, while Poland's is US$3,590. Generally, these levels of quality of life, as well as the prospect of relatively swift accession to the EU, tend to decrease the potential for minority-based violence in these countries.

Albania is an exceptional case, not just in this cluster, but in Europe as a whole. It was the poorest country on the continent even before World War II, and the isolationist policies of its postwar Communist regime contributed to its destitution. The difficult early stages of transition from central planning to a market economy brought Albania close to collapse in 1993–94. On most indicators of quality of life and economic activity, Albania ranks the lowest in Europe. It has a relatively low endowment of arable land per capita, and many in the urban areas continue to depend on humanitarian aid to meet their most basic requirements. In 1997, Albania's GNP per capita (US$750) and its level of urbanization (38%) were the lowest in Europe. Clearly, economic crisis and political instability have tended to exert a negative influence on interethnic relations: for example, there have been reports of violence targeted at the Greek minority in the South of the country. Albania has agreed to allow troops from Greece to participate in restoring social peace in these areas. In September 1998, ex-President Salih Berisha tried to play the ethnic card to his advantage by accusing the peacekeeping forces of participation in the disturbances, but, significantly, failed to make much impact (see *Cosmos*).

Slovenia is the only country in central and eastern Europe that does not include significant minority areas. Slovenes amount to around 91% of the country's total population, and over 94% of them are Roman Catholic. The largest ethnic minorities are Croats (3% of the total) and Serbs (2%). Although they are much smaller, Hungarian and Italian minorities enjoy constitutionally assigned representation in the unicameral National Assembly. Thus, minority politics has been merged into the everyday process of democratic competition. In addition, Slovenia is the most economically and socially successful state in central and eastern Europe. It enjoys the highest GNP per capita (US$9,680) in the region, and also leads the region on most indicators of quality of life, such as life expectancy and infant mortality. Slovenia's prosperity and political stability may well improve its chances of rapid acceptance into the EU, as compared even to the other countries now engaged in "fast track" negotiations on membership, and this is likely to provide another very strong incentive for social accord.

## Conclusion

Since the late 1980s, the devolution of power in central and eastern Europe, and the rapid economic stratification both within and between states in the region, have substantially transformed cultural identities and local interests. However, newly visible minorities and increased social contradictions do not necessarily translate into violent conflict; and policymakers at every level need to abandon the assumption that a single, "ideal" minority policy can prevent extreme action. Parallel to the wave of globalization, spurred by the revolution in communications technology, a process of increasing geographic diversification is taking place on the regional and local levels. Place-specific policies that address the concrete concerns of particular groups have a much greater chance of engendering and enhancing tendencies toward cooperation.

## Further Reading

Batsavage, Rich, *Kosovo: Challenge to Balkan Stability*, Washington, DC: Woodrow Wilson International Center for Scholars, Smithsonian Institution, 1999

The author, a senior analyst on the Bosnian Task Force at the Office of the Secretary of Defense of the United States, comments on the interest of the United States and other countries in the maintenance of Balkan stability. In his view, that stability is threatened by a possible spillover of violence from Kosovo to neighboring Albania and Macedonia. He also suggests that even a negotiated solution carries risks, as it may set off other movements for autonomy within the former Yugoslavia.

Brown, Keith, *Determined Histories: Macedonia in the International Arena*, Washington, DC: Woodrow Wilson International Center for Scholars, Smithsonian Institution, 1999

The author, a lecturer in anthropology at the University of Wales in Lampeter, warns against tracing today's confrontations into the past and presenting them as "ancient hatreds." He also points out that maintaining a neutral stand on a nation's history may brand a scholar as hostile to that nation. His report links scholarly ambivalence about the historical depth of Macedonian identity to the activities of Macedonia's neighbors.

CIA: *The World Factbook 1998*, Washington, DC: Central Intelligence Agency, 1998

This comprehensive reference work on states, other territories, and international organizations is the principal source for the population percentages and other data given in this chapter. It is available both in book form and on the World Wide Web (at www.odci.gov/cia/publications/factbook).

*Cosmos*: "Albania Again in Crisis," in *Cosmos*, Volume 2, number 9, Athens: Institute of International Relations, Pantheon University, 1998

This short but very informative article presents a Greek perspective on the economic and political turmoil in Albania in 1998–99. It suggests three main goals for Greek foreign policy in this respect: protection of the human rights of the Greek minority; establishment of a stable and friendly Albanian government; and prevention of illegal immigration into Greece.

De Blij, H. J., and Peter O. Muller, *Geography: Realms, Regions, and Concepts*, Chichester and New York: John Wiley, 1998

This influential textbook describes and explains 13 great geographic "realms" of the modern world, and provides a geographic perspective on contemporary transformations. It is a comprehensive source of valuable political, economic, social, and cultural information.

Goldman, Minton, *Global Studies: Russia, The Eurasian Republics, and Central/Eastern Europe*, Guilford, CT: Dushkin/McGraw-Hill, 1999

This book includes country reports, statistical information, and maps of eastern Europe and the successor states of the Soviet Union. The second part features articles from the world press on the most important political, economic, and social developments in the countries in transition.

Kolarova, Rumyana, "Tacit Agreements in the Bulgarian Transition to Democracy: Minority Rights and Constitutionalism," in *Roundtable: A Journal of Interdisciplinary Studies*, 1993

This well-researched article analyzes the institutionalization of minority rights in Bulgaria since 1989. It includes coverage of the historical setting of the minority question, and the strategies for social and political liberalization and democratization.

Liebich, Andre, "Getting Better, Getting Worse: Minorities in East Central Europe," in *Dissent*, Summer 1996

This article reviews minority problems in central and eastern Europe, showing how new minorities, notably Roma and Albanians, have replaced the traditional ones, due to their higher growth rates. Liebich concludes that territorial autonomy for minorities remains an absolute taboo, especially in the wake of the recent collapse of federal states in the region.

*Monitor Daily*, Sofia, January 11, 1999

Prelec, Marko, *The Fear of Islam in Croatian Politics*, Washington, DC: Woodrow Wilson International Center for Scholars, Smithsonian Institution, 1999

This report refutes the myth of ancient Balkan ethnic hatreds, with the exception of the conflict with the Ottoman Empire. The author finds the core of Croatian fear of Islam today in the enormous influence of President Tudjman.

Seymore II, Bruce, editor, *The ACCESS Guide to Ethnic Conflicts in Europe and the Former Soviet Union*, Washington, DC: ACCESS, 1994

This useful book contains an essay by Paul Goble on types of nationalism, a listing of ethnic conflicts in Europe and the former Soviet Union, profiles of the most important confrontations, excerpts from selected UN documents, a chart of selected memberships in international organizations and agreements, and a guide to organizations, government contacts, and resources.

World Bank, *World Development Report*, Oxford and New York: Oxford University Press, annual publication

This invaluable and wide-ranging publication is the main source of the data on the economies of central and eastern Europe in this chapter.

Zhelyazkova, Antonina, "Bulgaria's Muslim Minorities," in John D. Bell, editor, *Bulgaria in Transition: Politics, Economics, Society and Culture After Communism*, Boulder, CO: Westview Press, 1998

The author reviews the historical background, demographic characteristics, and political institutions and activities of the Moslem minorities in Bulgaria, and assesses the influence of the economic transition on interethnic relations in a comparative perspective. She concludes that, despite the complexity of interethnic relations, Bulgarian nationalism is not particularly popular, and is mostly concerned with national identity, self-esteem, and the possibility of national and territorial fragmentation.

*Dr Boian Koulov* is a Visiting Assistant Professor in the Department of Geography and Earth Systems Science at George Mason University, Fairfax, Virginia.

# International Relations

## Chapter Eighteen

# Relations with the Wider Europe

## *Bogdan Szajkowski and*
## *Nieves Pérez-Solórzano Borragán*

The rapid demise of Communism and the consequent disintegration of the bipolar system of international relations was hailed, not so long ago, as "the end of history" or, less dramatically, as the triumph of market capitalism and liberal democratic values, and the beginning of the construction of peaceful and harmonious cooperation. However, the euphoria that accompanied the collapse of Communism induced a rather simplistic and mechanistic set of policy prescriptions. It was hoped that, with the lifting of the Iron Curtain, central and eastern Europe could simply return to being part of "Europe." Indeed, since 1989 all the countries in the region have officially expressed their desire to join international organizations that, as H. Grabbe and K. Hughes have put it, could "facilitate and consolidate reintegration into the world economy and departure from the Soviet sphere of influence" (see Grabbe and Hughes). The EU and NATO are generally regarded as the most important among these institutions, both because of the practical benefits of membership and because of what they represent politically.

## Defining Central and Eastern Europe

Central and eastern Europe, traditionally the playground of Europe's great powers, is not easy to define and the task will always be a contested one. As J. Batt has declared, "Central and eastern Europe seems easier to define by what it is not than by what it is" (see White,

Batt, and Lewis). After World War II, Poland, Hungary, Czechoslovakia, Romania, Bulgaria, and the eastern part of Germany became components of the Soviet bloc, being bound by the Soviet Union into a network of institutions that had the Warsaw Pact and Comecon at its core. As far as the West was concerned, they now formed, along with Yugoslavia and Albania, a newly defined region: "eastern Europe."

The boundaries of the region did not become any clearer or more widely agreed after 1989. As was only to be expected, public debate in the region and beyond was focused, not on what seemed the relatively minor question of the region's own definition – apart, of course, from its being resolutely ex-Communist – but on what constitutes "Europe" as a whole. Numerous and various calls were made for a redefinition of thinking about Europe, its core and its peripheries, its achievements and its goals, as well as the appropriate means for defining "European" aspirations and realizing them in practice.

A report entitled *Europe and the Challenge of Enlargement*, issued in 1992 by the European Commission (the executive body of the European Community, renamed the EU in November 1993), found it strikingly difficult to establish clear geographical limits for Europe in general or the "Europe" that it represented in particular. It argued that it "is neither possible nor opportune to establish now the frontiers of the European Union, whose contours will be shaped over many years to come" (see Commission).

We are faced, then, with a region that, having shaken off the Communist unity imposed from Moscow, can now be seen to cover a wide range of economic, political, and social conditions, and to be in a state of rapid and not wholly predictable transformation that varies in its effects from country to country. In the absence of any internally generated and practically unifying regional identity, it has become conventional to rank the countries of the region, significantly enough, by reference to their relations with the leading European and western institutions. There is a vanguard of three NATO members – Poland, Hungary, and the Czech Republic – which is closely followed by several other applicants for EU membership, leaving the troubled republics that so recently constituted the Yugoslav federation at something of a distance from the rest of the region. (Their recent history has been so complex and controversial that we do not have sufficient space to address it here.) For most of the countries of the region, however, relations with the wider Europe are central to their political and economic development, and, not least, to their search for individual and common identities.

## Relations with the EU

To overcome the difficulties intrinsic to the transition process, the countries of the region turned to their western neighbors, particularly the member states of what was still the European Community, for advice and financial support. The EU, as it has since become, has increasingly come to be seen as symbolizing economic prosperity and democratic success. It follows, for most policy-makers and opinion-formers in the region, that accession to the EU would be a concrete expression of their "return to Europe." At the same time, the collapse of Communism removed the eastern limits of the process of European integration that is centered on the EU and opened the door to enlargement (see Szajkowski).

A Joint Declaration was signed by the European Community and Comecon in June 1988, before Communism began to collapse in the region, taking almost everyone by surprise. Under its terms, the two organizations formally

established mutual recognition for the first time, a very important step compared to the previous lack of contacts between them. This in turn legitimized the initiation of diplomatic relations between western states and individual countries in what was still the Soviet bloc. By the end of 1988, Hungary and Czechoslovakia had negotiated trade and cooperation agreements with the European Community. Nevertheless, the initial reaction of the Community and its member states to the changes that swept through central and eastern Europe after 1989 was decidedly cautious. It offered technical assistance and support, but was reluctant to make any further commitment.

However, while proposals for a "new Marshall Plan" to assist the transition to a market economy and parliamentary democracy made little impact, in July 1989 the Group of Seven and the European Commission agreed to provide aid to any country in the region that committed itself to pursuing the twin goals of democratization and market liberalization. The Community's PHARE program was the most important outcome of these developments. It was aimed, to begin with, at providing financial and technical support for the reconstruction of Poland and Hungary, but it was extended to Czechoslovakia, Bulgaria, and the former Yugoslavia in 1990, and to the Baltic states in 1991. Nevertheless, neither the increasing number of trade and cooperation agreements nor the PHARE program succeeded in addressing the expectations of the new democracies.

The need to offer a more effective response to the new democracies and to acknowledge the new state of relations within Europe inspired the Community to initiate the negotiation of association agreements. The first two "Europe agreements" (as they were subsequently called) were signed in 1991. Agreements were eventually made with Poland, Hungary, the Czech Republic, Slovakia, Romania, and Bulgaria, providing for:

- free movement of services and capital, and the reciprocal right to establish enterprises;
- cooperation and assistance for transition, including financial resources directed through the PHARE program for

economic reconstruction, the formulation of legislation, and the establishment of market institutions;

- three main institutions for each associate country – an Association Council, an Association Committee, and a Parliamentary Committee; and

- a continuing process of political dialogue, which has been extended to more and more areas of policy as the EU itself has taken on new powers in relation to security and foreign relations.

Those countries in central and eastern Europe that signed Europe agreements were clearly attempting to escape from the post-Communist political vacuum, seeking the support of the Community's economic and political mechanisms for the success of their internal reforms. Nothing in any of these documents represented a commitment to their future accession to membership of the Community. In December 1992, however, a meeting of the European Council (the Community/EU body that brings together the heads of state and government of the member countries) recognized that "the Community's partners' ultimate objective is to accede to the Community" and accepted "the goal of eventual membership in the European Union for the countries of central and eastern Europe when they are able to satisfy the conditions required" (see Council 1992).

In the following year, a meeting of the European Council in Copenhagen took the issue further by deciding that

"the associated countries in central and eastern Europe that so desire shall become members of the European Union. Accession will take place as soon as an associated country is able to assume the obligations of membership by satisfying the economic and political conditions required" (see Council 1993).

The following specific conditions for accession to membership were laid down by the Copenhagen meeting:

- stability of the institutions guaranteeing democracy, the rule of law, human

rights, and respect for and protection of minorities;

- the existence of a functioning market economy, as well as a capacity to cope with competitive pressures and market forces within the Union; and

- an ability to take on the obligations of membership, most notably adherence to the goals of political, economic and monetary union (see Council 1993).

These "Copenhagen criteria" did not bind the EU to granting membership to any country that fulfilled them, but they helped to shape the new map of relations on the European continent. Ten countries that had signed Europe agreements were regarded as candidate members: Bulgaria, the Czech Republic, Estonia, Hungary, Latvia, Lithuania, Poland, Romania, Slovakia, and Slovenia. At the same time, Albania, Croatia, and the CIS countries were excluded.

In 1994, the German government, which was then occupying the rotating Presidency of the EU, decided to give a new impetus to integration with the countries of central and eastern Europe. The result of this initiative was the "pre-accession strategy" adopted by the European Council, meeting in Essen in December 1994. Subsequently, the Commission was asked to elaborate a White Paper on the applicant countries' preparations for taking part in the EU's internal market. It was hoped that the White Paper would provide guidelines to assist the associated countries. In the event, it went into considerable detail, identifying the key measures to be taken in respect of each sector of the internal market and suggesting a sequence in which the approximation of legislation to EU standards should be tackled. The recommendations covered such areas as the free movement of capital, the safety of industrial products, competition, agriculture, social policy, the environment, and transportation (see Carr).

By June 1995, all the associated countries in the region had submitted formal applications for EU membership. The Commission was then required to prepare official opinions in response to each of the applicants. (Additionally, given the challenge of EU enlargement for existing member states, the Commission elaborated a paper on the measures to be taken by the Union itself in order to adapt to the new situation.)

The Commission concluded, first of all, that all the candidate countries, except Slovakia, met the political criteria laid down at Copenhagen, even if a number of them still had to make progress concerning the actual practice of democracy, and the protection of human rights and minorities. In particular, there were still unresolved problems over the treatment of the Russian-speaking minorities in Estonia, the Roma populations of the region, and the Hungarian minorities in Romania and Slovakia. Overall, the candidate countries had proved that they were capable of maintaining institutional stability, but there were some doubts over the integrity of the judiciary in some of the countries and the Commission emphasized the importance of combating corruption more effectively.

The Commission also concluded that all the candidate countries in central and eastern Europe had made considerable progress in the transition to a market economy. Foreign direct investment was still rising, which was seen as a sign of economic health, even though the general levels of investment were still low in comparison with those in western Europe. Hungary, the Czech Republic, Estonia, Slovenia, Latvia, and Lithuania had received the largest inflows (as measured per capita), reflecting their relative success in pushing forward the privatization of state enterprises and structural reforms of their economies. The GDP per capita of some of the candidate countries (at purchasing power parity) was close to that of some EU member states: in particular, Slovenia's GDP per capita was 68% of the EU average and the Czech Republic's was 63%. There were other welcome trends in macroeconomic indicators: inflation was falling in Slovenia, the Czech Republic, Slovakia, Latvia, and Lithuania, and budget deficits were small or nonexistent, and were manageable across the region. However, the balance of trade for each of the countries under review was still negative, indicating that in some respects the transition still had some way to go.

On the basis of the Commission's opinions, official negotiations on accession started in the summer of 1998 with Poland, Hungary, the Czech Republic, Slovenia, and Estonia. The problem that now faces these and other countries in the region is that the consensus in favor of EU membership may not last. The imperative of enlargement has been presented by political leaders in the region as an integral and inevitable part of the overall process of transformation. However, according to the Eurobarometer surveys conducted on behalf of the European Commission, by 1996 there had already been a slight deterioration in the image of the EU throughout the region. Only around 40% of those questioned in the ten Europe agreement countries had a positive impression of the EU, 6% a "negative" one, while 23% declared themselves "neutral."

## Relations with the Council of Europe

The Council of Europe, the oldest of the various international organizations dedicated to promoting European integration, has launched numerous initiatives on safeguarding pluralist and parliamentary democracy, the indivisibility and universality of human rights, the rule of law, and a common cultural patrimony in its half-century of existence. After 1989, the Council of Europe created a "special guest" status for the new democracies of central and eastern Europe. It thus effectively made itself a "gatekeeper," responsible for checking these countries' credentials for participation in an integration process that had originally been intended to include them but had gone ahead without them for decades. By 1995, however, all the countries in the region, apart from the former Yugoslav republics, were members of the Council of Europe, despite some important reservations regarding Romania, Slovakia, and Latvia.

In relation to the countries of the region, the Council of Europe's most important programs are probably the following:

• the Demosthenes programs, which are focused on institution-building through the training of national policy-makers, civil servants, lawyers, youth leaders, and officials of nongovernmental organizations;

- the Themis program, which is designed specifically to train judges, prosecutors, notaries, and lawyers; and
- the LODE program for local democracy, which aims to foster the development of efficient grass-roots democracy, and the training of local officials and representatives.

Since 1993, an increasing proportion of these programs has been carried out in the form of joint activities by the European Commission and the Council of Europe. To handle the ever increasing need for improving and extending information flows to and from the Council, it has established information and documentation centers in Bratislava, Bucharest, Budapest, Ljubljana, Prague, Riga, Skopje, Sofia, Tallinn, Vilnius, and Warsaw, as well as in the capitals of some CIS countries.

## Relations with NATO

The collapse of the Soviet Union, the demise of the Warsaw Pact, and the unification of Germany left central and eastern Europe with a deep sense of instability. In this "security vacuum," the countries of the region turned to NATO, the world's most powerful military alliance and the only one with direct involvement in European affairs. Hungary, Poland, the Czech Republic, and Romania had all submitted formal applications for membership by the spring of 1996. NATO initiated formal contacts with delegations from the region and then decisively institutionalized relations by creating the North Atlantic Cooperation Council in December 1991. It has since been renamed the Euro-Atlantic Partnership Council. By 1999, this Council was an active forum for the discussion of security issues among the 19 members of NATO itself, now including the Czech Republic, Hungary, and Poland; nine other countries in the region (Albania, Bulgaria, Estonia, Latvia, Lithuania, Macedonia, Romania, Slovakia, and Slovenia); the 12 member countries of the CIS; and four traditionally "neutral" states (Austria, Finland, Malta, and Sweden).

The Council is integrally related to the Partnership for Peace initiative, which was launched at NATO's Brussels summit in January 1994, and which has been accepted in central and eastern Europe (apart from the obvious exception of Yugoslavia) as a second-best arrangement for countries that still expect to join NATO sooner rather than later. The Partnership for Peace is aimed at enhancing stability and security throughout Europe, and at going beyond dialogue and cooperation to create a real partnership. Detailed individual Partnership Programs have been agreed by most of the countries in the region and are now being implemented. The Partnership initiative was further strengthened in the spring of 1997 through the Enhanced Partnership for Peace, which envisages a larger operational role, more extensive political consultation, and increased opportunities for Partners to participate in decision-making and the planning of activities.

As has been mentioned, the Czech Republic, Hungary, and Poland joined NATO in April 1999. This first step in eastward enlargement is regarded by NATO decision-makers as benefiting the Alliance itself and the new partners alike. In 1998, for example, Javier Solana, then Secretary General of NATO, declared that enlargement would make NATO stronger and enhance cooperation throughout the Euro-Atlantic area; he also took care to emphasize that enlargement posed no threat to relations between NATO and Russia, and that it was not a costly process, since it will require an estimated additional outlay of only US$1.5 billion on commonly funded programs over the first 10 years (see Solana).

As for further enlargement, NATO has set out formal criteria that other applicants in the region will have to meet. In particular, they must demonstrate respect for OSCE norms; a commitment to economic freedom, social justice, and environmental responsibility; significant progress toward resolving any interstate or ethnic disputes; civilian control of the military apparatus; and an ability to make a genuine military contribution to collective defence (see Carr). For their part, decision-makers in the countries of central and eastern Europe generally expect that NATO membership will not only fill the security vacuum in the region but possibly facilitate future accession to the EU. NATO membership is also regarded as a tool for the promotion of democracy and stability, and as yet another element in the symbolic commitment to the "return to Europe."

## International Relations Within the Region

The end of Soviet dominance over central and eastern Europe and of the Cold War has resulted in the creation of new forms of regional cooperation. Russia, the principal successor state of the Soviet Union, has managed to maintain contact with the region through its membership of the Council of Baltic Sea States and the Black Sea Economic Cooperation group. These changes have come about in the context of four main trends in the pattern of regional cooperation, as identified by A. Hyde-Price:

- the continuing absence of effective structures for multilateral cooperation;
- the emergence of an independent and sovereign Ukraine;
- the break-up of three federations – the Soviet Union, Czechoslovakia, and the former Yugoslavia – which has left the region much more heterogeneous than it was under Communism; and
- the continuing impact of the presence of significant national minorities in most of the countries of the region, which are separated from each other by arbitrary frontiers (see Hyde-Price).

However, perhaps the most far-reaching trend affecting intraregional cooperation is what Saul Cohen has identified as its gradual transformation into "a gateway region within the international system" open to economic forces from its East and its West (see Hyde-Price).

The emergence of new forms of regional cooperation is most evident in three areas: "central Europe," which is as difficult to define as the region itself; the Baltic Sea region; and the Black Sea area. We shall briefly examine each of these in turn.

The structures of regional cooperation established by Poland, the Czech Republic, Hungary, and Slovakia, and joined in 1996 by Slovenia, are aimed at fostering their "return to Europe." A "Declaration of Cooperation on the Road to European Integration" was agreed at Visegrád in February 1991, creating the basis for the Central European Free Trade Association, also known as the Visegrád Group. The five countries have made no provision for the creation of organizational structures but have concentrated their efforts instead on developing multilateral cooperation, mutual consultation, and the harmonization of economic and social policies.

Cooperation in the Baltic Sea region is mainly promoted through the Council of Baltic Sea States, which was created in March 1992, and brings together Sweden, Norway, Finland, Denmark, Iceland, Lithuania, Latvia, Estonia, Germany, Poland, and Russia. The areas of activity for this organization, which prides itself on being relatively informal, include environmental protection, trade promotion around the Baltic, transnational crime, and crossborder police cooperation (see Huldt and Johannessen).

The Black Sea Economic Cooperation group was founded in June 1992. It brings together Turkey, Romania, Bulgaria, Greece, Albania, Russia, Ukraine, Georgia, Moldova, Azerbaijan, and Armenia, while Poland and Slovakia have been accorded observer status. Despite attempts by Turkey in particular to enhance the effectiveness of the group, with a view to fostering its strategic relations with Russia and showing the EU that it can provide leadership in southeastern Europe, its progress has been hindered by deeply rooted historical animosities among some of its members, as well as by their fragile political and economic environments.

Finally, most of the countries of central and eastern Europe have also become involved in the "Euroregion" initiatives promoted by the EU, which are aimed at enhancing crossborder cooperation between contiguous regions (see also Chapter 16). These initiatives illustrate the process of differentiation that is taking place within central and eastern Europe, since they are moving forward at varying speeds and with very diverse effects. However, they also serve to underline once again the commitment of most countries in central and eastern Europe to promoting integration with the wider Europe.

## Conclusion

As Robert Bideleux has rightly pointed out, "The so-called 'return to Europe' will not succeed if it is based upon wishful thinking and self-delusion" (see Bideleux). The process of transformation which started in central and eastern Europe in 1989 has brought about significant political, economic, and social changes. New democratic governments have been established, the economies of the region are undergoing liberalization, and the region is pervaded – though it cannot yet be said to be wholly defined – by a general determination to adopt the behavior patterns typical of liberal and pluralistic societies (see Pérez-Solórzano Borragán).

Unfortunately, however, the high hopes with which the 1990s began withered away as the region started to be gripped by aggressive nationalism, political instability, and the social costs of transformation. Most western decision-makers and opinion-formers continued to insist that the transfer of liberal democratic values and structures, accompanied, ideally, by substantial aid and a massive inflow of capital to the ex-Communist countries, would bring about a rapid transition; but reality has proved, as so often, to be far more complex. Although free democratic elections, multiparty parliamentary politics, market structures, and the free exchange of opinions have largely been achieved and are being maintained, in practice these and other institutions often tend to function in ways that are at variance with liberal democratic principles (see Szajkowski). It has become increasingly clear that the successful completion of the transition process will depend, crucially, on the full development of a number of important institutional relationships (as identified by Carr and others). First, the ex-Communist states are still characterized by the absence or weakness of the intermediate institutions that compose a civil society in the full sense, while the interactions of state bodies –

the legislatures, the judiciary, the executive arms – often leave much to be desired, basically because those who direct them mostly lack experience of transparent and constitutional government. Second, the dismantling of the Communist legacy of state enterprises, central planning, and government welfare systems is proceeding at different rates in different countries, while the creation and maintenance of the market structures that are to replace that legacy will continue to be hindered by political and social obstacles, just as they create new political and social problems that the peoples of the region are not fully prepared to face. Finally, as we have seen, the development of new relationships with countries outside the region, whether bilaterally or through international economic and security institutions, has also proceeded at varying rates across the region, and differentiation among the 15 countries of central and eastern Europe has the potential to create new sources of conflict and misunderstanding.

In short, the demise of Communism has left a vacuum that is in danger of being filled with conflict and instability. Western Europe is faced with an unprecedented opportunity to enhance the process of integration in which it has been fitfully engaged ever since 1945, yet there is no consensus on how best to handle this opportunity and prevent its collapse into mutual recrimination. In particular, it is striking that decision-makers and opinion-formers, whether in the region itself or in western Europe, have no clear idea as to when and how the dividing lines between the "East" and the "West" of the continent will at last disappear from the map. The EU officially committed itself in its "Agenda 2000" program to a forecast that the first group of countries from central and eastern Europe to attain EU membership would do so in 2002 and 2003. This already seems far too optimistic to many observers, who point out that the EU is already fully occupied with adjusting to monetary union, and combating fraud and corruption. Others have begun to ask when, if ever, the second group of applicants can realistically expect to join. Certainly, the gradual rapprochement between the countries of central and eastern Europe and the structures, institutions, and organizations of western Europe has developed too rapidly for some and too slowly for others. Nevertheless, it is generally the case that politicians and ordinary people alike, throughout large parts of the region, remain at a loss to understand why they are treated as second-class inhabitants of a common continent.

The consequences of NATO's enlargement to the East are even more difficult to assess or forecast. The conflict over Kosovo in the spring of 1999 provoked disagreements within the Czech Republic, Hungary, and Poland over the activities of the organization that they had only just joined. It is becoming clearer than it was before that the strategic interests and internal politics of these three countries – and still more of their neighbors in the region – do not necessarily coincide with those of the other members of NATO. Questions also remain about the prospects for further enlargement, especially in view of the likelihood that there will be even more decisive opposition from Russia to any such proposals. The security and international relations of the Baltic states are also clouded by uncertainty about future developments, both to their East and to their West, especially as Estonia is to be one of the first wave of new entrants to the EU while Latvia and Lithuania's accession has been postponed.

Above and beyond the specific trends and developments – whether economic, political, military, or social – that will shape decisions on these and other issues in the coming century, there remains the widespread acceptance that none of these challenges can be met in isolation. The conduct of international relations in the "common European home" requires overall agreement on the establishment of structures of cooperation and integration that can bring in all the countries of Europe. Yet even after 50 years of progress toward integration in western Europe, and 10 eventful years of transition in central and eastern Europe, the very concept of "Europe" itself remains to be defined.

## Further Reading

Bideleux, Robert, "Eastward Enlargement of the EU: Problems and Prospects," unpublished paper, presented to the International Seminar on the Enlargement of the European Union at the University of Salamanca, April 1998

Bideleux, Robert, and Ian Jeffries, *A History of Eastern Europe: Crisis and Change*, London and New York: Routledge, 1998

This is a very comprehensive and complete assessment of the history of the region, full of insights into the crucial links between past, present, and future.

Borko, Y., "The New Intra-European Relations and Russia," in M. Maresceau, editor, *Enlarging the European Union: Relations Between the EU and Central and Eastern Europe*, London and New York: Longman, 1997

This is one of several outstanding papers in a remarkable volume that offers a thorough, multidisciplinary, and up-to-date analysis of all aspects of relations between the EU and the ex-Communist countries.

Bryant, Christopher G. A., and Edmund Mokrzycki, editors, *The New Great Transformation? Change and Continuity in East Central Europe*, London and New York: Routledge, 1994

This book provides an essential guide to the process of transformation taking place in central and eastern Europe by raising important theoretical questions. It is based on clear conceptualization and first-hand experience in the field.

Carr, F., editor, *Europe: The Cold Divide*, London: Macmillan, and New York: St Martin's Press, 1998

This volume constitutes a mixture of contributions on the changing environment facing the EU, central and eastern Europe, and the CIS as they address the gigantic challenge of reshaping relations within their continent.

Commission of the European Community, *Europe and the Challenge of Enlargement*, Brussels, 1992

Commission of the European Union, *Central and Eastern Eurobarometer No. 6*, Brussels, 1996

Commission of the European Union, *Composite Paper: Reports on Progress towards Accession by Each of the Candidate Countries*, Brussels, November 1998

Council of the European Union, *Presidency Conclusions: Edinburgh European Council*, Brussels, 1992, and *Presidency Conclusions: Copenhagen European Council*, Brussels, 1993

Grabbe, H., and K. Hughes, "Central and East European Views on EU Enlargement: Political Debates and Public Opinion," in Henderson, Karen, editor, *Back to Europe: Central and Eastern Europe and the European Union*, London and Philadelphia: UCL Press, 1999

Harris, G., *Enlargement of the Union: Threat or Promise?*, unpublished paper, prepared for presentation to the Conference on European Community Studies, Seattle, May 1997

Harris is a privileged witness of the process of transformation taking place in central and eastern Europe. From his position within the Secretariat of the European Parliament, he offers an excellent portrait of the challenges that enlargement will present and of the benefits that it will bring about.

Huldt, B., and U. Johannessen, editors, *First Annual Stockholm Conference on Baltic Sea Security and Cooperation*, Stockholm: Utrikespolitiska Institutet, 1997

Hyde-Price, A., "Patterns of International Politics," in Stephen White, Judy Batt, and Paul G. Lewis, editors, *Developments in Central and East European Politics 2*, London: Macmillan, and Durham, NC: Duke University Press, 1998

Jacobsen, Hanns-D., "The European Union's Eastward Enlargement," in *European Integration Online Papers*, Volume 1, number 14, 1997

This paper (located on the Worldwide Web at http://eiop.or.at/eiop/texte/1997–014a.htm) analyzes the implications of the future eastward enlargement of the EU both for the Union itself and for the candidate countries, stressing the need for institutional transformation and adequate measures to facilitate the convergence of the newcomers.

Nicolaides, P., and S. R. Boean, *A Guide to the Enlargement of the European Union: Determinants, Process, Timing, Negotiations*, European Institute of Public Administration, 1997

This publication offers an accurate and enlightening depiction of the complex processes of submitting applications for EU membership and negotiating accession.

Pérez-Solórzano Borragán, Nieves, *Assessment of Central and Eastern European Interests' Representation at the European Union Level*, Brussels: College of Europe and European Interuniversity Press, 1998

This publication assesses the various channels of representation through which the countries of central and eastern Europe express their interests to the EU, and presents the social, economic, and political environment for the emergence of interest groups in the region.

Solana, Javier, "Do We Need New Allies? Yes, to Enhance Everyone's Security," in *The Wall Street Journal*, March 12, 1998

This is one of several articles written by Dr Solana on the importance of NATO enlargement, and the need to create an adequate security structure in Europe.

Szajkowski, Bogdan, *The Importance of Further Enlargement of the European Union to the New World Order*, unpublished paper, presented to the Congress on European Integration at the University of Salamanca, April 1995

This unpublished paper offers a comprehensive characterization of the "New World Order" and highlights the essential role of the EU in the shaping of political relations in Europe.

White, Stephen, Judy Batt, and Paul G. Lewis, editors, *Developments in Central and Eastern European Politics 2*, London: Macmillan, and Durham, NC: Duke University Press, 1998

This volume brings together a number of specialists in post-Communist studies to address such issues as the workings of the democratic system in each country, the pattern of international relations in the region, the environment, and voting behavior.

## Websites

The four principal international organizations discussed in this chapter have all placed very large amounts of information on the Worldwide Web. Documentation on the EU can be found at http://europa.eu.int; on the Council of Europe, at www.coe.fr; on NATO, at www.nato.int; and on the OSCE, at www.osce.org.

*Bogdan Szajkowski* is Professor of Pan-European Politics and Director of the Centre for European Studies at the University of Exeter in England, and *Nieves Pérez-Solórzano Borragán* is a part-time Lecturer in the Centre and a doctoral candidate in the Department of Politics.

# Appendices

## Appendix 1

# Chronology

This listing is focused on political, economic and military events that continue to affect the countries of central and eastern Europe as the 20th century nears its end. However, this Chronology excludes many topics mentioned elsewhere in the appendices. Inevitably, it overlaps with, but also accompanies, the Chronology in another volume in this series, *The CIS Handbook*.

| | | |
|---|---|---|
| **1939** | **February** | *Hungary* signs the Anti-Comintern Pact, allying itself with Germany, Italy, and Japan in the "Axis" group of nations. |
| | **March** | Germany destroys *Czechoslovakia*, the last remaining democracy in central and eastern Europe, occupies Bohemia and Moravia, forms an alliance with autonomous *Slovakia*, allows *Hungary* to seize Subcarpathian Ruthenia and parts of Slovakia, and allows *Poland* to seize the district of Zaolzia. |
| | | German troops occupy the Klaipeda (Memel) district of *Lithuania*. |
| | | The United Kingdom and France reject proposals from the Soviet government for an alliance that could defend central and eastern Europe against further German aggression. |
| | **April** | Italy invades *Albania*, and its ruler, King Zog, goes into exile. |
| | **July** | The government of *Poland* provides its British and French counterparts with copies of the German Enigma code machines, constructed by a team headed by Marian Rejewski, thus helping to secure the eventual victory of these countries and their allies in the coming world war. |
| | **August** | *Croatia* is given special status as an autonomous province within the Kingdom of *Yugoslavia*. |
| | **September** | World War II begins in Europe with the signing of a non-aggression pact by Nazi Germany and the Soviet Union, their partition of *Poland*, and the declaration of war on Germany by Britain and France. Up to June 1941, around 750,000 Poles are killed, deported, or allowed to starve to death in the Soviet-occupied zone. |
| | **October** | *Estonia*, *Latvia*, and *Lithuania* acquiesce in the stationing of Soviet troops on their territories, and in the beginning of the evacuation of their German minorities to Nazi Germany. |
| **1940** | **March** | Soviet forces murder and bury around 22,000 military officers, politicians, and other leading figures from *Poland* in a forest near Katyn; the massacre is uncovered in 1943, but not admitted until 1992. |

**June**          The Soviet Union occupies *Estonia*, *Latvia*, and *Lithuania*, and transfers Vilnius from occupied *Poland* to Lithuania (of which it remains the capital city).

                 Soviet forces invade *Romania*, and make Bukovina part of Soviet Ukraine.

**August**        Soviet forces seize Bessarabia from *Romania*, and divide it between Ukraine and the newly formed Soviet republic of Moldova.

                 Following fraudulent elections in July, "People's Assemblies" in *Estonia*, *Latvia*, and *Lithuania* vote to make all three countries members of the Soviet Union; from this month up to August 1941, at least 170,000 people are deported from all three countries to Siberia.

**September**     *Romania* cedes southern Dobrogea to *Bulgaria*, where it remains (as Dobrudja).

                 King Carol II of *Romania* abdicates in favor of his son Mihai (Michael), who appoints General Ion Antonescu Prime Minister; Antonescu invites the extreme nationalist Iron Guard to join his government, and takes the title of *Conducător* (Leader).

**October**       German forces enter *Romania*, and seize its oil fields and then its capital, Bucharest.

**November**      Greece begins an invasion and occupation of southern *Albania*.

**1941 March**    The government of *Yugoslavia* signs a pact with Germany and Italy, and is then overthrown after mass protests. The government of *Bulgaria* also allies itself to Germany and Italy.

**April**         The armed forces of *Hungary* and *Bulgaria* join German and Italian forces in an invasion of Greece and *Yugoslavia*. Germany and Italy seize *Slovenia*, and parts of Serbia; Italy also seizes Montenegro, part of *Macedonia*, and the Dalmatian coast of *Croatia*, and incorporates the province of Kosovo into *Albania*; *Bulgaria* seizes parts of Greece, of Serbia, and of Macedonia. Germany also helps the Ustaše, a Croatian nationalist movement with minimal public support, to create an "Independent State of Croatia," controlling most of that country as well as the whole of *Bosnia-Herzegovina*. The Freedom Front is formed to resist the occupiers in *Slovenia*, while a mainly-Serb royalist resistance movement, known as the Četniks, is established, under Draža Mihailović to fight the occupiers elsewhere in Yugoslavia.

**June**          *Hungary*, *Romania*, and *Slovakia* join in Nazi Germany's attack on the Soviet Union, which then signs treaties with the western Allies, including the exiled government of *Poland*.

                 *Romania* seizes control of Bukovina and Moldova.

                 The Communist Party of *Yugoslavia* establishes a resistance force, the Partisans, led by Josip Broz Tito, to fight against the occupying forces, the Ustaše, and (from November) the Četniks.

                 In *Croatia* and *Bosnia-Herzegovina*, the Ustaše regime, under its *Poglavnik* (Leader) Ante Pavelić, launches a "purification" campaign: around 500,000 Serbs, thousands of anti-Ustaše Croats, and many Jews, Roma, and others are murdered during its four years in power.

                 Communists and other resistance fighters in *Bulgaria* form the Fatherland Front.

| | |
|---|---|
| **July** | German forces occupy *Estonia*, *Latvia*, and *Lithuania*; during their occupation of these three countries, around 250,000 Jews and 125,000 others are murdered by the Nazis and their collaborators. |
| | Having already massacred hundreds of thousands of Jews, Poles, and other subject peoples, Nazi Germany begins construction of extermination camps, mainly in *Poland* (Maidanek, Auschwitz, Treblinka, Sobibor, Chelmno, and Belzec). By 1945, around 6 million Jews, at least 500,000 Roma, and tens of thousands of political opponents, homosexuals, and other victims have been deported from all over occupied Europe, including the western Soviet Union, and murdered. |
| **September** | Volunteers from among the police force in *Latvia* become the first of several groups from among peoples conquered by the Nazis to enrol in the Waffen SS, the military arm of the Nazi security service engaged in repression and murder in pursuit of "racial purity." |
| **December** | In occupied *Yugoslavia*, some units of the royalist Četniks begin collaborating with the Germans against the Communist Partisans (until May 1943), and the Četnik leader, Draža Mihailović, calls for the creation, within a revived Yugoslavia, of "a greater Serbia, which is to be ethnically clean." |
| **1942 January** | The Soviet Union persuades its western Allies to reject a proposal from the governments of *Poland* and *Czechoslovakia*, based in London, that their countries form a federation after the war, and invite neighboring countries to join it. |
| **1943 April** | The Jews remaining in the Warsaw ghetto in *Poland* launch an uprising against Nazi occupation and genocide, with the aid of many Christian Poles. |
| | The government of *Poland*, in exile in London, breaks off relations with the Soviet Union, accusing it (accurately) of having organized the Katyn massacre uncovered by German troops (see March 1940). |
| **August** | King Boris III of *Bulgaria* dies, and is succeeded by his son Symeon II, aged six. |
| **September** | Following Italy's surrender to the Allies, Germany takes control of *Albania*, Montenegro, and parts of *Macedonia* and *Croatia*, in addition to its conquests of 1941. |
| **November** | In *Yugoslavia*, the Partisans, now receiving aid and intelligence from the United Kingdom, establish a provisional government, known as AVNOJ, for the multiethnic and federal republic that they envisage. |
| **December** | At a conference in Tehran, Winston Churchill, Prime Minister of the United Kingdom, the Soviet leader Josef Stalin, and US President Franklin D. Roosevelt arrive at a secret agreement to redraw the boundaries of *Poland*, by transferring its eastern provinces to Soviet Ukraine and Belarus, and giving it most of the eastern provinces of Germany (implemented in 1945); they also agree to recognize the Partisans' provisional government in *Yugoslavia*, abandoning support for the royal government in exile and for the Četniks. |
| **1944 January** | The Soviet Army launches the first of the offensives that will extend Soviet control over much of central and eastern Europe by the end of the war. |
| **March** | German forces enter *Hungary* at the invitation of its government, which cooperates in the deportation of nearly 500,000 Jews to the extermination camps in the following months. |

**July**            The Soviet Union establishes a puppet government for *Poland*, based in Lublin, and headed by Bolesław Bierut.

The Soviet Army retakes Vilnius, the capital of *Lithuania*, from the Germans, then organizes the deportation of around 120,000 Lithuanians to Siberia and Central Asia up to 1953.

**August**          Underground groups opposed to the government of *Slovakia*, which is allied with Nazi Germany, launch the Slovak National Uprising.

In *Poland*, the resistance launches the Warsaw Uprising, which is eventually suppressed by Nazi troops, while the Soviet Army waits on the opposite bank of the Vistula River.

The Soviet Army retakes Riga, the capital of *Latvia*, from the Germans, then organizes the deportation of around 120,000 Latvians to Siberia and Central Asia up to 1953.

King Mihai of *Romania* dismisses Prime Minister Ion Antonescu, makes peace with the Allies, declares war on Germany, and flees Bucharest, the capital, while Antonescu is imprisoned by Communists.

King Petar II of *Yugoslavia*, in exile, disowns the Četnik resistance movement.

**September**       A provisional government of *Romania*, largely controlled by the Soviet Army, arrives in Bucharest, and confirms the transfer of Bessarabia and northern Bukovina to the Soviet Union.

The Communist-led Fatherland Front mounts a successful coup in *Bulgaria*, with aid from the Soviet Army.

Between the withdrawal of German troops from *Estonia* and the return of the Soviet occupiers, the national resistance movement establishes a provisional government in the capital, Tallinn, for four days. Around 100,000 Estonians take refuge in the West, and the Soviet government deports around 80,000 others to Siberia and Central Asia up to 1953.

In *Estonia*, *Latvia*, and *Lithuania*, pro-independence groups known as the "Forest Brothers" launch partisan campaigns of resistance against the Soviet occupation (in this and following months), which continue up to 1956.

**October**         At a meeting in Moscow, Churchill and Stalin reach agreement on the postwar division of influence in *Romania* (the Soviet Union 90%, the West 10%), *Yugoslavia* and *Hungary* (50/50), and *Bulgaria* (the Soviet Union 75%, the West 25%).

The western Allies begin to repatriate citizens of the Soviet Union, and of countries in central and eastern Europe; hundreds of thousands are murdered or jailed by the Communist regimes in the following few years.

In *Yugoslavia*, the Communist-led Partisans and the Soviet Army jointly take control of the capital, Belgrade.

In *Albania*, the Communist-led National Liberation Front emerges victorious from five months of fighting against Germany and rival resistance movements, and forms a government under Enver Hoxha, the leader of the Communist Party.

In *Hungary*, Admiral Miklós Horthy, Regent for the absent Habsburg monarchy and effective ruler since 1920, is deported to Germany, as the Arrow Cross and other right-wing groups join forces with the German army.

**November**
The provisional government of *Albania*, created in October, takes control of Tirana, the capital, and (with some reluctance) returns the province of Kosovo to the control of its Communist ally, *Yugoslavia*.

**December**
The Communist Party in *Hungary*, aided by the Soviet troops occupying the eastern half of the country, establishes a provisional government, in coalition with other parties, at Debrecen.

**1945 January**
The Soviet Army enters the ruins of Warsaw, the capital of *Poland*, destroyed by the Nazis after the suppression of the uprising in the city.

**February**
At the Yalta Conference, Roosevelt, Churchill, and Stalin agree on the division of Germany and the holding of free elections in *Poland*.

The Soviet Army conquers Budapest, the capital of *Hungary*.

**March**
A new, Communist-dominated government in *Romania* takes back control of northern Transylvania, a largely Hungarian-speaking area that had been seized by *Hungary* in 1940.

**April**
A National Front government for *Czechoslovakia*, dominated by Communists and their allies, is created in Moscow.

**May**
World War II ends in Europe (but continues in the Pacific and East Asia until August).

In *Czechoslovakia*, the Soviet army helps to bring the National Front government to power. Edvard Beneš, a liberal democrat elected President in 1935, returns from exile in London: he is reelected in 1946, but resigns in June 1948.

The Ustaše government flees from *Croatia*.

**June**
Ruthenia, part of *Czechoslovakia* until its seizure by *Hungary* in 1939, becomes part of Soviet Ukraine.

**August**
At the Potsdam Conference, Stalin agrees with US President Harry S Truman and Clement Attlee, Prime Minister of the United Kingdom, on the return of the Sudetenland to *Czechoslovakia*, and the expulsion of ethnic Germans from that country and from *Poland*, but they leave other issues to a general peace conference that never takes place.

President Edvard Beneš of *Czechoslovakia* issues a decree removing citizenship from all Germans resident or formerly resident in the country, except those who were victims of Nazism or remained loyal to Czechoslovakia.

**October**
President Beneš of *Czechoslovakia* issues a decree confiscating "enemy property" from Czechs and Slovaks who collaborated with Nazi Germany, as well as from the ethnic Germans deprived of Czechoslovak citizenship in August.

The labor federations of most countries in the region join the new World Federation of Trade Unions, alongside their counterparts from western Europe, the Americas, and the Soviet Union (but see December 1949).

**November**      In *Yugoslavia*, a constituent assembly controlled by AVNOJ, the Communist-led provisional government established in November 1943, proclaims a Federal People's Republic – later renamed the Socialist Federal Republic – comprising six national republics (*Bosnia-Herzegovina*, *Croatia*, *Macedonia*, Montenegro, Serbia, and *Slovenia*); Serbia is granted control of the provinces of Kosovo and Vojvodina.

The Communists win elections in *Bulgaria*, helped by an opposition boycott and manipulation of the results.

In *Hungary*, the Smallholders Party wins a majority in the first free elections for the National Assembly, the only such elections until 1990.

**1946 January**     The government of *Czechoslovakia* begins to expel ethnic Germans; by November around 1.5 million have been forced to leave.

In *Albania*, King Zog is deposed and a republic is proclaimed.

**February**      *Hungary*, formally still a kingdom ruled by the Habsburgs (who departed in 1918), is declared a republic, with Zoltán Tildy, the Smallholders' leader, as President.

**May**           Elections in *Czechoslovakia* give the Communists 38% of the votes (40% in the Czech lands and 30% in Slovakia). The Communist leader Klement Gottwald becomes Prime Minister.

**June**          Ion Antonescu, former dictator of *Romania*, is executed as a war criminal.

**July**          In *Yugoslavia*, Draža Mihailović, former leader of the royalist resistance movement, the Četniks, is executed as a traitor.

**November**      *Albania* and *Yugoslavia* agree to coordinate economic planning, and create a customs union (but see July 1948).

In *Romania*, the publication of election results ceases as the Communists appear to be losing and then resumes with the announcement that the Communists have won nearly 90% of the votes cast.

The government of *Czechoslovakia* announces that around 3 million ethnic Germans have been expelled from the country since the end of World War II.

**1947 January**     Elections in *Poland* are said to have given the Communists nearly 90% of the votes, but the United States and the United Kingdom reject this claim.

**February**      In Paris, the wartime Allies (the United Kingdom, France, the Soviet Union, and the United States) sign peace treaties with five former enemy states: *Bulgaria*, Italy, Finland, *Hungary*, and *Romania*. Bulgarian and Romanian territory lost to the Soviet Union is not returned; Hungary is required to return territories it seized from *Czechoslovakia* and Romania; Italy gives up all claims to any part of *Yugoslavia* or *Albania*, except the Territory of Trieste, which passes under UN control (to 1954).

**March**         The Soviet Union's domination of central and eastern Europe, its intervention in the Greek civil war, and its withdrawal of cooperation in occupied Germany lead US President Truman to commit his country to the defense of "free peoples who are resisting subjugation by armed minorities or outside pressure" (the "Truman doctrine"). His adviser Bernard Baruch coins the term "the Cold War" soon after.

| | | |
|---|---|---|
| **April** | | Father Jozef Tiso, leader of the wartime Slovak state, is hanged as a traitor in *Czechoslovakia*. |

**May** — Ferenc Nagy, Prime Minister of *Hungary*, resigns under Communist pressure while on a visit to Switzerland.

**June** — US Secretary of State George Marshall announces the European Recovery Program (the "Marshall Plan"). The Soviet government orders its satellite regimes not to take part.

**August** — The Communist Party in *Hungary* claims victory in fraudulent elections for the National Assembly. Lajos Dinnyés of the Smallholders Party stays on as Prime Minister, while the Communists complete their infiltration of the secret police, the media, and most government ministries.

**September** — The monarchy is abolished in *Bulgaria* and King Symeon II departs for Egypt.

**October** — Cominform is established by nine European Communist parties. It is widely seen as the successor to the Communist International, a vehicle for Soviet control of other Communist parties that was dissolved in 1943 (but see April 1956).

**December** — King Mihai of *Romania* abdicates, and flies into exile; the Romanian People's Republic is proclaimed.

**1948 February** — In *Czechoslovakia*, following resignations of ministers opposed to the Communists, the Communist Party uses limited public support and extensive strength in the state machine to establish a monopoly of power.

The Communist government of *Yugoslavia* rejects the demand of the Soviet leader Josef Stalin that it should form a federation with *Bulgaria*, initiating the Soviet-Yugoslav split.

**March** — Jan Masaryk, the non-Communist Foreign Minister of *Czechoslovakia*, is found dead. The Communists announce that he committed suicide but his supporters believe that he was murdered.

**June** — Edvard Beneš resigns as President of *Czechoslovakia* rather than sign the new Stalinist Constitution. The Communist leader Klement Gottwald moves up from the prime ministership to the presidency.

The Communist Party of *Yugoslavia* is expelled from Cominform on Stalin's insistence.

The Soviet Union begins its blockade of Berlin (to May 1949), often seen as the decisive act in separating central and eastern Europe from contact and exchange with western Europe.

**July** — *Albania* denounces its agreements with *Yugoslavia* on economic cooperation (signed in November 1946).

In *Hungary*, Zoltán Tildy, a leader of the Smallholders Party, is replaced as President by Árpád Szakasits, Chairman of the Communist Party, who remains subordinate to Mátyás Rákosi, the Party's General Secretary since 1945.

| **1949** | **January** | Comecon is established in Moscow by the Soviet Union, *Bulgaria*, *Czechoslovakia*, *Hungary*, *Poland*, and *Romania*; *Albania* joins in February. |
| | **February** | József, Cardinal Mindszenty, head of the Catholic Church in *Hungary*, is convicted of conspiring to overthrow the government and sentenced to life imprisonment (see October 1956). |
| | **March** | More than 100,000 citizens of *Estonia*, *Latvia*, and *Lithuania* are deported to Siberia and Central Asia. |
| | **April** | The formation of NATO seals the western alliance against the Soviet bloc. |
| | | The government in *Bulgaria* begins a series of trials of Communists accused of "nationalist deviations" from the Party line, which favors submission to the Soviet Union. |
| | **June** | In *Hungary*, Mátyás Rákosi and other "Muscovites" secure control over the Communist Party by purging members who did not spend the war years in the Soviet Union, or who allegedly show nationalist or reformist tendencies. At least 2,000 are executed and 150,000 jailed by 1955. |
| | **September** | *Yugoslavia* becomes the only country in the region to receive aid from the United States, in the form of a loan totaling US$620 million. |
| | **October** | After a trial in September, László Rajk, the former Foreign Minister of *Hungary*, is hanged as a traitor. The most prominent victim of Rákosi's purges, Rajk is "rehabilitated" in 1956. |
| | **December** | Traicho Kostov, a former Deputy Prime Minister of *Bulgaria*, is executed after a trial on charges of "Titoism" (excessive nationalism) and 10 other leading Communists are imprisoned on similar charges. |
| | | Labor federations from western countries withdraw from the World Federation of Trade Unions, which becomes a Communist organization, and create the rival International Confederation of Free Trade Unions. |
| **1950** | **May** | *Yugoslavia* and *Albania* break off relations with each other. |
| | **June** | *Yugoslavia* enacts a new law on enterprise management, establishing the system of "self-management" devised by Edvard Kardelj. |
| **1951** | **March** | A major purge of the Communist Party begins in *Czechoslovakia*. Around 600,000 individuals are expelled over the next few years. |
| | **June** | Archbishop József Grösz, Mindszenty's successor as head of the Catholic Church in *Hungary*, is convicted of conspiring to overthrow the government and sentenced to 15 years in jail. |
| **1952** | **December** | Repression in *Czechoslovakia* reaches its ultimate absurdity with the execution, after show trials, of Rudolf Slánský and 10 other leading Communists who have signed confessions of "Titoism" (excessive nationalism), Trotskyism, Zionism, and spying for the West (see April 1963). |
| **1953** | **March** | President Klement Gottwald of *Czechoslovakia* dies from pneumonia contracted at the funeral of Josef Stalin. |

**May–June**   A currency reform in *Czechoslovakia* eliminates much of the population's savings and provokes protests, including strikes by 32,000 workers.

**June**   A workers' uprising in East Germany evokes sympathetic protests in central and eastern Europe, but pleas for help are ignored by the West.

**July**   Imre Nagy, appointed Prime Minister of *Hungary* over the objections of the Party's General Secretary, Mátyás Rákosi, launches the "New Course," a set of policies for limited reform of the command economy.

**September**   Stefan, Cardinal Wyszyński, head of the Catholic Church in *Poland*, is arrested and interned after leading protests against a law giving the state the power to appoint members of the Church's hierarchy. He is released in 1956.

**1954  January**   *Yugoslavia* resumes diplomatic relations with the Soviet Union after six years of estrangement.

**October**   *Albania* signs the first of many bilateral agreements with the People's Republic of China.

*Yugoslavia* and Italy agree to divide the territory on the Adriatic Sea that has been in dispute since World War II. The city of Trieste returns to Italian control, while its hinterland remains part of *Slovenia*.

**1955  April**   Mátyás Rákosi, General Secretary of the Communist Party in *Hungary*, engineers the removal of the reformist Prime Minister, Imre Nagy.

**May**   The Warsaw Pact is created by the Soviet Union, *Albania*, *Bulgaria*, *Czechoslovakia*, East Germany, *Hungary*, *Poland*, and *Romania*.

**1956  March**   Bolesław Bierut, Prime Minister of *Poland*, dies suddenly in Moscow, soon after the Soviet leader Nikita Khrushchev denounces his predecessor, Josef Stalin. Both events seem to promise a degree of liberalization in the Soviet bloc.

**April**   Cominform, the international organization of Communist parties, is abolished, but Soviet domination of almost all the Communist parties in central and eastern Europe continues.

**June**   During an uprising in Poznań, *Poland*, sparked off by price increases, at least 53 people are killed by the army.

**July**   Mátyás Rákosi of *Hungary* is removed from the leadership of that country's Communist Party.

**October**   In *Poland*, attempts to collectivize farms are abandoned. Władysław Gomułka, newly appointed First Secretary of the Communist Party, launches limited reforms of the command economy and grants official recognition to workers' councils formed in many large enterprises.

In *Hungary*, public protests in Budapest and other cities lead to the formation of a new Communist/Smallholders coalition government, led once again by Imre Nagy, who releases Cardinal Mindszenty from prison, and negotiates withdrawal of Soviet forces. Meanwhile, Ernö Gerö, General Secretary of the Party since July, requests military support from the Soviet Union, only to be replaced by János Kádár on the orders of a Soviet delegation.

| | | |
|---|---|---|
| | **November** | Prime Minister Nagy declares *Hungary* neutral as between NATO and the Warsaw Pact. Soviet troops return, forcing the replacement of Nagy by János Kádár, while a Greater Budapest Central Workers' Council is formed to continue the uprising. The West ignores all pleas for support (and see June 1958). |

President Tito of *Yugoslavia* endorses the Soviet intervention in *Hungary* and protests by Yugoslavia's Hungarian minority are suppressed.

**December** The government of *Hungary* suppresses the Greater Budapest Central Workers' Council.

In *Yugoslavia*, the dissident Communist Milovan Djilas, formerly one of President Tito's closest collaborators, begins the first of a series of prison sentences imposed for writing and speaking against repression and corruption.

**1957 March** *Hungary* is formally readmitted to the Warsaw Pact.

**1958 April** The workers' councils formed in *Poland* in October 1956 are subordinated to the Communist Party, losing the last remnants of their autonomy.

**June** Imre Nagy, Pál Maléter, and Miklos Gimes, leaders of the 1956 reform movement in *Hungary*, are hanged in secret. Sandor Kopacsi, former head of the Budapest police, is sentenced to life imprisonment and four other reform Communists are given lesser prison terms.

**1959 December** The member states of Comecon – the Soviet Union, East Germany, *Albania*, *Bulgaria*, *Czechoslovakia*, *Hungary*, *Poland*, and *Romania* – sign a treaty on economic specialization, under which each country will seek to direct investment into certain designated industries as part of a common plan for the bloc; the scheme is never fully implemented.

**1960 June** The government of *Albania* publicly sides with China in its growing rift with the Soviet Union during a meeting of the World Federation of Trade Unions (in fact, state-controlled pseudo-unions) in Beijing.

**July** A new constitution proclaims the successful construction of a "socialist" society in *Czechoslovakia*, with almost all production in the state or cooperative sectors, and permits the use of the Hungarian, Polish and Ukrainian languages (but not of German or Romani).

**1961 August** The building of the Berlin Wall by the government of East Germany evokes formal protests from western governments, but it remains in place, symbolizing the apparent permanence of the "Iron Curtain" between liberal democracy in western Europe and Communism in "eastern" Europe (see November 1989).

**December** The Soviet Union and *Albania* break off relations with each other.

**1962 January** *Albania* is excluded from meetings of the Warsaw Pact (see also September 1968).

**November** Todor Zhivkov becomes Prime Minister of *Bulgaria* and completes a purge of the Communist Party, removing Vulko Chervenkov and other opponents of "de-Stalinization" from office.

In *Hungary*, János Kádár, General Secretary of the Communist Party and Prime Minister, announces that "he who is not against us is with us," summing up the relaxation of repression from 1961 onward.

| | | |
|---|---|---|
| **1963** | **March** | The government of *Hungary* grants political prisoners an amnesty, freeing many of those who were jailed for participating in the uprising in 1956. |
| | **April** | The government of *Czechoslovakia* "rehabilitates" Rudolf Slánský and 14 other leading Communists who were executed or jailed as traitors in December 1952. |
| **1965** | **March** | Following the death of Gheorghe Gheorghiu-Dej, the First Secretary of the Communist Party in *Romania*, Nicolae Ceauşescu is appointed General Secretary and a new constitution is adopted for the "Socialist Republic" of Romania. |
| **1966** | **February** | In *Albania*, the government initiates a "cultural revolution," largely imitating China's, involving purges of state and party officials, the insertion of party agencies into the armed forces, the banning of religious observances, and the dispatch of "intellectuals" to manual work in the countryside (to December 1969). |
| | **November** | The government of *Hungary* permits more candidates to stand in elections than there are seats available while retaining the Communist monopoly of power. |
| **1967** | **June** | The government of *Poland* launches a campaign against "Zionist tendencies" among the country's Jewish population, arousing anti-Semitic feeling and prompting more than half of the Jews in the country to emigrate by 1970. |
| **1968** | **January** | Alexander Dubček is elected First Secretary of the Communist Party in *Czechoslovakia*, initiating the limited economic and political reforms of the "Prague Spring." |
| | | The government of *Hungary* introduces the "New Economic Mechanism," relaxing price controls, allowing wages to be linked to profits, and decentralizing economic decisions. |
| | **March** | The government of *Poland* suppresses student protests in support of the Prague Spring and launches a campaign against "bourgeois tendencies" among intellectuals in universities, publishing houses, and other institutions. |
| | **June** | *Czechoslovakia* is declared a federation, and press censorship is abolished. |
| | **August** | *Czechoslovakia* is invaded without warning by troops from the Soviet Union and other Warsaw Pact states (except *Albania* and *Romania*). *Yugoslavia*, China, and the western powers make formal protests against the invasion but offer virtually no support to its victims. |
| | **September** | *Albania*, excluded from Warsaw Pact meetings since January 1962, is formally expelled from the organization after denouncing the invasion of *Czechoslovakia*. |
| | **November** | During a visit to Warsaw, the Soviet leader Leonid Brezhnev announces that the Warsaw Pact will continue "the defense of socialist gains" (the "Brezhnev doctrine"; but see October 1989). |
| **1969** | **January** | Ján Palach, a university student, sets fires to himself in Prague in protest against the Soviet occupation of *Czechoslovakia*. (A memorial to him is unveiled by Václav Havel, President of the *Czech Republic*, in January 1999.) |
| **1970** | **January** | In *Yugoslavia*, the ruling Communist Party of *Croatia* initiates a partial liberalization, permitting public manifestations of nationalist feeling against the wishes of the federal government. The political and cultural upheaval known as the "Croatian Spring" continues to December 1971. |

| | | |
|---|---|---|
| **April** | | Gustáv Husák, the new First Secretary of the Communist Party in *Czechoslovakia*, endorses the "temporary" occupation by Soviet troops and launches "normalization." |

**April**  Gustáv Husák, the new First Secretary of the Communist Party in *Czechoslovakia*, endorses the "temporary" occupation by Soviet troops and launches "normalization."

**December**  In *Poland*, increases in food prices spark off protests in Gdańsk, Gdynia, Szczecin, Łódź, and other cities. At least 300 people are killed by the police. Władysław Gomułka is replaced as First Secretary of the Communist Party by Edward Gierek, who cancels the increases.

**1971  January**  The federal structure of *Czechoslovakia* is negated by laws giving the federal government power to override decisions taken by the Czech and Slovak governments, and reinstating the central planning system.

**December**  Following strikes by students and others in *Croatia*, President Tito of *Yugoslavia* denounces the Communist leaders in Croatia for fostering nationalism and forces their resignations.

**1973  March**  The government of *Hungary* continues the program of economic liberalization but launches a new wave of repression in the universities, the mass media, and other cultural institutions.

**1974  February**  *Yugoslavia* promulgates a new constitution, said to be the longest in world history. It enhances the autonomy of its six republics, and of the provinces of Kosovo and Vojvodina, and also extends the system of "self-management."

**1975  August**  The United States, Canada, and 33 European states sign the Helsinki Accords on international frontiers and human rights at the first CSCE, but its provisions under the latter heading continue to be widely disregarded in the Soviet bloc.

**September**  In *Albania*, the government orders citizens with Greek or other non-Albanian family names to replace them with Albanian names.

**1976  September**  Following protests against price rises in June, dissidents in *Poland* form a Workers' Defense Committee (KOR), which later becomes an influential group within Solidarity.

**1977  January**  Opposition activists in *Czechoslovakia*, including the playwright Václav Havel, launch a movement known as Charter 77, in reference to its founding document, which calls on the government to honor its international commitments to human rights. More than 2,000 signatures are collected, but association with the dissident movement leads to discrimination in work and harassment by the police.

**August**  President Ceauşescu of *Romania* appears to accept demands for higher pay for 35,000 miners on strike in the Jiu Valley, but then orders the killing of their leaders and the imposition of martial law in the area.

**1978  May**  In *Poland*, the Committee of Free Trade Unions for the Baltic Coast is formed by shipyard workers, including an electrician named Lech Wałęsa.

**July**  After seven years of increasing tension, China withdraws all financial and technical aid from *Albania*, leaving it completely isolated.

**1979  June**  John Paul II, elected Pope in October 1978, visits his native *Poland*, drawing enormous crowds and challenging the Communist government to observe human rights.

| 1980 | **May** | The death of Josip Broz Tito, President for Life of *Yugoslavia*, ushers in a period of uncertainty and increasing instability in the country's politics. |
| | **July** | Price rises in *Poland* are met once again with protests; more strike committees and independent workers' unions are established. |
| | **August** | Following widespread strikes and protests in *Poland* – denounced by the Catholic hierarchy as threats to stability – Lech Wałęsa and the Deputy Prime Minister, Mieczysław Jagielski, sign the Gdańsk Agreement, legalizing strikes and free labor unions. |
| | **September** | Workers in *Poland* establish the union federation Solidarność (Solidarity), which is recognized by the government two months later. |
| 1981 | **April** | In *Yugoslavia*, the province of Kosovo is disrupted by protests and violence as the ethnic Albanian majority of its population demand that its status be raised to that of a republic within the federation. |
| | **December** | Solidarity starts to campaign for the creation of a non-Communist government. General Wojciech Jaruzelski, Prime Minister since February and First Secretary of the Communist Party since October, responds by imposing martial law, banning Solidarity, and jailing many of its leaders. |
| | | Enver Hoxha, leader of *Albania*, arranges for the removal and murder (or perhaps suicide) of the Prime Minister, Mehmet Shehu, claiming that he had been spying for the West throughout the Communist period. |
| 1982 | **December** | The government of *Poland* lifts martial law, but continues the ban on Solidarity. |
| 1983 | **August** | In *Yugoslavia*, the funeral of Aleksander Ranković, a prominent Serbian Communist and former head of the secret police, becomes the occasion for demonstrations in Serbia against the autonomous status of Kosovo, a province inhabited mainly by ethnic Albanians. Meanwhile, in *Bosnia-Herzegovina* Alija Izetbegović is jailed as an "Islamist counterrevolutionary." |
| 1985 | **February** | *Bulgaria* orders its citizens with Turkish family names to take Bulgarian names, and continues other forms of harassment of the Turkish minority. Around 1,500 are killed during 1985 and 1986. |
| | **July** | In *Hungary*, for the first time in any Communist country in the region, non-Communist independent candidates are permitted to run for election to the legislature (the National Assembly). |
| 1986 | **October** | President Ceauşescu of *Romania* responds to the country's energy crisis by sending in troops to manage power plants, imposing drastic cuts in supplies, and forcing farmers to replace machinery with draft animals. |
| 1987 | **April** | In *Yugoslavia*, Slobodan Milošević, General Secretary of the Communist Party of Serbia since May 1986, visits the autonomous province of Kosovo to express support for the Serb minority there, telling them: "no one will beat you." |
| | **September** | In *Yugoslavia*, Slobodan Milošević removes his rivals from posts in the Communist Party of Serbia, takes direct control of several newspapers and magazines, and launches a nationalist policy program. |
| | | In *Hungary*, the foundation of the Hungarian Democratic Forum initiates the revival of open non-Communist politics. |

| | | |
|---|---|---|
| **November** | | Protests in *Romania* over energy rationing and food shortages reach a climax with demonstrations in Brasov. |
| **1988** | **March** | President Ceauşescu of *Romania* launches "systematization" of the countryside, forcing thousands to relocate to state housing and suppressing traditional rural culture. |
| | | A group of law students in *Hungary* founds Fidesz, a liberal democratic youth group, in the face of police repression. |
| | **April** | The Popular Front, a movement for independence, is founded in *Estonia*, the first such openly active movement anywhere in Soviet-controlled territory. |
| | **May** | János Kádár, paramount leader in *Hungary* for 32 years, is persuaded to retire and is succeeded by a collective leadership. |
| | **June** | The European Community (now the EU) signs an agreement on trade with Comecon, which is followed by agreements with *Hungary* later in 1988, the Soviet Union and *Poland* in 1989, and *Czechoslovakia, Bulgaria, Romania,* and East Germany in 1990. |
| | | A National Independence Movement is established in *Latvia*. |
| | | Sajudis, a popular front movement for independence, is founded in *Lithuania*. |
| | **October** | Celebrations of the 70th anniversary of the founding of *Czechoslovakia* end in police brutality against supporters of Charter 77 and other dissidents. |
| | | In *Yugoslavia*, supporters of the Serbian leader Slobodan Milošević throw cartons of yogurt at government buildings in the autonomous province of Vojvodina, launching the "Yogurt Revolution," which installs a provincial leadership favorable to Milošević. |
| | **November** | The "Supreme Soviet" (legislature) in *Estonia* passes a declaration of sovereignty. |
| **1989** | **January** | In *Yugoslavia*, Momir Bulatović, a supporter of the Serbian leader Slobodan Milošević, becomes Prime Minister of Montenegro, thus helping to create a dominant pro-Milošević bloc within federal institutions. |
| | | *Estonia* declares Estonian the state language, and requires knowledge of it for recruitment to certain government and professional posts. |
| | **February** | As the government of *Bulgaria* continues its repression of the Turkish minority, members of that minority begin fleeing to Turkey, totaling an estimated 350,000 by August. |
| | **February–April** | Round table talks are held in *Poland*, bringing together delegations from the government, the Catholic Church, and Solidarity. Agreement is reached on free elections, a strong executive presidency, the revival of the Senate, and the legalization of Solidarity. |
| | **March** | In *Yugoslavia*, Slobodan Milošević imposes a new constitution on Serbia, eliminating the autonomy of the provinces of Kosovo and Vojvodina in violation of the federal Constitution. |

| | |
|---|---|
| **May** | The "Supreme Soviet" (legislature) in *Lithuania* passes a declaration of sovereignty. |
| | The popular front movements seeking to restore the independence of *Estonia*, *Latvia*, and *Lithuania* meet in the Estonian capital, Tallinn, to coordinate their activities (see also August). |
| **June** | Free elections are held in *Poland*, for the first time since 1928, resulting in a decisive victory for Solidarity, but the lower house of Parliament (the Sejm) continues to be dominated by Communists under the terms of the April agreement. |
| | In *Yugoslavia*, Slobodan Milošević marks the anniversary of the Battle of Kosovo Polje (1389), in which the Ottoman Turks defeated the Serbs, with a revival of monarchist and Orthodox symbolism. |
| | In *Hungary*, Imre Nagy and other leaders of the 1956 uprising are reburied with full honors, and National Round Table talks begin between the Communist Party, opposition groups, and other social organizations. |
| **July** | The "Supreme Soviet" (legislature) of *Latvia* passes a declaration of sovereignty. |
| **August** | Tadeusz Mazowiecki becomes Prime Minister of *Poland* and the first non-Communist head of government anywhere in central and eastern Europe since July 1948. |
| | On the 50th anniversary of the signing of the Nazi-Soviet Pact, more than 1 million citizens of *Estonia*, *Latvia*, and *Lithuania* join hands to form a "human chain" linking their three capital cities, Tallinn, Riga, and Vilnius. |
| **September** | The National Salvation Front is launched by anonymous elements within the Communist Party of *Romania* who seek the removal of President Ceaușescu. |
| | *Slovenia* declares sovereignty, asserting its right to leave *Yugoslavia*, which is guaranteed in the federal Constitution, but postponing its exercise. |
| | *Hungary* opens its western border to allow citizens of East Germany to leave for the West, helping to precipitate upheaval in East Germany itself and elsewhere in the region. |
| **October** | The Communist Party in *Hungary* gives up its monopoly on political power and renames itself the Socialist Party. A new Hungarian Republic is proclaimed. |
| | President Gorbachev of the Soviet Union formally abandons the "Brezhnev doctrine" (see November 1968), thus abandoning the Communist regimes of central and eastern Europe to collapse over the following months. |
| | Unrest in southern *Albania*, over cuts in pay and mistreatment of the Greek minority, is met with executions and torture. |
| | In *Bulgaria*, an environmental protest group, Ecoglasnost, begins demonstrating and petitioning in the capital, Sofia. |
| **November** | The government of East Germany opens the Berlin Wall, an act that precipitates and has come to symbolize the collapse of almost all the Stalinist regimes in central and eastern Europe. |
| | Todor Zhivkov, dictator of *Bulgaria*, resigns after 35 years in power and is replaced as President by Petur Mladenov. |

The "Velvet Revolution" begins in *Czechoslovakia*. Mass public demonstrations, addressed by the dissident Communist Alexander Dubček, the Charter 77 leader Václav Havel, and other reformists, are followed by a two-hour general strike, leading to the collapse of Communist power.

**December**    In *Bulgaria*, the Communist Party expels the former dictator Todor Zhivkov, abandons its monopoly on political power, and ends the campaign against the Turkish minority, while opposition groups form the Union of Democratic Forces.

In *Czechoslovakia*, a government dominated by non-Communists is formed, President Gustáv Husák resigns, and Alexander Dubček becomes Chairman of the Federal Assembly, which also elects Václav Havel as President.

Popular protests in *Romania*, beginning in Timişoara in opposition to the eviction of the ethnic-Hungarian priest László Tökés, lead to the overthrow and execution of the dictator Nicolae Ceauşescu and his wife Elena, and the formation of a provisional government under the National Salvation Front.

In *Yugoslavia*, Slobodan Milošević encourages the imposition by Serbian enterprises of sanctions on *Slovenia* in response to its declaration of sovereignty, but in violation of the federal Constitution.

*Estonia* conducts the first democratic elections for local governments to be held anywhere in Soviet-controlled territory.

**1990 January**    The Soviet Union begins full-scale withdrawal of its military forces from central and eastern Europe.

Václav Havel, the newly elected President of *Czechoslovakia*, visits both West and East Germany to apologize for the expulsions of ethnic Germans from his country after World War II.

Leszek Balcerowicz, Minister of Finance in *Poland*, launches a program of "shock therapy," increasing prices, abolishing subsidies, and making the currency convertible.

The League of Communists of *Yugoslavia*, at what is to be its last Congress, decides to abandon its monopoly of political power. The federal government replaces the currency, the dinar, with a new dinar, worth 10,000 of the old ones.

**February**    The "Supreme Soviet" (legislature) of *Estonia* abolishes the Communist monopoly of power and declares that the country's independent status continues unbroken from 1940, in preparation for elections (in March) that give a majority to groups favoring independence.

The government of *Yugoslavia* imposes martial law in the province of Kosovo, where the mainly ethnic-Albanian population demands the restoration of the province's autonomy.

**March**    Following the victory of the Sajudis movement in elections in February, and in the referendum, the "Supreme Soviet" (legislature) of *Lithuania* declares independence. The Soviet Union responds by imposing an oil embargo and other sanctions from April to June.

*Hungary* establishes a State Property Agency to manage its privatization program.

| | |
|---|---|
| **April** | Multiparty elections in *Hungary*, the first since 1947, result in victory for the center-right Hungarian Democratic Forum and associated parties. |
| **May** | Following multiparty elections in March and April, the first in *Yugoslavia* since 1938, Franjo Tudjman and his nationalist Croatian Democratic Union (HDZ) take control of *Croatia*, while Demos, a coalition of six reformist parties, is victorious in *Slovenia*. Elections are not held in the other four republics. |
| | In the "Supreme Soviet" (legislature) of *Latvia*, elected in March and April, a majority (including the Popular Front deputies and some Communists) approves a declaration of independence, but postpones making it effective to allow for negotiations with the Soviet Union. |
| | The "Supreme Soviet" (legislature) of *Estonia* declares independence and revives the 1920 Constitution. |
| | The first free elections in *Romania* since 1937 confirm the positions of Ion Iliescu as President and Petre Roman as Prime Minister. |
| **June** | Antigovernment demonstrations in Bucharest, the capital of *Romania*, are violently dispersed by miners from the Jiu Valley, led by Miron Cozma. |
| | Legislative elections in *Czechoslovakia* confirm the defeat of the Communists. |
| | Free multiparty elections in *Bulgaria*, the first since 1938, result in a majority in the National Assembly for the Socialists (former Communists). |
| | In *Yugoslavia*, the new Constitution of *Croatia* omits any reference to the Serbs or other national minorities. |
| | Pro-democracy protests erupt in Tirana, the capital of *Albania*, continuing into July. |
| **July** | In *Yugoslavia*, the government of Serbia abolishes the elected Assembly of the province of Kosovo, thus flouting both the Yugoslav and Serbian Constitutions. The Assembly itself meets in secret to declare Kosovo's independence from Serbia. |
| | In *Albania*, thousands fleeing from police repression of the pro-democracy movement take refuge in foreign embassies. Many are eventually allowed to emigrate. |
| | In Brussels, representatives of 24 leading western countries form the Group of 24 to provide aid and advice to the countries of central and eastern Europe engaged in economic reform. This initiative results in the creation of the EBRD. |
| **August** | Zhelyu Zhelev of the Union of Democratic Forces becomes President of *Bulgaria*. |
| **September** | *Croatia* declares sovereignty within *Yugoslavia*. |
| **October** | Following the unification of Germany, the repatriation of former Soviet troops and their dependents from former Warsaw Pact countries accelerates, while increasing numbers of ethnic Germans emigrate to Germany from all over the region. |
| **November** | All the countries of central and eastern Europe, except *Albania*, join with other members of the CSCE (now the OSCE) to sign the Charter of Paris for a New Europe, which includes commitments to multiparty democracy, market-based |

economies, the rule of law, and respect for human rights. The CSCE also agrees to begin monitoring human rights, thus abandoning the principle of nonintervention in the internal affairs of sovereign states.

The member states of NATO and the Warsaw Pact sign the first version of a treaty on reducing conventional forces in Europe (the CFE Treaty).

In *Poland*, Lech Wałęsa wins the first round of the country's first free election of a head of state by universal suffrage. He goes on to win the second round in December and begin his term of office as President (to December 1995).

In *Yugoslavia*, multiparty elections result in an Assembly dominated and divided by Moslem, Serb, and Croat nationalist parties in *Bosnia-Herzegovina*, and in an Assembly split between ex-Communists and nationalists in *Macedonia*.

**December**    In a referendum in *Slovenia*, 88% approve independence from *Yugoslavia*. Multiparty elections in Serbia are won by Slobodan Milošević, who becomes President of the republic, and his supporters, who already control most of the media and all the electoral processes. A non-Communist government is formed in *Macedonia*.

The government of *Albania* recognizes the Democratic Party, the first opposition group permitted since the Communist regime's predecessor, the dictatorship of King Zog, was established in 1928.

**1991 January**    The member states of Comecon agree to dissolve it.

*Estonia* and Russia sign a treaty recognizing each other's sovereignty and guaranteeing a free choice of citizenship (the latter provision being nullified by Estonia's citizenship law – see November 1991).

Following Soviet military actions in Vilnius, the capital of *Lithuania*, and in Riga, the capital of *Latvia*, in which 21 people are killed in total, Boris Yeltsin, then Chairman of the Supreme Soviet of Russia, signs mutual security agreements with both countries and with *Estonia*.

**February**    The government of *Bulgaria* abolishes most price controls and subsidies for energy and transportation, and liberalizes foreign exchange.

A referendum in *Lithuania* shows more than 90% supporting independence.

**March**    The Warsaw Pact is formally dissolved.

*Estonia*, *Latvia*, and *Lithuania* (along with Georgia and Armenia) opt out of the Soviet Union's referendum on a new union treaty to hold referendums on independence instead. In all three Baltic states, large majorities favor independence.

In *Albania*, the first round of multiparty elections is held under the close supervision of the Socialist (ex-Communist) authorities, who secure victory.

In *Yugoslavia*, the government of Serbia uses military force to disperse demonstrations by its opponents in Belgrade, the capital city. Serbia's delegation withdraws from the collective Federal Presidency, disabling the institution and initiating the collapse of the federation. The Serbian government then accelerates the collapse by sending aid and arms to Krajina in *Croatia*.

As fighting begins in Krajina – as well as in Eastern and Western Slavonia, also in *Croatia* – Presidents Tudjman of Croatia and Milošević of Serbia secretly reach agreement on partitioning *Bosnia-Herzegovina*.

The Paris Club of western governments forgives half of the foreign debt accumulated by *Poland*.

**April**     In *Yugoslavia*, the federal army begins operations in *Croatia* in support of the minority of Croat Serbs seeking union with Serbia.

In one of the first major investments by a western multinational in central and eastern Europe, Volkswagen of Germany buys a majority of the shares in Škoda of *Czechoslovakia*.

**May**     In *Yugoslavia*, a large majority voting in a referendum in *Croatia* favors independence.

**June**     Comecon is formally dissolved.

*Croatia* and *Slovenia* proclaim their independence from *Yugoslavia*.

A multiparty "government of national salvation" takes office in *Albania* (up to December).

**July**     After 10 days of fighting in *Slovenia* – during which its capital, Ljubljana, became the first European city bombed from the air since 1945 – a ceasefire is agreed between the governments of Slovenia and *Yugoslavia*.

**August**     Following the failure of the Moscow coup against the Soviet President, Mikhail Gorbachev, *Estonia* reissues its declaration of independence, while *Latvia* brings its declaration of independence (passed in May 1990) into effect. Both countries also ban the Communist Party.

*Romania* launches its first program of privatization.

**September**     The Soviet government recognizes the independence of *Estonia*, *Latvia*, and *Lithuania*, but only as from this point, not from 1940.

Protests over the impact of economic reforms in *Romania* culminate in a march by Jiu Valley miners, led by Miron Cozma, into the capital, Bucharest. Seven people are killed, in still disputed circumstances, during subsequent battles between the miners and the security forces (see also January 1997 and January-February 1999).

The UN imposes an arms embargo on all the republics in *Yugoslavia*. The embargo lasts until June 1996.

In *Macedonia*, a majority voting in a referendum favors independence.

*Albania* legalizes the private ownership of productive assets and starts its first privatization program.

**October**     In *Romania*, following the miners' march and other protests in September, Petre Roman is replaced as Prime Minister by Theodor Stolojan.

*Czechoslovakia* starts sales of privatization vouchers.

*Czechoslovakia* and Germany agree on the permanence of the border between them.

The army of *Yugoslavia* completes its withdrawal from *Slovenia* and begins the shelling of Dubrovnik in *Croatia*. The multiethnic Assembly of *Bosnia-Herzegovina* declares sovereignty.

*Slovenia* introduces its own currency, the tolar, in place of the Yugoslav dinar.

Following elections for the National Assembly in *Bulgaria*, the Union of Democratic Forces forms a coalition government including representatives of the Turkish minority.

**November**      *Estonia* revives a citizenship law enacted in 1938, effectively rendering Soviet immigrants and their descendants non-citizens. Similarly, *Latvia* limits its citizenship to those who held it before 1940 and their descendants.

**December**      *Czechoslovakia*, *Hungary*, and *Poland* sign association agreements with the European Community (now the EU).

In *Yugoslavia*, the republic of *Macedonia* declares independence, but it is initially recognized by only a few countries.

In *Albania*, the Democratic Party withdraws from the coalition government.

**1992  January**   The UN and the European Community broker a ceasefire in *Croatia* and the army of *Yugoslavia* begins withdrawing, leaving around 25% of the country under the control of self-appointed Serb governments.

**March**         In *Bosnia-Herzegovina*, a referendum on separation from *Yugoslavia* is boycotted by many (not all) Bosnian Serbs, but shows a large majority supporting independence.

In *Albania*, the Democratic Party and its allies defeat the Socialists in elections for the People's Assembly. The Democrats' leader, Salih Berisha, is elected President in April.

The UN Protection Force (UNPROFOR), established in February to help restore peace and security in the former *Yugoslavia*, begins operations in *Croatia* from a base in Sarajevo, the capital of neighboring *Bosnia-Herzegovina*.

**April**         *Yugoslavia* is refounded as a federation between Serbia and Montenegro, the largest and smallest of the former six republics (their populations and GNPs being in a ratio of around 16:1). This "rump" Yugoslavia has not received international recognition.

Yugoslav forces complete their withdrawal from *Macedonia*.

*Bosnia-Herzegovina* is recognized as independent by the United States and the European Community.

In *Slovenia*, the ruling coalition, Demos, splits, and the Liberal Democratic Party takes office. This party has been in government, alone or with coalition partners, ever since.

*Bulgaria* establishes its Agency for Privatization.

**May**        The UN imposes sanctions on the new federation of *Yugoslavia* because of its sponsorship of aggression against other former Yugoslav republics. Although the sanctions are often broken by some of Yugoslavia's neighbors, the economy plunges into crisis, eventually suffering its highest ever rate of inflation.

Also in *Yugoslavia*, Ibrahim Rugova is elected President of Kosovo in defiance of the martial law conditions imposed by the federal government.

**June**       Legislative elections in *Czechoslovakia* confirm the widely differing complexions of Czech and Slovak politics. Victorious politicians from the two parts of the federation agree to work for a peaceful separation (see January 1993).

*Estonia* becomes the first country to leave the Russian ruble zone when it revives its own national currency, the kroon.

UNPROFOR deployed in *Bosnia-Herzegovina* to protect the capital, Sarajevo, which is under siege by Serb (in fact Serbian) forces.

**July**       A revised version of the CFE Treaty is signed by 29 states.

**August**     Two British journalists, Penny Marshall and Ed Vulliamy, expose conditions in the concentration camp in Omarska, one of several established by Serbian forces in *Bosnia-Herzegovina*. The fate of that country becomes the main topic of an international conference on the former Yugoslavia, held in London by the UN and the UK government.

**October**    General Motors of the United States buys a majority shareholding in FSO of *Poland*.

In *Bosnia-Herzegovina*, ethnic-Croat militias aided but not controlled by elements in *Croatia* launch attacks on the national army and on Moslems, and seize Mostar, the capital of the province of Herzegovina.

**November**   The National Assembly of *Slovenia* enacts a law on privatization of state assets.

**December**   The CSCE condemns elections in "rump" *Yugoslavia* as unfair.

**1993 January**   Independent *Czech* and *Slovak* states emerge, and gain international recognition. Václav Havel becomes the first President of the *Czech Republic* and Václav Klaus its first Prime Minister, while in *Slovakia* the President is Michal Kováč and the Prime Minister is Vladimír Mečiar.

Cyrus Vance of the United States and David Owen of the United Kingdom, the UN's mediators in *Bosnia-Herzegovina*, issue the first of several international proposals to partition the country among the Serbs, Croats, and Moslems.

In *Albania*, Nexhmije Hoxha, widow of the dictator Enver Hoxha, is convicted of misappropriating public funds and jailed.

**February**   *Poland* introduces one of the most restrictive laws on abortion in Europe, despite evidence of public support for a more liberal policy, prompting concern that the Catholic Church is increasing its influence on public life.

*Slovakia* introduces its own currency, the koruna, initially at parity with the Czech koruna.

*Romania* and *Bulgaria* sign association agreements with the European Community (now the EU).

**April**       The IMF introduces a "Systemic Transformation Facility" for post-Communist economies, offering credit of various amounts in return for economic reforms, including limits on central bank financing of budget deficits, reduced subsidies for production, full liberalization of prices, and privatization.

*Poland* initiates the privatization of 600 large state-owned enterprises and the transfer of most shares in them to new investment funds.

Greece imposes a trade embargo on *Macedonia*, which it believes has ambitions to take over the Greek province of the same name (to September), while the UN and most states around the world recognize Macedonia's independence.

**May**         The UN proclaims five "safe areas" in *Bosnia-Herzegovina*: Bihać, Goražde, Srebrenica, Tuzla, and Zepa. The Vance/Owen plan for the partition of Bosnia-Herzegovina (see January) is rejected in a referendum conducted by the Bosnian Serb parliament in its first act of defiance against its sponsor, President Milošević of Serbia.

**June**        In *Poland*, Solidarity refuses to endorse candidates supported by President Lech Wałęsa, confirming the disintegration of the Solidarity movement.

A Democratic Left Alliance/Peasants' Party government is elected in *Romania*.

*Slovakia* accepts the IMF's plans for reducing the government deficit and accelerating privatization.

The government of *Croatia* supports the establishment of Herceg-Bosna, an ethnic-Croat "state" within *Bosnia-Herzegovina*.

*Lithuania* introduces its new national currency, the litas.

**July**        *Latvia* promulgates a new Constitution, confirming the restriction of citizenship to those who held it before 1940 and their descendants, and imposing language tests for posts in the public service. As a result, around 42% of the resident population, including tens of thousands born long after 1940, are excluded from participation in its revived democracy.

**August**      The withdrawal of ex-Soviet troops from *Lithuania* is completed.

**October**     In *Poland*, the Democratic Left Alliance (the former Communist Party) and the Peasant Party, which have become the largest parties in the lower house of Parliament (the Sejm) following elections in September, establish a coalition government excluding groups formed out of Solidarity, for the first time since 1989.

*Croatia* launches a successful counterinflation program. The monthly rate falls from 38% to zero.

**December**    The IMF begins paying a loan of nearly US$700 million to *Romania* on condition that the government implements economic reforms, including privatization and reductions in public spending.

*Hungary* becomes the first country in the region to introduce private pension funds.

**1994 January**  
*Romania* becomes the first country in the region to enter NATO's Partnership for Peace program, launched this month.

In *Yugoslavia*, where prices are rising by around 313,000,000% each month, the government revalues the dinar. Monthly inflation apparently falls to around 1% in February.

**February**  
Under pressure from the UN and NATO, Bosnian Serb forces briefly lift their siege of Sarajevo, the capital of *Bosnia-Herzegovina*, which is already the longest siege in Europe in the 20th century.

Greece reimposes its trade embargo against *Macedonia* (to October 1995).

**March**  
Disagreements between the President of *Slovakia*, Michal Kováč, and the Prime Minister, Vladimír Mečiar, lead to a vote of no confidence in Mečiar in the National Council (legislature) and the appointment of a new government, united largely by its opposition to him.

In Washington, DC, representatives of the national (mainly Moslem) government of *Bosnia-Herzegovina* and of the country's Croat population agree on a federation directed against Serbian aggression.

**April**  
At the request of the UN, NATO launches its first ever assault, in the form of airstrikes on Bosnian Serb forces besieging the UN "safe area" of Goražde in *Bosnia-Herzegovina*.

**May**  
*Croatia* replaces its temporary national currency, the Croatian dinar, with the kuna.

**June**  
Following elections in *Hungary*, the former Communists (as Socialists) return to power in coalition with the Alliance of Free Democrats.

**July**  
In the *Czech Republic*, a new law requiring the registration of places of residence effectively deprives Roma of citizenship and access to social services.

Ramiz Alia, former Communist President of *Albania*, is found guilty of abuse of power and violations of citizens' rights, and jailed for nine years.

**August**  
NATO bombards Serb heavy weaponry, which has been fired at Sarajevo in contravention of Serb pledges.

The last Russian combat troops stationed in *Estonia* and *Latvia* are withdrawn, leaving only a few hundred technicians and other specialist personnel behind.

**October**  
For the first time, government forces in *Bosnia-Herzegovina* retake territory seized by Serbs.

**November**  
In *Macedonia*, the ex-Communist Social Democratic Alliance of Macedonia wins elections, partly because of a boycott by opposition parties, and forms a coalition government with one of the two parties representing the Albanian minority.

NATO bombards an airbase in Krajina, *Croatia*, used by Bosnian and Croatian Serbs to launch attacks on targets in *Bosnia-Herzegovina*. Bosnian and Croatian Serbs jointly besiege Bihać in Bosnia-Herzegovina, and take around 450 UN personnel hostage (but release them in December). The International Criminal Tribunal for the Former Yugoslavia, based in The Hague, the capital of the Netherlands, issues the first of its indictments against persons accused of committing war crimes in *Bosnia-Herzegovina*.

**December**     In *Bulgaria*, the former Communists, now Socialists, return to power.

**1995**   **February**     "Europe agreements" with the EU come into force in *Bulgaria*, the *Czech Republic*, *Romania*, and *Slovakia*.

**March**     *Hungary* completes the implementation of an economic stabilization program agreed with the IMF by imposing austerity measures known as the "Bokros package" (in reference to the Finance Minister, Lajos Bokros).

A UN Preventive Deployment Force (UNPREDEP) arrives in *Macedonia* in the midst of widespread fears that conflict would erupt between that country and *Albania* or Greece.

The government of *Croatia* refuses to extend the mandate for the UNPROFOR troops stationed on its territory. They are replaced by a smaller UN Confidence Restoration Operation (UNCRO), disbanded in January 1996.

**May**     In the midst of a financial crisis in *Latvia*, the country's largest bank, Baltija Banka, collapses.

In *Croatia*, government forces retake Western Slavonia from Serb rebels.

In *Bosnia-Herzegovina*, NATO launches air strikes on Serb weapons depots and the Serbs take UN personnel hostage again.

**June**     *Romania* and *Slovakia* become the first of six countries in central and eastern Europe to present applications for membership of the EU. *Latvia* follows in October, *Estonia* in November; *Lithuania* and *Bulgaria* follow in December. *Estonia, Latvia*, and *Lithuania* also sign "Europe agreements" with the EU, giving all three countries EU associate status.

**July**     In *Bosnia-Herzegovina*, Serb forces seize Zepa and Srebrenica, two of the last remaining UN "safe areas." Up to 8,000 Moslem men are believed to be killed by Serbs near Srebrenica, in the worst single atrocity in Europe since World War II.

The International Criminal Tribunal for the Former *Yugoslavia* issues indictments charging the Bosnian Serb leaders Radovan Karadzić and Ratko Mladić with genocide and other crimes. However, certain governments in western Europe refuse to cooperate with the Tribunal in formulating charges against President Milošević of Serbia.

**August**     *Croatia* completes its reconquest of Krajina as UNCRO troops and officials withdraw. The UN Security Council condemns the Croatian action and demands an immediate cessation of hostilities. The defeated Serb nationalist "government" in that region and most of its Serb inhabitants (around 25% of all the Serbs in Croatia) flee to *Yugoslavia*.

In *Bosnia-Herzegovina*, the Croat-Moslem federation retakes more territory from the Bosnian Serbs and NATO launches more air strikes against Bosnian Serb positions.

**September**     Greece and *Macedonia* sign an agreement under which Greece lifts its trade embargo, while Macedonia agrees to change its flag and to be known as the Former Yugoslav Republic of Macedonia (FYROM), being seated under the letter "F" at international meetings.

**October**   In *Estonia*, the coalition government formed in March by the Coalition Party and the Rural People's Union is compelled to leave office after a scandal over illicit tapping of telephone calls, and is replaced by a coalition between the Rural People's Union and the Reform Party.

**November**   The *Czech Republic* becomes the first of the transition economies to join the OECD.

In *Slovakia*, Slovak is declared the sole official language, even though more than 14% of the population use Hungarian and other languages.

The leaders of *Yugoslavia*, *Croatia*, and *Bosnia-Herzegovina*, and of the Serb and Croat nationalities in Bosnia-Herzegovina, initial an Agreement at Dayton, Ohio (formally signed in Paris in December). The country is partitioned between the Moslem-Croat federation (51% of its territory) and the Serbs (49%), under the supervision of a UN Implementation Force (I-FOR), replacing UNPROFOR up to December 1996, as well as EU and OSCE officials. UN sanctions against Yugoslavia are lifted. At least 280,000 people have been killed in the conflict, of whom around 240,000 were Moslems; tens of thousands remain displaced; and many of the provisions of the agreement have yet to be realized (as of mid-1999).

**December**   The government of *Croatia* reaches agreement with rebel Serbs on the peaceful transfer of Eastern Slavonia, Baranja, and Western Sirmium to government control, after a period of supervision by a UN Preventive Deployment Force (UNPREDEP) and Transitional Administration (UNTAES) up to January 1998.

**1996  January**   Józef Oleksy, a former Communist, resigns as Prime Minister of *Poland* in the midst of accusations, by ex-President Lech Wałęsa and others, that he had passed state secrets to the Soviet intelligence services and then to their Russian successors.

President Algirdas Brazauskas of *Lithuania* dismisses the Prime Minister, Adolfas Šleževičius, who withdrew his savings from a bank just two days before it collapsed.

**February**   In *Bosnia-Herzegovina*, around 60,000 Serbs depart from the suburbs of Sarajevo as these areas are returned to the control of the government. Many of them end up among more than 1 million displaced people inside the country or among around 600,000 refugees elsewhere (as of 1998).

**March**   *Hungary* and *Slovakia* sign a treaty confirming the border between them, and guaranteeing the rights of the Hungarian minority in Slovakia.

*Croatia* enacts a special privatization program, involving the allocation of US$2 billion-worth of state-owned assets through the issuing of vouchers to victims of Communist repression (1945–91) and of the 1991 war, on condition that they return to their former homes.

**April**   *Macedonia* and *Yugoslavia* begin inconclusive negotiations on a definitive demarcation of the border between them.

**May–June**   Elections for the People's Assembly in *Albania* are boycotted by some opposition groups and the ruling Democratic Party is accused of falsifying the results. The elections are rerun in June and the Democrats win again.

**June**   Following elections in the *Czech Republic*, Václav Klaus continues in office as Prime Minister at the head of a weakened and divided government.

In *Bosnia-Herzegovina*, the Croats break away from the federation with the Moslems agreed in March 1994.

The government of *Slovenia* submits an application for membership of the EU (see September 1997).

**August**          *Croatia* and *Yugoslavia* sign an agreement on mutual recognition and exchanges of refugees.

**September**       *Romania* signs a Treaty of Friendship with *Hungary*.

Sude becomes the first of numerous pyramid schemes to collapse in *Albania* over the winter of 1996–97, impoverishing thousands of people, and setting off an economic and political crisis (see March 1997).

Elections in *Bosnia-Herzegovina*, marred by violence and widespread tampering with ballots, result in the three main Moslem, Serb, and Croat parties retaining power in their respective communities. Violent incidents, including forcible removals from homes, continue before and after the elections in all three communities, and their leaders frequently ignore the advice or instructions of NATO, OSCE, UN and EU officials issued under the Dayton Agreement.

**October**         *Estonia* accepts a border agreement with Russia, but Russia refuses to ratify it.

**November**        A new President, Emil Constantinescu, takes office in *Romania*. At the same time, the Democratic Convention of Romania, the Social Democratic Union (now the Democratic Party), and the Democratic Union of Hungarians in Romania form a coalition government. These are the first postwar President and government to have no links with the former Communist Party.

In *Yugoslavia*, municipal elections won by opposition parties in the Zajedno coalition are nullified by the government, sparking demonstrations in the capital, Belgrade, which continue for 88 days until the elections are validated in February 1997.

**December**        I-FOR, the UN force in *Bosnia-Herzegovina*, is replaced by a smaller Sustaining Force (S-FOR) up to June 1998. The Bosnian Croat entity known as Herceg-Bosna, founded in June 1993, is dissolved.

**1997 January**    *Romania* accepts proposals from the IMF and the World Bank for fast-track economic reform in return for an extended loan program.

Miron Cozma, leader of the Jiu Valley miners in *Romania*, is jailed for 18 months for his involvement in the violent protests that brought down Petre Roman's government in September-October 1991.

The *Czech Republic* and Germany issue a joint declaration in which the Czechs express regret for the expulsions of ethnic Germans after World War II and the Germans express regret for the occupation of former Czechoslovakia by the Nazis.

**March**           The government of *Albania* resigns in the wake of the collapse of numerous pyramid schemes. A state of emergency is declared by President Salih Berisha, who is reelected by the People's Assembly at a session boycotted by opposition parties. An interim coalition government takes office (to July), and a UN security force is deployed to supervise relief work and elections (from April to August).

**April**            Following an election victory, the Union of Democratic Forces forms the first government in postwar *Bulgaria* not dominated by Communists or ex-Communists.

**May**              Economic difficulties and pressure from the IMF push the government of the *Czech Republic* into adopting an austerity package that damages the prestige of Prime Minister Klaus.

**June**             The OSCE concludes that the presidential election in *Croatia*, which gave Franjo Tudjman a second term in office, was free but not fair because of the media bias in his favor.

**July**             NATO invites the *Czech Republic*, *Hungary*, and *Poland* to become members.

In *Yugoslavia*, the Zajedno coalition of Serbian parties opposed to the government splits between liberal and nationalist groupings; Slobodan Milošević becomes federal President. In Montenegro, Prime Minister Milo Djukanović takes control of the ruling Democratic Party of Socialists and expels President Momir Bulatović from it.

In *Albania*, Fatos Nano, who was released from prison in March and then led the Socialists (former Communists) to electoral victory in June, is reappointed Prime Minister. President Salih Berisha resigns and is succeeded by a Socialist, Rexhep Mejdani. The state of emergency declared in March is brought to an end.

**August**           The government of *Bosnia-Herzegovina* introduces a new currency, the marka. However, the Yugoslav dinar and the Croatian kuna remain in circulation in large parts of the country into 1999.

**September**        The Commission of the EU announces that the *Czech Republic*, *Estonia*, *Hungary*, *Poland*, and *Slovenia* (as well as Cyprus) will be invited to negotiate membership of the EU, to be achieved by 2003 at the earliest, while five other countries in the region – *Bulgaria*, *Latvia*, *Lithuania*, *Romania*, and *Slovakia* – are to continue preparing for membership at later dates.

**October**          In *Yugoslavia*, Milo Djukanović, formerly a supporter but now a critic of federal President Slobodan Milošević, is elected President of Montenegro, replacing Momir Bulatović. In the meantime, Bulatović has become federal Prime Minister and head of a new Socialist People's Party.

**November**         Václav Klaus resigns as Prime Minister of the *Czech Republic* but manages to keep control over his party.

The Kosovo Liberation Army (UÇK or KLA), established in 1993 to fight for the independence of Kosovo from *Yugoslavia*, makes its first public appearance in the province, after weeks of clandestine operations against Serbian forces.

**1998 January**     A caretaker government takes office in the *Czech Republic*, headed by Josef Tošovský, the governor of the central bank.

UN troops and officials complete their withdrawal from Eastern Slavonia in *Croatia* as control of the area passes from UNPREDEP and UNTAES to the Croatian government, but a Civilian Police Support Group remains to monitor events.

**February**         The IMF withholds the third tranche of its US$410 million standby loan to *Romania* in order to express its dissatisfaction with progress on the country's reform program.

*Hungary* and the IMF agree on allowing a standby loan arrangement to expire without renewal.

Under the direction of President Slobodan Milošević of *Yugoslavia*, Serbian police attack villages in the province of Kosovo, prompting threats of NATO intervention. The Albanian population of the province (around 90% of the total) elect a new Assembly and reelect Ibrahim Rugova as President, while the Kosovo Liberation Army, rejecting Rugova's reliance on peaceful methods, launches a major campaign against the Serbian forces in the province.

**March**
The EU signs "accession partnerships" with 10 countries in central and eastern Europe preparing for EU membership (see September 1997).

President Guntis Ulmanis of *Latvia* dismisses the army's chief of staff, Juris Dalbins, after he took part in a rally held in the capital, Riga, by Latvian veterans of the Nazi SS, but arouses international protest by refusing to condemn the rally itself.

After President Michal Kováč of *Slovakia* completes his term of office, Prime Minister Vladimír Mečiar takes on some presidential powers. He then uses them to issue amnesties for himself and others in relation to the 1995 kidnapping of Kováč's son, as well as to cancel a referendum on NATO membership and the system of presidential elections. Mečiar's successor as Prime Minister, Mikulas Dzurinda, annuls the amnesties in December.

**April**
The UN imposes an arms embargo on *Yugoslavia* in view of the conflict in Kosovo.

**May**
In *Yugoslavia*, voters in Montenegro give a large majority to the Democratic Socialists, led by President Milo Djukanović, in elections that are praised by OSCE observers as the most democratic ever held in any of the six former Yugoslav republics. A broadly inclusive coalition government takes office.

Elections in *Hungary* result in the creation of a center-right government (taking office in June) by Fidesz and two other parties.

**June**
Elections in the *Czech Republic* have an indecisive outcome, leading to a minority Social Democrat government led by Miloš Zeman.

In *Bosnia-Herzegovina*, S-FOR is replaced by a Dissuasion Force (D-FOR).

NATO conducts airborne exercises over *Albania* and *Macedonia*.

**July**
Severe flooding damages large areas of *Poland*, *Slovakia*, and eastern Germany.

*Slovakia* starts to receive electricity from a reactor at Mochovce, the first new nuclear power plant to be opened in Europe since the Chernobyl' disaster in Ukraine in 1986.

**September**
Elections in *Slovakia* inflict a firm defeat on the former Prime Minister, Vladimír Mečiar, who resigns his seat in the National Council (legislature) in favor of Ivan Lexa, formerly head of the secret service.

The federal government of *Yugoslavia* imposes a "war tax" to fund increased "security" operations in Kosovo. The government of Montenegro refuses to permit the collection of the tax in its territory but fails to prevent Montenegrin conscripts from being sent to Kosovo. The UN Security Council calls for a ceasefire.

**October**    Pandeli Majko, aged 30, succeeds Fatos Nano as Prime Minister of *Albania*, becoming the youngest head of government in Europe.

The US envoy Richard Holbrooke negotiates an agreement with Slobodan Milošević, the President of *Yugoslavia*, which averts NATO air strikes, permits unarmed OSCE monitors to operate as the Kosovo Verification Mission (KVM), and provides for an extraction force, to be based in *Macedonia*, which would intervene if the monitors were attacked.

A referendum in *Latvia* shows a majority in support of liberalizing the law on citizenship. Its Parliament, the Saeima, enacts a law to make Latvian the state language and the sole language of instruction in state schools.

**November**    Detailed negotiations begin on EU membership for the *Czech Republic*, *Estonia*, *Hungary*, *Poland*, and *Slovenia* (as well as Cyprus).

In *Macedonia*, elections result in victory for an alliance of the Internal Macedonian Revolutionary Organization-Democratic Party of Macedonian National Unity (VMRO-DPMNE) and the Democratic Alternative (DA), ending 43 years of rule by Communists and ex-Communists.

Montenegro, the smaller of the two republics remaining in *Yugoslavia*, opens a representative office at the EU headquarters in Brussels, its first such separate representation abroad.

**December**    In *Yugoslavia*, the government of Montenegro extends its defiance of the federal government both practically, by reopening its border with *Croatia*, and symbolically, by refusing to celebrate the 80th anniversary of the establishment of the former Yugoslav kingdom.

**1999 January**    In *Yugoslavia*, there are continuing violations of the October 1998 ceasefire agreement in Kosovo and of international law, by both sides to the conflict.

In *Romania*, coalminers striking for higher pay and job security fight pitched battles with riot police, who halt their march to the capital, Bucharest. The miners' leader, Miron Cozma, negotiates their withdrawal in talks with the Prime Minister, Radu Vasile.

Johannes Klaassepp, a former Soviet official who ordered deportations from *Estonia* in 1949, becomes the first person in the Baltic states to be convicted of crimes against humanity.

**February**    After farmers throughout *Poland* spend 10 days setting up roadblocks and mounting other protests, the government agrees to provide additional aid for agriculture; protests continue into March.

Talks on the future of Kosovo in *Yugoslavia* are held in Rambouillet, France, between delegations representing the Serbian government and Kosovar Albanian parties. They end with a statement by the Contact Group of six western nations that the territorial integrity of *Yugoslavia* is to be respected, that there is a consensus on autonomy for Kosovo, and that talks will resume in March.

*Bulgaria* and *Macedonia* sign an agreement to renounce all claims on each other's territory, and to recognize Macedonian as a separate language from Bulgarian.

In *Romania*, security services disperse miners and other protesters in the capital, Bucharest, and arrest their leader, Miron Cozma, on charges arising from earlier protests (see September 1991). Parliament endorses a government plan to cut public spending in preparation for a new line of credit from the IMF.

*Poland* and other countries in the region welcome the establishment by leading German companies of a new fund to compensate victims of Nazism, including around 300,000 Polish survivors of enslavement as laborers for such companies.

**March**     *Hungary, Poland,* and the *Czech Republic* are admitted to NATO in a ceremony at Independence, Missouri, the home town of Harry S Truman, US President when NATO was founded.

In *Bosnia-Herzegovina*, the legislature of the Serb entity votes to boycott all federal institutions in protest over two decisions by the UN/EU mission: to dismiss Nikola Poplasen from the presidency of the entity; and to make the city of Brcko neutral instead of handing it over to Serb control.

Following the Serbian government's rejection of the agreement on Kosovo concluded at Rambouillet in February, thousands of Kosovar Albanians are driven from their homes as the OSCE monitors leave the province for *Macedonia*. In Paris, the representatives of the Kosovar Albanians sign the agreement, which is endorsed by the western powers but not by Russia. Both Montenegro and the Serb entity in *Bosnia-Herzegovina* declare neutrality in the event of conflict between Serbia and NATO.

After the federal army of *Yugoslavia* increases its presence in Kosovo, despite the terms of the October 1998 ceasefire, and makes forays into the territory of *Albania*, NATO begins to carry out its decision (unanimous apart from Greece) to launch air strikes on targets throughout Yugoslavia.

**April**     NATO's air strikes on *Yugoslavia* continue and intensify.

*Albania*, the poorest country in Europe, provides refuge for displaced Kosovar Albanians with aid from NATO, the EU, and the UN. The government of *Macedonia* repeatedly closes and reopens its border with Kosovo, permits mistreatment of refugees by its troops, and demands more aid from the West. Member states of the EU and NATO offer refuge to up to 95,000 displaced Kosovar Albanians.

The government of *Albania* cedes control of its sea ports, air space, and military facilities to NATO.

In the *Czech Republic*, following the bankruptcy of the chemicals firm Chemapol in January, and facing deepening economic recession, the government announces plans for a new state development agency to take over up to 30 debt-ridden privatized companies and prepare them for resale.

According to a report by the EBRD, the aggregate GDP of the 15 countries of central and eastern Europe rose by 2.3% in 1998; in *Slovakia* and *Slovenia*, GDP regained the level reached in 1989.

*Bulgaria* and *Romania* put their air space at the disposal of NATO, while the *Czech Republic, Slovakia,* and *Slovenia* announce that they will permit the movement of NATO troops and material through their territories.

The IMF grants a standby credit of US$500 million to *Romania*, where a general strike is averted by an agreement on wages policy between the government and the major labor unions.

**May**

During the first two months of the conflict between NATO and *Yugoslavia* (March 24 to May 24), at least 830,000 Kosovar Albanians have been forced out of their homeland. Around 440,000 have taken refuge in *Albania*. At least 240,000 are in *Macedonia*, 89,000 of them in camps near the border, while around 60,000 others have been transported from that country to refuge elsewhere in the world. There are also around 64,000 refugees in Montenegro and 22,000 in *Bosnia-Herzegovina*. Meanwhile, unknown thousands are either hiding from Serbian forces inside Kosovo, or being held captive by them.

The government of Montenegro, still a component part of *Yugoslavia*, continues to pursue a separate foreign policy, notably by sending a delegation to Germany led by President Milo Djukanović and including Zoran Djindjić, leader of the Serbian opposition Democratic Party and former Mayor of Belgrade.

In *Macedonia*, the authorities continue to clash with officials of the UN High Commission for Refugees over the inadequacy of provision for Kosovar Albanians and Macedonia's attempts to remove them to *Albania* against their will (and thus against international law).

The government of the *Czech Republic* approves plans by the state electricity utility CEZ to complete a nuclear power station at Temelin, despite concerns over safety and costs.

The International Criminal Tribunal for the Former *Yugoslavia* indicts five Serbian leaders on charges of crimes against humanity: President Slobodan Milošević, the first head of state still in office ever to be indicted in this way; Aragoljub Ojdanić, head of the Yugoslav armed forces since November 1998; Nikola Sainović, Yugoslav Deputy Prime Minister in charge of the security forces; Milan Milutinović, President of Serbia and head of its police units; and Vlajko Stojilković, Interior Minister of Serbia.

In the first direct election for the presidency of *Slovakia*, ex-Communist Rudolf Schuster, the candidate favored by the coalition government, defeats the former Prime Minister Vladimír Mečiar and other rivals.

**June**

Following the Serbian Assembly's approval of the Group of Eight peace plan, Yugoslav and NATO generals sign an agreement on the withdrawal of Serbian troops from Kosovo and the suspension of air strikes.

The UN Security Council formally ratifies the peace agreement and NATO's peace-keeping forces move into Kosovo.

# Appendix 2

# Personalities

## Paramount Leaders of the Communist Regimes After World War II

In each case, "First Secretary" or "General Secretary" was the leading position in the ruling party. Leaders appointed to control the Baltic states, the former Yugoslav republics, and Slovakia during the Communist period are not included in this list, as they were subordinate to the Soviet, Yugoslav, and Czechoslovak regimes, respectively. Soviet leaders are listed in *The CIS Handbook*.

*Albania*

| | | |
|---|---|---|
| 1943–85 | Enver Hoxha | General Secretary (1943–54), Prime Minister (1944–54), First Secretary (1954–85) |
| 1985–91 | Ramiz Alia | First Secretary |

*Bulgaria*

| | | |
|---|---|---|
| 1945–49 | Georgi Dimitrov | First Secretary (1945–49), Prime Minister (1947–49) |
| 1949–50 | Vasil Kolarov | Prime Minister |
| 1950–54 | Vulko Chervenko | Prime Minister (1950–56), First Secretary (1949–54) |
| 1954–89 | Todor Zhivkov | First Secretary (1954–81), General Secretary (1981–89), Prime Minister (1962–71), President (1971–89) |
| 1989–90 | Petur Mladenov | General Secretary (1989–90), President (1989–90) |

*Czechoslovakia*

| | | |
|---|---|---|
| 1945–53 | Klement Gottwald | First Secretary (1927–53), Prime Minister (1946–48), President (1948–53) |
| 1953–68 | Antonín Novotný | First Secretary (1953–68), President (1957–68) |
| 1968–69 | Alexander Dubček and Ludvík Svoboda | General Secretary (1968–69) President (1968–75) |
| 1969–89 | Gustáv Husák | General Secretary (1969–87), President (1975–89) |

*Hungary*

| | | |
|---|---|---|
| 1945–56 | Mátyás Rákosi | First Secretary (1945–56), Prime Minister (1952–53) |
| 1956 | Ernö Gerö | First Secretary |
| 1956–88 | János Kádár | First Secretary (1956–88), Prime Minister (1956–58 and 1961–65), President of the Party (1988–89) |

*Poland*

| | | |
|---|---|---|
| To 1956 | Bolesław Bierut | Prime Minister (1944–47), President (1947–52), First Secretary (1948–56), Prime Minister (1952–54) |
| 1956 | Edward Ochab | First Secretary |
| 1956–70 | Władysław Gomułka | General Secretary (1943–48), First Secretary (1956–70) |
| 1970–80 | Edward Gierek | First Secretary |
| 1980–81 | Stanisław Kania | First Secretary |
| 1981–90 | Wojciech Jaruzelski | First Secretary (1981–89), Prime Minister (1981–85), Chairman of the State Council (1985–89), President (1989–90) |

*Romania*

| | | |
|---|---|---|
| 1944–65 | Gheorghe Gheorghiu-Dej | General Secretary (1944–54), Prime Minister (1952–55), First Secretary (1955–65), President of the State Council (1961–65) |

| 1965–89 | Nicolae Ceauşescu | General Secretary (1965–89), President of the State Council (1967–74), President of the Republic (1974–89) |

*Yugoslavia*

| 1943–80 | Josip Broz Tito | First Secretary (1937–52), Federal Prime Minister (1943–53), Federal President (1953–80) |
| [1980–89 | Federal Presidency | A collective leadership, with annual rotation of the office of President and no paramount federal leader] |

## Presidents and Prime Ministers in the Transition Period

*Albania*
Presidents: Ramiz Alia (1991–92), Salih Berisha (1992–97), Rexhep Medjani (1997– )
Prime Ministers: Fatos Nano (1991), Ylli Bufi (1991), Vilson Ahmeti (1991–92), Aleksander Meksi (1992–97), Bashkim Fino (1997), Fatos Nano (1997–98), Pandeli Majko (1998– )

*Bosnia-Herzegovina*
President: Alija Izetbegović (1990–96)
Chairman of the Presidency: Alija Izetbegović (1996–98), Zivko Radisić (1998– )
Prime Ministers: Jure Pelivan (1990–92), Mile Akmadzić (1992–93), Haris Silajdzić (1993–96), Hasan Muratović (1996– )
Co-Chairmen, Council of Ministers: Boro Bosić (1997–99), Haris Silajdzić (1997– ), Svetozar Mihajlović (1999– )

*Bulgaria*
Presidents: Petur Mladenov (1989–90), Zhelyu Zhelev (1990–97), Petur Stoyanov (1997– )
Prime Ministers: Andrei Lukanov (1990), Dimitur Popov (1990–91), Filip Dimitrov (1991–92), Lyuben Berov (1992–94), Reneta Indzhova (1994–95), Zhan Videnov (1995–96), Stefan Sofianki (1997), Ivan Kostov (1997– )

*Croatia*
President: Franjo Tudjman (1990– )
Prime Ministers: Stjepan Mesić (1990–91), Franjo Gregurić (1991–92), Hrvoje Šarinić (1992–93), Nikica Valentić (1993–95), Zlatko Mateša (1995– )

*Czechoslovakia (to December 31, 1992)*
President: Václav Havel (1989–93)
Prime Ministers: Marián Čalfa (1989–92), Václav Klaus (1992–93)

*Czech Republic (from January 1, 1993)*
President: Václav Havel (1993– )
Prime Ministers: Václav Klaus (1993–97), Josef Tošovský (1998), Miloš Zeman (1998– )

*Estonia*
Presidents: Arnold Rüütel (1990–92), Lennart Meri (1992– )
Prime Ministers: Edgar Savisaar (1990–92), Tiit Vähi (1992), Mart Laar (1992–94), Andres Tarand (1994–95), Tiit Vähi (1995–97), Mart Siimann (1997– )

*Hungary*
President: Árpád Göncz (1990– )
Prime Ministers: József Antall (1990–93), Péter Boross (1993–94), Gyula Horn (1994–98), Viktor Orbán (1998– )

*Latvia*
Presidents: Anatolijs Gorbunovs (1988–93), Guntis Ulmanis (1993– )
Prime Ministers: Ivars Godmanis (1990–93), Valdis Birkavs (1993–94), Mâris Gailis (1994–95), Andris Škele (1995–97), Guntars Krasts (1997–98), Vilis Krištopâns (1998– )

*Lithuania*
Presidents: Vytautas Landsbergis (1990–92), Algirdas Brazauskas (1992–98), Valdas Adamkus (1998– )
Prime Ministers: Kazimiera Prunskiene (1990–91), Gediminas Vagnorius (1991–92), Aleksandras Abišala (1992), Bronislovas Lubys (1992–93), Adolfas Šleževičius (1993–96), Laurynas Stankevičius (1996), Gediminas Vagnorius (1996– )

*Macedonia*
President: Kiro Gligorov (1990–  )
Prime Ministers: Nicola Kljušev (1991–92), Branko Crvenkovski (1992), Petar Gosev (1992–96), Branko Crvenkovski (1996–98), Ljubco Georgievski (1998–  )

*Poland*
Presidents: Lech Wałęsa (1990–95), Aleksander Kwaśniewski (1995–  )
Prime Ministers: Tadeusz Mazowiecki (1989–91), Jan Krzysztof Bielecki (1991), Jan Olszewski (1991–92), Waldemar Pawlak (1992), Hanna Suchocka (1992–93), Waldemar Pawlak (1993–95), Józef Oleksy (1995–96), Włodzimierz Cimoszewicz (1996–97), Jerzy Buzek (1997–  )

*Romania*
Presidents: Ion Iliescu (1989–96), Emil Constantinescu (1996–  )
Prime Ministers: Petre Roman (1989–91), Theodor Stolojan (1991–92), Nicolae Văcăroiu (1992–96), Victor Ciorbea (1996–98), Radu Vasile (1998–  )

*Slovakia (from January 1, 1993)*
Presidents: Michal Kováč (1993–98), vacancy (1998–99), Rudolf Schuster (1999–  )
Prime Ministers: Vladimír Mečiar (1990–91), Ján Čarnogurský (1991–92), Vladimír Mečiar (1992–94), Jozef Moravčik (1994), Vladimír Mečiar (1994–98), Mikulas Dzurinda (1998–  )

*Slovenia*
President: Milan Kučan (1990–  )
Prime Ministers: Lojze Peterle (1991–92), Janez Drnovšek (1992–  )

*Yugoslavia (Bosnia-Herzegovina, Croatia, Macedonia, Montenegro, Serbia, and Slovenia)*
Presidents of the Federal Presidency: Janez Drnovšek (1989–90), Borisav Jović (1990–91), Stipe Mesić (1991–92)
Prime Ministers: Ante Marković (1989–92), Milan Panić (1992)

*Yugoslavia (Serbia and Montenegro)*
Presidents: Stipe Mesić (1991–92), Dobrica Ćosić (1992–93), Zoran Lilić (1993–97), Slobodan Milošević (1997–  )
Prime Ministers: Milan Panić (1992), Radoje Kontić (1992–98), Momir Bulatović (1998–  )

**Alia, Ramiz** (1925–  ): First Secretary of the Communist Party in Albania from 1985 to 1991, President from 1991 to 1992. After fighting with the Communist resistance during World War II, Alia became a protégé of the dictator Enver Hoxha and was prominent in the Party's youth wing up to 1955, when he briefly became Minister of Education. From then on, he held a series of party posts, vying with Mehmet Shehu for recognition as Hoxha's heir. In 1981, however, Shehu died (allegedly a suicide) and in 1982 Alia became Chairman of the Presidium of the National Assembly (head of state). Three years later, Hoxha died and Alia succeeded him as First Secretary. Alia reopened contacts with Italy, Turkey, and Greece but made few changes in the regime until demonstrations compelled him to announce, in November 1990, that there would be multiparty elections. He then organized the ballot-stuffing and other measures that ensured a Communist victory in those elections, in April 1991. After almost one year as President, he and his fellow-Communists were swept from office by the Democratic Party. In July 1994, Alia was found guilty of abuse of power and violations of citizens' rights, and jailed for nine years.

**Antall, József** (1932–93): Prime Minister of Hungary from 1990 to his death. Antall was the son of a lawyer and Smallholders Party politician who was Minister of Reconstruction in the first postwar government. Antall himself trained as a historian and participated in the 1956 uprising. He spent the rest of the Communist period working in the Museum of Medical History in Budapest. When the Hungarian Democratic Forum chose to become a right-of-center political party, in the second half of 1989, he was invited to lead it. He became Hungary's first democratically elected Prime Minister, but had difficulties keeping his coalition government together. He died in office after a long battle with cancer.

**Beneš, Edvard** (1884–1948): President of Czechoslovakia from 1935 to 1948. Beneš, originally an academic, was the first Foreign Minister of Czechoslovakia and then its delegate to the League of Nations, before being elected President by Parliament in 1935. Four years later, after Nazi Germany and its collaborators took control of his country, he departed for exile in London. After World War II, he returned home, hoping to establish Czechoslovakia as a neutral country with a limited degree of state intervention in the economy. However, he was outmaneuvered by the Communists in the new coalition government and, under considerable pressure, he acquiesced in their seizure of power in 1948. Gravely ill, he resigned soon after in protest at the new Constitution.

**Berisha, Salih** (1944– ):  President of Albania from 1992 to 1997. Berisha was not politically active under Communism, although he had formal membership of the ruling party because of his prominence as a cardiologist. He quickly became a leading figure in the Democratic Party and led it to its election victory of March 1992. In office, however, his lack of political experience and his authoritarian tendencies made Berisha and his party increasingly unpopular. He was eventually forced out of power in the wake of the collapse of numerous pyramid schemes. Since then, Berisha and his supporters have campaigned to restore him to power, or at least to salvage his reputation.

**Bierut, Bolesław** (1892–1956): First Secretary of the Polish Communist Party from 1948 to his death, Prime Minister from 1944 to 1947 and again from 1952 to 1954, and President from 1947 to 1952. A socialist militant from his teens, Bierut spent most of the years from 1919 to 1944 in the Soviet Union. While most of the Polish Party's leading members were accused of "nationalist deviations" by the Soviet dictator Josef Stalin, and ended up in Soviet or Nazi concentration camps, Bierut's devotion to Stalin was handsomely rewarded. He imposed Stalinist methods and institutions on his native country and became notorious as one of the "Little Stalins" of the region, along with Klement Gottwald of Czechoslovakia and Mátyás Rákosi of Hungary.

**Brazauskas, Algirdas** (1932– ): President of Lithuania from 1992 to 1998. During the period of Soviet occupation, Brazauskas pursued a career as a civil engineer, directing construction on a hydroelectric power plant in Kaunas and then at that city's reinforced concrete plant, before taking on a series of posts in the government and Communist Party bureaucracy. He became prominent as a "reform Communist" in the 1980s and in 1988 the independence movement Sajudis supported his appointment as First Secretary of the Party in Lithuania. Brazauskas went on to ensure that, unlike in Estonia and Latvia, the Communists did not seek to obstruct progress toward independence. In 1989, he declared the separation of his Party from the Communist Party of the Soviet Union and, in his role as Chairman of the Supreme Soviet (legislature), endorsed the country's declaration of sovereignty. In 1990, he also endorsed the declaration of independence. He became acting President in October 1992 and won election to the post by a majority in the legislature in February 1993. He had to exercise his reserve powers over the government only once, in January 1996, when he dismissed the Prime Minister, Adolfas Šleževičius, who had withdrawn his savings from a bank just two days before it collapsed.

**Ceauşescu, Nicolae** (1918–89): Ruler of Romania from 1965 to his execution in 1989. Having become prominent in the Romanian Communist Party when it was an illegal organization, Ceauşescu progressed through its hierarchy after 1948 and was made First Secretary in 1965, after the death of Gheorghe Gheorghiu-Dej. He became President as well in 1974. Liberalization and a degree of genuine popularity in the early years of his regime were replaced by extremism and nepotism in the 1980s. Even then, however, Ceauşescu was careful to maintain good relations with western politicians and business leaders. Little attention was paid abroad to the activities of his secret police, the Securitate; the corruption and profligacy of his government, at a time when most Romanians were becoming increasingly impoverished; or the enforced resettlement of many villagers. Unyielding to the end, he was unprepared for the upheaval of December 1989. The televised trial and execution of Ceauşescu and his wife Elena proved an embarrassment to Britain and other western countries where the couple had received a number of state honors and even university degrees.

**Dimitrov, Georgi** (1882–1949): First Secretary of the Communist Party in Bulgaria from 1945, and also Prime Minister from 1947, up to his death. Dimitrov was an agent of the Communist International (Comintern), based in Berlin from 1929. He achieved worldwide fame in 1934, defending himself in a Nazi court against the charge that he and three other Bulgarian Communists had started the Reichstag fire. He was then deported to the Soviet Union, where he remained until the Soviet Army installed him as head of a new government in Bulgaria. Whatever doubts he may once have had, he became a staunch supporter of Stalin's policies. His four years in power were marked by the repression of non-Communist parties and religious groups, the imprisonment and execution of dissidents within the Communist Party and beyond, the collectivization of agriculture, and other forms of "Sovietization." In 1991, his remains were removed from his magnificent mausoleum in the Bulgarian capital, Sofia.

**Dubček, Alexander** (1921–92): First Secretary of the Communist Party of Czechoslovakia from 1968 to 1969, Chairman of the Federal Assembly from 1989 to 1992. Dubček, who was a Slovak, spent part of his early life in the Soviet Union, returning home shortly before the start of World War II, during which he fought in the Slovak resistance. From 1950, he was an official in the Slovak Communist Party, becoming its leader in 1963. As head of the Party in the whole of Czechoslovakia, he launched the "Prague Spring," which saw the initiation of limited reforms until the Warsaw Pact invasion. He was removed from office in March 1969, and expelled from the Party in 1970. He then took menial jobs until his triumphant return to public life in November 1989. He joined and led the Slovak Social Democratic Party, and appeared to be one of the few prominent politicians with some standing in both parts of the federation, but his "reform Communism" was no longer in tune with the times. He retired from chairing the Assembly in June 1992, and died, after a road accident, in November.

**Gheorghiu-Dej, Gheorghe** (1901–65): General Secretary of the Communist Party of Romania from 1944 to 1954, then First Secretary until his death, Prime Minister from 1952 to 1955, and President of the State Council from 1961 until his death. Among the Communist leaders who came to power in the region in the 1940s, only Gheorghiu-Dej, Tito of Yugoslavia, and Hoxha of Albania did not spend the war years in Moscow. Unlike Tito or Hoxha, however, Gheorghiu-Dej was not a resistance fighter either. An active Communist from 1926, he had been jailed in 1933 for organizing a rail workers' strike and he remained in prison until 1944, when he escaped to take over the Party leadership. Between 1949 and 1951, he led the "nationalist" faction that, unlike in the rest of the Soviet bloc, defeated the "Muscovite" faction of the Party, led in Romania by Ana Pauker. Having secured supreme power, he cultivated friendly relations with China and the West, but otherwise followed the Stalinist model, repressing dissent, imposing rapid industrialization, and frequently purging the Party. It was Gheorghiu-Dej who discovered and promoted the man who succeeded him, Nicolae Ceauşescu.

**Gierek, Edward** (1913– ): First Secretary of the Polish Communist Party from 1970 to 1980. Gierek spent most of the years from 1923 to 1948 in France and then Belgium, working as a coalminer and participating in Communist politics. He thus avoided joining either the "Muscovite" minority in the Polish Party, which was loyal to the Soviet dictator Stalin, or the "nationalist" majority, which Stalin dispersed and destroyed. After 20 years as a competent but colorless bureaucrat in Poland, Gierek succeeded Władysław Gomułka as Party leader. He continued the established policy of favoring heavy industry and repressing dissent, until widespread strikes in the summer of 1980 forced him to concede recognition to independent trade unions. The Solidarity movement was founded just a few days after ill health ended Gierek's career.

**Gligorov, Kiro** (1917– ): President of Macedonia since 1991. Trained as a lawyer in Skopje and Belgrade, Gligorov was working for a bank in Skopje when Yugoslavia was invaded by Germany, Italy, Hungary, and Bulgaria in 1941. He became a leading figure in the Macedonian resistance to the invaders and joined AVNOJ, the Communist-led provisional government of Yugoslavia, in 1943. After World War II, he spent the years 1945–69 in a variety of posts in the federal government in Belgrade, specializing in finance and economic planning, and took part in introducing market-oriented reforms of the Yugoslav economy. He then went on to serve as President of the Institute for Social Sciences, a member of the collective federal Presidency (1974–78), and President of the federal Parliament. During most of the 1980s, however, he withdrew from politics to undertake theoretical research. In 1989, the federal Prime Minister Ante Marković invited Gligorov to join his reformist government, but as Yugoslavia disintegrated Gligorov left Belgrade to return to Macedonia. As President, he negotiated his country's peaceful secession from the Yugoslav federation, culminating in the withdrawal of federal forces by April 1992. He was reelected in 1994: his current term of office ends in October 1999. Gligorov, who survived a car bomb that killed his chauffeur in October 1995, has become a symbol of Macedonia's independence and unity in the face of tensions among its numerous ethnic groups and difficulties in relations with neighboring countries, notably Greece and "rump" Yugoslavia.

**Gomułka, Władysław** (1905–82): General Secretary of the Polish Communist Party from 1943 to 1948, and First Secretary from 1956 to 1970. Gomułka, a locksmith by profession, joined the Party in 1926. His role as a union organizer led to his spending most of the 1930s in jail, while the Party was being purged on the orders of the Soviet dictator Josef Stalin. During World War II, he chose not to go into exile in Moscow, unlike many other future Communist leaders in the region, but stayed in Poland to play a leading role in the Communist resistance to the Nazi occupiers. As a result, he was distrusted by Bolesław Bierut, whom Stalin had chosen to run Poland. Gomułka was expelled from the Party in 1948, and jailed in 1951, but was "rehabilitated" after Bierut's death in 1956. As First Secretary, Gomułka initiated some reforms, notably abandoning the collectivization of agriculture, but he also presided over the revival of official anti-Semitism in 1967, and the purging of universities and publishing houses in 1968. Two years later, his colleagues, blaming him for the mass protests that followed his decision to raise food prices, forced him to resign.

**Gottwald, Klement** (1896–1953): First Secretary of the Czechoslovak Communist Party from 1927 to his death; Prime Minister from 1946 to 1948, and then President. Gottwald helped to found the Party in 1921, and became its leader six years later. At that stage, the Party was the only Communist Party in central and eastern Europe with a genuine mass membership and a degree of popular support. These facts may have helped Gottwald to retain his post. In any case, he was to be the only Communist leader in the region to remain in place through the purges of the 1930s and World War II, an indication of how much he was trusted by the Soviet dictator Josef Stalin. Like the other "Little Stalins" of the region – Mátyás Rákosi of Hungary and Bolesław Bierut of Poland – Gottwald spent the war years in Moscow, returning home to impose Stalinism with considerable enthusiasm, and thus, ironically, destroying any chance that the Party might ever regain popular support. It seems somehow fitting that he died after catching pneumonia at Stalin's funeral.

**Havel, Václav** (1936– ): President of Czechoslovakia from 1989 to 1992, President of the Czech Republic since 1993. Havel, who came from a wealthy Czech background, suffered political discrimination under Communism. For example, he was prevented from going to university. His first play was produced in 1963, but he did not gain prominence in the theatrical world until 1968. As an active dissident, he suffered continual police harassment and persecution, with three periods of imprisonment (in 1977, from 1979 to 1983, and in 1989). He emerged in November 1989 as the leading figure in Civic Forum. He resigned the presidency in June 1992, when the end of the federation appeared inevitable, but was elected President of the new Czech Republic by its Parliament in January 1993. He won reelection in January 1998, but by only one vote, due to opposition from members of the ODS party. Havel, whose powers under the Czech Constitution are very limited, has tended to avoid intervening in politics, but he has spoken up on behalf of the Roma and other minorities. His enthusiasm for the Czech Republic's entry into NATO in 1999 has intrigued those who remember him calling for the dissolution of both NATO and the Warsaw Pact in the 1980s.

**Horn, Gyula** (1932– ): Foreign Minister of Hungary from 1989 to 1990, Prime Minister from 1994 to 1998. Until the late 1980s, Horn's career was that of a typical Communist Party official. He graduated from the College of Economics and Finance in Rostov-on-Don in the Soviet Union in 1954, returning to Hungary to work in the Ministry of Finance. Controversy surrounds his precise role in the 1956 uprising: he has admitted that he served in a paramilitary unit alongside Soviet troops. He then served in both Party and government posts before becoming State Secretary in the Ministry of Foreign Affairs from 1985. As Foreign Minister, he opened Hungary's western border and negotiated the withdrawal of Soviet troops. In 1990, he was elected to the National Assembly as a Socialist deputy and he became leader of the Socialist Party later that year. From 1994 to 1998, he presided, apparently with some reluctance, over the implementation of economic reforms and an austerity program. Following the Socialist Party's electoral defeat in 1998, he resigned from its leadership.

**Hoxha, Enver** (1908–85): General Secretary of the Communist Party of Albania from 1943 to 1954, then First Secretary until his death, and Prime Minister from 1944 to 1954. Hoxha, the son of a landowner, spent the years from 1930 to 1936 studying and working in France and Belgium. He then taught French in Albanian schools until the Italian occupation authorities dismissed him in 1939. Two years later, he became a founder member of the Communist Party and its armed resistance movement. Like Tito in Yugoslavia, he thus established a degree of distance from the Soviet Union. Nevertheless,

again like Tito, he did not hesitate to impose Stalinist policies of political repression and rapid industrialization. Hoxha also pressed ahead with the collectivization of agriculture, which Yugoslavia abandoned. In 1948, he purged the Party of pro-Soviet and pro-Yugoslav factions alike, and proceeded to
orient Albania, first toward a dependence on China, and then, in the 1960s, toward complete isolation. Repeated purges kept the Party in line, all religious groups and ethnic minorities were ruthlessly
repressed, and at Hoxha's death Albania was still what it had long been, the poorest country in
Europe.

**Husák, Gustáv** (1913–91): General Secretary of the Communist Party of Czechoslovakia from 1969 to
1987, and President of the Republic from 1975 to 1989. Husák, a Slovak, combined membership of
the Party (from 1933) with an active career as a lawyer up to 1940, when he was jailed. After his
release three years later, he helped to organize the Slovak uprising of 1944, then occupied various
Party and state posts under the Communist regime. In 1951, however, he was jailed again, this time
as a "bourgeois nationalist," and was not released until 1960. He then retired from politics to become
a historian, until a fellow Slovak, Alexander Dubček, appointed him a Deputy Prime Minister in his
reforming government in 1968. Husák acquiesced in the Warsaw Pact invasion later that year and
then, with Soviet support, set about reimposing the Stalinist system that he had once been a victim
of. His extraordinary ideological journey ended with a return on his deathbed to the Catholicism of
his childhood.

**Iliescu, Ion** (1930–  ): President of Romania from 1990 to 1996. Iliescu was a leading figure in the
Communist youth movement in the 1950s and from 1968 to 1984 he was a member of the Party's
Central Committee. However, he was managing a publishing company when he sprang to prominence in 1989 as a leader of the National Salvation Front, which overthrew his former patron Nicolae
Ceauşescu. Some have condemned him for blocking rapid reform in the early years of the transition,
but most would probably agree that his caution was justified, or at least understandable. Despite his
continuing activity as leader of the Social Democratic Party, he is widely regarded as a spokesperson
for the past rather than the future.

**Izetbegović, Alija** (1925–  ): President of Bosnia-Herzegovina from 1992 to 1996, Chairman of the
(nonfunctioning) Presidency from 1996 to 1998. During World War II, Izetbegović witnessed the occupation of the Bosnian capital, Sarajevo, by the Germans, and then the absorption of the whole country
into Croatia under the Ustaše regime. After the war, he was jailed by the new Communist regime
for three years, apparently for advocating religious ideas, but later was able to study and become a
consultant to various enterprises. His first book, *The Islamic Declaration* (1970), is a discussion of the
need for democratic legitimacy in any Moslem state, while a later book, *Islam Between East and West*
(1982), envisages mutual tolerance in a multiethnic society. After five more years in jail (from 1983
to 1988), Izetbegović took part in founding the Democratic Action Party (SDA) in 1992. The SDA,
open in principle to all nationalities, won the largest numbers of votes and of seats in Bosnia-
Herzegovina's first multiparty elections later that year. In the conditions imposed upon his country
by war and then by the 1995 Dayton agreement, which Izetbegović signed with evident and understandable reluctance, he was rarely able to play more than a symbolic role as President.

**Jaruzelski, Wojciech** (1923–  ): First Secretary of the Polish Communist Party from 1981 to 1989, Prime
Minister from 1981 to 1985, Chairman of the State Council from 1985 to 1989, and President from
1989 to 1990. In 1939, the entire Jaruzelski family, which belonged to the Polish gentry, escaped from
the Nazi advance to take refuge in Lithuania, only to be deported to Siberia by the Soviets. Jaruzelski
himself returned to Poland six years later as a soldier, and combined careers in the army and the
Party from then on. He was Minister of Defense when the Party chose him to head a new government charged with repressing the Solidarity movement. Apparently believing that the only alternative would be a Soviet invasion, Jaruzelski imposed martial law, creating the only military regime in
Europe at that time. However, he was eventually forced to negotiate a peaceful transition to democracy with Solidarity's leaders, in response to pressure from the Soviet President Mikhail Gorbachev
and the Catholic Church – led by a fellow-Pole, Pope John Paul II – and, perhaps, to his own realization that the Communist regime could not resolve the growing economic and political crisis. In
retirement, Jaruzelski has concentrated on writing his memoirs and has refused to answer charges
that, as Defense Minister in 1970, he ordered the killing of striking shipyard workers in Gdańsk.

**Kádár, János** (1912–89): First Secretary of the Hungarian Communist Party from 1956 to 1988, then President of the Party until 1989; Prime Minister of Hungary from 1956 to 1958, and again from 1961 to 1965. Born János Czermanik, the illegitimate son of a Slovak woman and a Hungarian man who deserted her, Kádár was an unemployed mechanic when he joined the Communist Party in 1931. He was jailed by the Hungarian government from 1937 to 1940, by the invading Germans for a brief period in 1944, and again, after he had become deputy head of the Budapest police, by his own Communist government in 1951, this time as a "deviationist." After his release in 1954, he maintained his opposition to Hungary's "Little Stalin," Mátyás Rákosi, but during the uprising in 1956 he broke from other "reform Communists" to accept the Soviet government's offer of supreme power in Hungary. Over the next 32 years, he initiated a series of decentralizing and liberalizing reforms that gave his country the least repressive government and the most open economy in the Soviet bloc, but in May 1988 he was replaced by even more determined reformers. In May 1989, they dismissed him from the ceremonial presidency of the Party that had been created specially for him. He died two months later.

**Klaus, Václav** (1941– ): Minister of Finance of Czechoslovakia from 1989 to 1992, and Prime Minister from 1992 to 1993; then Prime Minister of the Czech Republic until 1997. Klaus engaged in economic research up to 1970, and was then an official of the central planning system until returning to a research institute in 1987. He was not an active dissident, but he made no secret of his allegiance to neoclassical economic theory and was quick to ally himself with the emerging Civic Forum in November 1989. As Minister of Finance, he pushed through his conception of economic reform based on an IMF stabilization package and accompanied by voucher privatization. He was the key figure in the creation and leadership of the Civic Democratic Party (ODS), which dominated Czech politics from its foundation until Klaus was forced from office. His arrogance and his ruthless debating style won him both friends and enemies.

**Kováč, Michal** (1930– ): President of Slovakia from 1993 to 1998. An economist working in various banks up to 1989, Kováč became Slovak Minister of Finance after the Velvet Revolution. He left the government in April 1991, and joined Vladimír Mečiar's Movement for a Democratic Slovakia. As the first head of state of independent Slovakia, he adopted a very correct approach in relations with the Czech Republic, while escalating conflicts with Mečiar, now Prime Minister, led Kováč to instigate a vote of no confidence against him in March 1994. After returning to power, Mečiar tried a series of unsuccessful devices to remove Kováč, and then took over most of the presidential powers after Kováč completed his term of office.

**Kučan, Milan** (1941– ): President of Slovenia since 1990. Kučan trained and worked as a lawyer in Ljubljana during the Communist period. He was also active in the Slovenian League of Communists, rising to the post of chairman of the Slovenian legislature before becoming President of the League in 1986. During the late 1980s, he sought economic and political reforms within the framework of the Yugoslav federation, only moving toward a position favoring independence when faced with obstruction from the federal authorities, which were increasingly dominated by Serbian officials. In September 1989, he accepted the legislature's declaration of sovereignty, though apparently with some reluctance. Faced with economic sanctions engineered by Serbia from December 1989, a legislature dominated by non-Communist parties from May 1990, and a huge vote for independence in a referendum in December 1990, Kučan found himself joining President Tudjman of Croatia in declaring independence from Yugoslavia in June 1991. No longer even formally a Communist, Kučan has since been content to occupy a position of limited power, presiding over Slovenia's development into the richest country in the region (as measured by GDP per capita).

**Mečiar, Vladimír** (1942– ): Prime Minister of Slovakia from 1990 to 1991, from 1992 to 1994, and again from 1994 to 1998. Formerly a boxer, and active in the Communist youth organization, Mečiar was expelled from the Party after 1968, and took a series of manual jobs. He subsequently became a lawyer. His rise to political leadership was supported by Alexander Dubček, among others, and he became Minister of the Interior of Slovakia – then still within Czechoslovakia – in January 1990. As Prime Minister, Mečiar appeared almost indestructible, building support with pugnacious and xenophobic rhetoric. While his style appealed to many among the older generation, he also built support among industrial workers whose jobs were threatened, and among businessmen who profited from his privatization program. His determination to maintain himself in power was a barrier to the development of democracy and constitutional politics, until his removal after electoral defeat. The amnesty that he granted to himself and others in relation to the mysterious kidnapping of President Kováč's son in 1995 was overturned by the government that replaced his. In 1999, Mečiar ran in the first direct election for the presidency of Slovakia.

**Meri, Lennart** (1929– ): Foreign Minister of Estonia from 1990 to 1992 and President since 1992. The son of a diplomat, Meri was educated in Berlin, Paris, and Tallinn. In 1941, following the Soviet conquest of his country, he was deported with his entire family to Siberia, but returned home with them in 1946. Under Soviet rule, Meri had a varied and distinguished career as a translator, writer, and film-maker, notably on the history and prehistory of Estonians and other Finno-Ugrian peoples, as in his most widely known book *Hõbevalge* (1976; *Silverwhite*). In 1988, he founded a cultural and educational agency, the Estonian Institute, creating missions abroad that were transformed into Estonian embassies and representative offices in August 1991. In the same year, he became a founding member of the Popular Front, which cooperated with its counterparts in Latvia and Lithuania to remind the world of the Nazi-Soviet Pact of 1939 and its dire consequences for all three Baltic states. In April 1990, Meri became Foreign Minister in the new post-Communist government. Two years later, he was appointed Ambassador to Finland, but spent only five months in the post before being elected President by the Riigikogu (Parliament). He has since avoided party political controversy, even in the midst of the telephone-tapping scandal that brought down the government in October 1995, and has focused on helping to prepare Estonia for eventual membership of the EU.

**Milošević, Slobodan** (1941– ): President of Serbia from 1989 to 1997, President of Yugoslavia (Serbia and Montenegro) since then. Milošević was born near Belgrade, the son of a Montenegrin Orthodox priest and an active Communist who split up during his childhood (both committed suicide when he was an adult). After his marriage to an influential Party activist and sociologist, Mirjana Marković (whose aunt had been secretary to President Tito), he became head of two major companies, Tehnogas and Beobanka, in quick succession. He entered politics in 1984, as head of the Belgrade League of Communists; in 1986 he overthrew his mentor, Ivan Stambolić, and took his place as leader of the Serbian League of Communists (now the Socialist Party). Throughout his political career, he has been supported and assisted by Professor Marković, leader of her own party, the Yugoslav United Left (JUL), since 1994. Many in Serbia, and beyond, admire Milošević's Serb nationalism and defiance of pressure from the West, up to and including the NATO air strikes in 1999; to others he is "the butcher of the Balkans" and responsible for initiating the breakup of the Yugoslav Federation and for sponsoring "ethnic cleansing" throughout Croatia, Bosnia-Herzegovina, and Kosovo.

**Rákosi, Mátyás** (1892–1971): First Secretary of the Hungarian Communist Party from 1945 to 1956, and Prime Minister from 1952 to 1953. Rákosi was working in Britain as a commercial agent when World War I began in 1914. Despite his socialist beliefs, he joined the army of the Habsburg empire and became a prisoner of war in Russia in 1915. By the time he returned to Hungary in 1918, he was a convinced Communist; he went on to serve as a minister in the Communist government that ruled the country from March to August 1919. After it was overthrown he went abroad again, returning home only to be jailed from 1925 onward. In 1940, he was deported to the Soviet Union. His third return to Hungary, in 1945, was as a loyal disciple of the Soviet dictator Josef Stalin. Indeed, along with Klement Gottwald of Czechoslovakia and Bolesław Bierut of Poland, he soon became known as one of the "Little Stalins" of the region, imposing a harsh regime on the country and upholding Stalin's worldview even after his mentor's death in 1953. As head of the Party apparatus, Rákosi resisted all his colleagues' attempts at reform until July 1956, when he was dismissed and exiled to Central Asia. There was to be no fourth return to Hungary for him.

**Tito, Josip Broz** (1892–1980): Communist leader of Yugoslavia from 1944 to his death. Josip Broz, a locksmith and metalworker of mixed Croat/Slovene descent, was conscripted into the army of the Austro-Hungarian empire, which his native Croatia was then a part of, in 1914. He became a Communist while a prisoner of war in Russia in 1917, took part in that country's revolution up to his return to Croatia in 1921, and was a frequent visitor to Moscow from then on. By 1937, he was leader of the Communist Party of Yugoslavia, under the Party name "Tito." At that time, he favored dismembering the Yugoslav Kingdom into separate national republics and was generally regarded as a loyal disciple of Stalin. However, unlike most of his counterparts elsewhere in the region, he did not go to live in Moscow during World War II. Instead, after leading the Partisan movement to victory, over both occupiers and internal rivals, he established a federal system, and distanced the country from Stalin's Soviet Union. He dominated Yugoslav politics for 35 years, balancing political repression, especially of nationalist movements, with a degree of economic and cultural freedom. He also helped to found the Nonaligned Movement in 1961. The personality cult around Tito culminated in his appointment as President for Life in 1974. Tito succeeded in keeping Yugoslavia united, but fragmentation was starting by the time he died. As one government official said, when they buried Tito they also buried Yugoslavia.

**Tudjman, Franjo** (1922– ): President of Croatia since 1990. Somewhat surprisingly, given his present position, Tudjman was a loyal Communist for some years, fighting in the Partisan movement in World War II, and reaching the rank of general in the Yugoslav army by 1961, when he moved into academia. He became a professor of history at Zagreb University in 1963. He was expelled from the Communist Party in 1967, and jailed twice (in 1972 and 1981), because of his increasingly outspoken nationalism. As leader of the Croatian Democratic Community (HDZ), a party that he and other nationalists founded in 1989, and as President of a newly independent Croatia, he has attracted considerable domestic support for his revival of national identity and for his economic reforms. However, he is also the focus of hostility, especially from Croatian Serbs and their allies, to his authoritarian style, and to his attempts to rehabilitate the wartime Croat regime, which was allied to Nazi Germany.

**Ulmanis, Guntis** (1939– ): President of Latvia since 1993. Ulmanis is a great-nephew of Dr Karlis Ulmanis, President of Latvia when the Soviet Union invaded the country in 1940. He spent the years 1941 to 1946 in exile in Siberia with his family and escaped a second deportation in 1949 only because he had been given his stepfather's surname. As an economist and local government official in Riga, the Latvian capital, he resumed the name Ulmanis. He was a member of the Communist Party from 1965 to 1989. Following the achievement of independence, he was appointed to the board of the central bank in 1992 and was elected to the Saeima (Parliament) in 1993 as a leading member of the Farmers' Union. He became President shortly afterward, being reelected by the Saeima in 1996. Ulmanis has consistently emphasized the need for Latvia to be integrated with the EU and other European organizations, and to relax its restrictive citizenship laws; the latter goal was achieved by a referendum in 1998. In 1996, he declared a moratorium on the use of the death penalty.

**Wałęsa, Lech** (1943– ): Leader of the Polish labor federation Solidarity from 1980 to 1990, President of Poland from 1990 to 1995, winner of the Nobel Peace Prize in 1983. In the early summer of 1980, opposition to the government spilled over into strikes in many areas and a sit-in at the state-owned shipyard in Gdańsk, where Wałęsa was an electrician. He emerged as a leader of the Solidarity movement and the authorities soon found themselves negotiating with him. The government declared martial law in December 1981, and imprisoned Wałęsa (until November 1982) as well as other Solidarity leaders; but this served only to enhance their status. Following the defeat of the Communists in the elections of 1989, Wałęsa became head of state in 1990, after a campaign in which he declared himself "100% Polish" and called on Jews in public life to "reveal their identities." By then, however, Solidarity had become deeply divided, with many accusing Wałęsa of developing authoritarian tendencies. In the elections of September 1993, a "Non-party Bloc" formed by Wałęsa's own supporters won only 16 seats, while the rump of the Solidarity Parliamentary Club failed to win any. In September 1998, Wałęsa announced the foundation of a new party; in May 1999, he announced that he would seek the presidency again in 2000. On the one hand, neither initiative seemed likely to gain much popular support; on the other, Wałęsa has made a career out of being unpredictable.

**Zhelev, Dr Zhelyu** (1935– ): President of Bulgaria from 1990 to 1997. Zhelev had started a promising career as a professional sociologist and a member of the Communist Party by 1965, when he was expelled from the Party for writing "subversive" literature. He was subjected to internal exile from 1966 to 1972; from 1974 to 1979 he was a senior research associate at the Bulgarian Academy of Sciences. In 1988, he and other intellectuals formed a reformist group, the Club for the Support of Glasnost and Perestroika, which became one of the elements in the Union of Democratic Forces (UDF) formed at the beginning of 1990, following the removal of the Communist dictator Todor Zhivkov. Zhelev became the first Chairman of the UDF and later in 1990, following free elections, he was made President by the National Assembly, even though the UDF held a minority of seats. He went on to win the first direct presidential election two years later. As a non-executive head of state, his most important contribution was to help the country become accustomed to the norms of parliamentary democracy, notably by appointing Prime Ministers who either enjoyed the support of majorities in the Assembly, or served as "caretakers" when stable majorities could not be formed. After completing his term of office, he became Chairman of the Liberal Democratic Party.

**Zhivkov, Todor** (1911–98): Communist ruler of Bulgaria from 1954 to 1989. A printer from a rural background, Zhivkov came to prominence in the partisan resistance during World War II, and took part in the Communist seizure of power in 1944. From 1954, he used his position as First Secretary of the Party to purge actual and potential rivals from its ranks, starting with his predecessor as First Secretary, Vulko Chervenko. From 1961, Zhivkov, his friends, and his relatives enjoyed 28 years of centralized power and ever-increasing wealth. Under his rule, Bulgaria cooperated closely with the Soviet Union, not only economically but also in spying on the West and murdering dissidents. In 1989, however, 300,000 Bulgarian Turks fled the country to avoid submitting to Zhivkov's suppression of their culture and his imposition of Bulgarian names on them. In the ensuing crisis, Petur Mladenov and other younger Communists, encouraged by the Soviet leader Mikhail Gorbachev, removed him from office. After a long trial, from 1991 to 1992, Zhivkov was found guilty of embezzling the equivalent of at least US$18 million from state funds; he then remained under house arrest until his death.

## Appendix 3

# Political and Economic Institutions

## Political Systems

**National governments under Communism:** The ruling parties, under various names, were all modeled on the Communist Party of the Soviet Union. In each of the seven nation-states, as well as in the Soviet-occupied Baltic states, a First (or General) Secretary, a small and powerful group known as the Politburo, and a larger but generally ineffective Central Committee monopolized political power. Together, they used the *nomenklatura* system of party appointments to official posts, and the internal security services, to dominate the formal institutions of government. These institutions in turn were generally based on the Soviet model, with a Council of Ministers and a legislature (usually bicameral).

**Post-Communist national governments:** All 15 countries in the region have adopted new constitutions, or revived and modified pre-Communist ones. All except Yugoslavia function as parliamentary democracies, in which the President, whether elected by the people or by the legislature, has limited powers and the Prime Minister is usually the leader of the largest party, or coalition of parties, either in a unicameral legislature or, where there are two houses, the lower house.

The Presidents of Albania, Bulgaria, Croatia, Macedonia, Poland, Romania, Slovakia (from 1999 onward), and Slovenia are directly elected by their respective peoples, for terms lasting four years in Romania but five years in the other seven countries. In principle, the collective Presidency of Bosnia-Herzegovina has three members, directly elected every four years by the Moslem, Serb and Croat communities; in practice, it has not yet become operational. The Presidents are (or have been) elected by the respective legislatures in the rest of the region: for five-year terms in the Czech Republic, Estonia, Lithuania, and (up to 1998) Slovakia; for four-year terms in Hungary and Yugoslavia; and for three-year terms in Latvia.

The legislatures of eight countries in the region are unicameral: the People's Assembly (Kuvënd Popullóre) of Albania, the National Assembly (Narodno Sobranie) of Bulgaria, the Parliament (Riigikogu) of Estonia, the National Assembly (Országgyüles) of Hungary, the Parliament (Saeima) of Latvia, the Parliament (Seimas) of Lithuania, the Assembly (Sobranje) of Macedonia, and the National Council (Narodna Rada) of Slovakia. All are elected to sit for a maximum of four years, except in Latvia and Lithuania, where the maximum term is three years.

The other seven legislatures are bicameral. In Croatia, the Assembly (Sabor) comprises an upper house, the House of Districts (Zupanije Dom), which has some members appointed by the President but is mainly elected every four years, and the House of Representatives (Zastupnicki Dom), also elected every four years. In the Czech Republic, the Parliament (Parlament) comprises the Senate (Senat), one third of which is elected every two years to serve for six, and the Chamber of Deputies (Snemovna Poslancu), elected every four years. In Poland, the National Assembly (Zgromadzenie Narodowe) comprises the Senate (Senat) and a lower house, the Sejm, both elected every four years. In Romania, both houses of Parliament (Parlamentul) – the Senate (Senatul) and the Chamber of Deputies (Adunarea Deputatilor) – are elected every four years. In Slovenia, the Assembly (Skupscina) comprises the State Council (Drzavni Svet), with representatives of local governments and economic organizations serving five-year terms, and the State Chamber (Drzavni Zabor), with members elected every four years. Finally, the two federations in the region have special arrangements for electing their upper houses. In Bosnia-Herzegovina, the Assembly (Skupstina) comprises an upper house, the House of Peoples (Dom Naroda), and the larger House of Representatives (Predstavnicki Dom); each of the three communities has equal representation in both houses, which are elected every two years. In Yugoslavia (Serbia and Montenegro), the Federal Assembly (Savezna Skupstina) comprises an upper house, the Chamber of Republics (Vece Republika), in which Serbia and Montenegro have equal representation, and the Chamber of Citizens (Vece Gradjana); both are elected every four years.

**Local government:** As in the Soviet Union itself, local government units in the former Soviet bloc, and in Albania, were given elaborate names and symbols. However, they were effectively branches of the national government, even in Czechoslovakia, the only country in this group to have a federal structure set out in its Constitution. In Yugoslavia, the attempt to decentralize functions from the federal government to the republics and autonomous provinces had a significant impact – for better and/or for worse, depending on one's view – but there was very little genuine transfer of powers from the republics to any smaller units.

Since 1989, most countries in the region have retained the local government units of the Communist period, but given them greater powers, while others have revived older structures. There have been several reforms of boundaries and functions, ranging from Macedonia's replacement of 34 counties with 123, in 1996, to Poland's replacement of 49 regions with 16, in 1998. Four countries (Hungary, Latvia, Lithuania, and Slovenia) each distinguish between rural local governments and urban ones, while the other nine unitary states have uniform divisions, generally in two tiers: counties or regions, and smaller municipalities within them. In Bosnia-Herzegovina, the Moslem-Croat Federation and the Republika Srpska have wide powers allocated to them under the Dayton agreement of 1995. In Yugoslavia, Serbia and Montenegro retain separate republican institutions.

# Economic Institutions

**Banking:** During the Communist period, banking functions were generally divided among three main institutions – a national bank issuing money and providing commercial banking, a central savings bank, and a foreign trade bank – although there were variations on this pattern, notably in the federal systems of Czechoslovakia and Yugoslavia. In Hungary in 1987, and then in other countries from 1989, the usual approach to reform, endorsed by the IMF, was to carve a central bank out of the national bank, privatize its commercial branches, and remove the monopolies enjoyed by the savings bank and the trade bank. In theory, the central bank would then be freed to control monetary policy, while the privatized institutions and their new private sector counterparts would compete for customers in a free market. In practice, as more realistic commentators predicted, the old state monopolies have mostly given way to private monopolies, either at national or regional levels. Meanwhile, the links between financiers and politicians have not always been broken; and few domestic institutions, whether privatized or newly founded, have been able to prosper without participation by foreign capital.

The central banks of Bulgaria, the Czech Republic, Estonia, Hungary, Latvia, Lithuania, Poland, Romania, and Slovakia have all become members of the Bank for International Settlements, while the membership of Yugoslavia's central bank has been suspended.

**Stock exchanges:** The Ljubljana Stock Exchange in Slovenia was the first to reopen anywhere in central and eastern Europe, in March 1990; others reopened that year in Warsaw and Budapest. Still more followed in quick succession: Zagreb in 1992, Prague, Bratislava, and Vilnius in 1993, Riga, Sofia, and Bucharest in 1995, and even Tirana, where there had never been a stock exchange before, in 1996. Initially, their development was hampered by deficient technologies, and, in the absence of effective regulation, some dubious or occasionally fraudulent transactions. Privatization issues have tended to dominate trading on most exchanges. Trading on all of them remains limited in comparison to their counterparts in western Europe or North America.

**Labor unions:** The Communist regimes adopted the Soviet system of "labor unions" that were no more than organs of the state, thus establishing an association between unions and repression that has lasted into the 1990s. The Solidarity movement in Poland was the first free union movement to make any headway against the official unions, but the extension of its activities into parliamentary politics was followed by bitter divisions and, eventually, a loss of members and influence. Improvised unions played a role in the overthrow of Communism, notably in Czechoslovakia and Romania, by helping to organize strikes and protests, but since 1989 union activity has been limited, throughout central and eastern Europe, as a result of apathy among workers and hostility among managers. Polish farmers, Romanian coalminers, and other groups in other countries have occasionally mounted protests against declining living standards, and the loss or reduction of state aid for their industries, inadvertently reinforcing the widespread idea that unions are institutions of the past, not of the future.

Unions in some countries in the region continue to be hampered by ideological rivalries. In Poland and Romania, there are unions belonging to all three international federations: the International Confederation of Free Trade Unions (ICFTU), the mainly Christian World Confederation of Labor (WCL), and the ex-Communist World Federation of Trade Unions (WFTU). In Bulgaria, the Czech Republic, Hungary, and Slovakia there is rivalry between ICFTU and WFTU affiliates.

## International Organizations

**Worldwide:** Czechoslovakia, Poland, and the former Yugoslavia became founder members of the UN and its agencies in 1945; Albania, Bulgaria, Hungary, and Romania were admitted in 1955; Estonia, Latvia, and Lithuania joined in 1991; Bosnia-Herzegovina, Croatia, and Slovenia joined in 1992; and the Czech Republic and Slovakia were admitted in 1993. The UN retains a seat, nameplate, flag, and mission for the former Socialist Federal Republic of Yugoslavia, and has not accepted the claim of "rump" Yugoslavia (Serbia and Montenegro) to be its successor.

Since 1947, almost all European countries, as well as states in North America and Central Asia, have taken part in the activities of the UN Economic Commission on Europe (UNECE). Even during the Cold War, it had some success in promoting consensus and standardization in trade, transportation, science and technology, and the environment, and since 1989 it has also undertaken research and training in support of the transition to market practices in the post-Communist countries.

Since the World Trade Organization began operations in 1995, Bulgaria, the Czech Republic, Hungary, Poland, Slovakia, and Slovenia have become members, while Albania, Croatia, Estonia, Latvia, Lithuania, and Macedonia have submitted applications for membership. Yugoslavia's membership has been suspended.

**During the Communist Period**: There was intensive liaison between the Soviet security service and its counterparts in the satellite countries, and over the years relatively informal political and economic deals also became increasingly important. However, the formal, overt framework of the Soviet bloc comprised three international organizations: Cominform, Comecon, and the Warsaw Pact.

Cominform (the Communist Information Bureau) was founded in Warsaw in 1947. It had only nine members at the outset: the ruling parties of the Soviet Union, Bulgaria, Czechoslovakia, Hungary, Poland, Romania, and Yugoslavia, together with their sister parties in France and Italy. This was in marked contrast to the worldwide membership of the Communist International (the Comintern), established by Lenin in 1919 but dissolved by Stalin in 1943. The Yugoslav Party was expelled in 1948, following Tito's rejection of Stalin's hegemony; and it was mainly in the hope of a rapprochement with Yugoslavia that the Soviet leader Nikita Khrushchev abolished Cominform only eight years later.

Comecon was formally known as the Council for Mutual Economic Assistance (CMEA): the term "Comecon" appears to have been coined in the West. The organization, which had its headquarters in Moscow, was established in 1949 by the Soviet Union, along with Bulgaria, Czechoslovakia, Hungary, Poland, and Romania. Albania, admitted one month after the other members, was expelled in 1961. East Germany joined in 1950, Mongolia in 1962, Cuba in 1972, and Vietnam in 1978; Yugoslavia became an associate member in 1964. Trade agreements were made with a number of countries and organizations, notably the European Community (in 1988), and Comecon regulated trade among its members. For most of the period, around two thirds of the international trade of each member was with the other members. Comecon also played an important role in the system of economic planning: under an agreement signed in 1959, each member state was directed to specialize in selected industries. Comecon was formally dissolved in 1991. Its International Bank for Economic Cooperation, founded in 1963, and its International Investment Bank, founded in 1970, have become Russian commercial banks.

The Warsaw Pact alliance was established under a Treaty of Friendship, Cooperation, and Mutual Assistance signed in the capital of Poland in May 1955 by Albania, Bulgaria, Czechoslovakia, East Germany, Hungary, Poland, Romania, and the Soviet Union. Albania was excluded from alliance meetings from 1961, and formally denounced the Pact in 1968. Despite its name, the political and military bodies that coordinated the alliance's activities were based in Moscow, and its supreme commander was always a Soviet officer. The Pact took joint action only once, when the forces of its member states, except those of Albania and Romania, invaded Czechoslovakia. Its last formal act, before its dissolution in July 1991, was to represent its member states in talks on the Treaty on Conventional Forces in Europe, signed in 1990.

After their departures from the Soviet bloc, Yugoslavia and Albania adopted contrasting attitudes to international organizations. Albania became increasingly isolated up to 1978, when it broke off relations with China, the last country to remain on good terms with it. Yugoslavia became an active member of the Nonaligned Movement, a group of countries founded in 1961 that initially proclaimed its neutrality as between the West and the Soviet bloc. It grew from 25 members to more than 85, but fragmented during the 1980s, mainly as a result of attempts by Cuba and some other members to push it closer to the Soviet position in international relations.

It should also be noted that a limited degree of cooperation between the Communist countries of Europe and the West continued throughout the Cold War. For example, ever since 1948, Bulgaria, Czechoslovakia and its successor states, Hungary, and Romania have collaborated with Austria and Germany in the Danube Commission, which supervises navigation on the river. Russia, Ukraine, and Yugoslavia are now also members of the Danube Commission, while Croatia and Moldova have observer status.

**Economic Cooperation since 1989:** The main focus of elite and public attention in foreign relations has been on making progress toward membership of the EU (as the European Community has been known since November 1993). As of 1999, 10 countries in central and eastern Europe had made "Europe agreements" with the EU, acquiring associate status (alongside Cyprus, Malta, and Turkey), access to the EU's single market except in agricultural goods and labor, and the prospect of eventual EU membership. Of these 10, the Czech Republic, Estonia, Hungary, Poland, and Slovenia are taking part in detailed negotiations on membership, while Bulgaria, Latvia, Lithuania, Romania, and Slovakia have "accession partnerships" with the EU, and are likely to join at some date after 2003.

All 15 countries have also benefited from bilateral aid and advice delivered through the EU's PHARE program. This was established in 1989, initially to aid Poland and Hungary, but was extended to other transition economies in the region in 1991–92.

Fourteen countries in the region, aside from Yugoslavia, have joined the EBRD, which grew out of the meetings of the Group of 24 western nations during 1989–90. It began operations in 1991. Its other members include almost all the countries of western Europe, and all the CIS states, as well as Australia, Canada, Egypt, Israel, Japan, South Korea, Morocco, New Zealand, the EU, and the European Investment Bank (an organ of the EU). In practice, most of the EBRD's activities have been in central and eastern Europe, where it has provided loans in support of economic reform, and taken shareholdings in privatized banks and other institutions.

In addition, the countries of the region, aside from Bosnia-Herzegovina, Croatia, and Yugoslavia, have made agreements on trade and cooperation with the European Free Trade Association (EFTA), which comprises Iceland, Liechtenstein, Norway, and Switzerland. The EFTA countries, except Switzerland, formed a European Economic Area with the European Community (now the EU) in 1992.

Two other organizations are focused on "central Europe," although the term is not clearly defined. The Central European Initiative, was started as the Pentagonale in July 1990, by Austria, Czechoslovakia, Hungary, Italy, and Yugoslavia. It became the Hexagonale when Poland joined in July 1991. In 1992, the successor states of the former Yugoslavia were suspended from membership, although all but Serbia and Montenegro have now joined. In 1993 the Czech Republic and Slovakia inherited Czechoslovakia's membership; Albania, Bulgaria and Romania (as well as Belarus, Moldova, and Ukraine) have also joined.

The Central European Free Trade Association (CEFTA), also known as the Visegrád Group, was founded in December 1992 by Czechoslovakia, Hungary, and Poland. The Czech Republic and Slovakia joined it automatically when they were formed in January 1993. By July 1994, the members had removed import duties from more than half the goods traded among them. A fifth member, Slovenia, joined in January 1996.

Another regional body, the Black Sea Economic Cooperation (BSEC) group, was established under the Declaration on Black Sea Economic and Environmental Cooperation, signed in June 1992 by Turkey, Bulgaria, Russia, Romania, Georgia, and Ukraine (which have Black Sea coasts), and Albania,

Greece, Azerbaijan, Armenia, and Moldova (which do not). Poland and Slovakia, which are even more distant from the Black Sea, have observer status at BSEC meetings.

Yet another organization, the Council of Baltic Sea States, was established in 1992, by Denmark, Estonia, Finland, Germany, Iceland, Latvia, Lithuania, Norway, Poland, Sweden, and Russia. The purpose of this "informal" body is to promote cooperation on the transition to free markets, as well as on energy and the environment, culture, crime, and communications.

In 1996, Albania, Bosnia-Herzegovina, Bulgaria, Croatia, Hungary, Macedonia, Romania, and Slovenia joined with Greece, Moldova, and Turkey in launching the Southeast Europe Cooperation Initiative (SECI). In close consultation with UNECE (see above), SECI works to promote cooperation on economic and environmental problems, and to encourage the private sector to collaborate in resolving them.

The Czech Republic, Poland, and Hungary are also members of the OECD, while Slovakia has been designated an OECD "Partner in Transition."

**Cooperation on Security and Related Issues since 1991:** Most of the countries in the region have joined most of the other organizations that bring the countries of Europe together. Thus, all 15 are members of the OSCE (which began as the CSCE in 1975, but changed its name in 1995), alongside the countries of western Europe, the CIS countries, the United States, and Canada. However, Yugoslavia's membership has been suspended since 1992. The OSCE addresses issues of security, economic cooperation, science and technology, the environment, and human rights. In particular, it is responsible for monitoring the observance of the 1990 Treaty on Conventional Forces in Europe (the CFE Treaty); it appointed its first High Commissioner on National Minorities in 1992; and it frequently monitors elections, ceasefire agreements, and other potential sources of conflict or crisis. In central and eastern Europe, its missions in Kosovo, Vojvodina, and Sanjak each had little or no effect, and have been terminated, but other OSCE missions continue in Albania, Bosnia-Herzegovina, Croatia, Macedonia, Estonia, and Latvia.

The Czech Republic, Hungary, and Poland joined NATO in 1999. Until then, they had been members, along with 41 other countries by 1999, of the North Atlantic Cooperation Council (1991–97), and then the Euro-Atlantic Partnership Council (from 1997). These Councils form the framework for NATO's Partnership for Peace program, which started in 1994, and which links NATO's member states with other countries in Europe and in the CIS. The program now includes nine countries in central and eastern Europe, but excludes Bosnia-Herzegovina, Croatia, and Yugoslavia (Serbia and Montenegro). Ten countries in central and eastern Europe (other than Albania, Bosnia-Herzegovina, Croatia, Macedonia, and Yugoslavia) are also associate partners of the Western European Union (WEU), founded in 1950. The WEU comprises all the members of NATO except Canada, Denmark, Iceland, Norway, Turkey, and the United States. It was designated the "defense component" of the EU in 1991.

Between 1990 and 1996, 14 countries in the region joined the Council of Europe, which has monitored human rights, democracy, the treatment of minorities, and cultural issues since its establishment by 10 western European countries in 1949. Yugoslavia's membership has been suspended, however, while Bosnia-Herzegovina has guest status. It should perhaps be mentioned that the Council of Europe and the European Court of Human Rights associated with it have no connection with the EU, its European Council or its European Court of Justice.

**Other:** Yugoslavia became a founder member of the Nonaligned Movement in 1961. Since 1992, Croatia has obtained observer status at its meetings, while Bosnia-Herzegovina, Bulgaria, Hungary, Poland, Romania, and Slovenia have guest status.

Hungary, alone among the countries of the region, is a member of the Missile Technology Control Regime. The Czech Republic, Hungary, Poland, and Slovakia are members of the European Organization for Nuclear Research (CERN). These four countries, and Romania, are members of the Nuclear Suppliers Group, which monitors exports of nuclear weapons materials and information. These five countries, and Bulgaria, are members of the Zangger Committee on guidelines for exports of nuclear weapons technology.

Albania joined the Organization of the Islamic Conference in December 1992; Bosnia-Herzegovina has observer status there.

Bulgaria and Romania joined the Agence de la Francophonie in 1991 and 1993, respectively. This international organization groups countries and other territories that use the French language.

## Appendix 4

# Ethnic Groups

## The Ethnic Composition of National Populations

The figures set out below are all estimates, except where the taking of a census is indicated. All the figures, including those based on census returns, should be treated with caution. Some may be unreliable because of events since the estimates were made, such as the emigration of many ethnic Germans to Germany. Others may be affected by tendencies to underestimate the social presence of disfavored groups and exaggerate the numbers of those in favored groups. Poland is a special case: it does not officially monitor ethnicity.

**Albania** (1998): 3.4 million; Albanians 95%, Greeks 3%, and others, including Vlachs, Roma, Serbs, and Bulgarians

**Bosnia-Herzegovina** (1998): 3.4 million; Serbs 34–40%, (Slavic) Moslems (or Bosniacs) 36–38%, Croats 21–22%, Roma 5%, Montenegrins 1%, others, including self-declared Yugoslavs, Turks, Arabs, Albanians, and Jews, 4–10%

**Bulgaria** (1993): 8.2 million; Bulgarians 86%, Turks 9%, Roma 4%, as well as Macedonians, Vlachs, and Greeks

**Croatia** (1997): 4.7 million; Croats 78%, Serbs 12%, Hungarians 3.7%, Italians 2.6%, as well as Albanians, Czechs, Slovenes, Montenegrins, and Jews

**Czech Republic** (1996): 10.3 million; Czechs (Bohemians, Moravians, and Silesians) 94.4%, Slovaks 3.6%, as well as Poles, Germans, Roma, Hungarians, Ukrainians, and Russians

**Estonia** (1997): 1.4 million; Estonians 65%, Russians 28.2%, Ukrainians 2.6%, Belarusians 1.5%, Finns 0.9%, as well as Ingrians, Latvians, Lithuanians, Tatars, Roma, and Chavash

**Hungary** (1993): 10.2 million; Hungarians 90.4%, Roma 4.8%, Serbs 2%, Germans 1.9%, Slovaks 0.9%

**Latvia** (1997): 2.4 million; Latvians 55.3%, Russians 32.5%, Belarusians 4.0%, Ukrainians 2.7%, Poles 2.5%, as well as Lithuanians, Jews, Roma, and Germans

**Lithuania** (1997): 3.6 million; Lithuanians 81.6%, Russians 8.2%, Poles 6.9%, Belarusians 1.5%, Ukrainians 1%, as well as Jews, Latvians, Tatars, and Germans

**Macedonia** (1994 census): 2 million; Macedonians 66.5%, Albanians 22.9%, Turks 4.0%, Roma 2.3%, Serbs 2.1%, Slavic Moslems 1.5%, as well as Greeks, Bulgarians, Vlachs, Jews, and members of 17 other recognized ethnic groups

**Poland** (1996): 38.6 million; Poles 97.6%, Germans 1.3%, Ukrainians 0.6%, Belarusians 0.5%, as well as Jews and Lithuanians

**Romania** (1992 census): 22.4 million; Romanians 88%, Hungarians 8%, Germans 1.6%, Roma 1%

**Slovakia** (1993): 5.4 million; Slovaks 85.7%, Hungarians 10.8%, Roma 1.5%, Ruthenes 1.4%, as well as Czechs, Ukrainians, Poles, Germans, Russians, and Serbs

**Slovenia** (1994): 2 million; Slovenes 91%, Croats 2.5%, Serbs 2.1%, Slavic Moslems 1.4%, as well as Italians, Germans, Slovaks, and Czechs

**Yugoslavia (Serbia and Montenegro)** (1996): 11.2 million; Serbs 63%, Albanians 17%, Montenegrins 6%, Hungarians 4%, Slavic Moslems 3.2%, Roma 2.4%, Vlachs 1.5%, as well as self-declared Yugoslavs, Croats, Slovaks, Bulgarians, Ruthenes, Ukrainians, Turks, Poles, Germans, Czechs, Russians, and Jews

## Ethnic Groups in Central and Eastern Europe

As with the percentages above, great care should be taken over all the figures set out below. They are all estimates, based on official sources and standard reference texts. They all fail to take account of intermarriage, religious conversion, and other forms of intermingling between groups and cultures: in central and eastern Europe, as elsewhere, claims to ethnic "purity" hardly ever have any basis in fact. References to a minority in a specific country do not necessarily indicate its absence from other countries in the region.

**Albanians:** Most Albanians are Moslems. Linguistically, they are divided into two main groups, each speaking a different set of dialects: the Ghegs, to the North, who include a Roman Catholic minority; and the Tosks, to the South, who include an Orthodox minority. There are around 3.2 million in Albania itself.

Among the comparable number of Albanians historically resident in other countries, around 1.7 million formed around 90% of the population in the Yugoslav province of Kosovo until 1998–99, when the Serbian government planned and executed a program of "ethnic cleansing." This involved forced movements of populations, as well as massacres and wholesale destruction of settlements, on a scale not seen in Europe since the defeat of the Nazis. Kosovo had always had an Albanian majority population, before and during the Serb conquest in the Middle Ages, under the Ottoman Turks (when it included parts of modern Macedonia), and after 1913, when Serbia seized control of it again. From 1945 Kosovo had been a constituent part, not of Serbia, but of the former Yugoslav federation, and had the same right to leave that federation as any of the six republics. All the recent violence in the province has followed directly from Serbia's unilateral abolition, in 1989, of the autonomous status that Kosovo had enjoyed since 1974, and its consistent refusal to negotiate in good faith with Ibrahim Rugova and other moderate representatives of the Kosovar Albanians.

The number of Albanians in Macedonia has long been subject to dispute, but probably exceeded 500,000 up to 1999. There were some reports of mistreatment in the early 1990s, but one of the two Albanian political parties joined the country's coalition government in 1994 and interethnic relations appeared to be improving. In 1999, Serbian forces began driving Kosovar Albanians into Macedonia, partly in an attempt to destabilize it. Tensions among Macedonia's multiethnic population have undoubtedly been exacerbated as a result.

There are also Albanian minorities in Bosnia-Herzegovina (around 25,000 people) and Croatia (around 12,000), as well as in Greece and Italy. The continuing conflict in and over Kosovo, the presence of Albanians in Greece and Macedonia, and the proximity of Albania itself have been cited to support claims that a "Greater Albania" is being planned. There is no reliable evidence that this is the case.

**Arabs:** The 30,000 Arabs of Bosnia-Herzegovina, often counted with other groups simply as Moslems, are descendants of those who settled in the country when it was ruled by the Ottoman Turks.

**Belarusians:** The 23,000 Belarusians in Estonia and the 45,000 in Lithuania are mostly descended from those who settled in those countries, willingly or not, when they were under Soviet occupation. However, most of the 105,000 Belarusians in Latvia, which, like Lithuania, borders Belarus itself, form part of a community established there in the Middle Ages, when large parts of these countries were included in the Commonwealth of Poland-Lithuania.

**Bosniacs:** see Moslems.

**Bulgarians:** Outside Bulgaria itself, where around 7.8 million mostly Orthodox Bulgarians form the majority of the population, there are Bulgarian minorities of around 67,000 people in Serbia and Montenegro, and around 11,000 people in Macedonia. The Bulgarian government has officially abandoned the claim, often asserted in the past by Bulgarian nationalists and Communists alike, that Macedonians are Bulgarians too.

**Croats:** In this book, as is customary in English-language publications, "Croat" refers to membership of the ethnic group, "Croatian" to citizenship of the multiethnic country. In addition to the 3.7 million Croats in Croatia itself, there are Croat communities in Bosnia-Herzegovina (around 650,000 people), Macedonia (around 3,000), Serbia and Montenegro (105,000), and Slovenia (around 48,000), as well as in Austria and Italy. Croats have long been set apart from Serbs, with whom they share the Serbo-Croat language, by differences in dialects·and their use of the Roman alphabet rather than Cyrillic; by the traditional loyalty of most Croats to Catholicism rather than Orthodox Christianity; and by their history of subjection to rule by the Habsburg emperors of Austria-Hungary up to 1918. The 20th-century experience of rivalry and conflict between Croats and Serbs, which culminated in war and massacres in the 1940s, and again in the 1990s, has not improved relations between them. Many observers have argued for recognition of the Istrian Croats as a separate ethnic group: see Istrians below.

**Czechs (Bohemians, Moravians, and Silesians):** The 8.5 million Czechs in the Czech Republic, the 60,000 in neighboring Slovakia, and the 2,000 in Slovenia are heirs to the Bohemians, Moravians, and Silesians who became separated from the Slovaks and formed a powerful state of their own, known as Moravia, in the Middle Ages. What is now known as Protestantism had its first large-scale success there and there are more Protestants than Catholics in the country today, but in the 17th century the kingdom of Bohemia, as it had become, was absorbed into the Austrian half of the officially Catholic Habsburg empire. Nowadays, the 1.4 million Moravians and 45,000 Silesians are counted as Czechs in official statistics, but most of them speak distinct dialects and many have shown support for forms of autonomy within the Czech Republic. The 14,000 Czechs in Croatia, and the 8,000 Czechs in Serbia and Montenegro, are descended from settlers who arrived in the days of the Habsburg empire (up to 1918).

**Estonians:** The 940,000 Estonians in Estonia itself include an unknown number of Livs, descendants of what was once a separate Finnic people, who now speak Estonian but retain some distinctive cultural traditions. Most Estonians are Lutherans. There are also 5,000 Estonians in Latvia, including some Livs.

**Friuli:** see Italians

**Germans:** The *Drang nach Osten*, as Germans themselves call their historic movement Eastwards, began in the Middle Ages. By the end of World War I it had left sizable German minorities in all the countries of central and eastern Europe, as well as in the former Russian empire. However, in 1939–40, at the beginning of World War II in Europe, most of the formerly dominant German minorities in the Baltic states departed for Germany. In addition, at the end of the war around 9 million Germans were expelled, or fled, from Poland and Czechoslovakia. In the 1990s, hundreds of thousands more exercised their right, under the German Basic Law of 1949, to leave the region and settle in Germany itself. Nevertheless, significant German minorities remain, notably in the Czech Republic (52,000), Hungary, Poland, Romania (25,000), Serbia and Montenegro (10,000), Slovakia (5,000), and Slovenia (20,000). The existence of the German minority in Slovenia was officially acknowledged for the first time in January 1998. Poland is unique in reserving seats in its legislature for representatives of its German minority. The Czech Republic and Slovakia continue to resist claims from former German residents and their descendants in relation to property seized when they were expelled in the late 1940s.

**Greeks:** The Greek minority in southern Albania – which Greeks call Northern Epirus – may number as few as 60,000 or as many as 300,000. It was treated with hostility by the former Communist regime, which required its members to adopt Albanian names and suppressed their Orthodox Christianity. Claims and counterclaims about the treatment that they now receive continue to sour relations between Albania and Greece. Most of the 21,000 Greeks in Macedonia live near the border with Greece itself.

**Hungarians:** The Hungarians, who call themselves Magyar, are a Finno-Ugrian people culturally and linguistically distinct from the Slavic, Germanic, Romanian and other peoples among whom they have lived for more than 1,000 years. Today, around 9 million Hungarians form the majority of the population in Hungary itself and there are Hungarian minorities in Romania (mainly in the province of Transylvania), Yugoslavia (nearly 400,000, mostly in the province of Vojvodina), Croatia (around

170,000), the Czech Republic (around 21,000), Slovakia (around 570,000), and Slovenia (around 20,000). Except in the case of the Czech Republic, all these minorities are descendants of those who settled in these provinces and countries when they were parts of the Kingdom of Hungary. This was a major European power in the Middle Ages and it retained extensive lands in a Dual Monarchy with Austria under the Habsburgs up to 1918. In the past, lingering prejudice against them was fed by resentment of a former ruling power and, in some cases, by the declared attitudes of Hungarian governments, especially those allied to Nazi Germany in World War II. However, toleration, imposed under Communism and encouraged under liberal democracy, has now become the norm.

**Istrians:** The Istrians, said to number around 245,000 in Croatia and 37,000 in Slovenia, are often counted as members of the respective majority peoples of those countries. However, they have preserved a distinctive culture that mingles Slav, Italian, and German traditions, reflecting the complex history of the Istrian Peninsula. In Croatia in the 1990s, they have generally supported parties seeking local autonomy, rather than the Croat nationalist parties that are dominant elsewhere.

**Italians:** The 120,000 Italians in Croatia and the 27,000 in Slovenia mostly still live in or near the Istrian Peninsula and other parts of Dalmatia that were Italian territory until 1945. However, the presence of Italians in what is now Croatia can be traced back to the early Middle Ages, when, for example, the city now named Dubrovnik was the center of an Italian state called Ragusa. The Italians in Croatia include around 7,000 people known as the Friuli, who, like the Friuli of Italy, speak a language that resembles the Romansch language of Switzerland but with elements from the Venetian form of Italian.

**Jews:** Before the Nazis and their collaborators murdered around 6 million Jews during World War II, the countries of central and eastern Europe, above all Poland, were home to the largest and most diverse Jewish populations anywhere in the world. Some Jewish communities, the Ashkenazim, had been settled in the region since the early Middle Ages; others, the Sephardim, had found refuge there from persecution in Spain and Portugal in the late 15th century. Nevertheless, like the Roma, the Jews continued to suffer varying degrees of persecution and discrimination throughout Christian Europe. After World War II, many survivors of the *Shoah* (the Holocaust) departed for the new state of Israel and many more left the Soviet bloc when anti-Semitism was revived in the 1960s.

Today, there are around 17,000 Jews in Bosnia-Herzegovina, around 5,000 in Bulgaria, 130,000 in Hungary, 13,000 in Latvia, 6,000 in Lithuania, 2,000 in Macedonia, fewer than 10,000 in Poland, 3,000 in Serbia and Montenegro, 6,000 in Slovakia. A group of around 290 people in Lithuania speak a Turkic language but practice a unique, non-rabbinical variant of Judaism.

**Latvians:** The 1.4 million Latvians in Latvia are still the majority of the population, though they form a much lower proportion of the total than before World War II and the Soviet occupation. A distinction is sometimes made between mostly Lutheran Western Latvians and mostly Catholic Eastern Latvians. Alternatively, this people can be divided, chiefly by their dialects, into Latgalians in the East, Zemgalians in the South, Courlanders or Kurzemians in the West, and Vidzemians in the North. There are also 2,000 Latvians in Estonia, and 4,000 in Lithuania.

**Lithuanians:** There are a little more than 3 million Lithuanians in Lithuania itself, where they are customarily divided into four groups speaking different dialects – the Suvalkieciai in the South, the Dzukai in the Southeast, the Aukstaiciai in the Northeast, and the Zemaiciai in the West. Most Lithuanians are Catholics, but there are significant minorities of Lutherans and Orthodox believers as well. There are also 2,000 Lithuanians in Estonia and 30,000 in Latvia.

**Macedonians:** In addition to the 1.4 million Vardar Macedonians who form the majority population in the Republic of Macedonia – which they share with 26 other ethnic groups – there are Aegean Macedonians in Greece and Pirin Macedonians in Bulgaria. These three groups share a common language and culture, including widespread adherence to the autonomous Macedonian Orthodox Church. However, they have been separated since 1913, when Macedonia was seized from the Ottoman Turks and divided among Greece, Bulgaria, and what was then the Kingdom of Serbia. Greek fears of Macedonian expansionism or reunification lie behind the trade embargo twice imposed on independent Macedonia. Communist Bulgaria tried to assimilate its Macedonian minority, denying that it even existed as a distinct group, but tolerance has increased, at least to some extent, during the present transition period. Meanwhile, as the events of the spring of 1999 have indicated once again, at least some sections of the ruling elite in Serbia still cling to the belief that Macedonians are "really" Serbs. In their view, the country should be incorporated into Serbia, or a Serb-dominated Yugoslavia, as it was from 1913 to 1945.

**Magyar:** see Hungarians

**Montenegrins:** Historically closely linked to the neighboring Serbs, the people of Montenegro developed a distinct national identity as subjects of a line of Orthodox Prince-Bishops, each succeeded by his nephew, until 1851, and then of secular princes. Unlike the Serbs, they were never defeated or conquered by the Ottoman Turks. As citizens of Yugoslavia since its formation in 1918, Montenegrins were initially subjected to attempts to assimilate them into the Serb population, but since 1945 they have been recognized as a distinct national group with their own republic. In addition to the 630,000 in Montenegro and Serbia, there are 32,000 in Bosnia-Herzegovina and around 10,000 in Croatia.

**Moslems:** There are followers of Islam in almost every European country, but the term has a special, more restricted meaning in this context: the Moslems of the former Yugoslavia, descendants of Slavic converts under the Ottoman empire, who were designated as a nationality under Communism.

The Moslems in Bosnia-Herzegovina, numbering around 1.1 million, are sometimes called "Bosniacs," as, for example, in the Dayton Agreement of 1995. The claim that they have always been distrusted and disliked by their Serb and Croat neighbors has little foundation in fact. Intermarriage among the communities has been very common, there was no large-scale intercommunal conflict in Bosnia-Herzegovina between 1945 and 1992, and the government elected in the latter year must have had many non-Moslem supporters to achieve its majority in the Assembly that declared independence. Nevertheless, at certain periods, including the 1990s, many Moslems have understandably responded to intercommunal conflicts, typically generated by external forces, by returning to the religion that has given them their name, even though historically most have taken relatively little interest in it.

There are also Slav Moslem minorities in Bulgaria (see under "Turks" below); in Croatia and Slovenia, where the respective communities of 50,000 and 28,000 Moslems are also referred to as Morlakhs; in Macedonia, where there are around 30,000; and in "rump" Yugoslavia, where the 340,000 Slavic Moslems are generally known as Sanjaki Moslems, referring to the Sanjak region where most of them still live.

**Poles:** In addition to the 37.4 million Poles who form the overwhelming majority of the population in contemporary Poland, there are 63,000 Poles in the Czech Republic, 60,000 in Latvia, 250,000 in Lithuania, 6,000 in Slovakia, and 12,000 in Serbia and Montenegro. There are also Polish minorities in some CIS countries, as well as smaller Polish commmunities, generally established during or after World War II, in western Europe. The broad geographic dispersal of the Polish people reflects their dramatic history, which has included dominance within the medieval Commonwealth of Poland-Lithuania; subjugation to Prussian, Austrian, and Russian occupiers from the late 18th century to 1918; conquest by Nazi Germany and the Soviet Union during World War II; and Communist rule up to 1989. Throughout this history, most Poles have adhered to the Catholic Church. As a result, national identity and religious faith have often become intermingled, as (for example) in Ireland or Quebec. The link has been reinforced since 1978, when Karol Wojtyła (1920– ), Cardinal Archbishop of Kraków, became John Paul II, the first non-Italian Pope in more than 450 years.

There are at least four main dialects of the Polish language – Mazovian, Malopolska, Silesian, and Wielkopolska – each originating in a historic region of Poland and associated with local cultural variations. There is some dispute over whether Kashubian, which is still spoken by around 200,000 people on or near the Baltic coast and the German border, is a dialect of Polish, an offshoot of German comparable to Yiddish, or the language of a distinct people, the Kashubians.

**Roma:** This has become the preferred term for the formerly nomadic people who are sometimes still called "gypsies" in reference to their supposed origins in Egypt. In fact, they originated in the Indian subcontinent, arriving in southeastern Europe in the 14th century and then spreading around the world. Like the Jews, the Roma were subjected to prejudice and discrimination throughout Christian Europe, culminating in the campaign of genocide directed against all "non-Aryans" by the Nazis and their collaborators during World War II. At least 500,000 Roma were murdered in what they call *O Porraimos*, "the Devouring."

Under Communism, except in the former Yugoslavia, Roma traditions were officially despised and suppressed, and concerted efforts were made to compel them to abandon nomadism. The situation of the Roma has not improved since Communism collapsed. There are now significant Roma minorities in Bulgaria (850,000 people), Hungary (around 500,000), Romania (460,000), and "rump" Yugoslavia (260,000), as well as in Albania (around 34,000), Bosnia-Herzegovina (around 65,000), the Czech Republic (around 32,000), Latvia (8,000), Macedonia (47,000), and Slovakia (80,000), but they are present throughout the rest of the region as well.

**Romanians:** The Romanians have maintained their Romance language and culture for centuries, despite absorption into the Turkish Ottoman empire from the 16th century to the 19th century, and conflicts with Hungary, the former Soviet Union, and Yugoslavia during the 20th century. The 21 million Romanians in the modern state of Romania are generally regarded as distinct both from the people of neighboring Moldova and from the Vlachs of the former Yugoslavia (see below). However, all three peoples share a common linguistic and cultural heritage, including the coexistence of four types of Christianity: Catholic, Calvinist, Orthodox, and Uniate (Christians of the Orthodox rite who are in communion with Rome).

**Russians:** There are three distinct groups of Russians in central and eastern Europe. The 2,000 Russians in Slovakia, and the 5,000 in Serbia and Montenegro, are mostly members of communities formed during the 19th century. The 6,000 Russians in the Czech Republic are descendants of "White" (anti-Communist) Russians who migrated after the Bolshevik Revolution in 1917. However, the much larger Russian minorities in the Baltic states – numbering around 420,000 in Estonia, 765,000 in Latvia, and 300,000 in Lithuania – are descended from those settled in these countries, willingly or not, during the decades of Soviet occupation.

**Ruthenes:** see Ukrainians

**Serbs:** In this book, as is customary in English-language publications, "Serb" refers to membership of the ethnic group, "Serbian" to citizenship of the multiethnic country. In addition to the 6.7 million Serbs in "rump" Yugoslavia (Serbia and Montenegro), there are Serb minorities in Bosnia-Herzegovina (around 1 million people), Croatia (around 480,000), Macedonia (around 45,000), Montenegro, Slovakia (around 2,000), Slovenia (around 40,000), and Hungary (around 200,000). In the province of Kosovo, now part of Serbia – although Serbia's claim is debatable in terms of international law – Serbs have never exceeded 25% of the population in modern times. The Serb minority there was declining to around 5% of the total when ethnic cleansing was relaunched on their behalf in 1998–99.

Most Serbs, whichever country they live in, share a heritage of Orthodox Christianity that is focused on Kosovo in particular, since it was in that province, with its Orthodox monasteries and churches, that the Ottoman Turks defeated and destroyed the medieval kingdom of Serbia in 1389. The history of the Serbs in the 20th century has enhanced the belief, already widespread among them, that they are under threat from neighboring ethnic groups, even though each of these groups has long been less numerous and less powerful than the Serbs. Having been the dominant group in Yugoslavia between 1918 and 1941, Serbs became the main targets of Croatian nationalist repression during World War II and then suffered the effects of positive discrimination in favor of other nationalities under Communism. Partly as a result of these experiences – but partly also in response to worsening economic conditions and government propaganda – there has been a resurgence of Serb nationalism in the 1980s and 1990s.

**Slovaks:** The Slovaks and the Czechs have common origins, but their histories began to diverge in the 10th century. From then on, the Slovaks were subjugated successively by the Hungarians, the Ottoman Turks, and then the Hungarian half of the Habsburg empire, up to the creation of Czechoslovakia in 1918. One long-term effect of this history is that Catholicism is the majority faith among Slovaks, although there are also members of Lutheran, Orthodox, and Uniate churches (the last-named being churches of Orthodox tradition that are in communion with Rome). There are now around 4.6 million Slovaks in their homeland, 380,000 in the Czech Republic, at least 100,000 in Serbia (mostly in the province of Vojvodina), and around 5,000 in Slovenia.

**Slovenes:** By far the majority in Slovenia itself, where they number around 1.8 million, Slovenes form national minorities in other parts of the former Yugoslavia, as well as in Austria and Italy. In particular, there are around 25,000 in neighboring Croatia. The Slovene language is closely related to

Serbo-Croat but distinct from it. Most Slovenians are Catholics, partly reflecting the fact that their country was under the control of the Austro-Hungarian Habsburg empire up to 1918.

**Turks:** Reflecting the territorial extent of the former Ottoman empire, there are Turkish minorities in Bosnia-Herzegovina (around 50,000 people), Bulgaria (around 740,000), Macedonia (around 85,000), and "rump" Yugoslavia (around 21,000). The Bosnian and Macedonian Turks, descendants of settlers under the Ottoman empire, still use dialects of Turkish, increasingly as their second language, but are otherwise largely assimilated with the Slavic Moslems. In Bulgaria, the meaning of the term "Turk," which generally refers only to Turkish-speaking Christians or Moslems, is sometimes extended to include the Pomaks, who are Bulgarian-speaking Moslems. All three groups were persecuted under Communism, the first two being ordered to take Bulgarian names. Thousands fled to Turkey in 1950–51 and again in the 1980s. Their position has improved during the 1990s and many former exiles have returned to Bulgaria.

**Ukrainians (including Ruthenes):** The 11,000 Ukrainians in the Czech Republic and the 97,000 in Slovakia are descended from those who lived in the Czechoslovak province of Ruthenia up to World War II, when it was absorbed into Ukraine itself. Their numbers in Slovakia include around 75,000 Ruthenes or Rusyns, long established in and around the Carpathian Mountains, whose language has been variously classified as a dialect of Ukrainian or as a distinct Eastern Slav language. There are also 35,000 self-declared Ruthenes in Serbia and Montenegro. Around 23,000 other Ukrainians in Serbia and Montenegro speak yet another dialect. In the Baltic states, however, most Ukrainians – 39,000 in Estonia, 67,000 in Latvia, 35,000 in Lithuania – are descended from those sent there, willingly or not, during the decades of Soviet occupation. As in Ukraine itself, most of the Ukrainians in these countries adhere, in differing proportions, to one of three rival forms of Christianity: the Ukrainian Orthodox Church, which is in communion with the Russian Orthodox Church; the Ukrainian Autocephalous Orthodox Church, which was persecuted under Communism but revived in 1992; and the Uniate Church, which uses Orthodox rites but is in communion with Rome.

**Vlachs:** Although the Vlach minorities in Albania, Bulgaria, and the former Yugoslavia are often referred to as Romanians, they have historically been separated from the main body of that people. Their forms of the shared language and culture were molded by centuries under the rule of the Austro-Hungarian (Habsburg) empire, while other forms, in Romania itself and in Moldova, have Turkish and Slavic elements. The number of Vlachs in Serbia and Montenegro is disputed, with estimates ranging from 150,000 to 300,000. There are also around 10,000 Vlachs in Macedonia.

**Yugoslavs:** This term, which literally means "Southern Slavs," was coined in the mid-19th century but came into general use only after 1929, when the Kingdom of the Serbs, Croats, and Slovenes, established in 1918, was officially renamed Yugoslavia. Under Communism, a small but growing minority declared themselves Yugoslavs, in contrast to traditional ethnic and religious identities, either for ideological reasons or, perhaps more often, to indicate mixed ethnic origins. The revival of ethnic nationalisms, exacerbated by the historically false but politically powerful assertion that ethnicity and religious faith are one and the same, has rendered the term all but meaningless except as referring to the inhabitants of "rump" Yugoslavia (Serbia and Montenegro). Its broader connotation may yet be revived if current tensions are ever abated.

## Appendix 5

# Bibliography

This bibliography is intended to draw the attention of readers to some of the most useful and stimulating English-language books on the region, and the various countries in it, available in the late 1990s. It therefore excludes periodicals, websites, and publications in other languages. It should also be seen as a supplement to the suggestions for further reading at the end of each chapter.

## Reference

Croucher, Murlin, editor, *Slavic Studies: A Guide to Bibliographies, Encyclopedias, and Handbooks*, in two volumes, Wilmington, DE: Scholarly Resources, 1993

This impressive work offers guidance to further research in several languages, not only on the Slavic nations in central and eastern Europe but also on the former Soviet Union, Russia, and other CIS countries.

*Eastern Europe and the Commonwealth of Independent States 1999*, London: Europa, 1999

This is the fourth edition of a reference work dealing with 27 post-Communist countries (12 in the CIS, 15 in central and eastern Europe). Prefaced by 12 introductory essays, each country survey has standardized entries on geography, history and economy, as well as chronologies, statistics, and data on public institutions.

Ference, Gregory C., editor, *Chronology of 20th-century Eastern European History*, Detroit, MI, and London: Gale Research, 1994

An invaluable collection of historical data on what are now 27 ex-Communist countries, as well as the former East Germany, spanning the years up to the end of 1993. The chapters are arranged country by country and, in the cases of Czechoslovakia and Yugoslavia (as well as the Soviet Union), they include the successor states of these federations. The chronologies are accompanied with maps, photographs, biographies of prominent individuals, and a useful bibliography.

White, Stephen, editor, *Political and Economic Encyclopedia of the Soviet Union and Eastern Europe*, Harlow: Longman, 1990

This comprehensive reference text was already being overtaken by events as it was prepared and published, but it is still worth seeking out for data on the region in the Communist period.

## The Region up to 1989

Batt, Judy, *Economic Reform and Political Change in Eastern Europe*, London: Macmillan, and New York: St Martin's Press, 1988

This remains a groundbreaking study of the development of the Comecon countries, focusing on Hungary and Czechoslovakia in particular.

Davies, Norman, *Europe: A History*, Oxford and New York: Oxford University Press, 1996

This best-selling work includes an unusually large amount of information on a region that has often been neglected or misunderstood in the West. In contrast to those scholars who claim an impossible neutrality, the author does not conceal his Catholic faith or his detestation of Communism and he engages in lively polemic against other views, on 20th-century developments in particular.

Garton Ash, Timothy, *We the People: The Revolutions of 89 Witnessed in Warsaw, Budapest, Berlin and Prague*, Cambridge: Granta Books, 1990

This book vividly evokes the hopes, fears, and confusions surrounding the events of 1989, which took almost the whole world by surprise. It stands out among the many accounts of these events because of the author's rare combination of scholarly knowledge and journalistic skill.

Harman, Chris, *Class Struggles in Eastern Europe*, London and Chicago: Bookmarks, 1988

An account of the creation and maintenance of Stalinism in the region, focusing on the upheavals in East Germany in 1953, Poland and Hungary in 1956, Czechoslovakia in 1968, and Poland in 1980–81. The author writes from an independent Marxist perspective, but the book will be of interest even to readers who do not share his views – especially to those who imagine that Marxism and Stalinism are one and the same.

Held, J., editor, *The Columbia History of Eastern Europe in the Twentieth Century*, New York: Columbia University Press, 1992

A collection of scholarly essays that usefully places the Communist period in a larger perspective

Nove, Alec, *Alec Nove on Communist and Post-Communist Countries*, edited by Ian Thatcher, Cheltenham and Northampton, MA: Edward Elgar, 1998

This volume of pieces by the late Alec Nove, a leading expert on the Communist economies, provides a unique insight into developments from the late 1960s to mid-1990.

## Recent Developments Across the Region

Ábel, Istvan, Peter Siklos, and Istvan Székely, *Money and Finance in the Transition to a Market Economy*, Cheltenham and Northampton, MA: Edward Elgar, 1998

A comprehensive volume on the various roles of money in the transition process

Alden, Jeremy, and Philip Boland, *Regional Development Strategies: A European Perspective*, London and Bristol, PA: Jessica Kingsley, 1996

Given that the countries of the region, almost without exception, are seeking closer relations with the EU, this book provides a useful guide to current strategies of structural funding.

Amsden, Alice H., Jacek Kochanowich, and Lance Taylor, *The Market Meets its Match: Restructuring the Economies of Eastern Europe*, Cambridge, MA: Harvard University Press, 1994

The authors describe and explain the failure of the simplistic market medicine administered in the first five years of transition, in a major critique of the economic policies adopted in the CIS, as well as in central and eastern Europe.

Anderson, Ronald, and Chantal Kegels, *Transition Banking: Financial Development of Central and Eastern Europe*, Oxford: Clarendon Press, and New York: Oxford University Press, 1998

Anderson and Kegels examine the evidence that has begun to emerge on the development of the financial sectors in the transition countries.

Baldersheim, H., et al., editors, *Local Democracy and the Processes of Transformation in East-Central Europe*, Boulder, CO: Westview Press, 1996

A book that helps to bridge the gap between central planning and market economics. It emphasizes the role of local governments and nongovernmental organizations in the promotion of individual regions that are now competing for foreign direct investment.

Banac, Ivo, editor, *Eastern Europe in Revolution*, Ithaca, NY: Cornell University Press, 1992

Banac provides a background to the revolutions of 1989, revealing contrasts and similarities, and also deals with the problems encountered during the early years of the transition, which were generally underestimated at the outset.

Bonin, John, *Banking in Transition Economies: Developing Market-oriented Banking Sectors in Eastern Europe*, Cheltenham and Northampton, MA: Edward Elgar, 1997

Selected issues of financial reform are considered through in-depth comparative evaluations of the different approaches adopted in the post-Communist countries.

Bonin, John, and Istvan Székely, editors, *The Development and Reform of Financial Systems in Central and Eastern Europe*, Aldershot and Brookfield, VT: Edward Elgar, 1994

Various aspects of financial reform in the region are explored from a comparative perspective.

Braverman, Avishay, Karen M. Brooks, and Csaba Csaki, editors, *The Agricultural Transition in Central and Eastern Europe, and the Former USSR*, Washington, DC: World Bank, 1993

An assessment of the requirement for, and the likelihood of, the reform of agriculture in post-Communist countries, providing some insight into the theory (and ideology) prevailing in the international economic agencies

Carter, F. W., and D. Turnock, editors, *Environmental Problems of Eastern Europe*, London and New York: Routledge, 1993

A collection of essays summarizing the scale and nature of the environmental problems inherited from Communism. The book mentions the role of green movements in the revolutions of 1989, and underlines the importance of environmental quality for regional development in general, and for attracting foreign direct investment in particular.

Earle, John S., et al., editors, *Privatisation in the Transition to a Market Economy: Studies of Preconditions and Policies in Eastern Europe*, London: Pinter, and New York: St Martin's Press, 1993

An important technical work on privatization, one of the fundamentals of the transition process. It deals with the various strategies adopted across the region, and explains why the process has been considerably delayed in some countries.

Estrin, Saul, editor, *Privatisation in Central and Eastern Europe*, Harlow and New York: Longman, 1994

A wide-ranging book compiled by an editor who has been much involved in the formulation of strategy in some countries. The contributors generally advocate policies of radical change and "shock therapy" with almost the same fervor that Communists used to display.

Fair, D. E., and R. J. Raymond, editors, *The New Europe: Evolving Economic and Financial Systems in East and West*, Dordrecht and Boston: Kluwer, 1993

Most observers underestimated the scale of economic reconstruction that would be necessary after the revolutions of 1989. This book explains the difficulties and evaluates the progress made in the various countries of the region.

Fernández-Armesto, Felipe, editor, *The Times Guide to the Peoples of Europe*, revised edition, London: Times Books, 1997

This impressive survey of all the ethnic groups, major and minor, that share the continent is focused on contemporary conditions, but also includes summaries of each group's history in relation to the state or states that they have inhabited. By presenting central and eastern Europe, in particular, from what is still an unusual angle, it provides a thought-provoking supplement to studies of states and national economies.

Gorzelak, Grzegorz, *The Regional Dimension of Transformation in Central Europe*, London and Bristol, PA: Jessica Kingsley, 1995

The most important book so far published on issues of regional development in some of the countries covered here. It is particularly useful for the northern states of the region, especially Poland, and includes international perspectives in relation to "growth axes" linking the capital cities.

Gray, Gavin, *Eastern Europe*, London: Euromoney, 1996

Despite its title, this is a study of the economic and financial aspects of the transition from Communism in 27 countries, not only in central and eastern Europe, but also in the CIS. The author packs a great deal of information into a text which is more thoughtful, and enduring, than most in the genre of business reportage.

Helmenstein, Christian, *Capital Markets in Transition Economies: Central and Eastern Europe*, Cheltenham: Edward Elgar, 1998

This collection of comparative assessments of the emerging capital markets and related financial developments in the former command economies covers both the countries examined in this book and the CIS countries.

Swinnen, J., editor, *Policy and Institutional Reform in Central European Agriculture*, Aldershot and Brookfield, VT: Avebury, 1994

A lengthy assessment of agricultural reform in the post-Communist countries

Turnock, David, editor, *Privatization in Rural Eastern Europe: The Process of Restitution and Restructuring*, Cheltenham and Northampton, MA: Edward Elgar, 1998

A collection of scholarly essays on agriculture in each of the main countries of the region, accompanied by a general overview of agricultural reform, written by the editor

UN Development Program, *The Shrinking State: Governance and Human Development in Eastern Europe and the Commonwealth of Independent States*, New York: UN Development Program, 1997

This is an important and timely study of the grave social effects of the withdrawal of the state from a wide range of activities, notably education, health, and other social services. It has had strikingly little impact on policy-making either within the post-Communist countries or beyond them.

Vasko, T., editor, *Problems of Economic Transition: Regional Development in Central and Eastern Europe*, Aldershot: Avebury, and Brookfield, VT: Ashgate, 1992

An early study of regional problems during the transition from Communism. It pays considerable attention to the need for new transport services to provide "missing links," and to the prospects for specialization at the "mesoregional" level, transcending national boundaries.

## Specific Countries up to 1989

Bell, John D., *The Bulgarian Communist Party from Blagoev to Zhivkov*, Stanford, CA: Hoover Institution Press, 1986

A detailed and rewarding study of the Party from its foundation in 1917. This volume is one in a series of *Histories of Ruling Communist Parties* published by the Hoover Institution.

Biberaj, Elez, *Albania: A Socialist Maverick*, Boulder, CO: Westview Press, 1990

Perhaps the best, and certainly the most wideranging, among studies of Communist Albania, its internal development, and its external relations

Crampton, Richard J., *A Short History of Modern Bulgaria*, Cambridge and New York: Cambridge University Press, 1987

Still the most useful and accessible one-volume history of the country in English, this book covers the century from Bulgaria's liberation from Turkish rule up to the mid-1980s.

Davies, Norman, *God's Playground: A History of Poland*, Volume 2, *1795 to the Present*, Oxford: Clarendon Press, 1981, and New York: Columbia University Press, 1982

The best English-language history of modern Poland, by a scholar who is openly sympathetic to Polish nationalism and shares the Catholicism of the majority of Poles

Gadney, Reg, *Cry Hungary! Uprising 1956*, London: Weidenfeld and Nicolson, and New York: Atheneum, 1986

A day-by-day account of events in Budapest and elsewhere in October and November 1956, illustrated with numerous photographs

Hall, Derek, *Albania and the Albanians*, London and New York: Pinter, 1994

A comprehensive overview of the development of Albanian society

Hiden, John, and Patrick Salmon, *The Baltic Nations and Europe: Estonia, Latvia and Lithuania in the Twentieth Century*, Harlow and New York: Longman, 1991

A valuable historical presentation of these three states, placing their years of Soviet occupation and their struggles to regain independence in the context of European development throughout the century

Hoxha, Enver, *The Artful Albanian: The Memoirs of Enver Hoxha*, edited by Jon Halliday, London: Chatto and Windus, 1986

This extraordinary book is still worth searching out (it is sometimes listed under its editor's name) because it reveals a great deal about Hoxha's view of the country he dominated for more than 40 years.

Kopacsi, Sandor, *In the Name of the Working Class*, translated by Daniel and Judy Stoffman, Toronto: Lester and Orpen Dennys, 1986; London, HarperCollins, 1989

A fascinating eyewitness account of events in Budapest from 1956 to 1958, by the former head of the city's police force, who supported the reform movement within the Hungarian Communist Party, was jailed in 1958, and later emigrated to Canada.

Lampe, John, *Yugoslavia as History: Twice There Was a Country*, Cambridge and New York: Cambridge University Press, 1996

This is a readable history of the first two Yugoslavias – the kingdom before World War II and the federation after it – which pays attention to economic as well as political developments.

Leff, Carol Skalnik, *National Conflict in Czechoslovakia: The Making and Re-making of a State, 1918–1987*, Princeton, NJ: Princeton University Press, 1988

This historical account of Czechoslovak statehood provides a background for understanding the conflicts that emerged so forcefully after 1989.

Simecka, Milan, *The Restoration of Order*, London: Verso, 1984

This brief, classic account of the "normalization" in Czechoslovakia after the Warsaw Pact invasion in 1968 was written by an opposition activist who lived through it.

Swain, Nigel, *Hungary: the Rise and Fall of Feasible Socialism*, London and New York: Verso, 1992

The best general introduction in English to the Hungarian economy up to 1989

Teichova, Alice, *The Czechoslovak Economy 1918–1980*, London and New York: Routledge, 1988

This remains an accessible and reliable factual account of the development of Czechoslovakia during the period.

Tökes, Rudolf L., *Hungary's Negotiated Revolution: Economic Reform, Social Change and Political Succession, 1957–1990*, Cambridge and New York: Cambridge University Press, 1996

An unwieldy but interesting account of the roots of the system change

Winnifrith, Tom, editor, *Perspectives on Albania*, London: Macmillan and New York: St Martin's Press, 1992

A collection of essays on various aspects of the country, addressing both the Communist period and what went before it. The essays vary in range and quality, but the book as a whole offers a large amount of information and insight.

# The Transition in Specific Countries

Allcock, John B., John J. Horton, and Marko Milivojević, editors, *Yugoslavia in Transition: Choices and Constraints*, Oxford and New York: Berg, 1992

This collection of papers in honor of Fred Singleton (1926–88), a British scholar prominent in Yugoslav studies, is a useful sourcebook covering all aspects of Yugoslav society leading up to the collapse of the former federation.

Bennett, Christopher, *Yugoslavia's Bloody Collapse: Causes, Course and Consequences*, London: Hurst, and New York: New York University Press, 1995

One of the best studies of the breakup of Yugoslavia, emphasizing manipulation by political interest groups

Bristow, John A., *The Bulgarian Economy in Transition*, Cheltenham and Brookfield, VT: Edward Elgar, 1996

The only comprehensive treatment yet published on the economy in transition. It covers the period from 1989 to the end of 1994, and concentrates almost entirely on economic matters, with some reference to politics, but little on social issues.

Bútora, Martin, and Péter Hunčík, editors, *Global Report on Slovakia: Comprehensive Analyses from 1995 and Trends from 1996*, Bratislava: Sándor Márai Foundation, 1997

The contributors, a team attached to an independent Slovak think tank, provide a remarkably comprehensive overview of political, economic and social life in the country.

Cohen, L. J., *Broken Bonds: Yugoslavia's Disintegration and Balkan Politics in Transition*, Boulder, CO: Westview Press, 1995

This study covers the history of the political system of Yugoslavia, the transition to democracy, the first multiparty elections, and the breakup of the country.

Dedek, Oldrich, et al., *The Break-up of Czechoslovakia: An In-depth Economic Analysis*, Aldershot and Brookfield, VT: Avebury, 1996

This is a detailed account of the mechanics of the separation of the Czech and Slovak economies.

Dyker, David, and Ivan Vejvoda, editors, *Yugoslavia and After: A Study in Fragmentation, Despair and Rebirth*, Harlow and New York: Longman, 1996

A useful collection of essays on various aspects of the breakup of the former Yugoslavia, including chapters on the successor states and Kosovo

Heller, Wilfried, editor, *Romania: Migration, Socioeconomic Transformation and Perspectives of Regional Development*, Munich: Südosteuropa-Gesellschaft, 1998

A collection of papers dealing with research, by Romanians and others, on the spatial aspects of change since 1989. There is balanced coverage of economic, social and political issues, as well as a wealth of bibliographic and cartographic information.

Holy, Ladislav, *The Little Czech and the Great Czech Nation: National Identity and the Post-Communist Transformation of Society*, Cambridge: Cambridge University Press, 1996

Holy discusses perceptions of the Czech national identity and how they relate to recent political developments.

Malcolm, Noel, *Bosnia: A Short History*, London: Macmillan, and New York: New York University Press, 1994

An outstanding analysis of a country that has been misrepresented, and mistreated, for centuries. Malcolm provides the vital background for understanding how a well-established multiethnic society was torn apart, not by "ancient hatreds," but by the intervention of its larger neighbors, while the world watched.

Malcolm, Noel, *Kosovo: A Short History*, London: Macmillan, and New York: New York University Press, 1998

An impressive scholarly history of the province, which is both informative and readable

Morgan, Peter, *A Barrel of Stones: In Search of Serbia*, Aberystwyth: Planet, 1997

A first-hand account of life and opinion in Serbia in the 1990s

Shen, Raphael, *The Restructuring of Romania's Economy: A Paradigm of Flexibility and Adaptability*, Westport, CT: Praeger, 1997

A detailed economic survey of the early transition years, based on interviews with many of the politicians and experts involved. It should be noted that it pays no attention to alternative programs, and has been somewhat undermined by the entry of a new government into office in 1996.

Silber, Laura, and Allan Little, *The Death of Yugoslavia;* London: Penguin and BBC Worldwide, and New York: Penguin, 1995

Using research and interviews for a BBC television series with the same title, a prominent US expert on the Balkans and a distinguished British journalist show how Slobodan Milošević and other Yugoslav leaders tore their federation apart.

Sjöberg, Örjan, and Michael J. Wyzan, editors, *Economic Change in the Balkan States: Albania, Bulgaria, Romania, and Yugoslavia*, London: Pinter, and New York: St Martin's Press, 1991

This collection of essays deals with states that have experienced very great problems of adjustment as levels of investment have remained low.

Vickers, Miranda, *Between Serb and Albanian: A History of Kosovo*, London: Hurst, and New York: Columbia University Press, 1998

An excellent historical account of the development of the crisis in the province

Vickers, Miranda, and James Pettifer, *Albania: From Anarchy to a Balkan Identity*, London: Hurst, and New York: New York University Press, 1997

A readable journalistic account of the tumultuous political and social events surrounding the collapse of Communism in Albania

Vulliamy, Ed, *Seasons in Hell: Understanding Bosnia's War*, London: Simon and Schuster, and New York: St Martin's Press, 1994

A harrowing eyewitness account of the war in Bosnia-Herzegovina by a courageous British journalist. Vulliamy, who gave evidence at the International War Crimes Tribunal, does not pretend to be neutral in the face of atrocities.

Weclawowicz, Grzegorz, *Contemporary Poland: Space and Society*, London: UCL Press, and Boulder, CO: Westview Press, 1996

A review of recent economic, political and social change in Poland, with special reference to the post-Communist period

Wojtaszczyk, Konstanty Adam, *Poland: Government and Politics*, Warsaw: Elipsa, 1997

A review of Poland's political and social transition from Communism

Wolchik, Sharon, *Czechoslovakia in Transition: Politics, Economics, Society*, London and New York: Pinter, 1991

Wolchik gives an accessible factual account of the background to the end of Communist rule in Czechoslovakia, and describes the first years of the transition.

# Index

# Index

The breakup of federations in central and eastern Europe is reflected in the special use of four terms in this Index. All entries for "the Czech lands" cover the period up to 1993, those for "the Czech Republic" the period from 1993. All entries for "former Yugoslavia" refer to the state created in 1918, renamed in 1929, refounded in 1945, and dissolved in 1992. Finally, "rump Yugoslavia" refers to the Federal Republic established by Serbia and Montenegro in 1992 but not recognized internationally.

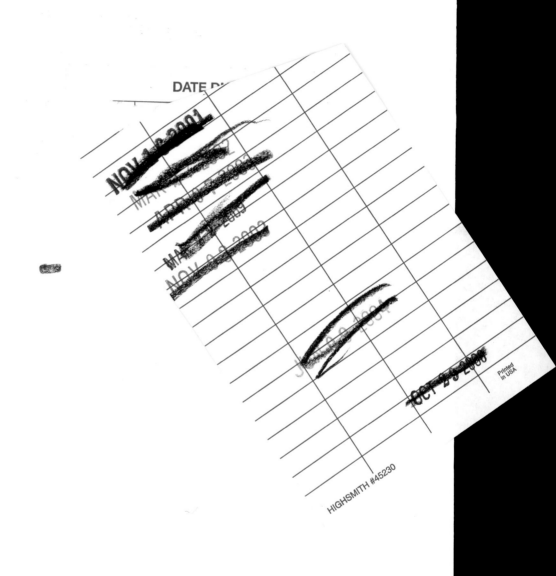

DATE D

NOV 1 8 2001

MAR

MA

NOV

HIGHSMITH #45230

Printed
In USA